BEVERAGES

Kartik R. Bhat

Associate Editor–Acquisitions: Neeraj Bhalla
Editor–Production: Nikhil Rakshit

ISBN: 978-81-317-8895-0

First Impression

Published by Dorling Kindersley (India) Pvt. Ltd., licensees of Pearson Education in South Asia.

Head Office: Pearson Education, 7th Floor, Knowledge Boulevard, A-8 (A), Sector-62, Noida, India
Registered Office: 11 Community Centre, Panchsheel Park, New Delhi, 110017, India

Compositor: Mukesh Technologies Pvt. Ltd.

Printed in India at Repro India Limited

About the Author

Kartik R. Bhat is presently a senior lecturer of Food and Beverage Services at Garden City College, Bangalore. Prior to join this assignment, he has worked as a faculty of Food and Beverage at Welcomgroup Management Institute, which is now known as ITC Hotel Management Institute. He has also worked as an assistant food and beverage manager at ITC Maurya Sheraton, New Delhi, India. He has an experience of more than 12 years in the hospitality industry as well as in the teaching field. He has a passion for beverages as a subject, and has extensively travelled many places to add value to the content, which the reader of this book shall benefit from. He has also won many bartending competitions at the beginning of his career.

Kartik R. Bhat has completed his BHM from Welcomgroup Management Institute (Management Training Integrated Course), BTS (from IGNOU), PGDBA (HR) and PGDRM (Retail Management) from Symbiosis, Pune,

The author has envisioned about improving the knowledge of beverages in general, including working professionals of Food and Beverage establishments. This would not only help the readers in improving the service standards at their restaurants, bars and other food and beverage establishments, but also help them to better understand beverage as a subject. People across all the industries may use this book to gain knowledge, which would help them to socialize with their superiors, colleagues and counterparts.

I would like to dedicate this book to the almighty Lord, who is the creator of everything on the earth. Without the lord's creation, there would be no scope to make beverages, which have given human the willingness to live and enjoy his/her life.

Contents

Chapter 12 Tequila 125

Chapter 13 Brandy 131

Chapter 14 Whisky 146

Preface

Beverages are an integral part of human life. The various natures of beverages are consumed by a human being since his/her birth in the form of fruit juices, milk and milk-based products etc. Due to the immense variety available on beverage lists for the consumer, things can get a bit confusing. This book helps the reader understand each one of them. All these, especially in India, can be attributed to the increased influence of the western culture on the Indian subcontinent, through employment opportunities and foreign direct investments. Socializing plays a vital role for building bridges, and this is achieved through cocktail parties and other get-togethers. Almost all these social parties follow a one drink protocol, making beverages a great method for ice-breaking. While Indian traditional ceremonies or marriages mostly prefer nonalcoholic beverages such as juices, kahwa, coffee, tea etc., the westerners prefer alcoholic beverages. Therefore, to accommodate oneself to this emerging global culture, it is essential to understand alcoholic beverages for two basic reasons. First understanding and knowing how to consume a beverage, its relevance and history not only adds value as a conversation starter, but it prevents alcohol abuse as well. Secondly, even in modern India, alcohol is considered as a taboo substance. But, in reality, alcohol, if consumed in limited quantity, is an elixir and can bring pleasure to the human body and mind.

This book helps increase awareness among all professionals, thereby increasing their knowledge and sociability. It is very important especially for Food and Beverage handlers to know the basics of beverages as they are the key marketers of beverages in their respective establishments.

This book will help Hotel Management professionals; especially the aspiring professionals pursuing their degrees and diplomas in hotel management and oenology. The specific details on various beverages of the world, the production processes, important information, facts and details along with frequently asked questions will empower the reader to get correct and precise information. The knowledge and practical experience that I have gained in my career spanning over twelve years in food and beverage management and teaching have helped me give the relevant information necessary for all Food and Beverage professionals, especially ones interested in bar operations or oenology.

Entrepreneurs, who are planning to start their own micro-brewery, bars or pubs, will find this information very useful.

Acknowledgements

There have been many friends, colleagues and family members without whom I could not complete this book. All of them are familiar with my gratitude towards them. I would like to thank in particular:

- Mr Kapil Grover—Director, Grover Vineyards, for the contribution towards the wine chapter.
- Mr Vishal Nagpal—Director Operations, the Biereclub, Bangalore, for their expertise and contribution towards the Beer chapter.
- The Bacardi International Limited, for providing all support to this book. Particularly for their association with brands, such as Bacardi (rum), Bombay Sapphire & Oxley (gin), Grey Goose & 42 Below (vodka), Cazadores (tequila), Otard (cognac), Dewar's & Aberfeldy (whisky), Noilly Prat & Martini (aromatized wines), Martini Spumante (Italian wine) and Benedictine (liqueur). I would like to thank Mr Nitin Tewari, theTrade Ambassador of Bacardi India.
- The Brown-Forman Company, for providing all information and photographs pertaining to Jack Daniel's Whiskey and Southern Comfort Liqueur labels. I would like to thank Ms Susman Christy, Ms Michelle Green, Jennifer Powell and Mr Amrit Kiran Singh for all their prompt support. Please note the following:

  The Jack Daniel's trademarks appear courtesy of Jack Daniel's Properties, Inc.
  JACK DANIELS'S and Old No. 7 are registered trademarks of Jack Daniel's Properties, Inc.

  &

  The Trademark of Southern Comfort appears courtesy of Southern Comfort Properties, Inc. Southern Comfort is a registered trademark of Southern Comfort Properties, Inc.

- Drambuie Liqueur Co. Ltd of 8 Grand Union Office Park, Packet Boat Lane, Uxbridge, UB8 2GH UK, and its employees Ms Kim Hulse and Ms Miranda Rennie, Marketing Director, Drambuie Liqueur Co. Ltd, for sharing a number of very useful brand images and interesting details of this iconic liqueur.
- MONIN FRANCE and its India office, for their valuable contribution towards the Flavored Syrups and Liqueurs chapter. I would like to thank in particular Mr Ravi Kathuria—Director, Business Development, MONIN, SAARC countries, and Mr Nilesh Karia and the entire team at MONIN. I would also like to thank them for proving the images pertaining to Angostura Bitters.
- Mr Yvonne Van de Bospoort and the entire management of LIBBEY GLASSWARE, for providing all the photographs pertaining to glassware and other equipment used in bars.
- Inmaculada Menacho, Consejo Regulador Jerez-Xérès-Sherry Manzanilla-Sanlúcar de Barrameda Vinagre de Jerez for the contribution to the hapter on Spanish Wine (sub-section on Sherry).
- The Graham's Port Company, for their contribution towards the Portuguese Wines chapter (sub-section on Port).
- Ms Shymala Ganesh, for the photographs related to Sake.
- Chilipili Coffee Estates at Coorg, Bangaluri, for their contribution to the Coffee chapter.
- Mr Sudhir Nair—Executive Chef, Royal Orchid Hotels, for his expertise on food and wine pairing.

- The creators and management of allfranceinfo.com website, for their support toward the French Wines chapter.
- Mr Periyannaraj Sadayapillai Raj who provided the images for tea from Upland tea estates, Sri Lanka.
- My students who gave me encouragement to write this book. In particular, Mr Mohammad Hadi Saeidy (Iran), Mr Ameya Ghate (India) and Mr Periyannaraj Sadayapillai (Sri Lanka).

I would like to specially thank H.E. Dr, Joseph V.G.—Chairman of Gardencity Group of Institutions, for his encouragement and support.

I would also like to thank my mentor, Mr Viju Varghese—Director, Hospitality and Tourism, Gardencity College, for his guidance, support and encouragements. I would like to thank my colleagues who have stood by me in this endeavour.

I would like to thank my teacher Brigadier Manoranjan Singh VrC. (Retd.), who taught me the fundamentals of Hoteliering at Welcomgroup Management Institute during my graduation.

I would like to thank Neeraj Bhalla, Nikhil Rakshit, Uma Tamang and the entire editorial team at Pearson Education for their valuable time, honest effort, and encouragement for the timely completion of this book.

I would like to thank the pillars of my life—my parents, late Mrs Devika R. Bhat and Mr B.R. Bhat without whom I would not have reached this stature in my life. I also thank my sister Mrs Smriti Bhat Gracias and Wing Commander Deepesh Gracias for their unrelenting support in helping me to complete this book.

—Kartik R. Bhat

About the Book

This book is aimed at bringing the students in touch with the practical reality about the Beverage Industry rather than a guided theoretical experience. This book discuses the detailed history of all beverages. Through associations with producers and manufacturers of various alcoholic and non-alcoholic beverages, it gives a first-hand exposure to the reader about the details of each and every beverage.

The wine chapters begin by discussing the growth of the grape vine with details of production and pictures taken at Grover Vineyards, Bangalore—the leading wine producer in India. Furthermore, the wine regions, especially from the old world countries, such as France, Italy, Germany and others, have been discussed in detail, highlighting important regions, communes and vineyards along with their tasting notes and history. Hence the reader's foundations on oenology will be strong.

The Beverage Industry's contributions to this book shall help students in meticulously understanding each type of beverage. The Biere Club—micro-brewery in Bangalore has shared the production process of their famed beers, Chilpili Estates showed us growing the coffee plantations and coffee processing in the coffee capital of India, namely Coorg in Karnataka. The tea plantations of Srilanka also show us tea processing in a better way.

Bacardi International has associated with this book, which owns the world's famous Bacardi rum brand, the Grey Goose Vodka brand, Bombay Sapphire gin brand, the Cazadores Tequila brand, the Dewar's Label along with Aberfedly, which are their famous whisky brands. Apart from this they have given details about their Liqueur Benedictine, which has been in production since 1510 AD. All these information has added value to the overall readability and content of this book.

The Brown-Forman Company, which is the parent company owning the Jack Daniel's Whiskey company, has played an important role in sharing information pertaining to the most famous American Whiskey and details about its production process including the photographs. They have also given information pertaining to their signature liqueur Southern Comfort.

The author is highly grateful to all the beverage companies and the people involved in making this book. This will help the reader to develop a better understanding about beverages of various natures and help them gain knowledge about how to cherish and enjoy the different types of beverages made from the produce of God's own Garden called, 'Mother Nature'.

Apart from this, the book is written in a simplistic manner along with many historical details, making it a very interesting and informative read to everyone.

BEVERAGES—INTRODUCTION AND HISTORY

CHAPTER OUTLINE

LET'S DEFINE

'A beverage is a potable drink, excluding water, which could be non-alcoholic or alcoholic, consumed to rejuvenate, refresh or stimulate the body as per its particular characteristic.'

1.1 A BRIEF HISTORY

Beverages are one of the most sought-after substances in the world. It not only helps to keep the consumer rejuvenated throughout the day, but also provides a good counterpart to the various food substances consumed. For example, a morning tea is now a quint essential substance along with the early morning bread and butter toast. Hence, it is essential to know, in general, the details of various beverages.

During the Middle Ages, there were numerous developments in the consumption of beverages. For example, rustic beers and wild fruit wines became increasingly popular, especially among Celts, Anglo-Saxons, Germans and Scandinavians. However, wines were the most preferred beverage in the Roman countries (*i.e.*, Italy, Spain and France).

With the collapse of the Roman Empire and decline of urban life, religious institutions, particularly monasteries, became the repositories of the brewing and wine-making techniques, which had been developed earlier. While rustic beers continued to be produced at homes, the art of brewing was essentially mastered by the monks, who carefully guarded this knowledge. Around the 13th century, *hops* (a flavouring agent and preservative used in beer production) were discovered. They became a common ingredient in beers, especially in the Northern Europe.

The monasteries also maintained the art of viticulture. Importantly, they had ample resources, security and stability in those turbulent times to improve the quality of their vines over time. During the Middle Ages, the best vineyards were owned and tended by the monasteries.

By the beginning of the first millennium, the most popular form of festivities in England were known as 'ales', and both *ale* and beer were the most prized products to be given to the lords for rent. In the 12th century, German towns were granted the privilege of brewing and selling beer in their immediate localities. A flourishing artisan brewing industry developed in many towns, inculcating a strong civic pride among the citizens.

Distillation was another important development during the Middle Ages. It was Albertus Magnus (1193–1280 AD), who first clearly described the distillation process. This distilled spirit was known as *aqua vitae*, meaning water of life (later named as 'Brandy'). Brandy was derived from the Dutch word *brandewijn*, meaning burnt (or distilled) wine.

In the mid-14th century, plagues such as Black Death spread across the masses in Europe. This dramatically changed people's perception of their lives and place in the cosmos. Some dramatically increased their consumption of alcohol in the belief that this might protect them from the mysterious diseases, whereas others thought that through moderation in all things, including alcohol, they could be saved. The consumption of distilled spirits, which was meant exclusively for medicinal purposes, increased in popularity.

As the end of the Middle Ages approached, the popularity of beer spread in England, France and Scotland. Beer brewers were officially recognized as a guild in England, and the adulteration of beer or wine became punishable by death in Scotland. Importantly, the consumption of spirits as a beverage began to occur.

Interesting Facts

Coca-Cola

'Coca-Cola's secret ingredient when it was established was supposed to be kola-nut from the kola tree, and the leaves from the coco (from which "cocaine" is extracted). The rest is left to speculation.'*

The soft drink was first sold to the public at the soda fountain in Jacob's Pharmacy in Atlanta on May 8, 1886. About nine servings of the soft drink were sold every day. Sales for that first year added up to a total of about $50. The funny thing was that it cost John Pemberton over $70 in expenses; therefore, the first year of sales was a loss. Until 1905, the soft drink, which was marketed as a tonic, contained extracts of cocaine as well as the caffeine-rich kola nut.

In 1887, Asa Candler, another Atlanta pharmacist and businessman, bought the formula for Coca-Cola from inventor John Pemberton for $2,300. By the late 1890s, Coca-Cola was one of America's most popular fountain drinks, largely due to Candler's aggressive marketing of the product. With Asa Candler, now at the helm, the Coca-Cola Company increased syrup sales by over 4000% between 1890 and 1900. Advertising was an important factor in John Pemberton and Asa Candler's success; by the turn of the century, the drink was sold across the United States and Canada. Around the same time, the company began selling syrup to independent bottling companies licensed to sell the drink. Even today, the US soft drink industry is organized on this principle.

Death of the soda fountain and the rise of the bottling industry: Until the 1960s, both small town and big city dwellers enjoyed carbonated beverages at the local soda fountain or ice-cream saloon. Often housed in the drug store, the soda fountain counter served as a meeting place for people of all ages. Often combined with lunch counters, the soda fountain declined in popularity as commercial ice-cream, bottled soft drinks and fast food restaurants became popular.

New Coke: On April 23, 1985, the trade secret 'New Coke' formula was released. Today, products of the Coca-Cola Company are consumed at the rate of more than one billion drinks per day.

*Kola-nut: It comes from two evergreen trees of the cocoa family, which contains high amounts of caffeine.

1.2 CHARACTERISTICS OF BEVERAGES

All beverages have basic qualities and also some specific enhanced characteristics, which is why people prefer each beverage for a particular time, place, occasion or festival. Certain characteristics that differentiate one beverage from the other are the following:

1. Thirst-quenching properties.
2. Value as social drinks. For example, be it a tea party or a cocktail soiree.
3. Nutritional value.
4. Pairing with food items, that is, fish when had with a glass of wine is said to taste better than with any other beverage.
5. Medical properties of various beverages.

Keeping in mind all the above-mentioned characteristics, it is of utmost importance to understand the different types of beverages and their classification.

1.3 CLASSIFICATION OF BEVERAGES

Beverages are many, but choices are a few. We all know that beverages are many whenever we go shopping to fill our shopping cart; however, we end up purchasing only the limited things that are of interest to us. For each time of the day in every part of the world, different beverages are consumed.

Some wake up and have a cup of coffee, whereas some prefer tea. Some have a glass of juice and many prefer milk. As the day progresses, the cocktail dinners begin with the flow of beverages such as rum, gin and vodka; in addition, some wonderful-smelling liquors with aromas of fruit or spices are consumed to tantalize our senses.

For an in-depth understanding of the types of beverages, it is important to learn the various categories of beverages; they are classified into various categories according to production methods and content. They can be broadly classified into the following types:

1. Non-alcoholic beverages
2. Alcoholic beverages

Figure 1.1 explains in detail the beverage classification chart.

Non-alcoholic Beverages

Non-alcoholic beverages are those beverages that are *not* fermented and distilled for the production of alcohol and are consumed without any alcoholic content.

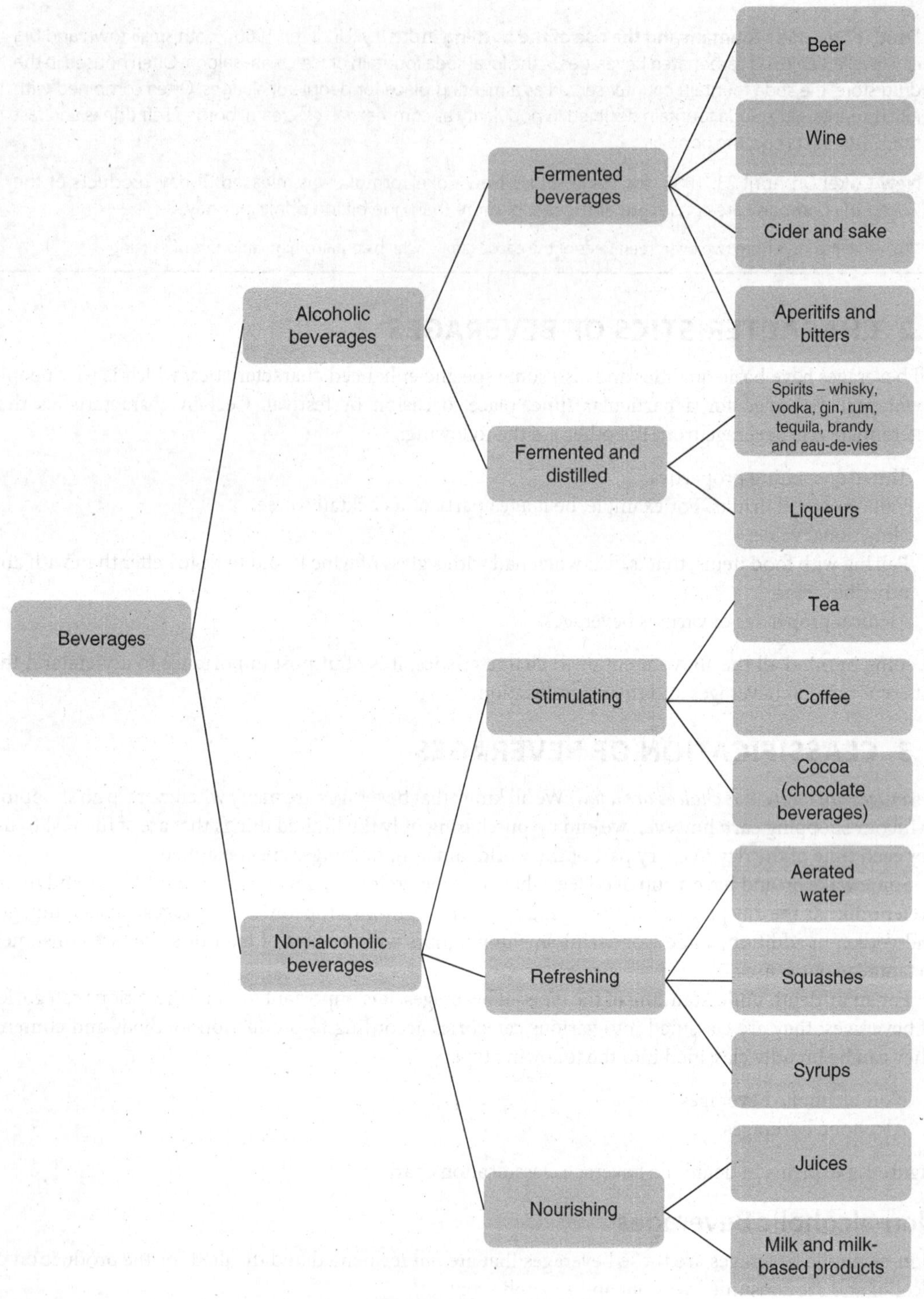

Figure 1.1 The beverage classification chart.

There are three broad categories of non-alcoholic beverages, which are as follows:

1. **Stimulating beverages:** Stimulating beverages refer to those beverages that have the property to stimulate the senses and rejuvenate the body. Some examples of stimulating beverages are tea, coffee and cocoa (drinking chocolate).

   Let us understand in brief, the properties of these beverages and what makes them so popular for consumption. The details of each beverage shall be discussed in the subsequent chapters.

   (i) **Tea:** Tea is the terminal bud of tea plantation. The botanical name of tea is *Camellia sinensis*. It has properties to rejuvenate the human body and has been medically proved to be highly beneficial to human health.

   The ancient Aztec tribe making cocoa.

   (ii) **Coffee:** Coffee is the most popular non-alcoholic beverage in the world. We are all aware that the world-over, coffee lounges are the most popular 'hang-out' places. The aroma of coffee itself is divine. The seed of the coffee cherry is what contains the flavour, and the caffeine tinkles the senses. The most popular varieties of coffee are Espresso and Cappuccino. Chapter 3 discusses coffee in detail.

   (iii) **Cocoa:** It is popularly known as chocolate. Cocoa is a tropical fruit, which contains the cocoa beans. These are used to produce chocolate drinks and all chocolate-based products. Chocolate in the solid form is called, 'a bar of chocolate'. However, drinking chocolate also known as *cocoa* is a very popular drink. In fact, for many centuries, the ancient inhabitants, especially the Aztec tribes of South America, have consumed cocoa and referred it as *the drink of the Gods.*

2. **Refreshing beverages:** The name itself is self-explanatory; these beverages are mostly chilled beverages that are consumed on a hot summer day for refreshing the mind and body. The following are the types of refreshing beverages:

   (i) **Aerated beverages:** These are carbonated beverages that may have a particular flavour or essence added to it or the flavour could be added subsequently just before serving. Certain sodas (referred as cold drinks in India), such as Coca-Cola, Pepsi and Fanta, are examples of aerated beverages that have a particular flavour already added to it. While a fresh lime soda is one when fresh lime juice is mixed with club soda, which is served either sweet or salted.

   (ii) **Squashes:** Squashes are non-alcoholic, fruit-flavoured concentrated syrups that are usually made from fruit juice, water and sugar. These are generally concentrates and are consumed after dilution with water or club soda. Squashes are common in the United Kingdom, Ireland, India, Scandinavia, South Africa and Kenya, and have a large market share in competition with fruit juices and soft drinks. Typically, a squash is created by mixing one part concentrate with four or five parts water (depending on concentration and personal taste) directly into a glass or jug.

DID YOU KNOW

Tea leaves contain more than 700 chemicals, among which the compounds closely related to human health are flavonoids, amino acids, vitamins (C, E and K), caffeine and polysaccharides. Tea plays an important role in improving beneficial intestinal microflora, as well as providing immunity against intestinal disorders and in protecting cell membranes from oxidative damage. It also prevents dental caries due to the presence of fluorine. Moreover, tea plays a well-established role in normalizing blood pressure, lipid-depressing activity, prevention of coronary heart diseases and diabetes by reducing the blood-glucose activity.

(iii) **Syrups:** In cooking, a syrup is a thick, viscous liquid, containing a large amount of dissolved sugars, but showing little tendency to deposit crystals. The viscosity arises from the multiple hydrogen bonds between the dissolved sugar, which has many hydroxyl (OH) groups and water. Technically and scientifically, the term, 'syrup' is also employed to denote viscous, generally residual liquids, containing substances other than sugars in solution. Artificial maple syrup is made with water and an extremely large amount of dissolved sugar. The solution is heated, so that more sugar can be put in than what is normally possible, thereby making it super-saturated.

Amaretto syrup

Apple pie

Apple pie cafe

Basil syrup

(*Courtesy*: MONIN International, France.)

3. **Nourishing beverages:** Nourishing beverages are those that have the properties to add nutrients, proteins, vitamins etc. that, as the name itself suggests, can nourish the human body. Nourishing beverages normally refer to malted beverages or milk-based beverages; however, we should not exclude fresh fruit juices that themselves have vitamins and nourishing properties for the human body. The types of nourishing beverages are as follows:

   (i) **Milk and milk-based products:** Milk and milk-based beverages, such as malted beverages, milkshakes and yogurt-based smoothies, all come under this scheme of things. Examples of malted beverages are Horlicks, Bournvita, Boost etc.

   (ii) **Juices:** All canned and fresh fruit juices such as orange, mango, cranberry, pineapple and apple come under the category of juices.

All the non-alcoholic beverages, mentioned here, have been explained as per their categorization as per their reference.

Cassis/ black currant syrup

Blood orange (sanguine) syrup

Blue curacao syrup

Blue berry syrup

Bubble gum flavor

Caramel syrup

Cardamom syrup

Chocolate cookie syrup

Chocolate mint syrup

Coconut syrup

Cranberry syrup

Crème cookie syrup

Cucumber flavor

Green apple syrup

(*Courtesy*: MONIN International, France)

Alcoholic Beverages

LET'S DEFINE

'An *alcoholic beverage* is a drink containing ethanol, which is commonly known as alcohol.'

Alcoholic beverages are divided into three general classes: beers, wines and spirits. Low alcohol content beverages such as beer and wine are produced by the fermentation of sugar or starch-containing plant material. High alcohol content beverages, such as spirits are produced by fermentation followed by distillation.

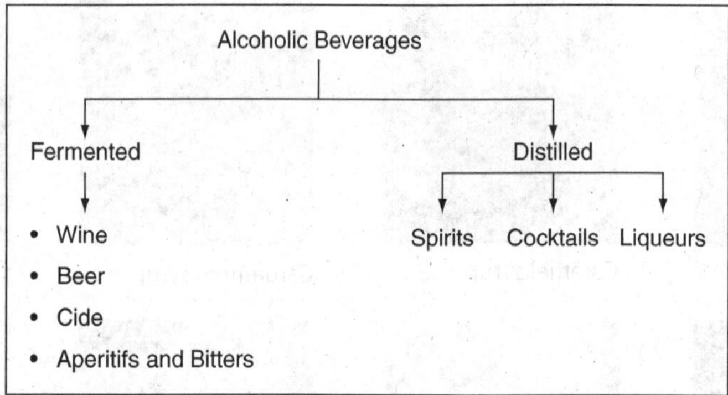

Figure 1.2 Alcohol classification chart.

Production of alcohol can be done by the following methods:

1. Fermentation or brewing
2. Distillation

Fermentation or Brewing

LET'S DEFINE

'Fermentation is the anaerobic enzymatic conversion of organic compounds, especially carbohydrates, to simpler compounds, especially to lactic acid or ethyl alcohol, by producing energy in the form of adenosine triphosphate (ATP). It is used commercially in the preparation of alcoholic beverages. Moreover, fermentation is the basic process in the manufacture of antibiotics'.

The chemical process that breaks down organic materials is called fermentation. This process is carried out by microbes such as bacteria, moulds and yeasts (Figure 1.3). For example, moulds or fungi act upon mixtures of molasses and mineral salts to produce penicillin. Yeast breaks down the sugar obtained from malted grain into ethyl alcohol and carbon dioxide gas, which is used in beer. Sugar from grape juice is also broken down in the same way, which is used in wine (please refer Chapter 5 on beer-making to understand the 'brewing of beer' in detail).

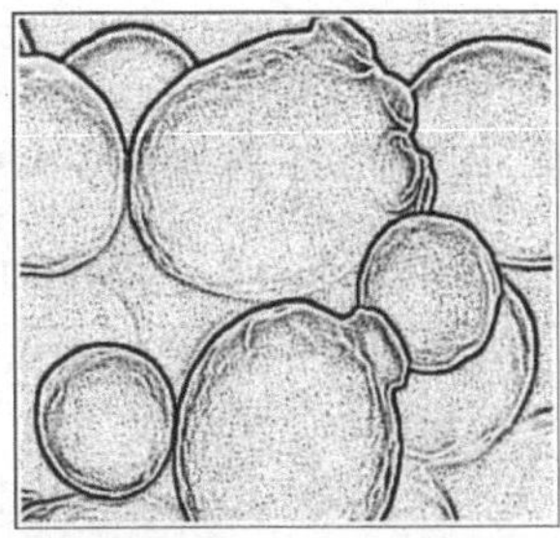

Figure 1.3 Yeast used for beer making—*saccharomyces cerevisiae*.

Distillation

LET'S DEFINE

'A method of separating a substance that is in solution from its solvent or of separating a liquid from a mixture of liquids having different boiling points. The liquid to be separated is evaporated (as by boiling), and its vapour is then collected after it condenses. The condensed vapour, which is the purified liquid, is called the *distillate*.'

The first clear evidence of distillation came from the Greek alchemists working in Alexandria in the AD 1st century. The Alexandrians were using a distillation alembic or still device in the AD 3rd century. The medieval Arabs learned the distillation process from the Alexandrians and used it extensively; however, there is no evidence that they distilled alcohol. Fractional distillation was developed by Tadeo Alderotti in the 13th century.

The term 'hard liquor' is used in North America to distinguish distilled beverages from un-distilled ones (implicitly weaker).

Ancient method of distillation—the sketch depicting the tribal communities trying to master the art of distillation.

1.4 INTERESTING FACTS ABOUT ALCOHOL

1. Alcoholic drinks have different amounts of alcohol in them, which are as follows:
   (i) Beer has about 5% alcohol, although darker beers and ales can have more.
   (ii) Wine has usually 12–15% alcohol.
   (iii) Hard liquor has about 45% alcohol.
2. Certain types of alcoholic drinks get into your bloodstream faster. A carbonated (fizzy) alcoholic drink, such as champagne, will be absorbed faster than a non-carbonated drink.
3. Alcohol slows your breathing rate, heart rate and how well your brain functions. These effects may appear within 10 minutes and peak at around 40–60 minutes.

4. Alcohol increases the risk of motor vehicle accidents; head, neck, stomach and breast cancers and suicide and homicide rates.
5. Alcohol stays in your bloodstream until it is broken down by the liver. The amount of alcohol in your blood is called 'blood-alcohol level'. If you drink alcohol faster than the liver can break it down, this level will rise. Your blood alcohol level is used to legally define whether or not you are 'drunk'. The blood alcohol legal limit usually falls between 0.08–0.10 in most parts of the world. A list of blood alcohol levels and the likely symptoms are as follows:
   (i) 0.05—reduced inhibitions
   (ii) 0.10—slurred speech
   (iii) 0.20—euphoria and motor impairment
   (iv) 0.30—confusion
   (v) 0.40—stupor
   (vi) 0.50—coma
   (vii) 0.60—respiratory paralysis and death
6. Drinking during pregnancy can harm the developing baby. Severe birth defects are also possible.
7. Excessive consumption of ethanol may cause a delayed effect, which is called hangover. The hangover starts after the euphoric effects of ethanol have subsided, typically in the night and morning after alcoholic drinks were consumed.

LET'S SUMMARIZE IN POINTS

- At the end of this chapter, we can conclude that we would have gained the knowledge of what exactly a *beverage* is, along with its historical references and categorization.
- Beverages are classified into alcoholic and non-alcoholic beverages.
- Non-alcoholic beverages are further divided into stimulating, refreshing and nourishing beverages.
- Alcoholic beverages are categorized under fermented or brewed beverages and fermented and distilled spirits.
- There are various points discussed on laws of the world associated with alcohol along with the health benefits and effects of alcohol on the human body.
- We should also learn the most important series of questions in the following section, which would aid us to recap this chapter in particular.

1.5 FAQs

Short-Answer Type Questions

1. Define a beverage.
2. Who invented Coca-Cola?
3. What is the difference between nourishing and stimulating beverages?
4. Name the three most interesting facts of alcoholic beverages.
5. Give in one sentence the types of refreshing beverages.

Long-Answer Type Questions

1. What is the historical reference pertaining to Middle Ages referring to the evolution of beverages?
2. Give the beverage classification chart outlining the details of both alcoholic and non-alcoholic beverages.
3. Categorize non-alcoholic beverages as per their relevance.
4. What is blood alcohol level? Define the state of the human body pertaining to the same in detail.
5. What is brewing?
6. What is the difference between fermentation and distillation?
7. Why is Coca-Cola named as such? Describe its history.
8. Who are the Aztecs? Give a brief history pertaining to this tribe.
9. What are the various uses for alcohol?
10. Mention the various symptoms and effects of excessive alcohol consumption.

2 TEA

CHAPTER OUTLINE

LET'S DEFINE

'Tea refers to an aromatic beverage prepared from the cured leaves of the shrub *Camellia Sinensis* by infusing them either with hot water or boiling water. It also refers to the leaves, buds and the internodes of this shrub that is used for making a cup of tea.'

The beverage of all sophisticated ladies and gentlemen is, without doubt, 'tea'. It may be because of the association of tea with sophistication that till date most diplomatic meetings are known as 'tea parties'.

Tea has been an essential trade item since the colonial days. We all know the relevance of the Boston Tea Party in the history of great nations which changed the tea trade across the world (refer to the 'did you know section' ahead).

Tea has a bitter and acidic taste, which many people prefers and it is considered to be the most consumed beverage after water. It is a morning and evening beverage. People who consume it are charged or rejuvenated by its taste and flavour. Tea contains catechins, a type of antioxidant, which may be the reason behind the belief, 'tea rejuvenates the body, mind and soul'.

Apart from the usual tea, herbal tea infusions are also popular. The herbal teas have various herbs added to them, for example, Indian basil also known as *Tulsi* is a popular variant of herbal tea in India.

In the next few paragraphs, we will understand the tea plant, the history of tea, the varieties of tea, their making and the health benefits of the world's most popular beverage.

2.1 HISTORY OF TEA

The tea shrub is said to have its origins from northeast India, Burma, south-west China and Tibet.

Tea has a very unique history. The consumption of tea is dated back to the 10th century BC wherein it was first recorded. By 200 BC, during the Qin Dynasty, tea had become a very common drink in China. During the 19th century, Europe started the tea trade with China; due to the trade, tea spread to various parts of the world and it is now consumed extensively almost everywhere.

Catherine of Braganza, the wife of Charles II, took the tea habit to Great Britain around AD 1660, but it was not until the 19th century, that tea became as widely consumed as it is today in Britain.

Timeline of Tea

2700 BC: Tea was discovered and credited to the Chinese Emperor Shennung.

222: Tea will be mentioned as a substitute for wine for the first time in the Chinese writings of the next half century.

708: Tea-drinking habit gains popularity among the Chinese in part because water is boiled to prevent intestinal diseases. Tea is also valued for its claimed medicinal values.

725: T'ang Dynasty: *Cha*, tea in Chinese, becomes a part of daily life.

800s: Lu Yu wrote the first Chinese authoritative book on tea, the *Cha Ching*.

1484: The tea ceremony was introduced by a Japanese named Yoshimasa.

1500: Ming Dynasty: In imitation of spouted wine earthenware, the first teapots were made at Yixing, near Shanghai, which is famous for its clays. Black, green and Oolong teas become prevalent.

1591: The Japanese tea master Sen Rikyū formalized the tea ceremony.

1597: The first English mention of tea appears in a translation of Dutch navigator Jan Hugo van Lin-Schooten's Travels. He called the beverage *Chaa*.

1610: Tea reaches Europe, carried by the Dutch from Banten, Java.

1618: Imperial Russia was attempting to engage China and Japan in trade, while the East India Company was trying to do the same, and gaining access to the Vast Economies of the East. The Chinese Embassy in Moscow presented several chests of tea to Czar Alexis.

1680: Madame de la Sabliere, the wife of the French poet Antoine Rambouillet, introduces France to the custom of drinking tea with milk. Pouring the milk into the cup of hot tea cooled the tea slightly, making it less apt to break her cherished eggshell porcelain tea cups.

1773: The Tea Act passed by the British Parliament lightens the duties on tea imported into Britain to give relief to the East India Company.

***1774*:** The British ship London docks at New York on 22 April; the Sons of Liberty prepare to follow the example set at Boston four months earlier.

***1780*:** The smuggling within the tea trade was thought to be as large as the legal trade.

***1784*:** The British Parliament further lowers the British import duties on tea. The lower duties end the smuggling that has accounted for so much of the nation's tea imports and hurt the East India Company, as the rewards become too small to justify the risks.

***1790*:** Boston merchants start a triangular trade with clothing, copper and iron to the Columbia River to be bargained for furs. The sea captains will sell the cargoes at Canton and return round the Cape of Good Hope with Chinese porcelains, teas and tiles.

***1796*:** In Russia, the samovar, adopted from the Tibetan 'hot pot', made its preview. It could run throughout the day and serve up to 40 cups of tea at a time. Again showing the Asian influence in the Russian culture, guests sipped their tea from glasses in silver holders, very similar to Turkish coffee cups.

***1797*:** English tea consumption reaches an annual rate of two pounds per capita, a figure that will increase fivefold in the next century.

***1820*:** The book *A Treatise on Adulteration of Food and Culinary Poisons* by the English chemistry professor Fredrick Accum shows among other things that counterfeit China tea is made from dried thorn leaves coloured with poisonous verdigris. Caffeine is isolated by the German chemist Friedrich Ferdinand Runge.

***1823*:** Acting for the British Government, Charles Bruce smuggles knowledgeable coolies out of China and puts them to work transplanting young tea bushes into nursery beds to begin tea plantations.

***1824*:** Cadbury Chocolate has its beginnings in a tea and coffee shop opened by Birmingham, England. John Cadbury employs a Chinese to preside over his tea charter. The Royal Navy reduces its daily rum ration from half a pint to a quarter pint and tea becomes a part of the daily ration.

***1825*:** British colonists in Ceylon plant coffee bushes.

***1866*:** More than 90% of Britain's tea still comes from China. The Great Tea Race from Foochow to London pits 11 clipper ships that race to minimize spoilage of the China tea in their hot holds. The skippers crowd on sail but the voyage still takes close to three months.

***1869*:** The coffee rust *Hemileia vastatrix* appears in Ceylon plantations and will spread throughout the Orient and the Pacific in the next two decades. It will destroy the coffee-growing industry and soaring coffee prices will lead to wide-scale tea cultivation. The English clipper ship Cutty Sark, built for the tea trade, sails for Shanghai to begin a 117-day voyage with 28 crewmen to handle the 10 miles of rigging that control her 32,000 square feet of canvas.

***1890*:** Thomas Lipton enters the tea business to assure supplies of tea at low cost for his 300 grocery stores. He offers 'The Finest the World Can Produce' at 1d 7p lb. when the going price is roughly a shilling higher. He buys tea estates in Ceylon, in order to sell tea at a reasonable price.

***1904*:** Due to the unbearable heat, iced tea is invented by Richard Blechynden and popularized and commercialized at the St. Louis World's Fair when sweltering fairgoers pass him by to get ice cream cones.

Today, automation has contributed to improved quality control and reduced labour. Sensor and computer controls have been introduced to machine automation, so that unskilled workers can produce superior tea without compromising on quality. The combination of nature's bounty and manmade technical breakthroughs combines to produce the most exceptional tea products that are sold on the market today.

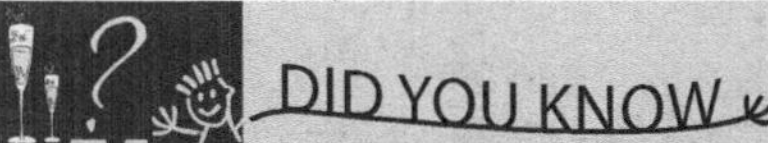

Boston Tea Party

In May 1773, The British Parliament gave money to the British East India Company, so they could lower their tea prices. The Americans were angered because the British East India Company would trade only with pro-British merchants.

In September 1773, the British East India Company put 500,000 pounds of tea on the market. They did this because they had so much extra tea on hand and many of the members of British Parliament were investors in the tea market. If there was too much tea available for sale, tea would be cheaper and the members of British Parliament would lose money.

The Boston Tea Party took place on 16 December 1773, when colonists threw tea into the Boston Harbor. They did this because they did not like the British tea taxes.

Tea is being thrown out into the sea opposing the British in America. Tea is being thrown out into the sea opposing the british in America. (Courtesy: *Art Today*).

Three ships had come from England and wanted to dock in Boston Harbor. Because the ships would not go back to England, Samuel Adams, John Hancock and 80 other men disguised themselves as Natives Americans and threw all the tea into Boston Harbor. The Boston Tea Party was the idea of Samuel Adams. His cousin John Adams did not like mob action, but he wrote this about dumping the tea: 'There is a dignity, a majesty, a sublimity, in this last effort of the patriots that I greatly admire.'

The British people in the British Parliament did not admire this action. They were angered and passed the Intolerable Acts as punishment for the Boston Tea Party. The worst part of these acts was that they closed the Boston Harbor and said that the city had to pay for the tea that had been dumped into the Harbor.

The colonists sang a song about the Boston Tea Party. It started like this: 'Rally, Mohawks! Bring out your axes, and tell King George we'll pay no taxes on his foreign tea.'

2.2 CULTIVATION

Tea like all other beverages cannot be consumed directly off the tea shrub. It needs to be processed very delicately. The flavourful dried leaves of this shrub are used for making the beverage. First, we need to study the tea plant and the ideal conditions it requires to grow.

2.3 THE PLANT CAMELLIA SINENSIS

The biological name of the tea plant is *Camellia sinensis*. The tea plant is an evergreen shrub and grows in tropical and sub-tropical regions of the world. It has more than 200 varieties of the species *Camellia sinensis*; each has a unique flavour and taste. The 'terminal buds' of the tea plant are used to make tea.

A tea plantation in Sri Lanka. (Courtesy: *Periyannaraj Sadayapillai, Sri Lanka.*)

Climatic Conditions

The climatic conditions required for the growth of a flavourful and aromatic bush are as follows:

- Soil: acidic soil,
- Temperature: 10–30°C,
- Rainfall: 2,000 mm/annum, and
- Ground level: 600–2000 metres above the sea level.

The soft seedlings are developed in a nursery for 10 months on an average, which protects them from harsh weather conditions. After they have strengthened, the plants are transferred to open fields to develop under the shade of wide branched trees. It takes about three years before the plants are ready for harvesting.

A tea plant will grow up to 16 metres (52 feet) into a tree if left undisturbed. However, the cultivated plants are pruned to waist level for the ease of plucking the terminal buds at the topmost tip of the plant.

Varieties of the Plant

As mentioned, the *C. sinensis* shrub has more than 200 varieties of the species *C. sinensis*. However, primarily two varieties are used.

1. **The China tea plant (*C. sinensis*)**—used for most Chinese and Japanese teas.
2. **The clone Assam tea plant (*C. sinensis* var. *Assamica*)**—used for most Indian teas apart from Darjeeling (which differs in aroma).

Tea estates in Sri Lanka. (Courtesy: *Periyannaraj Sadayapillai, Sri Lanka.*)

The tea plants are categorized based on the size of the leaves. The different sizes are as follows:

- Assam type, which has the largest leaves,
- China type, which has the smallest leaves and
- Cambod type, which has the intermediate-sized leaves.

2.4 TEA PROCESSING

The method of processing tea is similar to all varieties, be it black tea, Oolong tea or green tea. The taste of the various types of tea may vary, but processing steps are very similar (Figure 2.1).

Plucking

Plucking is the process in which the terminal buds of the shrub are carefully picked along with two young leaves (as shown in the photo in p. 19). This is done twice a year during early spring and early summer or late spring. It is rarely done in the winter season, if the weather permits. Picking the leaves is usually done by hands, as it is very difficult to get machines to the hill slopes where most teas of the world are grown. In addition, hand picking reduces the risk of damaging the leaves as compared to machine picking. It has to be done by the 'twist of the wrist' rather than pinching the plant, which may damage the stalk.

Withering/Wilting

As soon as the leaves are picked, they begin to wilt and the enzymatic action begins. Withering helps in removing the excess water from the leaves and allows slight oxidation of the leaves. The leaves are left under the sun or in rooms with free flow of air. It is a very important step, because, first, the leaves lose the excess moisture of up to a quarter of its weight. Second, the tannin in the leaves reacts with the air, breaks down the leaf proteins into amino acids and exposes the caffeine, making it freely available. This essentially brings out the flavour of the tea.

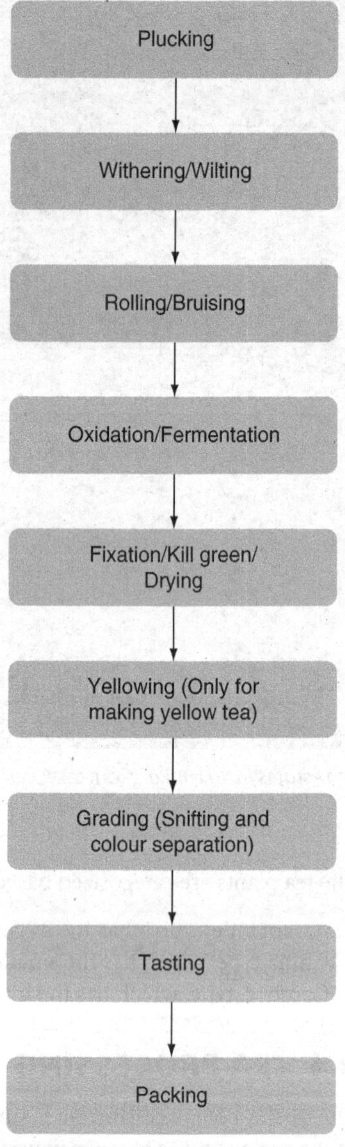

Figure 2.1 Tea processing.

Rolling/Bruising

This process is usually done by putting the leaves on a conveyor belt to help bruise the leaves. The bruising process exposes the leaves to the oxidative enzymes and the oxidation process begins. This leads to the release of the leaves juices, which aid in the oxidation process and change the profile of the tea.

Rolling is the process used to curl the leaves either by hand or by rolling machine. The leaves are moist; in this process, they start curling and lose more moisture. This step causes the essential oils and juices of the leaves to come out, enhancing the taste of the tea. The leaves can be given a shape of twists or rolled into balls/ spheres depending on the shape that is required. In many types of Oolong tea, the rolled strips are rolled in spheres or semi-spheres. There are many shapes that tea leaves are given in this process, for example, spheres, semi-spheres, pellets or even cones.

Oxidation/Fermentation Process

This is a process specifically used for black and Oolong teas. In this process, the teas are kept in a climate-controlled room that is dark for beginning the oxidation process. This process enables the chlorophyll in the leaves to be broken down, releasing the tannins in the leaves. This process is referred to as fermentation. The tea manufacturer, based on the desired quality of the tea required, varies the duration of the fermentation process. For example, for light Oolong tea that is a semi- or partially fermented tea, the

After withering, 1800 kg of leaves will reduce to 900 kg due to the loss of moisture in the leaves. After the total processing of the leaves, 1000 kg of leaves will reduce to 200 kg. Hence, to make Pekoe tea, 80% of the moisture is lost.

Tea being plucked with a 'twist of the wrist' by a plantation worker in Sri Lanka.
(Courtesy: *Periyannaraj Sadayapillai, Sri Lanka.*)

Withering fans (left) and empty withering beds (right) at Uplands Tea Estates, Sri Lanka. (Courtesy: *Periyannaraj Sadayapillai, Sri Lanka.*)

fermentation may be anywhere from 5–40°C oxidation. In darker Oolong teas, it is 60–70% oxidation and in black teas, it is 100% fermentation/oxidation. Oxidation is 'the most important' step to give tea its fragrance, taste, tea liquor colour, strength and briskness. Under or over oxidation/fermentation can result in grassy flavours or overly thick winey flavours.

Fixation/Kill-green/Drying

This process actually stops the previous oxidation process. This involves heating the tea leaves moderately, which will deactivate their oxidative enzymes. Traditionally, the tea leaves are heated in a hollow metallic, cooking vessel, *i.e.*, *wok* or the leaves are even steamed. However, now, with the advancements in technology, kill-green is done by baking in a rolling drum.

Drying process is the step taken just before the tea is ready for sale. This process is done by various methods, such as panning, air drying or baking. The usual process for drying is baking at a temperature of 120°C. However, care should be taken as to not overcook the leaves. The drying of the produced tea is responsible for many new flavours, particularly in green tea.

Tea leaves left to wither in Uplands Tea Estate factory before processing. (Courtesy: *Periyannaraj Sadayapillai, Sri Lanka.*)

Tea leaves left to wither in Uplands Tea Estate factory before processing. (Courtesy: *Periyannaraj Sadayapillai, Sri Lanka.*)

Fermentation room at Uplands Tea Estate factory in Sri Lanka. (Courtesy: *Periyannaraj Sadayapillai, Sri Lanka.*)

Dried tea leaves on a conveyor belt being sent to the next process of grading. (Courtesy: *Periyannaraj Sadayapillai, Sri Lanka.*)

Yellowing (Only for Making Yellow Tea)

In this procedure, a few leaves are left, after the kill-green process, in a closed container and are heated. This causes the green leaves to yellow, resulting in a beverage with a distinctive yellowish-green tinge due to the transformation of the leaf chlorophyll. The leaves being exposed to 'close to human body temperatures'; amino acids and polyphenols in the processed tea leaves undergo chemical changes to give this tea its distinctive and brisk yet mellow taste. This special variant is called 'yellow tea'.

Aging/Curing (Optional for Post-fermented Teas)

Aging is usually not required for most teas. However, some teas require a secondary fermentation or baking for them to reach their baking potential. A green tea, 'Pu-erh', for instance, prior to curing into post-fermented tea is often bitter in taste and harsh; however, after the curing process, it becomes sweet and potable. However, Oolong teas are benefitted by aging under charcoal fire.

Grading

Before the tea is graded, it undergoes two basic steps. First, fibre extraction also known as snifting is carried out to remove the unwanted leaf nodes, fibres and stems. Next, the tea is separated as per its colour (*i.e.*, black, brown, etc). After these two vital steps are completed, grading of tea is done. More details about grading of tea are discussed in Section 2.6.

Tasting

A panel of experts and connoisseurs taste the overall quality of the tea and judge it on various parameters, such as taste, colour, aroma and tannin content. The tea also undergoes laboratory test to check for its caffeine content.

Packing

After the tea is graded and tasted, it is packed and ready to be shipped to various destinations all over the world.

The steps, mentioned here, are essential for processing any kind of tea. Further in this chapter, we shall study in detail the different types of tea and the basic differences in their production processes.

Flavoured teas, such as jasmine, hibiscus, cherry, vanilla, orange, lemon and pearl grey are manufactured by spraying the tea with the respective flavouring agents or by infusing the flavours in the tea by marrying the ingredients with the tea for long periods of time.

2.5 TYPES OF TEA

White Tea

This tea is grown exclusively in the Fujian province of China. It is a lightly oxidized tea. In this tea, the leaves are allowed to whiten in sunlight, before they are processed to prevent oxidation. This preserves the characteristic flavour of white tea.

The unopened buds are white and silvery; hence, the tea acquired the name white tea. It is one of the most expensive teas, as it is grown only in a particular region and the plant has to blossom before the first rainfall, else the harvest of the year to produce this exquisite tea is lost. White tea is harvested only once a year. This is the reason why it is considered very special and one of the most expensive teas in the world.

Brands of White Tea

The brands of white tea are Darjeeling White Tea, Schonmei, White Peony and Silver Needle.

Green Tea

Green tea is one of the most widely accepted teas in the world. It undergoes minimal oxidation. It is also originated in China. It constitutes a major percentage of overall tea production in China.

Green tea is processed and grown in a variety of ways and is slightly different than other tea types. First, it is harvested three times a year, April–May, then June–July and finally July–August. It is then processed and stored at a temperature of 0–5°C that is called *Aracha*. Second, the tea is refined by a final firing.

At this stage, the leaves are refined throughout the year (*i.e.*, they are slow fired for a year). Due to this, the leaves get longer life and a better flavour. Third, the green tea is graded according to the leaf size. After this, the tea goes for the final process called 'blending' and then packing.

Green tea.

Brands of Green Tea

Some of the renowned brands of green tea are Long Ding, Qing Ding, Hui Ming, Gun Powder, Rain Flower, White Cloud, Huoqing, Defang, Tata Tea, Tetley and Mecha.

Yellow Tea

The manufacturing of yellow tea follows the same process of green tea. However, in addition to the drying phase, an additional yellowing step is undertaken. This converts the green leaves to yellow (refer Yellowing in Section 2.4).

Brands of Yellow Tea

The famous brands of yellow tea are Junshan Yin Zhen, Huo Shan Huang Ya and Meng Ding Huang Ya.

Oolong Tea

Oolong tea is a traditional Chinese tea, which is semi-oxidized, or fermented to about 70%. It is produced through a unique process under intense sun light. Its manufacturing process also involves application of external heat. The leaves in the rolling process are made into spheres or semi-spheres and finally giving this tea its unique appearance. It has a very unique method of brewing.

The process involves adding 3 grams of tea per 200 ml of hot water at a temperature of 93–96°C for 3–10 minutes. Oolong tea is served in a 2-oz. cup (*i.e.*, 30–60 ml approx.). The consumption of Oolong tea is very high in China. It is known to have a lot of health benefits..It prevents obesity, reduces high blood pressure, strengthens teeth preventing tooth decay and relieves physical and mental stresses. It helps in controlling skin ailments, such as eczema and rashes, improves vitality and life span.

Brands of Oolong Tea

The brands of Oolong tea are Red Robe, Gold Turtle, Iron Monk, White Comb and Cassia.

Black Tea

As we know, in India, black tea is the most popular variety of tea. It is a 100% oxidized/fermented tea type. The oxidation process breaks down the chlorophyll, which allows the caffeine in the leaves to surface and dissolve in the brew, because of this process, the black tea contains more amounts of caffeine than other varieties.

Black tea is considered to be the tea with strong flavour and aroma. While green tea usually loses its flavour within a year, black tea retains its flavour for many years. This is one of the reasons for tea to be compressed into bricks and used as currency in Tibet, Mongolia and Siberia in the 19th century.

Table 2.1 Popular Blends of Tea and Their Characteristics

Origin	District	Main Method of Manufacturing	Description
India	Darjeeling	Orthodox	Light, pungent and distinctive flavour
	Assam	CTC	Good colour and strong
	Nilgiris	Orthodox	Light, golden and smooth
Sri Lanka	Uva	Orthodox	Golden, pungent and distinctive character
	Dimbula	Orthodox	Golden and smooth
	Nuwara Eliya	Orthodox	Delicate, very pungent and distinctive character
Kenya	East of Rift	CTC	Golden and strong flavour
	West of Rift	CTC	Good colour and strong flavour

The literal translation in Chinese language for black tea is 'red tea' due to the colour of the tea liquor. However, in India, Western countries and most other countries of the world, it is called black tea, referring to the colour of the fermented tea leaves.

The oxidation process for black tea takes between 45–90 minutes or even up to 3 hours and it is done at high humidity, at a temperature ranging from 20–30°C. Black tea is further classified as either orthodox or CTC (*i.e.*, crush, tear and curl). This method was developed in 1932.

While unblended black teas are classified as per their estate of origin, their year and their flush (first, second or autumn), orthodox processed teas, on the other hand, are further graded according to the post-production leaf quality, based on the 'Orange Pekoe System', while CTC uses a different grading method.

Types of Black Tea

Other than the classification based on the estate of origin, their year and their flush (first, second or autumn), the black teas are classified based on their country of origin, which plays a vital role in its overall quality and hence grading.

Post-fermented Tea

In processing post-fermented tea, which is done after the fixation process, this variety of tea goes through a secondary fermentation. These teas are commonly known as Pu-erh, Liu'an and Liubao and post-fermented teas in English. These teas have a unique taste and flavour; one has to develop a palate to enjoy these tea varieties.

The details given above summarize the types of teas and their unique processing, leading to the same tea leaves with a variety of tastes and aromas.

Other Blends

Apart from the above-mentioned types, some teas are flavoured with additives. Usually, the flavouring is added to the black tea or some times to green tea. There are a wide range of such teas available in the market; some of them are hibiscus, jasmine and rose flavoured. Table 2.2 gives information about some of the famous blends.

Table 2.2 Famous Blends of Teas

Blend	Characteristic
Assam Tea	It is a famous breakfast black tea blend preferred by many people for its rich aroma. It is strong and full-bodied tea. It is native to Assam Tea Plantations, coming from the plant *C. sinensis* var. *Assamica*.
Darjeeling Tea	It is a fuller-bodied tea as compared to the Assam variety. It is a black tea variety. It is both a breakfast tea and an evening tea. It is recommended to be consumed without milk.
English Breakfast Tea	It is a blend made popular by Queen Victoria herself. It is made with a combination of Assam, Darjeeling, Ceylon and Kenyan tea varieties. This blend is best enjoyed by adding sugar and milk.
Earl Grey Tea	It is a blend of black tea, which is flavoured with the oil of Bergamot orange. It is best to drink without milk.
Lemon/Citrus Tea	It is a variant of tea with lemon essence. However, many people prefer to consume this blend with a squeeze of fresh lemon juice.
Hibiscus Tea	It is quite popular in Latin America. It is originally made with the petals of the hibiscus plant. Now, many teas are flavoured with the essence of hibiscus due to its refreshing qualities.
Indian Masala Blend Tea	Many people refer to this as a spiced tea or *masala chai*. It is a black tea that is infused with the spices, such as cardamom, cinnamon, cloves, fennel, nutmeg and ginger and enriched with a generous quantity of milk and sugar. It is very popular in India and the Middle-Eastern countries.
Individual Hotel Blends Tea	Many hotels, such as the Taj or ITC in India are often making their own tea blends by unique combinations of Assam and Darjeeling blends. They do not make these on their own, but from famous tea house like Twinnings.
Jasmine Tea	It is very famous due to the presence of numerous oriental restaurants all over the world. It is often served as an accompaniment in oriental restaurants in a *Chinese tea cup*.
Lapsang Souchong Tea	It is a Chinese black tea with a smoky flavour. It gains such a flavour due to its aging over pinewood smoke. It is recommended to be consumed without milk.
Mint Tea	It is a very popular blend adopted from Morocco. It is infused with mint flavour. In Morocco, the original version is served with a large sprig of mint in the cup.
Rose Tea	It is made by mixing tea with rose petals during oxidation. It is very refreshing. It tastes best when served without milk.
Sri Lanka Tea	It is a pale-golden coloured tea with a good flavour. Lemon blend is still used as a trade name. It is served with lemon or milk.
Vanilla Tea	It is flavoured with vanilla essence. It is famous in the tropical regions, such as the Caribbean, Brazil, etc.

Herbal Teas

Herbal teas are better known as *tisanes*. They are not made from the leaves of the tea plant, but from the flowers or leaves of other plants and herbs. They include a variety of teas. Some of the popular varieties are Indian Holy Basil (*Tulsi*), Chamomile tea, Hibiscus tea (made with Hibiscus petals), Ginseng tea (popular substitute for coffee in China and Korea) and *Neem* tea.

2.6 GRADING OF TEA

Like all products or services in the world, for each type and variety of tea to command a specific price and value, it needs to be graded as per its quality. There are two aspects that affect the grading of tea. They are as follows:

- The size of the tea leaf: Larger the leaves, better the grading.
- The method of production of the tea: There are two basic methods to manufacture tea. First method is harvesting tea by hand. The second method is a fully mechanized method called CTC process (crush, tear and curl). It is considered that the latter, *i.e.*, the mechanized method, is not good for the leaves, as the leaves get damaged and thus the CTC-processed teas are considered to be of a lower grade.

As opposed to black tea, no single accepted method of grading is developed for green and Oolong teas. The grading of green and Oolong teas is affected by many factors such as the variety of the tea plant, the region and the area in which the tea was grown and the stage at which the picking of the tea leaves took place.

Grades of Tea

Most of us use only tea dust or fannings, but there are many grades of tea available which are listed in the following:

1. **Dust:** This consists of small pieces of tea leaves and tea dust. It is the lowest grade in the classification of black tea.
2. **Fanning:** This consists mainly of pieces of tea leaves. It is a low-grade tea.

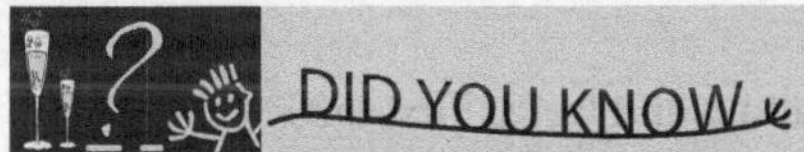

Chamomile Tea

It is another variant of herbal tea. Often confused to be made from the leaves of the tea plant (*Camellia sinensis*), but this type of tea is made from the flowers of several daisy-like plants from the Asteraceae family. It is believed to have medicinal properties of relieving stress and induces sleep. It is best served with lemon and honey (without milk).

Kahwah Tea

This type of tea is made in Afghanistan, Pakistan and the Kashmir valley. It has been popularized by the Kashmiri *pundits* in Delhi among the non-Kashmiris. It is an infusion made with green tea leaves, a few strands of saffron, Kashmiri roses, cinnamon and cardamom. Some even go to the extent of putting cashew nuts in the brew. Traditionally, Kahwah Tea is made in a *samovar* (a brass-kettle with charcoal placed in the centre cavity of it keeping the tea hot for a long time). It is a celebratory drink, served at weddings and important ceremonies. It is a rich and flavourful beverage, which can be best enjoyed during the bone-chilling winters nights. This tea is always consumed without milk.

The photograph shows how the various sizes of tea leaves are separated and graded. (Courtesy: *Periyannaraj Sadayapillai, Sri Lanka.*)

3. **BOP/Broken Orange Pekoe:** This consists of pieces of the larger leaves or small tea leaves. It is a medium-grade tea.
4. **OP/Orange Pekoe:** This consists of large whole tea leaves picked without the flower bud of the tea plant.
5. **FOP/Flowery Orange Pekoe:** These are the whole tea leaves along with the flower buds of tea plants.

Other than these five categories, there are two more important qualities and traits. First quality is 'Golden' where gold hues occur in the tea leave evidencing their quality and the other quality is 'Tippy' that signifies an abundance of young tea buds. The following are the classifications made based on the two qualities, 'Golden' and 'Tippy' as:

1. **GFOP/Golden Flowery Orange Pekoe:** The whole tea leaves with golden tips complemented by the flowers of the tea plants.
2. **TGFOP/Tippy Golden Flowery Orange Pekoe:** This consists of the tea bud and two uppermost tea leaves complemented by the flowers of the tea plant. This is the highest category in the grading of the tea.

However, in the highest grading of tea leaves, there are two more quality refinements, which are:

1. **FTGFOP/Fine Tippy Golden Flowery Orange Pekoe:** This is the choicest of tea leaves.
2. **SFTGFOP/Super Fine Tippy Golden Flowery Orange Pekoe:** This is the highest existing grade of tea leaves.

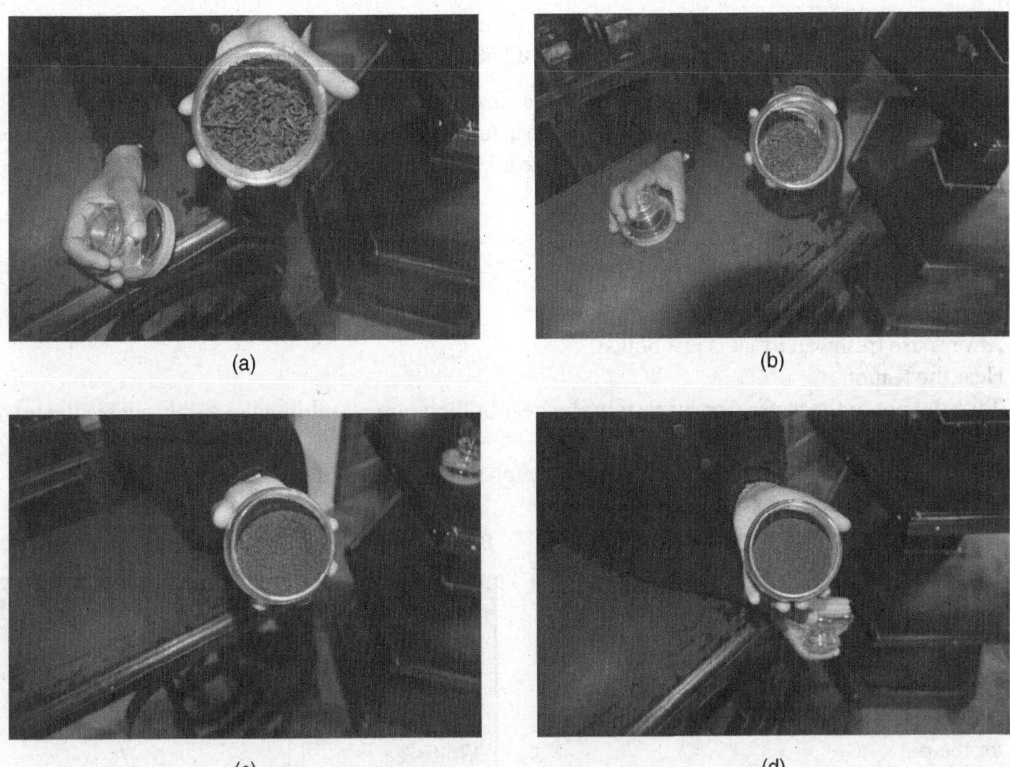

(a) (b) (c) (d)

(a) Flowery Orange Pekoe; (b) Orange Pekoe; (c) Broken Orange Pekoe; and (d) Fanning. (Courtesy: *Periyannaraj Sadayapillai, Sri Lanka.*)

The classifications (discussed in p. 26) are the detailed structure followed all over the world to grade the various categories of tea. Unfortunately, in most domestic households, the tea consumed, is prepared mostly by using the dust category tea leaves. The quality improvement and improvement in the living standard of the India people will lead to more appreciation of the finest and choicest of teas.

2.7 TYPES OF TEA PREPARATIONS AND MAKING A CUP OF TEA

The various tea preparations and the golden rules for making a cup of tea are as follows:

Indian tea: It is made either in metal or in China pots. Milk is usually offered and sugar served separately.

China tea: It is made from a special blend of tea that is more delicate in flavour, but strong. It is usually made in China pots and drunk on its own. To increase the flavour and taste, a slice of lime can be added. The slices of lime will be offered on a doily on a side plate and a small fork and sugar is offered separately.

Russian tea: It is made mostly from Indian or Ceylon tea. It is served with the slices of lime in quarter plates. The slices of lime can be put in the cup itself and some slices served separately. Sugar is usually offered separately.

Ice tea: Make strong tea and chill well. This tea is then strained and stored for future, which is served in a tumbler on a doily with a teaspoon with a slice of lemon. Mint is served as garnish.

Tisanes: An infusion of herbs and dry plants that is drunk hot on its own and sweetened lightly. The word is derived from the Greek word 'ptisane' that means barley water. Today, most tisanes are made from medicinal plants and some are fruit flavoured. Herbal infusions that are often used for medicinal purpose are gaining popularity.

Five Golden Rules for Making Tea

1. Use a good quality tea.
2. Always use freshwater that is just boiled.
3. Heat the teapot.
4. Take the pot to the water. The water must be near boiling point, as this will possibly enable the leaves to infuse properly.
5. Brew the tea. Do not allow it to boil. Brew only for 3–5 minutes and stir well before pouring.

Making Tea

1. Water used to make tea should be lime-free. Tap water makes tea cloudy.
2. Rinse the teapot well with boiling water before putting the tea into it. The requirements are one teaspoon of tea per person and one teaspoon for the pot.
3. Pour the water onto the tea just as it reaches the boiling point, stirring time to time.

Table 2.3 Brewing Temperatures for Making Tea

Type	Brewing Temperature (°C)
Green Tea	75–80
Yellow Tea	70–75
White Tea	65–70
Oolong Tea	80–85
Black Tea	92–95

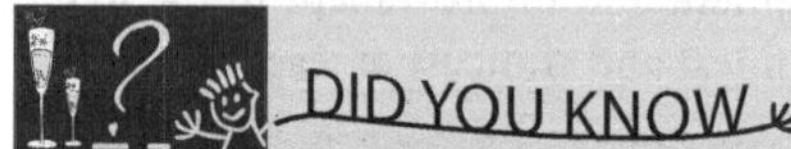

'Steeping' is the process of making a cup of tea, which is also known as brewing.

The standard procedure for brewing a good cup of tea is given below. This is applicable to all variants of tea except Oolong tea.

Add 2 grams of tea per 100 ml of hot water. Steeping temperature should be between 81–87°C for 2–3 minutes. The tea is steeped 2–3 times to form tea liquor with the help of a tea infuser (refer to the photograph given here).

The tea infuser, as shown in the photograph, is a hollow container with holes making it porous. The tea leaves are place in the centre of this container and it is dipped into the teapot/vessel containing hot water (similar to a tea bag).

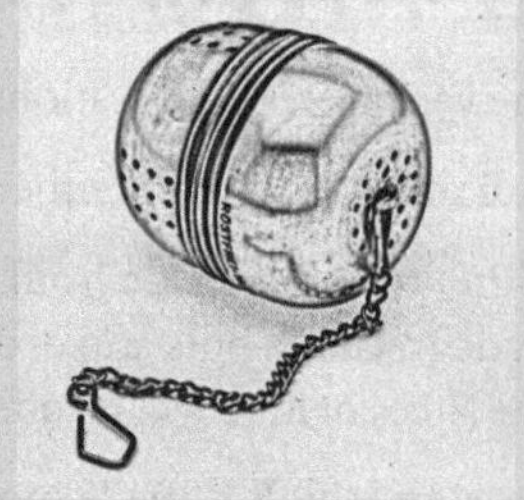

The tea infuser.

4. The infusion time is 3–5 minutes after which the flavour does not improve. The infusion becomes lesser if boiled longer.
5. Just before serving, stir the tea in the teapot and strain using a strainer.
6. Always remember the water should be 95°C hot and not boiling when you pour it over the tea leaves.

2.8 TEA STORAGE

Processed or unprocessed tea contains essential oils that give the tea its taste and aroma; if it is left exposed to the open air, the essential oils shall be lost due to their volatile nature.

Tea is vulnerable to five things, which are air, light, odour, heat and moisture. These elements can make tea stale.

The best place to store tea is an airtight container, preferable tin or ceramic. Tea has to be kept in a cool and dry place. Black and Oolong teas can be stored and kept for two to three years under ideal conditions. Tea that is less oxidized has a shorter shelf life as compared to oxidized teas.

2.9 SOME TEA RECIPES

Iced Tea Recipes

Thai Iced Tea

Ingredients:

- Guarana or California Chai made with three bags and cooled,
- 16 oz. Water,
- 8–12 Ice cubes,
- 1 oz. Cream,
- 4 oz. Milk,
- 2 oz. Almond syrup,
- 2 oz. Coconut syrup and
- 1 oz. Passion fruit syrup.

Method:

Combine the above ingredients in a blender. Blend in bursts on high till all the ice is chopped fine and the mix is even. Pour into tall glasses and garnish each with a cinnamon stick.

Fruit Tea Punch

Ingredients:

- 2 Bags golden green tea,
- 1½ Cups water,
- 1 Cup honey,
- 1 Cup orange juice,
- ½ Cup fresh lemon juice,
- 1 Cup fresh fruit, crushed and
- 1 Pint ginger ale.

Method:

Make the tea as per the instructions given on the tea bags. Allow it to cool. Mix all ingredients except ginger ale. Just before serving, add ginger ale and crushed ice. If the punch is too strong for you, you can dilute it with ice water or more ginger ale.

Spiced Tea

Ingredients:

- 4 Bags of your favourite tea,
- ½ Cup (4 oz.) sugar,
- 1 Cup (8 oz.) water,
- 1 Stick cinnamon,
- 6 Whole cloves,
- 3 Cardamom pods (optional),
- 2 Tablespoonful tea leaves,
- 4 Cups (32 oz.) boiling water,
- Juice of one large lemon and two oranges,
- Ice cubes,
- Iced water or soda water (club soda) to taste and
- Orange and lemon slices to decorate.

Method:

Boil the sugar, water and spices for 5 minutes and then remove from heat. Put the tea bags in a large pot, pour the boiling water over and leave for 5 minutes.

Strain into large bowl, add the strained syrup and leave to cool. Stir in the strained lemon and orange juice, then add ice cubes and dilute with iced water or club soda to taste. Decorate with the slices of orange or lemon. This can be served for 8–10 people.

Tea Punch

Ingredients:
- ½ Pint golden green tea,
- 6 oz. Sugar,
- ½ Pint orange squash,
- 4 Tablespoonful lemon juice,
- 2 Small bottle ginger ale,
- 1 Large bottle lemonade and
- 1 Orange, sliced.

Method:
Put the hot tea in a bowl, add the sugar and stir until the sugar dissolves. Add the orange squash and lemon juice and strain and then chill it. Just before serving, mix the ginger ale and lemonade and decorate with orange slices. This can be served for 12 people.

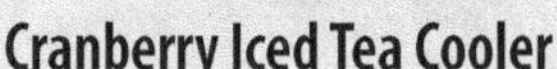

Cranberry Iced Tea Cooler

Ingredients:
- 2 Quarts CRAN-AID iced tea,
- 1 Can (6 oz.) frozen cranberry concentrate, partially thawed and undiluted,
- 1 Cup orange juice and
- ¼ Cup sugar.

Method:
Iced Tea: Place four CRAN-AID tea bags in a glass or porcelain container. Pour two quarts boiling water over the tea bags and steep 7–10 minutes. Squeeze and remove tea bags and allow the tea to cool.

In large pitcher, combine the cranberry and orange juices. Stir them until they are well mixed. Then, pour in the ice tea. Add the sugar and mix until you dissolve the sugar. Cover and place in refrigerator to chill about 1 hour. Serve in ice-filled glasses.

Hot Tea Recipes

Hot Tea Punch

Ingredients:
- 5 Bags of your favourite tea,
- 6 Cups water,
- ¾ Cup sugar,
- 2 Cinnamon sticks,
- 8 Whole cloves,

- 1½ Cups orange juice and
- ⅓ Cup fresh lemon juice.

Method:
Bring the first four ingredients to boil in heavy large saucepan over high heat, stirring until the sugar dissolves. Boil for 6 minutes and then remove it from heat. Add tea bags, cover it and let it steeps 10 minutes. Discard tea bags. Add orange and lemon juices to punch. (It can be prepared one day in advance and then cover and refrigerate it. Reheat before continuing.) Using slotted spoon, remove whole spices. Serve hot.

Indian Chai/Tea

Ingredients:
- 3 Teabags black tea,
- 4 Cups water,
- 1 to 3 pieces of 1-inch cinnamon sticks,
- 1-Inch piece of ginger root cut into four slices,
- ½ Teaspoonful (2 ml) cardamom seeds,
- ½ Teaspoonful (2 ml) black peppercorns,
- ½ Teaspoonful (2 ml) whole cloves,
- 1 Teaspoonful (5 ml) whole coriander seeds,
- 1 Cup (225 ml) milk and
- Honey or other sweetener to taste.

Method:
Bring water to boil in a saucepan. Add spices, cover it and simmer 20 minutes. Add teabags and steep 10 minutes. Add milk and heat to drinking temperature—do not boil. Strain mixture through a cheesecloth or cotton dish towel. Serve with honey or other sweetener to taste.

Hot Ginger Tea

Ingredients:
- 4 Ginger aid tea bags,
- 2 Pieces 3-inch cinnamon sticks,
- 8 Whole cloves,
- 6 Cup boiling water and
- 2 Orange slices.

Method:
Put tea bags, cinnamon sticks, cloves, ginger and sugar into a large teapot. Pour boiling water over and allow to steep 3 minutes. Remove tea bags and steep 5 minutes. To serve, pour tea into cups and float a quarter slice of orange in each cup.

Black Saffron Tea

Ingredients:

- 4 Bags golden green tea,
- 6 Green cardamoms,
- 4 Teaspoonful sugar,
- ½ Teaspoonful saffron threads,
- 4 Cups water and
- 4 Bags golden green tea black.

Method:

Add the cardamom, sugar and saffron to the water and make it boils. Simmer until reduced by half. Again make it boils, add tea bags and steep 8 minutes. Strain out tea and spices. Serve hot.

Almond Tea

Ingredients:

- 4 Tea bags of your favourite tea,
- ½ Teaspoonful lemon zest, finely grated, rind
- 4 Cups boiling water,
- ½ Cup sugar,
- 2 Tablespoonful lemon juice,
- 1 Teaspoonful almond extract and
- ¼ Teaspoonful vanilla.

Method:

Steep tea and lemon rind in boiling water for about 5 minutes. Stir in sugar, lemon juice, almond and vanilla. Serve hot.

2.10 INTERESTING FACTS ABOUT TEA

- Until the 19th century, blocks of tea were used as currency in Siberia.
- The Irish consumes highest amount of tea in comparison to the other nations in the world.
- As tin boxes were too expensive; therefore, a New York-based importer, Thomas Sullivan, looked for a cheaper alternative to send his tea samples to the clients. He adopted a way to store tea in 'gauze packets', made of mesh. This packaging confused his customers and instead of removing the tea from the gauze packets, they put the gauze packets containing tea in hot water and without any intention. Thomas Sullivan had invented the tea bag.

Traditional Japanese teaware used for serving green tea. (Courtesy: *Shamala Ganesh, Bengaluru.*)

- The Tibetans drink tea made from salt and yak butter.
- Tea is the most popular and cheapest beverage next to water in the world.
- The British East India Company introduced tea to the Indian sub-continent and started it's first plantations in the early 1800s. Prior to this, tea was not known to the Indians. To encourage the habit of tea drinking among the Indians, the British rulers introduced 'tea breaks' for the working class in this country. People would get a single 'tea-break'. This practice increased the popularity of this beverage that was made with milk showing the British influence, which is widely followed in India till today.

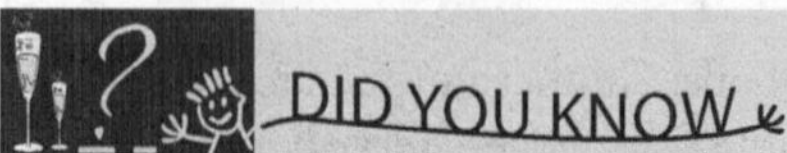

Tea was introduced by the British in India in the early 19th century. Prior to this, the Indian culture was not accustomed to tea in their day-to-day lives. The tea cultivation in various parts of India brought about large supply of this beverage in the subcontinent. Most teas processed from British India were black teas.

It was due to the British influence that Indians were introduced to tea. The British strategy was remarkable in increasing domestic demand in India. The working class in India was given exclusive 'tea breaks' in the morning and early evenings between their works. People interested to take a break automatically had tea.

These British 'tea breaks' are followed till this day and has India addicted to this wonderful beverage.

2.11 BENEFITS OF DRINKING TEA

Tea is said to have various benefits. It has various medicinal properties—it lowers cognitive impairment, helps lower cholesterol and it has anti-cancer and anti-diabetic properties. Other than these properties, tea is said to boost mental alertness, lowers stress hormone levels and increases the metabolic rate. Certain types of teas such as Oolong tea have a positive effect to prevent tooth decay and help in keeping breath fresh.

Tea contains caffeine and it may have a negative effect on the body. Excess caffeine in the body is said to increase sleeping disorders.

This concludes our understanding of one of the world's most preferred and popular beverages.

LET'S SUMMARIZE IN POINTS

- In this chapter, we have learnt about the tea plant *Camellia sinensis* and the various steps involved in tea processing.
- Tea is processed after picking to bring out the flavours and the caffeine, making this stimulating beverage very popular.
- Tea is the second most consumed beverage after water.
- Green tea, Oolong tea, black tea, white tea, yellow tea, Pu-erh tea (post-fermented tea) and various other flavoured teas and tea blends are popular.
- Making a perfect cup of tea is an art and a skill.

2.12 FAQs

Short-Answer Type Questions

1. Which country does tea originate from?
2. Give the biological name of the tea plant.
3. Give the varieties of the tea plant.
4. Give three specific climatic conditions required for growing the tea plant.
5. In which country was tea first used as a currency and when?
6. What are TGFOP, GFOP, OP and BOP?
7. What is CTC?
8. Fanning can be described as __________?
9. How do Tibetans drink tea?
10. Give three medicinal benefits of drinking tea.

Long-Answer Type Questions

1. Describe the following in detail:
   (i) White tea,
   (ii) Yellow tea and
   (iii) Post-fermented/Pu-erh tea.
2. Give in detail with diagram, the production process of tea.
3. How is tea graded? Give five grades of black tea.
4. Give the difference between black tea that comes from India, Sri Lanka and Kenya.
5. How is tea stored?
6. Name five hot/cold tea recipes.

2.13 KEY TERMS

- Antioxidants
- Briskness
- Caffeine
- Catechins
- CTC
- Enzymes
- Infusion
- Oxidation
- Terminal bud
- WOK

COFFEE

CHAPTER OUTLINE

LET'S DEFINE

'Coffee is a wonderful beverage, which is made from the beans of *Coffea canephora,* made after processing, roasting and brewing in hot water. This beverage is highly rejuvenating and has addictive qualities.'

Coffee is a wonderful beverage. An early morning cup of coffee or a late night 'cuppa' brings a smile to everyone's face. It has become synonymous now with relaxation and fun time with friends and colleagues. This is all due to the wonderful coffee shops lining the streets worldwide, where people enjoy having a free moment with family, friends or even small informal meetings.

Coffee has its own pleasing and soothing aroma that relaxes the mind naturally. This can be attributed to its caffeine content. It is one of the most popular and addictive beverages in the world; that is why it is one of the most traded crops in the world till date.

3.1 HISTORY

The word 'coffee' comes from the Arabic word *kahwa* referring to this aromatic bean, which is the seed of the coffee cherry.

The Ethiopian ancestors of the *Oromo* people (who are ethnic group found in modern day Ethiopia, Northern Kenya and Somalia) are said to have been the first to recognize the stimulating and energizing effects of coffee.

However, it is difficult to find evidence to support this theory. The story of 'Kaldi', a 9th-century Ethiopian goat herder, who is believed to have discovered coffee did not appear in writing till 1671.

However, especially in the Middle Eastern countries, Sheik Omar is attributed with the discovery of coffee. 'Sheik Omar' was known to cure the sick through prayer. The story tells us how he was exiled from Mocha (Yemen) to a desert cave near Ousab. Starving, Omar chewed berries from a nearby shrub, but it was bitter. He tried to roast them, but they became hard. He then tried to boil them to make them soft, which resulted in a fragrant brown liquid. Upon drinking this fragrant liquid Omar sustained for days. Stories of Omar reached Mocha and he was recalled and made a saint. From Ethiopia, it then spread to the rest of the Arab world, including Egypt and Yemen.

The most credible evidence of coffee drinking comes from Yemen in the middle of the 15th century. From Yemen, it was exported to the rest of the Middle East.

Sufi Baba Bundan, the first person to smuggle coffee out of the Middle East, strapped coffee beans to his chest and brought it to India in 1670. He then cultivated the bean in Mysore. It is from here in India that coffee spread across to Indonesia, Italy and the rest of Europe and then made its way to the Americas.

Coffee in American History

Coffee as compared to alcoholic beverages was not that popular in America. However, during the war in 1812, everything changed. The British temporarily cut off access to tea imports, igniting the American palate for coffee.

As brewing methods improved and also due to the American Civil War, coffee became an everyday product in the United States of America. On the other hand, the British conquest of India, made tea available in Britain at a very cheap price and was relatively easier to make. This made Britons prefer tea over coffee. This practice and preference of beverages is noticeable even today in the consumption patterns of both nations.

In South America, coffee was brought to the French territory Martinique in the Caribbean from which most of the cultivated coffee has originated. Coffee thrived in this climate. Today, Brazil cultivates and supplies a large percentage of the world's demand for coffee. It was in 1727 that coffee was brought into Brazil; however, only after Brazil got independence in 1822, did coffee cultivation come into prominence. Many rainforests were cleared near Rio de Janeiro and Sao Paulo to harvest this amazing beverage.

3.2 THE PLANT

Several species of the genus *Coffea* produce the berries from which the coffee is extracted. Out of several, there are primarily two main species that are cultivated:

1. *Coffea canephora*—this is also known as *C. robusta*.
2. *Coffea arabica*—this is the most regarded species.

All coffee plants are evergreen shrubs, growing to 15 feet in height if not pruned. The berries are green when immature, then ripen to yellow and then crimson and finally turn black on ripening. Every berry has two seeds; however, 5–10% of the berries have only one seed, which is called a pea berry. Berries in general ripen in 7–9 months.

The flower of the coffee plant (left) that converts to the red ripe coffee cherry (right).

3.3 CULTIVATION AND VARIETIES OF COFFEE SPECIES

Coffee is cultivated around the world. However, the species cultivated varies from country to country. Coffee is generally cultivated by directly planting the seeds in the soil or in greenhouses where they develop into seedlings and are then transferred to the fields.

Two main species which are grown are *C. arabica* and *C. robusta*. While *C. arabica* is preferred over the other *species* (i.e., *C. robusta*).

The different size of the leaves—from left to right: the leaf of the Arabica plant, the leaf of the Robusta plant and an immature leaf.

Table 3.1 shows the differences between *Robusta* and *Arabica* coffee species.

Table 3.1 Differences Between *Arabica* and *Robusta* Coffees

Arabica Coffee	Robusta Coffee
Arabica has more flavour and aroma and is less bitter than *robusta*.	*Robusta* has fewer flavours and is bitter but has more body (*i.e.*, thicker on the tongue) as compared to *Arabica*.
Contains lesser caffeine than *robusta*.	Contains 40–50% more caffeine than *Arabica*.
Cultivated in most parts of the world and is a preferred variety.	It is often used as a substitute and is added to coffee blends to give foam and body to the beverage.

3.4 COFFEE PROCESSING

Picking

A coffee plant usually starts to produce flowers 3–4 years after it is planted. The cherries appear after about five years of planting the seed. The cherries ripen in 8–9 months after the flowers appear on the plant.

Picking methods have evolved over the years in regard to coffee plantations. Brazil is the largest producer of *Arabica* coffee in the world and it has mechanized the process of picking cherries of the plant. While most of the countries still pick the cherries by hand, this is a very labour-intensive process.

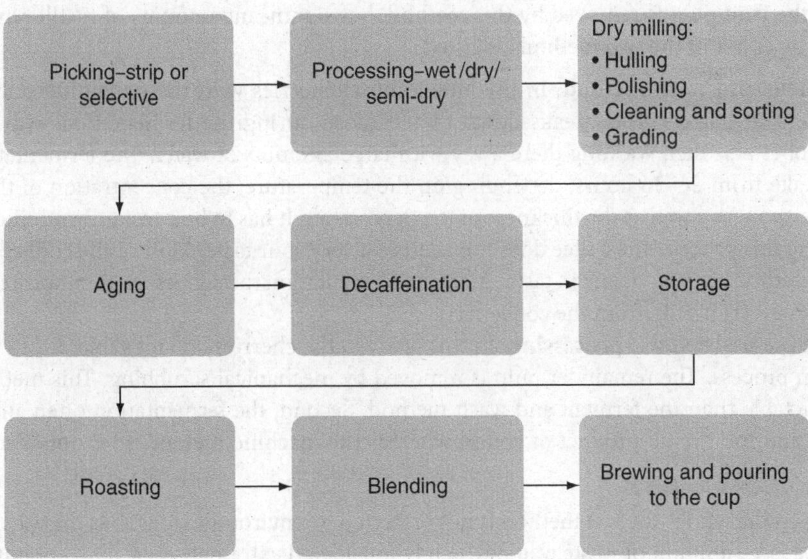

Figure 3.1 Flowchart showing the production process of coffee.

Coffee is harvested in any one of the following two ways:

1. **Strip method:** Harvesting of the entire crop is done at one time, that is, the branch is stripped of the cherries at one time.
2. **Selectively picked:** Only the ripened cherries are picked by hand. This method is used to pick the cherries for premium *Arabica* coffees.

Selective picking done at Chilipili plantations at Coorg, India.

Processing

After the coffee beans have been picked, they need to be processed to expose them, which will produce the wonderful aromatic cup of coffee.

There are basically three methods of processing coffee, namely, wet method, dry method and semi-dry method. Let us discuss them one at a time.

1. **Wet method:** We know that coffee is a cherry and the seed of that cherry is used to make the aromatic beverage. Therefore, to remove the outer covering of the cherry, the wet process/method is used. This method needs substantial amounts of water and specific equipment to scrub the fruit covering off the coffee bean.

   The coffee cherries are sorted by immersing them in water. The green cherries are the unripe ones and will float to the top, whereas the ripe cherries being heavier will sink to the bottom. The unripe cherries are skimmed of the surface and separated. The cherries are then pressed though a screen. Some of the fruit pulp is removed by this method, but significant amounts of it still remain. This is removed by either of the two methods as listed:

   (i) **Ferment and wash method:** In this method, the cherries with the remaining pulp are left to ferment in barrels. This breaks down the cellulose during the fermentation with the help of microbes and then washing them away with large amounts of water. The fermentation process can take from 24–36 hours, depending on the temperature, the concentration of the microbes and enzymes as well as the thickness of the parchment. It has to be constantly monitored, so that during this process, the coffee does not acquire a very sour taste. Most of the coffees made using this method are very acidic in taste. After the fermentation the coffees are then washed to remove the excess fruit pulp from the coffee seed.

   (ii) **Machine-assisted wet processing:** In this process, the cherries are not subjected to the fermentation process. The remainder pulp is removed by mechanical scrubbing. This method is more predictable than the ferment and wash method. Second, the fermentation often affects the flavour and the overall product of coffee, whereas the machine method does not affect the coffee comparatively.

   However, on the whole, the wet method is not preferred by environmentalists, as the washing process results in a large amount of waste water, which is considered extremely toxic and a pollutant.

   After the pulp is removed, the bean is surrounded by two additional layers, the silver skin and parchment. The beans then must be dried, either in the sun or in the machine to approximately 10–13%

moisture content. Drying in the sun reduces the moisture content from 13–14%, approximately. After which, the beans are subjected to machine drying, to achieve 10% moisture content.

Coffee cherries picked and laid out (left) in the tank and are then washed (right).

2. **Dry process:** This is the oldest method of processing coffee. In this method, the coffee beans are first sorted by an ancient method, separating the ripe cherries from the unripened cherries, dirt, soil, twigs, leaves etc. After this, the cherries are sieved to remove any remaining unwanted debris.

   (i) **Drying:** The cherries are then laid out to dry in the sun on concrete blocks or clay bricks. This process takes up to four weeks approximately. In large estates, the cherries are put through machine driers also, after drying them out in the sun for a shorter period of time. Once the cherries have been dried, they are subjected to hulling, sorting and grading along with certain other processes.

   The dry process is used for 95% of the coffee produced in Brazil. However, this process is not very popular in rainy regions, where the humidity in the atmosphere is very high.

3. **Semi-dry process:** This is a unique method of coffee processing. This method mostly practiced in parts of Brazil and Indonesia. In this method, the coffee cherry's outer skin is separated from the bean through mechanical pulping machines. The coffee beans still coated with mucilage are then stored for a day. After this, the mucilage is washed off and the coffee bean is allowed to dry. The coffee bean has a moisture content of 30–35% from this method after drying.

The process shows the hulling machine (wet method)—the soaked coffee cherries are put through the huller to remove the parchment.

Milling

Milling is also known as dry milling. It involves hulling, polishing, cleaning, sorting and grading. These are the final steps in coffee processing, which help in removing the last layers of dry skin and the remaining fruit residue from the dry coffee. A detailed explanation of each of these steps are explained below.

1. **Hulling:** Hulling is the process in which the residual elements of the fruit parchment are separated from the dry coffee bean. It could be the removal of the dried fruit parchment as a result of the dry process the dried mucilage of the semi-dry process or the crumbly parchment skin of wet-processed coffee.
   Hulling is done with the help of machine, which can range from simple mill stones to sophisticated machines.
2. **Polishing:** This process is sometimes described as a process that is detrimental to the taste of the coffee, as it raises the temperature of the coffee through friction. This is done to remove any silver skin left on the bean, which may result in a by-product called *Chaff* during roasting.
3. **Cleaning and sorting:** This process is completed by the following two steps:
   (i) **Sorting by size and density:** Most fine coffees go through machines that sort the beans based on their size and density and also removing unwanted rock, leaves and miscellaneous debris. First, the beans are blown by machines into the air. The *heavier ripe beans* fall to the closest bins, whereas the *lighter unripe beans* fall into the further most bins. Other machines shake the beans through a series of sieves separating the larger ones from the smaller.
   (ii) **Sorting by Colour:** The final step is cleaning and sorting. This step is done either by hand or by machines. Most of the finest coffees in the world are sorted by hand. Many times this process is done twice even thrice, to check if there are any unripe or green beans that are to be removed.

The coffee cherries sans their parchment is laid out for drying before it is graded and roasted.

This procedure is done by machines by making the beans pass in front of sensors that sort the beans as per their brown colour. If the bean is not brown enough, it is rejected. However, this method using a machine needs expensive capital investment and hence is not very popular and is never used in small units. It is used in places and countries where the standard of living is very high and the daily wages are high.

4. **Grading:** The coffee is based on its size, where and at what altitude it was grown, how it was picked, the method it was processed, the cup taste etc. In each sample, the amount of whole beans, known as pea berries, *vis-à-vis* the broken beans makes a difference to the grading of the coffee.

A whole bean known as a pea berry.

The location of growing the coffee along with the growers' standards for quality control established in those estates is very important. Good quality-control standards command a high premium. For example, the Jamaican blue mountain coffee is grown in a premium estate on the elevated land of Jamaica, thereby commanding a high premium for the finest quality of coffee, which is so scarce in the world.

Other Processes

The other processes include the following: (1) ageing, and (2) decaffeination, which can be describes as follows:

1. **Ageing:** As Europe expanded its reach, it was not long before that Europe was trading with nations all across the globe. Coffee reached Europe from Ethiopia and India. It used to take several months over the various seas for the coffee to reach its destination. On the ships, the coffee aged and got a particular taste. However, due to the opening of the Suez Canal, the voyage time reduced considerably. This made the beans not to acquire its peculiar aged flavour.

   Therefore, ageing as a process was introduced. It was not considered to be a very good procedure, as the coffee is believed to lose much of its essential oils in this stage.
2. **Decaffeination:** Caffeine is a stimulant and a highly addictive substance. This is available in coffee naturally. This is the reason why coffee is considered very addictive and believed to rejuvenate the mind and body. Unfortunately, caffeine has more risks as compared to its benefits. For instance, it increases the risk of heart ailments etc. (discussed further in this chapter).

   This is the reason why many coffee lovers, who enjoy the taste and aroma of this wonderful beverage, prefer it without caffeine, hence this method of decaffeination was invented. Decaffeination can be done by several methods. However, all the methods achieve 0.1% caffeine content or less, which is considered decaffeinated coffee.

Storage

Coffee has many essential oils that are very volatile and can evaporate, leaving the coffee beans without flavour, aroma or taste. Therefore, utmost care has to be taken while storing this beverage. It should be ideally stored in a cool and dry place, preferably air-tight containers, or where the air comes in least contact with the coffee bean.

Roasting

Most of the coffee beans available in the market are roasted, but only in few markets are coffee beans sold for home roasting. Roasting brings out the distinct flavours out of the coffee bean. The caffeine in the coffee bean is exposed on roasting making it soluble in water and giving the coffee its *punch* or rejuvenating affect.

The process: Coffee roasting is done after coffee processing and before coffee brewing. The following are the essential steps in the roasting process.

1. **Sorting:** The green beans are put on to a *hopper*, where the sticks, leaves and twigs are separated from the beans.
2. **Roasting:** Roasting is a very delicate process that requires care. First, the beans are laid out on a conveyor belt. The beans are heated to a great degree. This makes the green beans palatable and gives the coffee its aromatic flavour. The photographs presented in Table 3.2 shows the various degrees of roasting with their temperatures:
3. **Cooling:** The roasted beans are left under blowers that pass cool air to stop over roasting of the bean. In some large-scale production units, the beans are cooled by mist.

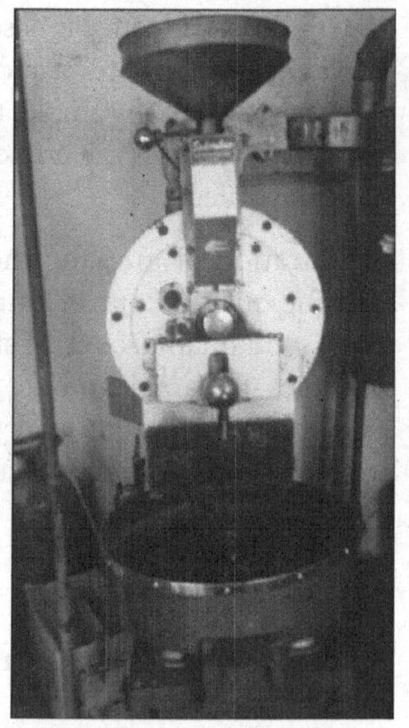

A coffee roasting machine in Coorg—Coffee district in Karnataka, India.

Different Roasts of the Coffee Bean

Table 3.2 Different Roasts of the Coffee Bean

	22°C (72°F) **Green Beans**—Green coffee beans as they arrive at the dock. They can be stored for up to two years.		165°C (329°F) **Drying phase**—As beans are roasted, they lose water and increase in size. Arabic coffee is prepared using this roast.
	195°C (383°F) **Cinnamon Roast**—The lightest drinkable roast, immediately before first crack. Light brown, toasted grain flavours with sharp acidic tones.		205°C (401°F) **New England Roast**—Moderate light brown, still acidic but not bready, a traditional roast for north-eastern U.S. coffee, at first crack.
	210°C (410°F) **American Roast**—Medium light brown, the traditional roast for the Eastern U.S. first crack ending.		220°C (428°F) **City Roast**—Medium brown, the norm for most of the United States good for tasting the varietal character of a bean.

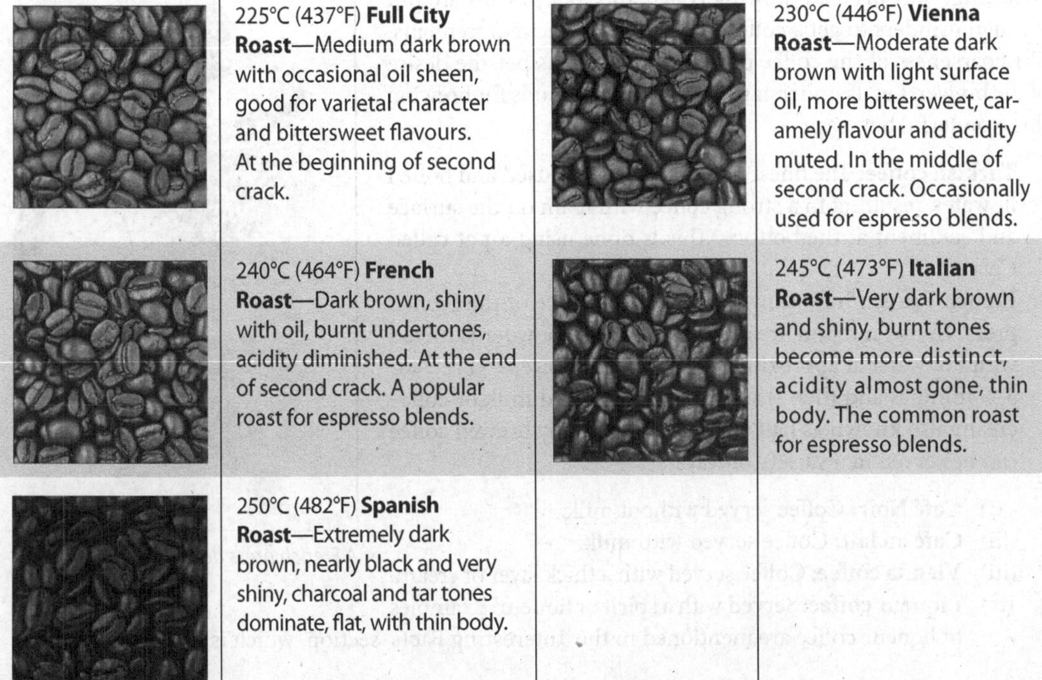

225°C (437°F) **Full City Roast**—Medium dark brown with occasional oil sheen, good for varietal character and bittersweet flavours. At the beginning of second crack.	230°C (446°F) **Vienna Roast**—Moderate dark brown with light surface oil, more bittersweet, caramely flavour and acidity muted. In the middle of second crack. Occasionally used for espresso blends.
240°C (464°F) **French Roast**—Dark brown, shiny with oil, burnt undertones, acidity diminished. At the end of second crack. A popular roast for espresso blends.	245°C (473°F) **Italian Roast**—Very dark brown and shiny, burnt tones become more distinct, acidity almost gone, thin body. The common roast for espresso blends.
250°C (482°F) **Spanish Roast**—Extremely dark brown, nearly black and very shiny, charcoal and tar tones dominate, flat, with thin body.	

4. **Packaging:** After roasting the beans, they are packed in air-tight bags/containers to seal their freshness. It is in these packaging units where the blending process is initiated.

Illy Coffee—perfect blend of Coffee.

Blending

There are many coffee companies, each producing their unique blend of coffee beans, either from different degrees of roasting or their different origins from where they are grown as per their grades. This process gives each company its own best selling formula.

Brewing

Methods of brewing that are practiced in the world are many. Before brewing the coffee, the roasted beans need to undergo a step. This step is grinding.

Grinding: Just prior to brewing coffee, the coffee beans are put through grinders to get a coffee as per the specific requirements. The coarseness of the coffee powder is decided as per the desire of the brewer. Let us understand the various methods for brewing this wonderful beverage.

A French press design by Bodum.

1. **Turkish coffee:** The finest powder of coffee is used and boiled in water, resulting in a strong coffee with foam on the surface and sediment at the bottom. This is done using a pot called *Cezve*.
2. **French Press:** Photo shown here is a reference of the French press. In this method, freshly ground coffee powder is mixed with hot water at approximately 92–95°C, allowed to brew for 3–5 minutes and then is served with skimmed milk or coffee cream also known as half and half. This freshly brewed coffee can be served in a variety of ways:
   - (i) **Café Noir:** Coffee served without milk.
   - (ii) **Café au lait:** Coffee served with milk.
   - (iii) **Vienna coffee:** Coffee served with a thick layer of cream.
   - (iv) **Liqueur coffee:** Served with a spirit or liqueur. Examples of liqueur coffee are mentioned in the 'Interesting Facts' section, which is discussed further.

Interesting Facts

Liqueur Coffees

Many coffees are made with an addition of a particular spirit and have a name coined after them. Some of them are listed as follows:

Speciality Liqueur Coffee Name	Liquor/Spirit
Highland Coffee	Scotch Whisky
Irish Coffee	Irish Whiskey
Bailey's Coffee	Baileys Irish Cream
French Coffee	Grand Marnier liqueur
Café Royale, French Coffee or Parisienne Coffee	Cognac or Armagnac
German Coffee	Schnapps
Italian Classico Coffee	Amaretto

Speciality Liqueur Coffee Name	Liquor/Spirit
Calypso Coffee, Spanish Coffee or Jamaican Coffee	Rum with either Tia Maria or Kahlua
Monk's Coffee	Benedictine Liqueur
Seville Coffee	Cointreau
Witch's Coffee	Strega
Russian Coffee	Vodka
Skye Coffee	Drambuie
The Real Foul One	Absinthe

3. **Italian method:** In this method, the coffee is brewed through an espresso machine (Figure 3.2).

   The standard measurement for an espresso is 8 grams of coffee powder per oz of coffee (1 oz. = 29.8 ml).

   The espresso method forces hot pressurized water through the ground coffee powder. Due to this, the coffee has a very strong, aromatic and concentrated flavour. A good espresso has reddish-brown foam called *crema*, which floats on the surface.

   The variants of coffee prepared by this Italian method through the espresso machine are listed as follows:

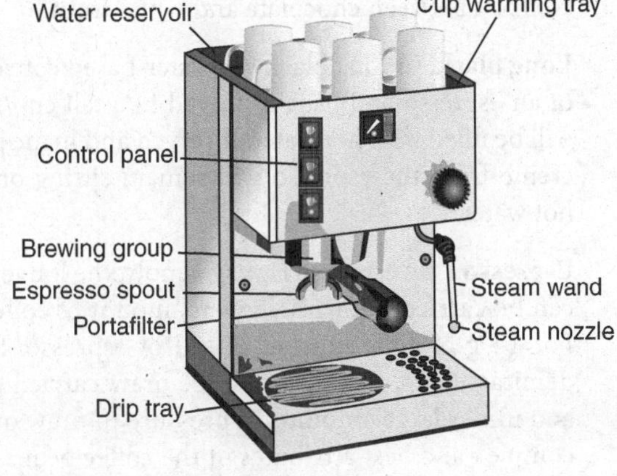

Figure 3.2 The espresso machine.

Styles of Coffee Preparation Based on the Italian Method

Cappuccino: A cappuccino is recognized by the frothy milk top and is often served sprinkled with chocolate powder; this drink is served to the following proportions:

Cappuccino

- $\frac{1}{3}$ **Espresso**
- $\frac{1}{3}$ **Steamed milk**
- $\frac{1}{3}$ **Froth**

The froth on these need not be mounded up in a heap on top of the milk—in fact, this is a common misperception. If you have a good barista the froth will be incorporated through the milk when it is being poured provided enough air is put through the milk at time of preparation. When it is poured the froth will sit at the top of the drink.

Latte

Café latte: A latte consists of an espresso and steamed milk served with a small layer of froth on top (usually about 1cm thick). Because of the way the latte is poured from the milk jug, it is often possible for a trained barista to create 'latte art' on top as can be seen in photo given as later.

Café mocha: Mocha is basically a latte with chocolate powder incorporated into the drink, to give that coffee/chocolate flavour. It is served similarly to a latte and latte art can also be achieved on these. When latte art is carried out on mocha, they can look very good due to the stronger contrast between chocolate and white froth.

Espresso

Long black: A long black is a water-based coffee; it consists of an espresso and usually served in a tall cup/mug, which will be filled with hot water. If served and made properly the crème from the espresso will remain sitting on top of the hot water.

Espresso: An espresso is very simply, the longest pour that can be carried out with a given amount of coffee grounds. For 14 g of coffee makes 60 ml of espresso. Served in a demitasse cup, this is the coffee brew carried out quickly and under large amounts of pressure to draw out all of the complex and best attributes of the coffee beans.

Ristretto

Ristretto: This is a similar concept to an espresso, which is served in a demitasse cup. The difference here, however, is that the ristretto is the first 15–20 ml of the extraction. Within this first amount is the sweetest, purest and most intense part of the extraction.

Macchiato: The macchiato is also served in a demitasse cup; it comprises of an espresso stained with a dollop of milk froth.

Affogato: Affogato, which is also based on an espresso, is generally served as an espresso with a scoop of ice cream.

Macchiato

4. **Cona coffee (vacuum infusion method):** This is a unique method involving two glass bowls. These glass bowls are separated by a filter at the centre, which is connected by a tube.

The lower bowl contains hot water. The upper bowl is empty and is placed above the lower bowl with a filter in between. The ground coffee powder is added to the bowl on top. The machine is then switched on. As the water boils, it rises into the upper bowl, hence dissolving the coffee. As the heat is reduced, the coffee descends to the lower bowl leaving the spent coffee sediment behind in the upper bowl. The coffee produced is full of flavour and the aroma and is served at approximately 82–85°C.

5. **Stove Espresso (stove Percolator):** It is also called as Espresso Percolator. Photo given here, shows the base or the lower half (base) of the Percolator is filled with hot water, whereas the coffee is kept in the filter at the centre of the equipment. As the heat is applied from the bottom—preferably heated by a stove—the coffee gushes up through the filter and collects in the pot above.

    The coffee cannot return to the pot below it, as it is not inter connected, unlike the bowls in the *cona* method. The resulting coffee is rich, flavourful and often referred to as '*A Homemade Espresso*'.

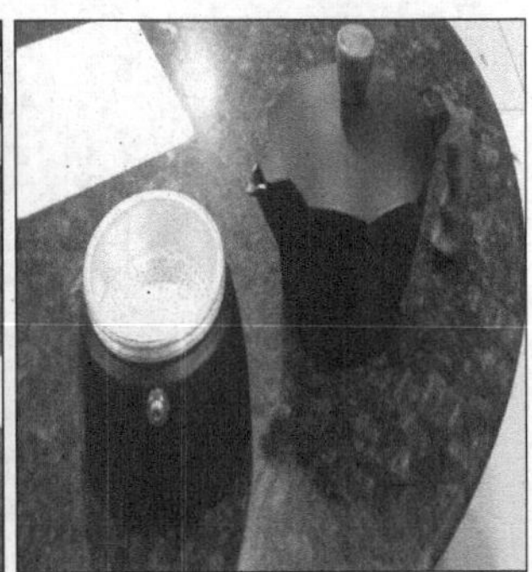

A stove percolator that makes strong espresso coffee decoction (left) and the photograph (right) shows two parts of the percolator—a base containing the hot water above which is the filter containing the coffee powder; the second part, which is the top container, is left with the coffee decoction after being subjected to heat.

6. **Indian method (better known as South Indian coffee):** South Indian coffee is a beverage with a rich coffee flavour having a heavy body. The heavy body can be attributed to the addition of chicory to the coffee powder. The ratio is 70–80% coffee powder to 20–30% Chicory.

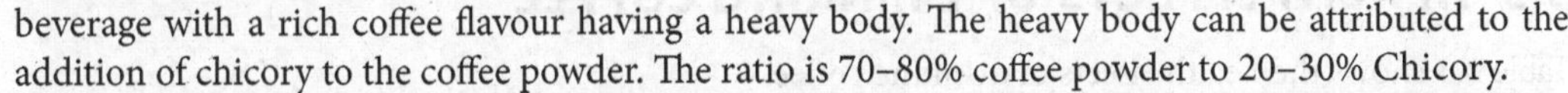

The coffee powder blended with the chicory is brewed in a south Indian coffee filter. This brewing method can take up to 3–4 hours, depending on the quantity of the coffee to produce the decoction. This coffee is often known as ribbon coffee and originated from the Indian State of Tamil Nadu. This is due to the ribbon effect created by the skilled 'Indian barista' while making this beverage.

DID YOU KNOW

Root Chicory

Root chicory (*Cichorium intybus* var. *sativum*) has been in cultivation in Europe as a coffee substitute. The roots are baked, ground and are used as a coffee substitute and additive, especially in the Mediterranean region (where the plant is native), although its use as a coffee additive is also very popular in India, parts of south-east Asia, South Africa and southern United States, particularly in New Orleans. It has also been popular as a coffee substitute in poorer economic areas and has gained wider popularity during economic crises, such as the Great Depression in the 1930s. Chicory, with sugar beet and rye was used as an ingredient of the East German Mischkaffee (mixed coffee), introduced during the 'coffee crisis' of 1976–1979. Coffee spread across to Indonesia, Italy and the rest of Europe and then made its way to the Americas.

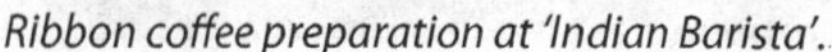

Ribbon coffee preparation at 'Indian Barista'.

Coffee percolator and the filter.

7. **Percolator coffee:** Most American homes have a coffee percolator. The coffee powder is put onto a filter paper or mesh filter and the hot water is poured on top of it. After which it is allowed to brew in a percolator jug.

3.5 HEALTH EFFECTS OF DRINKING COFFEE

Table 3.3 shows the health effects of drinking coffee.

Table 3.3 Benefits and Risks of Drinking Coffee

Benefits	Risks
Reduced risk of all stone ailments/diseases.	Increases the risk of cancer due to the high amount of rodent carcinogens.
Reduced risk of Parkinson's disease.	Gastrointestinal problems causing gastritis and ulcers.
Cognitive performance, that is, increases the ability to recall and reflex time, making the mind more alert.	Anxiety and sleep disorders, which is due to the levels of caffeine in the cup.
It is an anti-diabetic.	Cholesterol—coffee increases the cholesterol levels in the body due to the cholesterol present in coffee such as cafestol or kahweol.
Helps in liver protection, hence a hot cup of coffee may be related to 'getting rid of the high'.	It increases the risk of high blood pressure.

It is a natural laxative.	Can cause Iron deficiency anaemia.
It is an anti-oxidant.	It increases the risk of coronary artery disease.
Prevention of dental caries.	
Reduces the risk of gout.	

3.6 SOME INTERESTING FACTS ABOUT COFFEE

1. October 1st is official 'Coffee Day' in Japan.
2. More than 20 million people worldwide work in the coffee industry.
3. Brazil produces around 40% of the world's coffee supply.
4. Coffee beans are really berries. Each berry contains two beans (pips).
5. Black coffee with no sugar contains no calories.
6. Coffee has been used as a beverage for over 700 years.
7. A coffee tree lives between 60–70 years.
8. Caffeine, which is found in coffee, increases the effect of some painkillers, especially aspirin and paracetamol.
9. Worldwide, more than 1400 millions cups of coffee are drunk every day.

DID YOU KNOW

Kopi Luwak, or civet coffee, is one of the world's most expensive and low-production varieties of coffee. It is made from the beans of coffee berries that have been eaten by the *Asian Palm Civet* and other related civets, and then passed through its digestive tract. A civet eats the berries for their fleshy pulp. In its stomach, proteolytic enzymes seep into the beans, making shorter peptides and more free amino acids. Passing through a civet's intestines, the beans are then defecated, keeping their shape. After gathering, thorough washing, sun drying, light roasting and brewing, these beans yield an aromatic coffee with much less bitterness, widely noted as the most expensive coffee in the world with prices reaching $160 per pound.

Kopi luwak is produced mainly on the Islands of Sumatra, Java, Bali and Sulawesi in the Indonesian Archipelago, and in the Philippines (where the product is called motit coffee in the Cordillera and Kapealamid in Tagalog areas) and in East Timor (where it is called *kafé-laku*). Weasel coffee is a loose English translation of its name *càphê Chun* in Vietnam, where popular, chemically simulated versions are also produced. However, two farms have 300 civets in the wild in Dak Lak, the farmers collect the coffee seeds, and they produce 300 kg only of authentic Vietnamese chon coffee. The civets live in the wild and are fed beef. The processed civet beans are processed and imported to the UK to the farmers' sole UK supplier.

3.7 SPECIALITY COFFEES OF THE WORLD

Table 3.4 displays a wide range of speciality coffees available worldwide.

Table 3.4 Speciality Coffees of the World

Country	Region	Characteristics
Brazil	Santos and Rios	Medium body, mild, sweet
Colombia	Medellin, Armenia and Manizales	Full-bodied, rich in acidity and high aroma
Costa Rica	Tarazu and Tres Rios	Full body, rich in acidity, smooth clean cup
Ethiopia	Harar and Yirgacheffe	Medium body. Fruity, winey flavours, good body. Floral, fruity, rich, soft-toned acidity
Guatemala	Antigua, Cuban, San Marcos, Atitlan and Huehuetenango	High acidity, medium body, multi-dimensional complex flavour
Hawaii	Kona	Medium to full body. Rich, high-toned acidity and complex aroma
India	Kerala, Karnataka, Tamil Nadu and Monsoon Malabar	Low-keyed detectable sweetness. Heavy on palate, muted acidity, good for espresso blends
Jamaica	Blue Mountain	Full body, moderate acidity, balanced, complex flavours
Java	Java	Medium body, rich, low-toned acidity
Kenya	Mount Kenya	Wine like acidity, full body, complex taste
Mexico	Coatepec, Oaxaca, Chiapas and Tapachula	Delicate flavour, medium body, brisk, bright acidity
Nicaragua	Matagalpa and Jinotega	Medium to full body, complex flavours of chocolate and spice
Papua New Guinea	Papua New Guinea	Lighter body, higher toned floral acidity and delicate sweetness
Peru	Northern Chenchamayo and Ayacucho; Cuzco and Urubamba	Delicate to brisk acidity, medium body, sweet, mild flavour
Puerto Rico	Yanco	Full-bodied, balanced, with vibrant complexity
Sulawesi	Sulawesi	High-toned acidity, lighter body than Sumatra
Sumatra	Mandehling, Lintong and Gayo Mountain	Rich, resonant, deep-toned acidity, full body, wine, lighter body and less resonant
Tanzania	Mount Kilimanjaro and Mount Mere	Rich, wine-like acidity, full body
Yemen	Mocha	Rich, winey, medium to full body, wild natural notes

LET'S SUMMARIZE IN POINTS

In this chapter, we have learnt the following:

- History of coffee—How the wonderful beverage has found its place in most homes in the world from just a dessert shrub.
- The harvesting and processing of coffee along with various steps.
- The roasting process
- Blending process
- Brewing process along with the various methods of brewing.
- Health effects of coffee, benefits versus the risks.
- The interesting facts about coffee.

3.8 FAQs

Short-Answer Type Questions

1. What is an affogato?
2. Give the biological name of the coffee plant.
3. What is colour sorting?
4. How is grading done? What are the various parameters for judging the same?
5. What is the name of the equipment used in preparation of Turkish coffee?
6. Name five famous coffee brands.
7. What is *kapi* and ribbon coffee?
8. What is *luak* coffee or Kopi Luwak?
9. Describe ageing step in coffee production.
10. Describe decaffeination.

Long-Answer Type Questions

1. Give the history of coffee and how it was discovered.
2. Give five differences between Arabica and Robusta coffee.
3. Give the three methods of coffee processing before dry milling.
4. Name the steps and explain the wet milling method.
5. Name the five processes of brewing coffee with their explanations.

3.9 KEY TERMS

- Amaretto
- Amino acids
- Chaff
- Chicory
- Crème
- Decaffeination
- Fermentation
- Grinding
- Irish whisky
- Latte art
- Parchment
- Peptides
- Plunger
- Rum
- Scotch whisky
- Semi-automatic espresso
- Skimmed milk
- Tia Maria
- Kahlua

COCOA

CHAPTER OUTLINE

Chocolate is a food made with the seeds of a tropical tree called the *cacao.* The word *cocoa* apparently comes from the two Maya Indian words meaning *bitter juice.* The word *chocolate* meaning *sour water* also came from two Maya Indian words.

We should note that chocolate is a stimulating beverage, as it contains amounts of minerals and vitamins essential for the human body. Hence, this beverage is also called by the ancient tribes of South America as 'the drink of the Gods'.

4.1 HISTORY

Historians do not know how long the Maya Indians of Central America and the Aztec Indians of Mexico had cultivated cacao beans. They cultivated them before Columbus arrived in America in 1492. Botanists believed that the cacao tree originated in Amazon–Orinoco river basin in South America. In this area and the upper Amazon tributaries, present-day botanists and geneticists are searching for the original types of cacao, which may have the resistance to the diseases that plague this tree in cultivation.

The cacao bean played an important role in the traditions, religion and legends of the Aztecs. They believed that one of their prophets had brought the beans down from paradise and sown them in his garden.

The Aztecs thought by eating this fruit, the prophet acquired universal wisdom and knowledge. The Aztecs used the cacao beans as money. They also ground the beans to make a rich beverage.

In 1528, Hernando Cortes, the conqueror of Mexico, took some cacao beans to Spain. In about 1606, they were introduced to Italy. Shortly after, people in Austria and France began to use them. Eventually, their popularity spread to England. By 1707, cacao had become a fashionable drink in London. Today, chocolate is popular in most parts of the world. Countries in which large amounts of chocolates are eaten include Belgium, Germany, Great Britain, Norway, Switzerland and the United States of America.

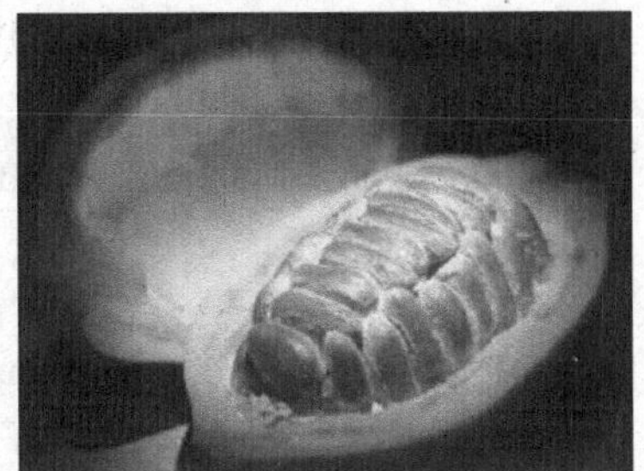

Cacao—'the drink of the Gods'—ancient Aztec saying.

4.2 THE CACAO TREE

The cacao tree produces seeds, or cacao beans, from which all the chocolate is made. These trees flourish in a warm and moist climate. They live in an area about 20° north and south of the equator. Most of the world's cacao beans come from the west coast of Africa, where Ghana, the Ivory Coast and Nigeria are the largest producers. Brazil is the largest cacao bean producer in the western hemisphere.

The cultivated cacao trees grow about 25 feet (7.6 metres) high. It produces leaves, flowers and fruits during all seasons of the year. The flowers are small. They grow singly and in clusters on the main stems on the branches and on the trunk. The ripe fruit, or pod, may be red, yellow or golden, pale green or a combination of these colours. When the seeds are dried and fermented, they are ready for commercial use.

Because of a mistake in spelling, probably made by the English importers many years ago, these beans became to be known as *cocoa beans* in English-speaking countries.This caused many people to think the beans came from the coconut palm tree instead of *cacao tree.*

The fruit of the cocoa plant containing the cocoa beans.

4.3 HARVESTING THE CACAO BEANS

Workers cut the pods from the trees with knives attached to long poles, or with machetes. They gather the pods into heaps, cut them open and scoop out the beans. The beans are then placed in piles, covered with banana leaves or burlap and are allowed to ferment for 7–10 days. After fermentation, the beans are dried in the sun or in an artificial heat to prevent molding. Then, workers place them in bags for shipment.

4.4 MANUFACTURING CHOCOLATE

Chocolate manufacturers receive many types of beans; they blend them, so that they yield the flavour and colour desired in the final product. The first steps in processing the seeds include cleaning, roasting, hulling, blending and grinding. Cacao seeds with their shells removed are called *nibs*. The nibs are quite dry; they even contain about 54% *cacao butter*, which is the natural fat of the cacao bean. In the grinding process, the nibs are ground fine and the cacao butter is released. The mixture of cacao butter and finely ground nibs forms a free-flowing substance known as chocolate liquor.

4.5 CHOCOLATE PRODUCTS

The chocolate products are all manufactured from the chocolate liquor. They include baking chocolate, cacao, milk chocolate and sweet and semi-sweet chocolate.

1. **Cacao:** In making the cacao powder, huge hydraulic presses force some of the cocoa butter out of the heated chocolate liquor. The mass remaining in the huge hydraulic presses is in the form of large, hard cakes. Manufacturers change this remainder into its final usable form by grinding it into fine reddish-brown powder. People can prepare a hot beverage from the cacao powder by adding sugar, hot milk and sometimes vanilla. Confectioners, bakers, ice cream manufacturers and other food producers use cacao in their products.
2. **Milk chocolate:** It probably ranks as the most popular of all the chocolate products. Chocolate liquor, whole milk solids and granulated sugar are the basic ingredients in this form of chocolate. Extra cacao butter, obtained from cacao powder production, is added to this chocolate liquor. First, the ingredients are mixed well. Then, the mixture passes through a series of large, steel roll refiners. The shearing and rubbing action of these rolls reduces the mass to a smooth paste. Machines called conches then process the chocolate for about 72 hours. In these machines, a large cylindrical stone rolling a stone bed pushes the chocolate back and forth. This rubbing action smoothes out any rough edges on the chocolate particles, helps develop the desired flavour and finishes blending the entire mass. Milk chocolate is sold in the form of bars and as a coating on some candies.
3. **Sweet chocolate and semi-sweet chocolate:** These are processed in the same way as milk chocolate. However, manufacturers do not add milk solids to the mixture in making these products. Manufacturers sell large amounts of sweet and semi-sweet chocolates to confectioners for making chocolate-covered candies. Increasingly large amounts of semi-sweet chocolates are used to make homemade cookies, candy, cakes and other items.

4.6 FOOD VALUE OF CHOCOLATE

Chocolate serves both as a confection and as a food. It possesses a pleasing and widely popular flavour and also ranks high in food value. It contains carbohydrates, fats, proteins and several vitamins and minerals. People whose work requires physical endurance, including soldiers, explorers and athletes, rely on chocolate as a source of quick energy for carrying out their tasks.

4.7 MAKING A GOOD CUP OF CACAO

A *good cup* of hot chocolate or hot cacao can be made by mixing the wonderful cacao powder or a chocolate bar in hot milk, preferably, or in hot water. Cacao butter is removed from cocoa powder, which makes it drinking chocolate, unlike the chocolate bar that contains cacao butter along with antioxidants as well as sugar.

4.8 HEALTH BENEFITS OF COCOA CONSUMPTION

Chocolate and cocoa contain a high level of flavonoids, especially epicatechin, which may have beneficial cardiovascular effects on health. Prolonged intake of flavanol-rich cocoa has been linked to cardiovascular health benefits, though it should be noted that this refers to raw cocoa and to a lesser extent, dark chocolate, since flavonoids degrade during cooking and alkalizing processes. Studies have found short-term benefits in LDL cholesterol levels from dark chocolate consumption. The addition of whole milk to milk chocolate reduces the overall cocoa content per ounce while increasing saturated fat levels, possibly negating some of cocoa's heart-healthy potential benefits.

Hollenberg and colleagues of the Harvard Medical School studied the effects of cocoa and flavanols on Panama's Kuna Indian population, who are heavy consumers of cocoa. The researchers found that the Kuna Indians living on the islands had significantly lower rates of heart disease and cancer compared to those on the mainland who did not drink cocoa as on the islands. It is believed that the improved blood flow after the consumption of flavanol-rich cocoa may help to achieve health benefits in hearts and other organs. In particular, the benefits may extend to the brain and have important implications for learning and memory.

Foods rich in cocoa appear to reduce blood pressure; however, drinking green and black tea may not, according to an analysis of previously published research in the April 9, 2007 issue of *Archives of Internal Medicine*, one of the JAMA/archives journals.

In June 2009, Mars Botanicals, a division of Mars Inc., the candy-maker and food company, launched Cirku, a cocoa extract high in flavanols.

A 15-year study of elderly men published in the *Archives of Internal Medicine* in 2006 found a 50% reduction in cardiovascular mortality and a 47% reduction in all-cause mortality for the men regularly consuming the most cocoa, compared to those consuming the least cocoa from all sources.

DID YOU KNOW

In India, most hotels refuse to sell milk to the customer. Instead, if the customer/guest persists, milk is sold as *Hot Chocolate* or *Cocoa* on the bill/check. This is because as per the Indian PFA Act (Prevention of Food Adulteration Act), the fat content of milk cannot be defined or verified in a hotel, and there is a possibility that milk sold as full milk having 6% fat content could actually have 5–7% fat content.

As hotels cannot verify this on a daily basis, which is a very lengthy process, they prefer to sell them as whole milk, thereby avoiding any legal hassles.

LET'S SUMMARIZE IN POINTS

In this chapter, we have studied the following:

- Cacao is a food made from the seeds of a tropical tree called the *cacao.*
- Historians do not know how long the Maya Indians of Central America and the Aztec Indians of Mexico had cultivated cacao beans. They cultivated the beans before Columbus arrived in America in 1492.
- The cacao tree produces seeds, or cacao beans, from which all the chocolate is made. These trees flourish in a warm, moist climate.
- The chocolate products are all manufactured from the chocolate liquor. They include baking chocolate, cacao, milk chocolate and sweet and semi-sweet chocolate.
- Chocolate contains carbohydrates, fats, proteins and several vitamins and minerals.
- Chocolate and cocoa contain a high level of flavonoids, especially epicatechin, which may have beneficial cardiovascular effects on health.

4.9 FAQs

1. What is cocoa?
2. What is the meaning of hot chocolate?
3. Describe the history of cocoa.
4. What are the benefits of cocoa consumption?
5. Name the types of chocolate and the manufacturing methods.
6. How do you make a good cup of cocoa?
7. What is the process of harvesting cocoa beans? In addition, where is it grown in large quantities in the world?
8. Name various chocolate products.
9. Explain in detail the chocolate-making process.
10. Describe the detailed food value of chocolate.

4.10 KEY TERMS

- Amazon
- Aztec Indians
- Cardiovascular
- Columbus
- Epicatechin
- Flavonoids
- LDL Cholesterol
- Orinoco
- PFA Act

Beer

CHAPTER OUTLINE

LET'S DEFINE

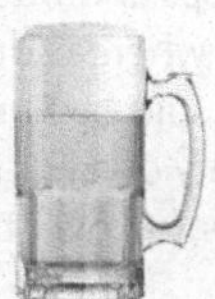

'Beer is a fermented alcoholic beverage made from cereal grains such as barley, wheat and rice flavoured with hops, which adds bitterness and is a natural preservative. Beer on an average contains 4–6% alcohol volume by volume (ABV).'

Beer is one of the oldest and most consumed beverages in the world. It is the third most consumed beverage after water and tea. It is the result of saccharification of starch and the fermentation of the resulting sugar. The starch enzymes for the fermentation process are derived from malted grains such as malted barley, malted wheat or even un-malted maize/corn and rice, which are substitutes with lower costs.

Most often, the fermented malted beverage is flavoured with hops, which gives beer its characteristic bitter taste and also acts as a natural preservative.

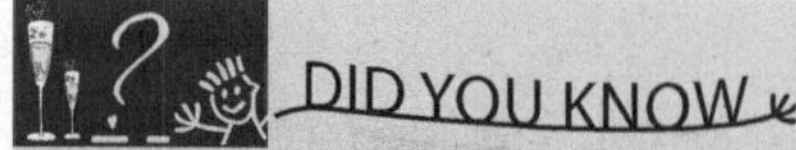

Some of mankind's earliest known writings refer to the production and distribution of beer such as the *Code of Hammurabi*, which included laws regulating beers and beer parlours. *The Hymn of Ninkasi* was a prayer dedicated to the goddess of beer, served both as a prayer and as a method to memorize the recipe of beer.

5.1 HISTORY OF BEER

Table 5.1 explains the evolution of beer.

Table 5.1 Evolution of Beer

Period	Events
9500 BC	Cereal was first formed and recorded in the written history of ancient Egypt and Mesopotamia. Archaeologists speculate that beer was instrumental in the formation of civilizations.
3500–3100 BC	Godin Tepe in the Zagros Mountains of western Iran; in Sumerian writings there is a reference to beer making in the *Hymn of Ninkasi* (explanation given above).
2500 BC	The Elba tablet discovery in 1974 in Syria, established the fact that the city produced a host of beers including a beer called *Elba*, which was named after the city. Factual data suggests that around 3000 BC, Germanic and Celtic tribes were spreading beer throughout Europe. During the period, beer was made with grain, fruit, honey and herbs and in most cases narcotic herbs. This is what made beer gain popularity initially. It was not until the 8th century, wherein hops was added to beer, mentioned by a Carolingian Abbot in 822 BC and in 1087 BC by Abbess Hildegard of Bingen.
1516	In 1516, William IV the Duke of Bavaria adopted a purity law called *Reinheitgebot*, which is the oldest food-quality regulation still being used in the 21st century. According to this law, the only permitted substances to brew beer are *malted barley, hops and water.* Beer before the Industrial Revolution was produced on a domestic scale, whereas during the Industrial Revolution in the 7th century, beer was produced and sold by European industries. The development of hydrometers (to measure the density of a liquid) and thermometers (to measure temperature) allowed the brewer more control over the process and greater knowledge of the results.

5.2 ESSENTIAL INGREDIENTS TO MAKE BEER

1. **Water:** Water constitutes 80% (or more) of what makes beer. Hence, the best quality of water is always sought after by every brewer. Water is the key element that gives the beer its unique character. This is one of the reasons why most breweries are located close to a water source. For example, Dublin has hard water to make stouts such as Guinness, which is one of the most popular beers in the world. While Pilsen has soft water and is famous for making light pale lagers such as pilsner urquell, another

unique style that is copied all over the world, better known as pilsner beers. Nowadays, brewers adjust the pH levels and filter the water.

2. **Starch source:** The key ingredient for beer making is the starch source. The starch source provides the sugar, which is essential for the fermentation process. Beer is either made from malted barley, (refer to the malting process later in this chapter) or other grains, such as wheat, rice or even corn in some parts of the world. Biere Weisse, a famous German style of beer, is made from wheat. However, the two most famous grains used to produce beer are barley and corn, respectively.
3. **Yeast:** The next most important ingredient in beer manufacturing is yeast. The particular sub-species of yeast and in that the particular string of yeast also makes a great difference to the final character of the beer. Most breweries preserve their string of yeast as a prized and secret ingredient. This makes the difference in character from one beer brand and the next. To understand in a simple manner, yoghurt that mothers make in India at home is different in each and every household. This is due to the specific string of cultured yeast, which differs in each home, even if the source of milk is the same. Other factors that influence the yeast are temperature, oxygen, the yeast nutrients and level of sugar present in the wort.

   The two types of yeast used in beer manufacturing are *Ale Yeast* or top-fermenting yeast also known as *Saccharomyces Cerevisiae*, which is commonly used for making bread. The other type is the *Lager Yeast* or bottom-fermenting yeast, which is also known as *Saccharomyces Uvarum* or *Saccharomyces carlsbergensis*. This yeast was first discovered in Carlsberg of Denmark. Top-fermenting yeast rise to the top after fermentation, whereas bottom-fermenting yeasts settle down to the bottom of the tank after fermentation.

Hops pellets, which are the extracts of the hops flowers, are added to the wort. (Courtesy: *The Bjere Club, Bengaluru.*)

4. **Hops:** Hops is the flower of the hop vine, this is the principle flavouring agent of beer. Hops give beer its characteristic, bitter taste. Initially, hops were added for its preservative qualities as it is a natural antibiotic. However, with modern-day inventions and advances in refrigeration technologies, hops are still added not for its preservative qualities, but for the distinct bitter taste, which has become the characteristic of beer itself. Its also contribute floral, citrus and herbal aromas and flavours to the beer, as they are rich in tannins (which clarify, stabilize and preserve the beer) and resins (aromas).

   Hops bitterness levels are calculated in *International Bitter Units* (IBU) For example, the International standards define each beer to have the following bitterness levels:

   (i) Lagers have 25 IBUs
   (ii) Ales have 30 IBUs
   (iii) Stouts have 28–30 IBU
   (iv) Weisse Beers have 15 IBUs

5. **Clarifying agents:** Many brewers use a clarifying agent to make sure their brew is crystal clear without any sediment. There are a variety of clarifying agents such as Isinglass (the swim-bladder of the sturgeon fish). Irish moss (it is a seaweed), egg albumen, gelatin and other artificial agents.

5.3 THE BREWING PROCESS—THE PROCESS HAS BEEN DOCUMENTED AT THE BIERE CLUB, BENGALURU (A MICROBREWERY)

The brewing process that has been documented at the Biere Club, Bengaluru is depicted in Figure 5.1.

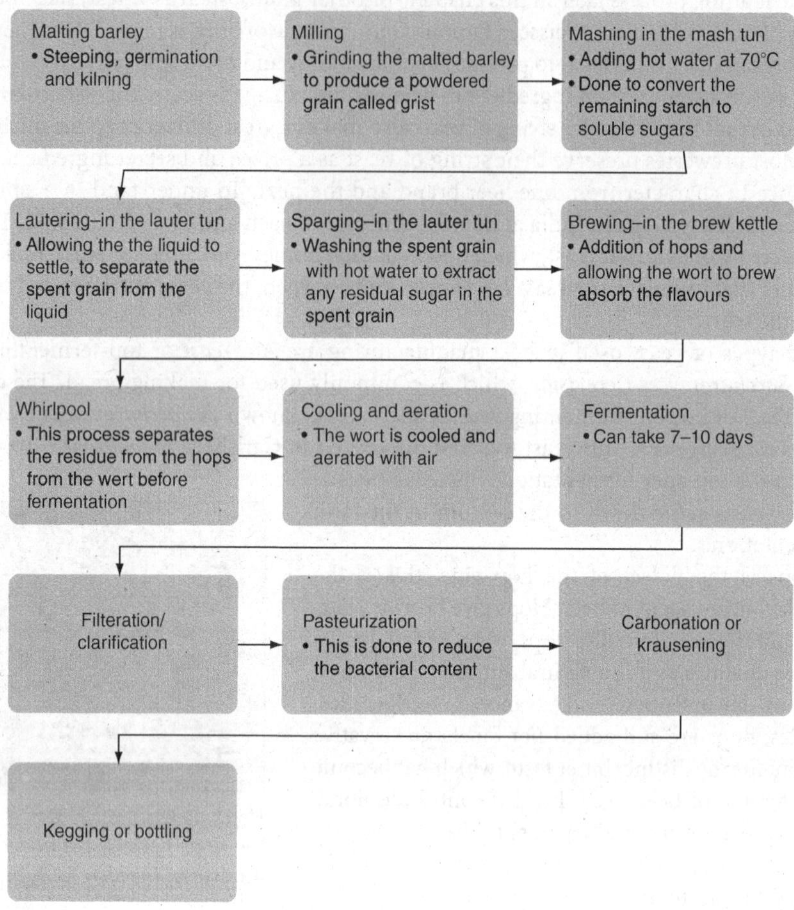

Figure 5.1 Brewing process.

1. **Malting:** Malting is the process wherein the cereal grain (barley) undergoes three sub-processes.

   (i) **Steeping:** The cereal grain is allowed to soak in water.

   (ii) **Germination:** The cereal grain germinates with the activation of natural enzymes, which convert the insoluble sugars into soluble sugars.

   (iii) **Kilning:** This process fires or bakes the grain to arrest the germination process and retain the soluble sugars in the grain. If this process is skipped, the germinating grain would turn into seedlings and if planted, would create new plants.

   Malting is an essential process that results in soluble sugars in the grain, which is essential in the production of alcohol. As we are aware that for the starch to be converted into sugar, the grain that contains the starch must germinate or sprout.

Sprouting results in an enzyme called *amylase*. In the 1830s the when this phenomenon was beginning to be researched and understood, this substance was called diastase meaning 'separation' in Greek.

Starch exists in long chains with a chemical formula of $C_6H_{10}O_5$. The enzyme amylase when in water defragments the starch molecule ($C_6H_{10}O_5$) and includes the water molecule (H_2O) to form a maltase sugar molecule ($C_{12}H_{22}O_{11}$), which is a soluble sugar. The other enzymes used in the preparation of beer are 'zymase' and 'proteases'. The proteases acts on the insoluble protein matter in the beer, resulting in a clear and haze-free beverage.

Malted barley—used for producing lighter ales and lagers (left) and for producing stouts (right).

2. **Milling:** Milling is the process where the malted barley is put onto the grinders to produce a powder called *grist*. It is immediately mixed with warm water and transferred to the mash tun.

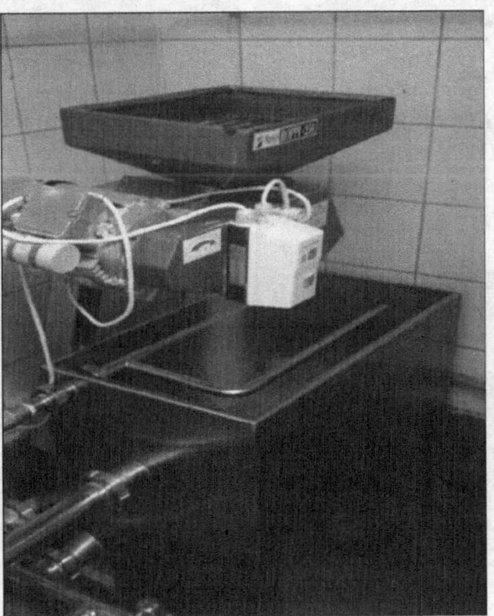

The grinder above is mixing the powdered grist with warm water.

3. **Mashing—in the mash tun:** The mashing process undergoes in a large vessel called the mash tun. Hot water at an approximate temperature of 60°C is heated up to 75°C and is added to the grist to dissolve the sugars in the water. This produces a sugary liquid with sediments of the grain. From the mash tun, it is transferred into the lauter tun.
4. **Lautering—in the lauter tun:** Lautering is the process of separating the spent grain from the sugary liquid, which is called *wort*. The lauter tun has a transparent wall, for the master brewer to monitor the sediment as it settles. After the grain settles, the liquid is

The mash tun the grist and water are mixed, whereas it is heated to 65–70°C. This helps to mix the soluble sugars into the liquid.

The lauter tun (left) and the transparent dome depicting the clarity of the liquid after the lautering process (right). Only after this, the liquid is clear (without any haze) and it is sent to the next process, the brew kettle.

filtered from the bottom of the lauter tun and is monitored for its clarity. The process is continuous and is done until the resulting liquid is not cloudy. Once the liquid is clear, it is transferred to the next vessel called the brew kettle.

5. **Sparging—in the lauter tun:** Sparging is the process of washing the spent grain with hot water to extract any residual sugars from the spent (used) grain. This liquid also undergoes lautering process and is then transferred to the brew kettle.

The hot water is poured over the spent grain in the lauter tun.

6. **Brewing—in the brew kettle:** Brewing is the process in which the now-made sugary liquid called *wort* is mixed with hops and brought to a boil in the vessel known as the brew kettle (at 100°C). The hops are allowed to brew in the wort to impart the bitter 'hoppy' characteristic, which has now become a distinctive characteristic to the beer itself. Hops used can be the flowers of the plant, but modern-day brewers prefer the hops pellets that leave lesser residue.

   It is in this copper vessel that the beer gets infused with the resins present in the hops, which helps in imparting the bitter taste to the beer. Second, hops increase the shelf life of the beer itself. Third, with the wort and hops boiling, the sugars in the wort caramelize, adding to the colour of the beer. Before the wort is transferred to the whirlpool, the sugar content is checked with a saccharometer. If the sugar levels are not satisfactory, additional grain sugar is added to the wort.

The brew kettle spins the wort as it increases the temperature to 100°C. Moreover, we can see the hops are being added.

LET'S DEFINE

'Brewing is the process of infusing the flavours of leaves, buds, flowers etc. of a plant to the brewing liquid, for example, water (brew liquid) in case of tea or coffee or wort (brew liquid) in case of hops, which are added to make beer.'

7. **Whirlpool or hop jack:** This is a whirlpool separator, a machine that spins the wort like a whirlpool (hence the name), which separates the sediments of the hops by concentrating them to the centre of the tank. Next, the liquid is sent for cooling.

(a)

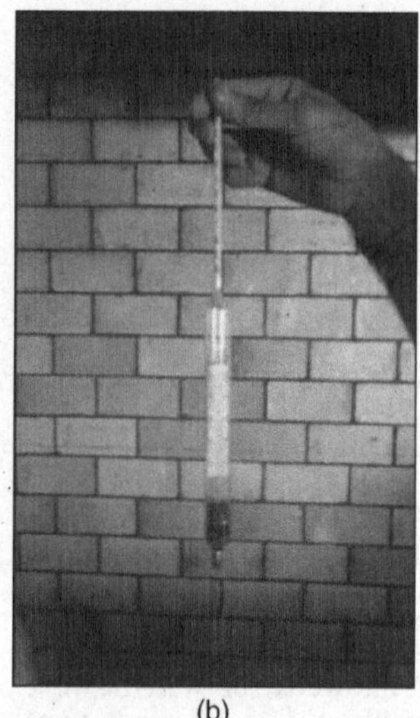

(b)

(a) The whirlpool separator; (b) A saccharometer that measures the baum level (sugar level).

8. **Cooling and aeration:** This is an important process in which the wort, which is at 90–95°C, is cooled to 10°C in the case of lagers and 20°C in the case of *ales*. As the yeasts used are different for ales and yeast, the temperatures also vary for both types. Cooling to this temperature is done to create a favourable temperature for the yeast to grow and multiply. Faster the yeast multiples, faster the wort converts into beer. The beer after cooling is aerated with sterilized air to provide enough oxygen for the yeast to multiply in the fermentation process.

Cooling plates that help reduce the temperature of the hot wort essential before fermentation.

A stainless steel fermentation tank.

The photo here shows the modern-day cooling methods through cooling plates, which cools the wort from 90°–20°C in less than a minute. It is then passed to the fermentation tanks.

9. **Fermentation:** Fermentation is the next process in which the sugars in the wort are converted to ethanol (alcohol) with the addition of yeast. This process takes from four to seven days depending on the temperature, sugar content etc. of the wort (please refer to yeast as an ingredient, discussed earlier in the chapter).

   The yeast is not only responsible for producing alcohol but is also responsible for giving the beer its unique character. This is the reason why yeast is the most protected ingredient in every brewery. Most breweries develop their own unique string of yeast and closely guard it as their secret ingredient. After this, the fermented beer is allowed to settle and it goes through the process of filtration.

DID YOU KNOW

The chemical equations below summarize the fermentation of sucrose, whose chemical formula is $C_{12}H_{22}O_{11}$. One mole of sucrose is converted into two moles of ethanol and two moles of carbon dioxide:

$C_{12}H_{22}O_{11} + H_2O + \text{invertase} \rightarrow 2C_6H_{12}O_6$

$C_6H_{12}O_6 + \text{zymase} \rightarrow 2C_2H_5OH + 2CO_2$

C_2H_5OH is the chemical formula for ethanol.

10. **Filteration and clarification:** Immediately after the fermentation process, the desired alcoholic percentage is achieved. The fresh beer undergoes filtration through a perforated plate at the bottom of the tank. This separates the larger sediments and removes them from the beer.

    After this the resulting beer would still contain smaller suspended sediments most probably of dead yeast cells floating in it. To make the beer crystal clear, a clarifying agent is added (please refer to the clarifying agents earlier mentioned in this chapter). These clarifying agents make the suspended particles settle to the bottom of the vat vessels and are then easily removed.

11. **Pasteurization:**

LET'S DEFINE

'Pasteurization is a process of heating a food, usually a liquid, to a specific temperature for a definite length of time and then cooling it immediately. This process slows spoilage due to microbial growth in the food.'

This process is applied to make sure the beer is bacteria-free and also the yeast is killed to prevent a secondary fermentation in the bottle, which would otherwise result in excess carbon dioxide formation and bursting the bottle or can. Pasteurization of beer is done by heating it to a temperature between 75°–80°C for 10–15 minutes. Sometimes, a flash method is used wherein the beer is first heated to 75–80°C for one minute and then rapidly cooled to a temperature of 4°C or lower.

It also increases shelf life of the beer cans by up to 4 months and beer bottles by up to 6 months.

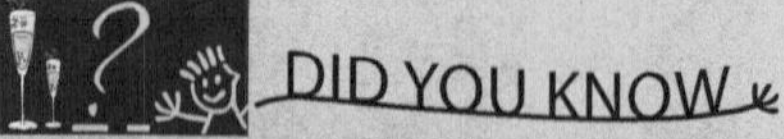

The yeast that is responsible for beer producing ironically is killed by the same alcohol that it produces. Yeast can survive in 16% alcoholic strength by volume after which it stops multiplying and soon perishes.

Keeping the above fact in mind, on an average, a beer contains 4–6% alcohol by volume (ABV). Hence, there is a large scope for a secondary fermentation to occur in the bottle. This is one of the reasons why pasteurization is an essential and vital step in beer manufacturing.

Fresh beers, also know as draught beers, are not pasteurized and are packaged in either kegs or cans. However, it has to be noted the pasteurization does diminish the overall taste of the beer but increases the stability of the beer.

12. **Carbonation or krausening:** Before the beer is packaged in kegs or bottled, the vital step of adding the sparkle, fizz or effervescence to the beer is done to make it more refreshing. This process is completed by carbonation process or krausening process.

    Earlier beers used to store in wooden barrels, but this lead to the beer gaining woody characteristics and flavour, which was not pleasant. Due to this, wooden barrels were replaced with metallic kegs for storing beer. Please note while a wooden barrel could contain a pressure of 50 psi, metallic barrels (also known as *kegs*) can contain a pressure of 300 psi.

    Beer keg.

    Carbonation is a simple process in which the beer is passed through compressor under pressure with carbon dioxide to add the carbon dioxide fizz to the beer in the bottle.

    The other process of adding the effervescence to the beer is done by the process of krausening. This process is done by adding approximately 15% of the fermenting wort; to the beer in storage, a short additional fermentation increases the carbon dioxide effervescence of the beer. After the carbonation process is completed, the beer is filtered and ready for packaging.

13. **Bottling:** Bottling and kegging is done immediately after the carbonation or krausening is complete, to avoid any loss of 'fizz'. Beer is stored in bottles, cans or kegs. There are various vessels in which beer is stored is mentioned as follows:

Capacities of Beer Containers

- Pin—4.5 gallons
- Firkin—9 gallons
- Kegs—10 gallons
- Kilderkin—18 gallons
- Barrel—36 gallons
- Hogshead—54 gallons

Interesting Facts

The Biere Club

A refreshing pint of beer at the Biere Club.

The Biere Club is the first and finest 'craft brewery' in Bengaluru city. Mr Arvind Raju, Ms Meenakshi Raju and Mr Vijaykumar Raju were the pioneers who established this Microbrewery (which produces its own beer) in 2011. The Biere Club promotes *Beer Discovery* through the production of beer in small batches with painstaking care, passion and respect for tradition. The beer that is brewed is made with the finest ingredients and is superior in every aspect—composition, colour, character, aroma and body.

This Microbrewery was established for the purpose of giving rise to a new culture of beer drinking in India. It serves and offers its consumers different types and kinds of beer educating people on beer and taking beer drinking to new level at par with wine culture.

5.4 STYLES OF BEER

There are varieties of beers in the market. Some differ in the content of alcohol, some by their colour taste etc. However, we are going to discuss the styles of beer, which differ from methods to making and each have become iconic. The various styles of beer need to be understood in detail, which is listed as follows:

1. **Ale:** An ale is an aromatic brew, made of only malt or a combination of malt and cereal and is usually fuller bodied and more bitter than the other styles of beer. Ale is fermented at a higher temperature at approximately between 15°–25°C and the yeast used is *S. Cerevisiae*, which rises to the top of the brew after fermentation, hence called top-fermentation brew.
2. **Porter:** Porter beers are the predecessors of stout-styled beers and are lower in alcohol with a darker colour and a bitter sweet taste. As its producers increased the alcohol content, it was referred to as an 'extra stout' porter and soon the stout became a different product. It can be considered a variant of ale.
3. **Stout:** It is very dark *ale* that is malty and in little bitter, flavoured and coloured by the addition of roasted barley to the brew.
4. **Lager:** It is a bright clear, light-bodied beer that has a sparkling effervescence. It is brewed from malt or occasionally from prepared cereals, such as corn grist or cracked rice, hops and water. The resultant wort is fermented for 7–10 days at a lower temperature between 9°–12°C, after which it is *lagered* (stored) for ageing and sedimentation. After this period,

Styles of beer (from left to right) American Pale Ale, Indian Pale Ale, Wheat Beer, Stout Beer, Lager Beer, Ale Beer. (Courtesy: *Biere Club, Bengaluru.*)

it is *krausened* or carbonated. Americans and Indians have a taste for lagers and are top-selling styles in both the United States and India. The yeast settles to the bottom of the container after fermentation and hence is called a bottom-fermentation brew.

5. **Pilsner:** It is a universal label for light beers. The *Pilsner Urquell* from Pilsen, Czechoslovakia, is the most famous Pilsner. All Pilsners are bright, light, lagered beers, but none come close to the original from Pilsen. Pilsner is almost too famous, that is the reason why some mistake it to be a separate style of beer, but it is a type of lager itself.

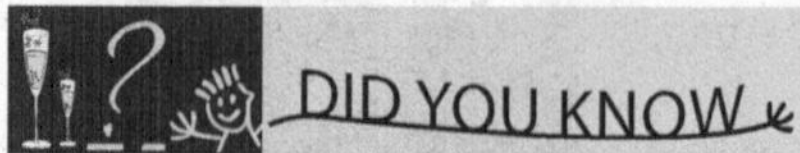

Indian Pale Ale is known by this name for a unique reason. As we know from Chapter 2 that, the Britisher brought tea to India, among other beverages beer was one of them. Since there were no breweries in India, the British asked brewers in Britain to ship beer in barrels. Unlike whisky, beer would get spoilt on its journey to India. To counter the problem, the British brewers created a beer with higher levels of alcohol (ABV) and also with more hops. On an average, these beers contain an alcoholic strength of 6–8% alcohol (ABV). The other ale variants are as follows:

- Regular Ale containing 5% ABV
- American Pale Ale containing 5% ABV
- Golden Ale containing 5% ABV
- Belgian Trappist beer containing 6–12 % ABV

The other lager variants are as follows:

- Dopplebock—An extra strong beer from Germany.
- Dortmunder—It is a blonde beer with a slightly bitter flavour.
- Munchner—A dark style of lager with an average 5% ABV.
- Vienna—It is an amber-coloured beer produced from amberish-brown-coloured malt with more than 5.5% ABV.

Other than the styles of the above-mentioned beer, there are more varieties but cannot be classified as a separate style. They are as follows:

1. **Bock beer or Bockbiere:** It is a special brew of heavy beer. It is usually darker and sweeter than regular beer. Some people think it is a variation of the *Einbecker beer from Einbeck town, Germany.* There is no legal definition for this variety of beer, but it differs from brewer to brewer.
2. **Malt liquor:** This is a malt beverage like beer, which has much higher alcohol content than regular beers. Alcoholic content in this beer is 6–7% as compared to an average beer, which has a 4–6% ABV. Its colour is usually light and pale.
3. **Weisse beer:** A popular German brew made from wheat grain. It is increasing in popularity due to its refreshing qualities. On an average these beers have an alcoholic strength of 5% ABV. *Hoegarden* is one of the most famous Belgian Weisse beers.

The styles discussed here, broadly covers all the styles of beer.

5.5 SERVICE OF BEER

Storage and Service of Bottled Beer

Bottled beer should be stored in a cool and dark place. Beer is extremely sensitive to light and the substances present in the hops turn cloudy when exposed to sunlight. Only when the hops are treated with hydrogen, they do not make the beer turn milky. Second, beer is supposed to be stored cold in a refrigerator, at a temperature between 4–6°C.

Serving

While serving bottled or canned beers, specific beer glasses such as beer pilsners and beer mugs should be used. Beer drinkers around the world prefer a foamy 'head' to their beers in the glass. Hence, we should first keep a glass (preferably chilled in the refrigerator called a *frosted glass* in most bars around the world) in an upright position and pour the beer in the centre of the glass. The glass should *not* be tilted as the beer then does not release enough carbon dioxide to form a desirable foamy 'head' as a top layer in the glass.

***Note*:** Beer glasses should be rinsed of all the soap solution else the carbon dioxide will breakdown and would destroy the foam of the beer.

Dispensing Draught Beer

There are three most important points to be considered while serving draught beer. These are as follows:

1. **Cleanliness:** Cleanliness is of utmost importance as beer is susceptible to airborne bacteria, sunlight and odours. Beer is one of the most delicate food products in a restaurant. The entire bar equipment has to be kept neat and clean, that is, the taps, pipes etc. It is recommended to clean the bar equipment at least once a week.
2. **Temperature:** Lager beers are supposed to be served at a temperature of 4°C, whereas *ales* at 8°C. While most places serve beer both the styles at 4°C or even colder, by doing so, the lower temperatures do not allow our palate to taste the essential esters and congeners, which impart the flavour to the beer.
3. **Pressure:** The pressure in the keg should be maintained as this is the reason for the beer to have effervescence ('fizz'). Pressure, especially in a keg, varies from the first glass to the last glass. An additional source of carbon dioxide or air is normally used to maintain the pressure. Usually carbon dioxide is a more trusted source as air can impart a foul smell to the beer. Most companies go to the extent of sterilizing the air before carbonation. A pressure gauge should be maintained in a bar to keep a check on the pressure at which the beer is dispensed.

Now, we have understood how to serve beer in general. We will study the procedure for serving beer in food and beverage establishments in Chapter 29.

5.6 FAMOUS BEER BRANDS FROM ACROSS THE WORLD

Various beer brands that are produced across the world are listed in Table 5.2.

Table 5.2 Beer Brands Made Across the World

Country	Brand of Beer
Australia	Fosters, Victoria Bitter, Swan, Emu and Melbourne Bitter
Canada	Labatt's Ale, Moosehead and Molson Dry
China	Tsingtao, Harbin, Yanjing, Zhujiang and Wusu
Czech Republic	Pilsner Urquell, Bernard, Radegast, Budweiser Budvar and Starobrno
Denmark	Carlsberg, Tuborg, Guld and Royal Spring
England	Bass Ale, Whitbread Ale and Cobra
France	Brassin de garde and Kronenbourg
Germany	Beck's, Dortmunder, Krombacher, Warsteiner and Bitburger
Holland	Amstel and Heineken
India	Eagle, Kingfisher, Kalyani, Sandpiper and Haywards
Ireland	Guinness stout and Harp
Italy	Perroni and Raffo
Japan	Asahi and Saporo
Mexico	Corona and Carta blanca
Norway	Ringness
Philipines	San Miguel
Sweden	Pripps and Kalback
Trinidad and Tobago	Carib and Stag

A yard of ale is a tall beer glass used especially in Irish Pubs to serve ale, approximately one yard long. The glass is shaped like a bulb at the bottom and tapers in the middle, widening towards the top. It has a volume of 1.4 l. This glass originated in England in the 17th century; it was used for drinking beer on special occasions. It was also known as Cambridge yard glass, long glass and yard glass.

5.7 SOME INTERESTING FACTS ABOUT BEER

1. Moderate consumption of beer, that is, alcohol is medically proven to reduce the risk of heart disease and stroke. However, long-term alcohol abuse results in liver disease.
2. Brewer's yeast is known to be a rich source of nutrients; therefore, as expected, beer can contain significant amounts of nutrients, including magnesium, selenium, potassium, phosphorus, biotin and vitamin B. In fact, beer is sometimes referred to as 'liquid bread'. Some sources maintain that filtered beer loses much of its nutrition.
3. Hops belong to the *Cannabis* family. Its female flowers contain *lupalin*, which contains the tannins and resins responsible for the aroma and stability of the beer.
4. To the unknown consumer, many bartenders pass-off their faulty beers as originals. If a beer is either cloudy, flat, sour or having sediments in them it is not suitable for drinking.

LET'S SUMMARIZE IN POINTS

- Beer is an alcoholic beverage made by fermenting barley or wheat.
- Ale is a top-fermentation beer and lager is a bottom-fermentation beer produced by *S. Cerevisiae* and *S. Uvarum* (or *S. Carlsbergensis*), respectively.
- Cleanliness, hygiene and temperature are three important factors while dispensing draught beer.
- Beer is served in beer mugs, pilsner glasses, beer steins, beer boots and stange beer glasses.
- Lagers are served at 4°C whereas ales are served at 8°C.
- Beer is rich in many vitamins and minerals. Moderate consumption of beer reduces risk of heart diseases.
- Beer should be stored in a cool, dark place. It is extremely sensitive to light and substances present in the hops turn cloudy when exposed to sunlight.

5.8 FAQs

Short-Answer Type Questions

1. Name five brands of beer from India, China, the United States, the UK and Denmark.
2. Name two yeasts used in the production of beer.
3. Give a brief description of hops.
4. Write a short note on styles of beer.
5. Give three hops in brewing.
6. What do you understand by the term *Krausening*?
7. What is Pasteurization?
8. Name the various ingredients used in the manufacture of beer.
9. What is Biere weisse?
10. Define brewing.

Long-Answer Type Questions

1. Give in detail the process of brewing.
2. Give the difference between ales and lagers.
3. Explain in detail the ingredients used for the manufacture of beer.
4. Explain the process of pasteurization in detail. Give its importance.
5. Give five brands of beer from various countries.
6. Give the health facts about beer along with its nutritional benefits.

5.9 KEY TERMS

- Aeration
- Ale
- Baum level
- Brewing
- Code of Hammurabi
- Ethanol
- Fermentation
- Fining
- Head
- Heat exchange
- Hop back
- Hops
- Hymn of Ninkasi
- IBU (International bitterness units)
- Isinglass
- Krausening
- Lager
- Lautering
- Mashing
- Pasteurization
- Pint
- Reinheitgebod
- Saccharification
- Saccharometer
- Sparging
- Starch
- Whirlpool separator
- Sucrose
- Wort
- Yeast

SAKE

CHAPTER OUTLINE

LET'S DEFINE

'Sake is an alcoholic beverage of Japanese origin that is made from fermented rice. It is sometimes spelled as saki or Sake.'

Sake is a popular fermented beverage made from rice and it originates from Japan. The word 'Sake' means 'the essence of the spirit of rice'. It is also called *Ninhonshu* in Japanese. Many people confuse this beverage to be a wine or spirit, as it is sometimes called a Japanese rice wine. However, in essence, Sake is a rice beer. This colourless beverage made without carbonation unlike beer.

6.1 HISTORY

The origins of Sake are unclear. However, the earliest reference was from *Kojiki*, Japan's first written history compiled in AD 712. Sake production was a government monopoly till the 10th century. However, from the 10th century to the next 500 years, Sake brewed in temples and shrines.

At the beginning of the 20th century, the brewing technology became more sophisticated and grew by leaps and bounds. The year 1904 marked the opening of *The Sake Brewing Research Institute.* This lead to the identification of yeast strains, especially for their brewing properties. Second, enamel-coated tanks replaced the wooden barrels. Wooden barrels were seen as being unhygienic and hence were discarded and not used in Sake brewing till date.

The traditional stoneware used in the service of warm Sake.

After the Second World War, Japan faced shortages of rice. This was a big blow to the Sake-brewing industry. The brewers, for this reason, started adding pure alcohol and glucose to the rice mash, which in turn increased the yield by 75%, but influenced the quality considerably. After the War, came other beverages of the world such as beer, wine and spirits. The recovering breweries had a stiff competition and by 1960, beer consumption had crossed Sake consumption in Japan.

The demand for Sake reduced gradually, but its quality improved with progress of times. In today's beverage industry, it holds a special place as an exotic and connoisseur beverage on most renowned restaurant's beverage list.

6.2 PRODUCTION OF SAKE

1. **Rice preparation:** First, polished rice is soaked in water for about 12 hours. Then, it is steamed in a *Koshiki* (a rice steaming tub). Some steamed rice is treated with a 'spore' (a type of yeast called *Aspergillus Oryzae*), which produces an enzyme that converts the starch in the rice to sugar. This step can take up to 35 hours and produces a culture string called *Koji*, in this enzyme.
2. **Preparing the yeast:** To develop the fermenting yeast culture, some *Koji* is added to a thin paste of steamed rice and water, with a little quantity of yeast starter. The yeast begins to multiply as it acts on the sugar that is produced due to the *Koji.* This process usually takes two to three weeks. The mash becomes a ripened *Moto.*
3. **Fermentation:** The *Moto, Koji* and water are added to fresh steamed rice and the fermentation process begins. Sake's quality is determined by the size of the rice kernels left after the fermentation. Good-quality Sake is made from rice that has been polished down by 50% of its original size. In the fermentation tank, two conversions take place. First, the starch converts to sugar by using the *Koji.* Second, the sugar converts into alcohol by using the yeast culture known as *Moto.* The fermentation process for Sake takes place between 15–16°C for three weeks. However, the best varieties undergo a four-week fermentation process between 14–15°C.
4. **Filtration and maturation:** The fermented Sake is first filtered. It is then rested and transferred into casks where it is matured for a short period.
5. **Pasteurization and bottling:** First, the Sake is pasteurized and then bottled or casked. Export varieties are not distinguished in grades. However, Sake meant for domestic sale in Japan is graded as special, first grade and second grade.

6.3 SERVICE OF SAKE

Sake usually has 14–16% alcohol by volume (ABV). It has a sweet first taste and a dry after taste. Traditionally, Sake is served warm because heating releases its heavy bouquet. To warm Sake, place the opened bottle in a pot of boiling water (*a double boiler*). Remove the Sake when it has reached a temperature of 38–40°C. The Japanese serve the Sake in small ceramic bottles called '*Tokkuri*' and then poured into a small ceramic bowls called '*Sakazuki*', which holds a little more than an ounce.

Sake can also be consumed at room temperature or even chilled. Today, many Sake-based cocktail recipes are also available.

Ceramic bottles called Tokkuris along with the ceramic bowls called Sakazuki that are used for sipping Sake.

6.4 BRANDS OF SAKE

- '*Gembei-San*' or 'Onigoroshi' or just 'Gembei'.
- '*Otokoyama*'—This brand of Sake is pretty popular. It is very dry and can usually be found at good Sushi shops and Japanese restaurants.
- '*Karatamba*'—Another pretty popular dryer than *Gembei*, but not as dry as *Otokoyama*.

These are all '*Junmai*' Sakes, which mean at least 30% of the rice has been removed. More refinement means more expensive; a '*Junmai Daiginjo*' will have 50% of the rice polished away and will cost about double the price.

Other well-known brands of Sake are *Oni-Korishi* from *Shizuoka*, *Kamotsuru*, *Gekkeikan Sake*, *Takara Sake* and *Ozeki Nigori* (which is unfiltered Sake and looks like water infused with milk).

Two brands of Sake bottles.

LET'S SUMMARIZE IN POINTS

- Sake is an alcoholic beverage of Japanese origin that is made from fermented rice. It is sometimes spelled as saki or Sake.
- Sake is a colourless beverage made without carbonation unlike beer.
- In the beginning of the 20th century, the brewing technology became more sophisticated and grew by leaps and bounds. The year 1904 marked the opening of *The Sake Brewing Research Institute*.
- Sake usually has 14–16% alcohol by volume (ABV). Traditionally, it is served warm because heating releases its heavy bouquet.
- The Japanese serve the Sake in small ceramic bottles called '*Tokkuri*' and is then poured into a small ceramic bowl called '*Sakazuki*', which holds a little more than an ounce.
- *Gembei*, *Otokoyama*, *Karatamba* and *Junmai – Junmai Daiginjo* are popular brands of Sake.

6.5 FAQs

Short-Answer Type Questions

1. What is *Koji* in Japanese?
2. What is *Moto* in Japanese?
3. What does the word *Sake* mean?
4. Name the service equipment used for serving Sake in Japan.
5. Give the fermentation temperature for producing Sake.

Long-Answer Type Questions

1. Give the production process of Sake in detail.
2. Describe in detail the service of Sake.
3. Explain the detailed reaction to convert the starch in rice to soluble sugars, with Japanese terminology.

6.6 KEY TERMS

- ABV
- Aspergillus Oryzae
- Kojiki
- Kojiki
- Koshiki
- Moto
- Ninhonshu
- Sakuzi
- Tokkuri

CIDER AND PERRY

CHAPTER OUTLINE

7.1 CIDER

LET'S DEFINE

'Cider is a fermented alcoholic beverage made from apple juice.'

In countries, such as Canada and the United States, Cider refers to a non-alcoholic beverage, whereas hard Cider refers to the alcoholic counterpart commonly called 'Cider' in the UK, France, Spain, Germany, Argentina and Australia. In Australia, it is produced Tasmania is land, as apples are cultivated there. In India, Cider is produced in the state of Himachal Pradesh, where apples are in abundance.

Types of Cider

There is no ready reference for the history of Cider or where it has evolved from. Cider has a variety of flavours and it varies from region, method of production, quality of the apples produced and so on.

Ciders can range from being dry to sweet and are categorized accordingly. They also vary in appearance from cloudy to clear. Ciders are usually brownish to golden in colour. The inexpensive ones resemble sparkling wine and can also be very clear, but are mostly produced in mass. The traditional brands, however, are darker and cloudier, giving a more intense apple aroma and flavour.

Production of Cider

For making good-quality Cider, best quality apples are to be selected. Most Cider producers use apples for consumption to make their Cider, whereas regional Cider makers prefer a mix of eating apples and Cider apples, which are higher on sugar.

The well-known varieties of Cider apples differ from the regions where they are cultivated. The two most prominent regions are as follows:

1. Cider apples from Kent, England.
2. Cider apples from West Country, England.

Further, we shall understand the various steps involved in making Cider.

1. **Scratting and pressing:** Scratting is the process of 'grinding down' apples to make it into pulp known as *pomace or pommage.* Traditionally, this was done by pressing stones or a Cider mill, powered by hand, water mill or horsepower. Nowadays, it is powered by electricity and is an automated process. Next, the *pomace* is transferred to the Cider press and is built up into layers known as cheeses into a block. Sweet straw is placed in between the presses to avoid exposure to the air, thereby preventing oxidation. Ten to twelve layers are made and then subjected to increased degrees of pressure, until all the juice, that is, the *must* is squeezed out.

   The *must* is then strained with a sieve and transferred in oak casks or barrels.
2. **Fermentation:** The next step is fermentation. The fermentation temperature ranges from 4–16°C. This is low for fermentation and is unique for making Cider, as the temperature slows down the fermentation process reducing the loss of delicate aromas.

   Before the fermentation process consumes all the sugars, the fermenting juice or *must* is 'racked' (refer Racking, later on in this chapter) to different vats or barrels. These vats or barrels are filled to the brim (top), leaving no room for air to oxidize the juice. The remaining sugar enables the fermentation to continue. The carbon dioxide thus produced creates a foamy layer on the top of the barrel, leaving no space for air at all. Racking process is repeated if the liquor is cloudy.

   The Cider is ready only after a 3-month fermentation period and matured for up to 2–3 years. The average Cider bottle contains an alcoholic strength between 2–8% ABV.
3. **Blending and bottling:** Ciders from different vats (containers) can be combined to meet the market's taste and demand. It is at times bottled using the *Méthode Champenoise* (Champagne method), which produces good-quality results (refer *Méthode Champenoise* in Chapter 19). However, often Ciders are bottled like beers and a secondary fermentation enables them to get carbonated before bottling. Else carbonation is done with the help of compressors before bottling. Ciders are also either bottled or put into kegs similar to beers.

LET'S DEFINE

'Racking is the process of allowing the liquor to rest in a vat or barrel until all the suspended particles settle to the bottom of the vessel or container. After this is done, the bottom containing all the sediments, such as dead yeast cells, fruit skin and remaining pulp is removed.' The process of removing the sediments is called *removing the lees.*

Brands of Cider

Table 7.1 Brands of Cider

Country	Brand of Cider
India	Mincy's under the brand name Wonderwyne, Green Valley and Gold Home
Ireland	Bulmers (Ireland)—marketed as Magners outside Ireland, Burrow Hill Cider
England	Aspall Cider Blackthorn Cider Constellation Europe Sheppy's Dabinett Apple Cider Merry Down Apple Cider Brothers Cider—British makers of Pear Cider (Perry), H.P. Bulmer—British brewers of Scrumpy Jack, Strongbow, Strongbow Sirrus, Woodpecker, White Lightning, Pomagne and Bulmers Original

Health Benefits of Cider

Apple Cider has a high concentration of phenolics, which may be helpful in preventing heart disease, cancer and other ailments. Apples are a good source of phenolics in general.

We have studied in detail about Cider; now we shall understand Perry, a beverage very similar to Cider.

7.2 PERRY

LET'S DEFINE

'Perry is a fermented alcoholic beverage made from the juice of pears. It is also popularly known as *Poire* in French.'

The CAPTION—"A refreshing glass of apple cider".

Perry and Cider have a lot in common and in some parts of the world, Perry is also called, 'Pear Cider'. However, connoisseurs prefer to call it Perry and not Pear Cider.

Pears: Like Cider apples, pears that are used to produce Perry are also specific. The cultivated pear species in Europe, where the beverage is most consumed, was brought by the Romans. Perry pears are higher in tannin and are more acidic than pears meant for eating and cooking.

History of Perry

Perry making can be traced back to the Roman Empire itself. After the collapse of the Roman Empire, pear cultivation continued in the region, which is modern-day France. As per the references, England imported pears from France in the medieval period.

Perry may have grown in popularity after the 'English Civil War', where the soldiers billeted in the three counties of Worcestershire, Gloucestershire and Herefordshire, where pears were cultivated and Perry was an established beverage. Furthermore, conflicts with France in the 18th century made the beverage reach the zenith in terms of popularity, as wine imports from France became difficult.

Perry from England is a still and dry beverage, whereas *Poire* or Normandy Perry developed a bottle fermented, sparkling style with a great amount of sweetness.

Production of Perry

Perry production is quite similar to traditional Cider making. While making Perry, the pear mash pomace is allowed to rest to loose tannins and only then is the juice extracted. After the initial fermentation, the drink undergoes a secondary malolactic fermentation while maturing.

Perry production is the same as Cider and its alcoholic strength is also between 1.5–8% ABV. For details, please refer to the production of Cider, which is discussed earlier in this chapter.

Brands of Perry

Most producers of Cider also produce Perry. Some of the prominent brands of Perry are shown in Table 7.2.

Table 7.2 Brands of Perry

Country	Brands of Perry
The United Kingdom	Blackthorn Cider Constellation Europe, Shepton Mallet, England
Sweden	Briska, Kopparberg, Herrljunga Cider, Rekorderlig Cider and Gravendals
New Zealand	Old Mout Cider, Macs and Monteiths Brewery
Australia	Westons, St Helier and Magners

7.3 SERVICE OF CIDER AND PERRY

Perry and Cider are served in the same way as beer, that is, in a beer mug or a suitable glass. The following steps are necessary to be followed while serving Cider or Perry:

1. Take a chilled glass used for beer, for example, a beer mug or a beer Pilsner glass.
2. Keep it upright on the table and pour to the centre of the glass.
3. Cider and Perry are sparkling beverages and they are served in a way similar to champagne service, but in a beer glass. These beverages do not form a foamy head unlike beer.

7.4 INTERESTING FACTS ABOUT CIDER

1. Draught Cider and bottled Cider are the different kinds available in the market. Cider is also available in kegs.
2. Draught Cider may be dry or still or slightly sweet and sparkling. The sweetness is added in the form of sugar or concentrated apple juice.

3. Draught Cider is usually unfiltered and has a hazy appearance. When completely dry, it is often called farmhouse Cider.
4. Keg Ciders are pasteurized, filtered Ciders, bright in appearance and are usually sweetened and carbonated.

LET'S SUMMARIZE IN POINTS

- Cider is an alcoholic beverage prepared from apple juice, whereas Perry is an alcoholic beverage from France, which is made from the juice of pears.
- Ciders can range from being dry to sweet and are categorized accordingly. They also vary in appearance from cloudy to clear.
- Conflicts with France in the 18th century made the beverage reach to the zenith in terms of popularity as wine imports from France became difficult.
- Perry and Cider are served in the same way as beer, that is, in a beer mug or a suitable glass. Unlike beer, they do not form any head.

7.5 FAQs

Short-Answer Type Questions

1. Define Cider.
2. What is unique about Cider apples?
3. Where is Cider produced in India?
4. Give three health benefits of Cider consumption.
5. Give two differences in the methods of making Cider and Perry.
6. Define Perry or *Poire*.
7. Define racking.
8. Give five brands each of Perry and Cider.
9. Where in France is *Poire* extensively produced?
10. Give the difference between Perry from England and Perry from Normandy France.

Long-Answer Type Questions

1. Give the production methods of Cider.
2. Give the production methods of Perry.
3. Describe in detail the history of Perry.
4. Write a detailed note on:
   (i) Cider apples
   (ii) Perry pears
5. Mention 10 brands each from Cider and Perry.

7.6 KEY TERMS

- Draught Cider
- Dry
- Lees
- Malolactic fermentation
- Medieval period
- Méthode Champenoise
- Must
- Normandy
- Pasteurization
- Phenolies
- Pommace/Pommage
- Racking
- Sweet
- Tannins

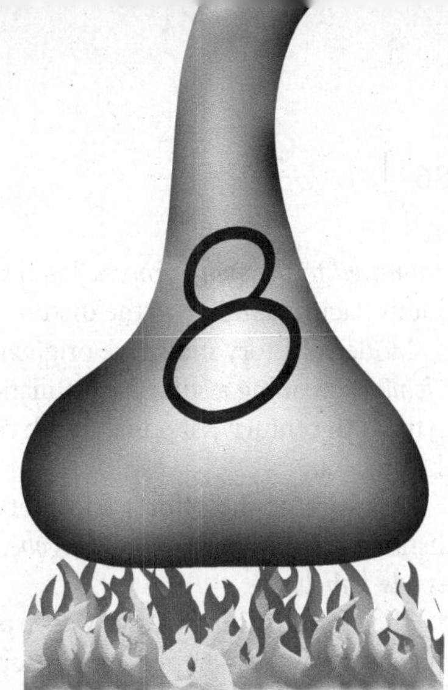

Distillation

CHAPTER OUTLINE

So far, we have learnt about the various types of fermented or brewed alcoholic beverages. Now, we will study the fundamentals of distillation and the manufacture processes of spirits in general.

Distillation applies on a very simple principle; alcohol vaporizes at a lower temperature than water on heating, at approximately 77–78°C, whereas water vaporizes at 100°C. Therefore, if the liquid containing alcohol is heated beyond 78°C while keeping it below 100°C, it will result in separating the alcohol from the base liquid.

If the alcohol vapours are not allowed to escape into the air, but are collected in a separate vessel allowing them to recondense into a liquid, it will result in higher alcoholic strength by volume. To produce a potable and fine alcoholic spirit, the procedure is more difficult than it appears.

8.1 HISTORY

Apparently, the science of distillation was known to the ancient Egyptians. The Chinese also obtained a spirit from rice beer long before the Christians. Arak was being distilled from sugarcane and rice as far back as 800 BC. Aristotle (384–322 BC), a great philosopher from Greece, stated in his book *Meteorology* about *how sea water can be made more potable by distillation and wine along with other liquids can be submitted to the same process.* Even Captain Cook, on his voyages, found the natives of the islands in the South Pacific familiar to the distillation process.

Modern history may have originated with the Arabs, as they were the first to use the words *Alcohol and Alembic*, meaning a still. The distillation process is attributed to an Arabian alchemist known as *Albukassen* in the 10th century. Later in the 13th century, Raymond Lully, a Majorcan chemist and philosopher, described the process.

Unaware of the efforts and methods of the Arabs, the Celts of Eire and Scotia were producing a distilled potable spirit called *Uisgebeatha or Uisgebaugh* meaning, 'water of life' (*Uisgebaugh is pronounced as wis-kah-bah*).

The first distilling vessel was a pot still. It comprised of two parts; one, an onion-shaped still and the other a worm-shaped condenser. This type of still is used even to this date. The *pot still* has a broad copper pot as its base, with a long tapering neck. The worm condenser is a copper tube that connects to the copper still through a copper pipe. The worm passes through a cold water jacket to assist in rapid condensation of the vapours. This type of still is commonly used to produce brandies, whiskies—both Scotch and Irish—rums and a few liqueurs. The pot still is said to produce a liquor with pronounced flavours due the presence of more esters and congeners in the final distilled beverage.

In 1826, Robert Stein invented the continuous still. He hailed from a family that distilled a famous Scotch whisky. This still was later perfected by Aeneas Coffey, whose patent replaced the Stein version. This is the reason for the continuous still to be known as the Coffey or patent still. This type of still is used to produce lighter liquors and grain whiskies.

8.2 DISTILLED SPIRITS

Further, in this chapter, we shall understand the various types of spirits. All potable alcoholic beverages are produced first by fermenting a liquid high in sugar, for example, wine or beer, which are consumed after fermentation. All other alcoholic beverages are then subjected to the distillation process to produce spirits higher in alcoholic content. For example, whisky, brandy, gin, vodka etc. Let us understand each spirit in brief.

Brandy: This is a potable spirit obtained by distilling wine or a fermented mash of fruits, aged in wood. Examples are Cognac and Armagnac from France, Grape brandies of the United States of America, Mexico, Spain, Israel and India. Brandies are made from other fruits, such as Kirsch from cherries, Calvados or Apple Jack from apples and Mirabelle and Quetsch from plums among many others.

Whisky: It is a spirit suitably aged in wood (usually oak wood) that is obtained from the distillation of a fermented mash of grain. Examples are Scotch whisky, Canadian whisky, Irish whisky, Rye whisky and Bourbon whisky.

Rum: A potable spirit aged in wood obtained from the distillation of the fermented mash of sugarcane juice or molasses. Some examples are Jamaican rum, Barbados rum, Cuban Ron, Puerto Rican Ron, Haitian Rhum and Batavia Arak among others.

Gin: A flavoured beverage obtained by redistilling a neutral spirit with a high alcoholic strength (ABV), in the presence of juniper berries and other flavouring agents. Examples are English and American gin (London Dry Type), Dutch gins (*Genever* or *Hollands*) and fruit-flavoured gins. Famous brands include Bombay Sapphire, Tanquerays and Beefeater gin.

Vodka: A neutral spirit distilled from the fermented mash of potatoes or grain. It is a spirit distilled or treated with charcoal or other material to obtain a resulting vodka without character, aroma, taste or colour. If the distillate is flavoured, the vodka is characterized and named after the flavouring material used.

Tequila: A potable spirit distilled from the fermented mash made from the blue agave plant. Primarily found in the area around the city of tequila in the Mexican State of Jalisco. The word '*tequila*' has exclusively been claimed by Mexico. Other countries are not permitted to use this word if they are making a distilled beverage using the Blue Agave plant.

Liqueurs and cordials: A liqueur is a neutral spirit that has been flavoured with fruit, herbs, nuts, spices and flowers or cream and bottled with added sugar. All liqueurs and cordials are sweetened. Examples include Amaretto, Chartreuse, Crème Liqueurs, Grand Marnier and Triple Sec.

There are other spirits that are made, such as Aquavits, Bitters and Liqueurs. We have defined the broad categories of spirits above, but further on, we shall consider each type in separate chapters.

8.3 TYPES OF STILLS

There are two types of stills—pot still and patent still that is also known as continuous still.

Pot Still

This is an older method of distillation. It is a modified version of the Alembic used by the Arabs in the 10th century. Figure 8.1 helps us better understand the working of a pot still. Figure 8.1 depicts the following steps:

1. The fermented wort, also known as the lower wines, is heated with wood fire, petroleum gas or even steam.
2. This leads to the evaporation of the alcohol vapour at 79°C. The alcohol comprises of methyl alcohol (methanol), ethyl alcohol (ethanol) along with esters and congeners. The methanol evaporates first

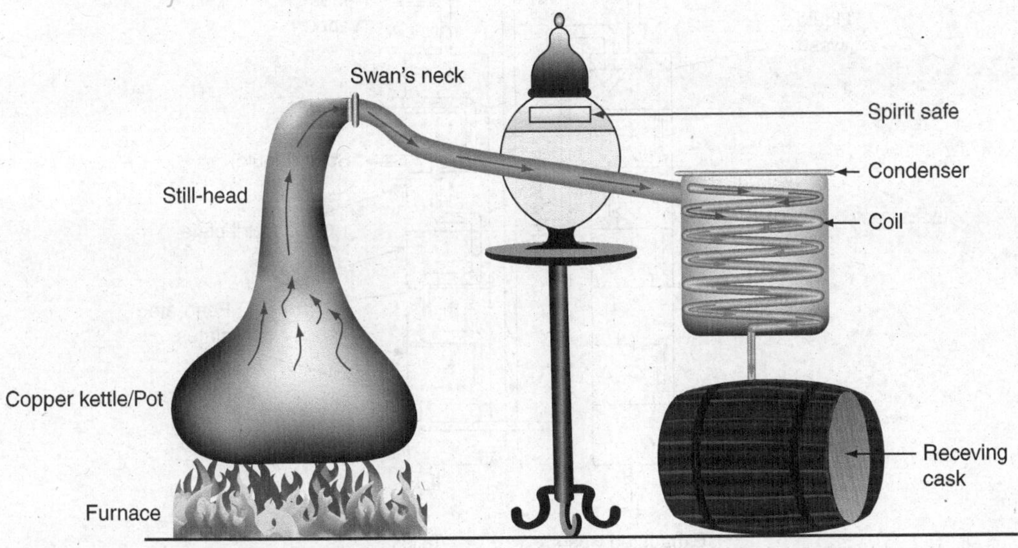

Figure 8.1 The working of a pot still.

and is not potable referred to as *heads*. The second part containing the ethanol vapours, which is the important potable vapour used to produce the distillate and referred to as the *hearts*. The third part is also known as the *tails*, which are the burnt leftovers of the lower wines; it can cause the distillate to develop a bad odour or taste.

3. The spirit safe is a transparent box where the *master distiller* can monitor the vapours. The distiller cuts off the heads and tails that are not potable. The master distiller specifically collects the 'hearts' of the beverage, which is potable containing ethyl alcohol congeners and esters.
4. Condensation coils are cooled with water where the heat exchange occurs, leading to the condensation of the vapours.
5. The distillate is collected in tanks or stainless steel vats. The pot still distillation method results in a distillate with 35% ABV. This is the reason, double distillation is mandatory to produce an alcohol of 70% ABV before maturation.

Patent Still

Figure 8.2 helps us better understanding the working of a patent still.

Description and Method of Working

The column still or patent still uses a continuous process to distil the base liquid or wash.

- First, the cold liquid base wash, which enters from the *rectifier column*, gets heated and enters the *analyser column*. It comes in contact with the steam at 102°C resulting in the alcohol vapours to evaporate into a gaseous state.

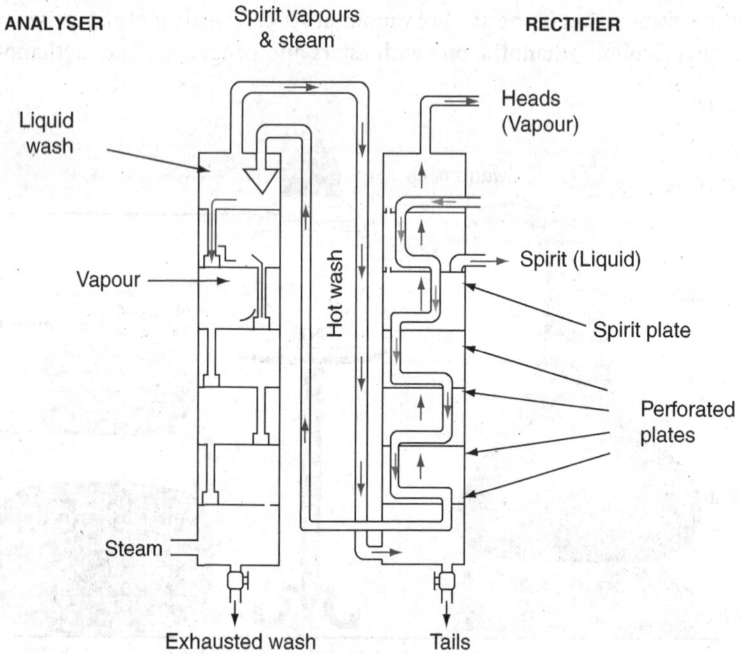

Figure 8.2 Working of the patent still.

- The alcohol vapours touch the plates in the *analyser column* (refer the diagram), hence, undergoing a continuous distillation process.
- The evaporated alcohol or spirit vapours along with steam go through the connected pipes into the *rectifier column.*
- The resulting alcohol vapours along with the steam pass through the perforated plates of the *rectifier column* (as shown in the diagram). The *heads* evaporate and are let off from the topmost pipe of the *rectifier column*; while, the tails condense and settle to the bottom of the rectifier column from where they are let off.
- The hearts or the essential potable spirits are collected from the middle of the *rectifier column.* This continuous distillation process results in a highly concentrated spirit with an average of 90–95% alcoholic strength. Due to this, the resultant distillate from this still has a lesser concentration of esters and congeners, making it neutral as compared to the resultant distillate from a pot still.

8.4 METHODS OF PROVING (PROOF)

Before distillation of spirits became a science, the primitive distillers had a very simple method for determining the potable strength of a liquor. Equal quantities of the sprit and gunpowder were mixed. Then, a flame was applied. If the flame did not burn, the spirit was too weak. If it burnt brightly, it was too strong. If the flame burnt evenly with a blue flame the spirit was said to have been *proved.* With today's progress in the field of distillation, we know that the potable mean is 50% proof or 50% ABV. There are various methods of proof. The famous ones are listed below:

1. **ABV**—It stands for *Alcohol by Volume.* It represents the absolute percentage of alcohol in the bottle. For example, 45% ABV refers to 45% alcoholic content in the bottle.
2. **US proof**—This method is followed in the United States. The alcoholic proof is defined as *twice* the value of ABV. Foe example, a 45% ABV would translate to a 90° proof in the US method.
3. **UK proof**—This method was defined as 7/4 times alcohol by volume. UK now uses the ABV standard instead of this proof method.

With this, we can understand the various methods of reading the alcoholic content in a bottle. The most famous one out of the three is the ABV method, which is practiced throughout the world.

8.5 INTERESTING FACTS ABOUT ALCOHOL

1. Drinking alcohol 'in limits' or sparingly does not physically damage the important organs of the body such as the heart, kidney, liver, stomach, brain or the nervous system.
2. Alcohol produces energy for the body without making the body work as it is absorbed directly into the blood stream.
3. The part of the body that is most quickly affected by alcohol consumption is the brain. Alcohol relaxes the brain and does not stimulate it like coffee or tea.
4. The best insulation against the effects of excessive alcohol consumption is consumption of food, as it lines the walls of the stomach. The best food is that which contains the fat of milk such as cream and butter. Olive and meat are also good food for this purpose. Spicy foods should be avoided as it may react with the alcohol.

There is no evidence to prove that alcohol causes any disease. However, the principle danger of alcohol consumption is social. It leads to a narcotized brain, one that is not awake. In a moment of crisis when a quick decision is required, the brain becomes less active, which leads to dangerous results.

We can conclude by saying that consumption of alcohol is not harmful. When consumed sparingly, it is known to be beneficial. Drinking alcohol should not be done for the *kick*, as in all probability, it will lead to alcohol abuse. Drinking should be done for relaxation and pleasure and it can be part of a good lifestyle.

8.6 SERVING ALCOHOL

The following are the various alcohol serving methods:

1. **Neat or straight:** The spirit is served at room temperature without any additives.
2. **Straight up:** It refers to an alcoholic beverage that is shaken or stirred with ice, strained and served.
3. **On the rocks:** In this method, the spirit is served on a bed of ice.
4. **With a mixer:** The spirit is served along with a *chaser*, for example, juice, club soda, water and aerated beverages.
5. **As an ingredient in a cocktail.**
6. **As a shooter:** Shots of the liquor with an added flavour served in ounces.

LET'S SUMMARIZE IN POINTS

- Distillation is a process in which alcohol vapours are separated from water by application of heat due to the difference in boiling points in both the liquids.
- There are two kinds of stills: the pot still and the patent still.
- Pot still invented by the Arabs is used to produce aromatic distillates with pronounced flavours. For example, whisky and rum.
- Patent still was invented by Aeneas Coffey. It is used in producing distillates with high alcoholic proof such as vodka and gin.
- Proving refers to measuring the alcoholic content in a beverage.
- Alcohol can be served neat, on the rocks, along with a mixer or as a shooter.

8.7 FAQs

Short-Answer Type Questions

1. Define distillation.
2. Who invented the pot still?
3. Who invented the patent still?
4. Give the salient features of the pot still.
5. What are the methods of proving?

Long-Answer Type Questions

1. Write a note on the following:
   (i) Brandy (ii) Whisky
   (iii) Vodka (iv) Gin
   (v) Tequila (vi) Liqueurs
2. Describe the working of the patent still with a diagram.
3. How is alcohol served?
4. Mention five interesting facts about alcohol.
5. Explain the working of a pot still citing a diagrammatic representation.

8.8 KEY TERMS

- ABV
- Arabs
- Arak
- Aristotle
- Congeners
- Esters
- Heads
- Hearts
- Patent still
- Pot still
- Proving
- Tails
- UK proof
- US proof

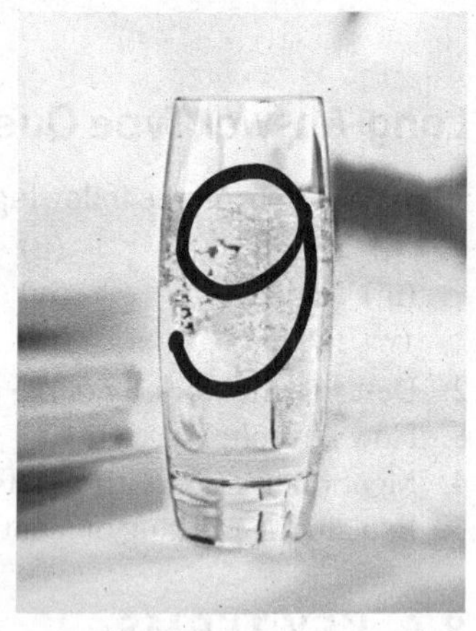

VODKA

CHAPTER OUTLINE

LET'S DEFINE

'Vodka is a neutral spirit distilled from potatoes or grains. It is a spirit distilled or treated with activated charcoal or other material to obtain a spirit without character, aroma, taste or colour. If the liquor is flavoured, the vodka is characterized and named after the flavouring material used'.

Today, vodka is one of the world's most popular spirits. It was rarely consumed outside Europe before the 1950s. It was in the latter half of the 1970s and 1980s that vodka gained popularity. This can be attributed to vodkas characteristic of being odourless and having a neutral flavour, making the smell of liquor undetectable on ones breath. Second, due to its neutral nature, it can be mixed with variety of drinks making it a universal base spirit as hence so popular.

9.1 HISTORY

The word 'Vodka' in Russian can be associated with the word 'Voda' meaning 'water'. In Northern and Eastern Europe (in countries, such as Czech Republic, earlier known as Czechoslovakia, Russia and Poland) spirits have long been distilled to a very high proof resulting in minimum flavour.

The history of vodka is often disputed. The Russians and Poles have claimed and disputed the rights over the invention of 'vodka' for many years.

According to some sources, vodka was first produced in today's Russia in the 9th century, whereas the Poles claim that it was distilled in Poland even earlier in the 8th century.

The vast distilleries of the Smirnoff in Moscow, Russia produced vodka from 1818, passed out of the family's control with the 1917 revolution. The formula reached America in the 1950s where it grew in popularity making it a fashionable beverage. From the United States, where drinking vodka was a trend, it spread to the rest of the world. Now Smirnoff is a popular brand of vodka in many countries, including India.

9.2 PRODUCTION PROCESS OF VODKA

Vodka is generally made by distilling a fermented mash, made of either wheat or corn (Figure 9.1). Vodkas can be made from other grains; however, vodkas made from wheat are considered to be superior. In Poland, however, potatoes are extensively used for making vodka.

As the name suggests vodka was associated with the word 'voda' meaning water. Vodka is a beverage without any colour, taste and odour and hence has been purified of all the congeners. Unlike whisky, which is distilled at a low proof to retain flavour, distillation of vodka is a continuous process and done at a high proof.

There are steps involved in the production of vodka. The process is listed as follows:

1. **Fermentation:** After the mash is ready, which is principally made from potatoes and other grains, such as wheat and corn which, yeast is added to this mash which contains high levels of sugar. After the fermentation process is complete, which normally takes approximately 7–10 days for the resulting liquid to achieve 8% alcohol levels (ABV). After this it is ready for distillation.
2. **Distillation & Filtration:** To get the characteristic, odourless flavourless vodka, the continuous still is preferred over the traditional pot still. The pot still may be a good option for making whisky, as it concentrates the congeners necessary to make a good whisky. Most vodkas are double distilled or even triple distilled in a continuous still. The resultant distillate is collected with a 96% ABV. This purest form of vodka is then passed through activated charcoal.

   The distillate is purified either by continuously passing it through tanks containing a minimum of 1 kg of vegetable charcoal per gallon for a minimum of 8 hours. Or the second process is followed in which the distillate is allowed to be in contact with vegetable charcoal for a minimum of 8 hours, but in a ratio of 3 kg of charcoal per 100 gallons of the spirit.

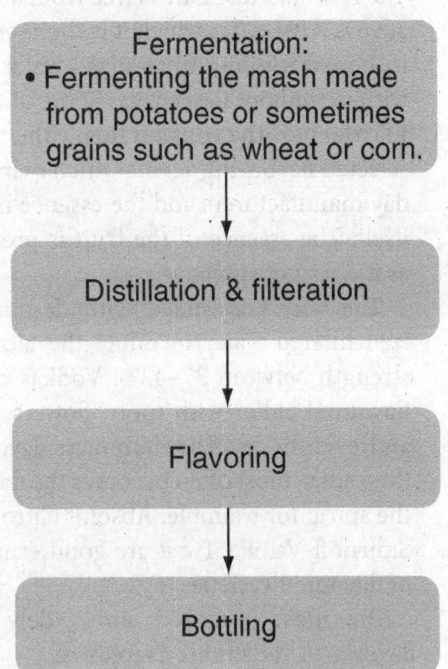

Figure 9.1 The flowchart displaying the production process of vodka.

DID YOU KNOW

Activated charcoal, (also known as activated carbon) has properties to absorb a variety of odours, hence widely used in vodka manufacturing. The best vodkas are the ones without any odour or particular flavour.

Vegetable charcoal.

The resultant distillate is free from all odours and colour. The vodka in this stage is in its purest form at 96% ABV. After which it is then sent to the next process of either flavouring or bottling. The vodka is diluted with de-mineralized water to an alcoholic strength between 39–44% ABV before bottling with or without flavouring. Some of the best vodkas in the world are bottled with 37% ABV.

3. **Flavouring:** The vodka is then either bottled (as mentioned above) after filtration or is flavoured with selected flavouring agents which marry (*i.e.*, mix well), thereby enhancing the flavour. Most modern-day manufacturers add the essence of flavouring agents and prefer not to add the fruit or fruit pulp itself. The essence of the fruit is preferred as it does not spoil.

The vodka is mixed with de-mineralized filtered water to dilute the alcoholic strength between 37–42%. Vodkas can be flavoured either with roots, flowers, fruits and even herbs. The dominant flavour of the vodka, most often becomes the name of the spirit, for example, Absolut Citron and Smirnoff Vanilla Twist are good examples of flavoured varieties.

The most preferred and widely used flavours of vodkas are as follows:

- Vanilla
- Blackcurrant
- Green apple
- Mandarin
- Raspberry
- Pears
- Lemon
- Grape fruit
- Peach

Figure 9.2 Flavoured vodkas from Grey Goose, a premium vodka brand (from left to right)—pear flavour (La Poire), lemon (Le Citron) and orange flavour (L'Orange)—(*Courtesy:* Bacardi International Limited).

Some other notable flavoured vodkas are as follows:

Zubrowka: It is a yellow-coloured vodka, flavoured with a type of grass, namely bison grass originating from the forests of eastern Poland.
Starka: This is amber-coloured vodka that is matured for ten years in oak casks.
Yubileyneya Osobaya: This is often confused as a liqueur, as it contains brandy, honey and other ingredients. It is popularly known as *Jubilee Vodka.*
Pertsovka: Pepper vodka that is prepared from a combination of capsicum, cayenne and cubeb peppers, having a sharp aroma and burning aftertaste and a dark brown colour.
Okhotnichya: A vodka containing heather honey and other herbs. It is often referred to as *Hunters Vodka.*

4. **Bottling:** The vodka is bottled after filtration, necessary dilution and flavouring. The vodka bottles are the best examples of clarity, as they show the purity of the vodka. Many famous distilleries use vodka to cleanse the bottles before bottling, as they believe water droplet can alter the taste of the final product. The best example of this is absolute vodka from Sweden.

9.3 FAMOUS BRANDS OF VODKA

Grey Goose and 42 Below, world famous vodka brands. (Image Courtesy: *Bacardi International Limited.*)

Famous brands of vodka have their unique history (Table 9.1). Smirnoff is a unique vodka and the following are some of its details:

Table 9.1 Famous Brands of Vodka

Brand	Country	Base
Belvedere	Poland	Rye
Cracovia	Poland	Potato

(Continued)

Table 9.1 Famous Brands of Vodka (Contd.)

Brand	Country	Base
Krupnik	Poland	Honey
Starka	Poland	Rye
Ultimat	Poland	Potato, Wheat and Rye
Wyborowa	Poland	Rye
Zubrowka	Poland	Rye
Moskuvskaya	Russia	Rye
Starka	Russia	Potato
Stolichnaya	Russia	Wheat and Rye
Stolnaya	Russia	Wheat
Absolut	Sweden	Wheat
Pinky vodka	Sweden	Wheat
Smirnoff	The UK	Grain
Vladivar	The UK	Grain
Bowman's	The US	Grain
Cirrus	The US	Potato
Grey Goose	France	Winter Wheat
Skyy	The US	Grain
Taaka	The US	Grain
Zodiac	The US	Potato
Pink	The Netherlands	Wheat
Bols	The Netherlands	Rye
Eristoff	Georgia	Wheat
Ciroc	France	Grapes
Finlandia	Finland	Barley
Danzka	Denmark	Wheat

GREY GOOSE VODKA

GREY GOOSE
World's Best Tasting Vodka

Grey Goose—awarded the World's Best Tasting Vodka, dates to its early creation in 1997 and begins with a selection of the very best ingredients from France, soft winter wheat and Gensac spring water. The unique production process is designed to bring out the naturally superior characteristics of the ingredients. Le Maître de Chai (Cellar Master) is responsible for creating this process which they and their team oversee every step, from field to bottle, to ensure that it remains the World's Best Tasting Vodka.

Name

Geese that reside in Cognac inspired the name Grey Goose. The geese are considered to be the part of the town and are celebrated within the region.

100% French Winter Wheat

This wheat is the same that is used in world-renowned French breads and pastries; it is certified CLASS 1. It is grown in the northernmost part of France in a region called Picardie known as the 'breadbasket of France'. The area is known for its temperate climate, moderate humidity and rich soil, ideal wheat-growing conditions. It takes 1.1 kg of wheat to create 1 litre of Grey Goose Vodka.

Gensac Spring Water

This is a water source exclusive to Grey Goose Vodka. It filters down from the Massif Mountains, underground and over Grande Champagne limestone to rest in a natural spring 500ft underground. It is deep enough to remain naturally pure and untouched by pollutants. The limestone acts as a natural filtration system. It softens the water and adds a slight sweet flavour that is characteristic of the taste of Grey Goose Vodka.

Distillation

The Grey Goose Vodka production process is designed and implemented by Le Maître de Chai and focuses on bringing out the naturally superior characteristics of the ingredients, while other traditional methods focus on removing faults and impurities after the distillation of lower quality ingredients.

It is a five-column distillation process and each of the five columns plays a unique role in developing the character of the spirit.

Smirnoff: It is a brand owned by the Diageo liquor conglomerate today, but was founded in Moscow by Pyotr Arsenievich Smirnov (1831–1898). He established this company in the 1860s and captured two-thirds of the Moscow market by 1886. The brand was the Tsar's favourite. In 1904, the Tsar nationalized the Russian vodka industry and the Smirnoff family had to sell its brand. In 1917, during the Revolution, the Smirnoff family had to flee Russia. They moved first to Constantinople and 4 years later to Lwow (now Lviv, Ukraine) and started selling the vodka under the Smirnoff brand name. The Kunette family, a close aid of the Smirnoff family, in Moscow before the revolution, bought the rights from the Smirnoff family to produce the vodka in North America. Due to low sales, the Kunette sold the rights to John Martin, president of Heublein. After the acquisition, the sales continued to be slow until the distributers started marketing Smirnoff as 'White Whisky No Taste No Smell.' They used whisky corks, which added to the popularity of this beverage in the United States.

Stolichnaya: It is considered as one of the best Russian vodkas in the world. Stolichnaya is a word coming from *Stolista* meaning, 'capital city'. Its origins are from the *Moscow State Wine Warehouse* opened in 1901. Stolichnaya is said have been created by V.G. Svirida. Stolichnaya is available in various forms, such as Stolichnaya Red Label at 40% ABV, Stolichnaya Gold or Kristal—40% ABV, Stolichnaya Blue Label—50% ABV and various other flavours, such as blackberry, blueberry, citrus, cranberry, apple and orange among others.

Absolut: Absolut is the largest brand of an alcoholic spirits in the world, larger than Bacardi and Smirnoff. It is owned by the French group Pernod Ricard. It is sold in more than 126 countries. It was first distilled in 1877 in Sweden under the brand name, *Tiodubbelt Renadt Brannvin*, meaning 'ten-fold purified vodka'. In 1917, this vodka was sold in Sweden under the name, '*Absolut Rent Brannvinn*'. It was in 1979 when *Absolut Vodka* was introduced in the international market. It is made from winter wheat; over 1 kg of grain is used to make a 1 Ltr. bottle. The wheat is grown in Sweden nourished by the refreshing local water. Absolut has a tradition to manually check each bottle for clarity and also wash the bottles with pure Absolut vodka to sanitize it before bottling. Absolut had one of the world's longest running and popular advertising campaigns, making it one of the world's most preferred beverages. The Absolut Bar started in Sweden and now spread across the globe, serves the precious vodka under sub-zero temperatures—the guests have to wear warm clothing, giving them a unique experience. Absolut vodka is available in the most amazing flavours, namely pepper, orange, peach, vanilla, dragon fruit, white grape, papaya, cherry, cranberry and many more. Absolut level is a super premium variety of the same brand.

9.4 VODKA AND LIFESTYLE—SERVICE OF VODKA

From being just a beverage to a lifestyle statement, vodka has evolved over the years. Due to its odourless quality going undetected over ones breathe, vodka is popular among the ladies. Bartenders also prefer this universal liquor across the globe to make cocktails that not only taste good, but are also a treat to the eye. Vodka-based cocktails have become an accessory for women, as they not only taste good, but also the colours often compliment their beautiful outfits.

9.5 INTERESTING FACTS ABOUT VODKA

The following interesting facts also contain a few health factor

1. In the 15th century, a type of vodka was used for making gunpowder in Sweden.
2. In Russia, vodka was first used for medical purpose, whereas in Poland, it was scented and often used as after shaves.
3. The exact origin of vodka is contested not only in Russia and Poland but also in Ukraine and Belarus.
4. Russians prefer vodka, as it replaced the need for water in winters as it never froze and warmed the body in the harsh weather due to its high alcoholic content.
5. Vodka will disinfect and alleviate a jelly fish sting.
6. Vodka in cold climatic countries such as Russia is essential for survival, as it prevents the blood vessels from freezing. It also ensures blood flow to the brain. The benefits of vodka other than above are the same as consumption of any other liquor.

Vodka and lifestyle. (Courtesy: *Bacardi International Limited.*)

Service of vodka—Grey Goose Vodka. (Courtesy: *Bacardi International Limited.*)

LET'S SUMMARIZE IN POINTS

In this chapter, we have learnt the following:

- Vodka is a colourless, odourless and flavourless spirit distilled from a fermented mash of potatoes or grains.
- It is derived from the word *voda* meaning water.
- Vodka is distilled at a very high proof in a continuous still by passing it through vegetable charcoal. It is flavoured and bottled.
- Vanilla, lemon, blackcurrant, green apple and raspberry are some of the widely used and preferred flavours.
- Vodka is widely used in making cocktails.

9.6 FAQs

Short-Answer Type Questions

1. What does 'voda' mean?
2. Where was vodka invented?
3. Give in brief the history of vodka.
4. What is activated charcoal, and what is it used for?
5. Name five flavours of vodka.

Long-Answer Type Questions

1. Give the detailed history of vodka.
2. Name the process involved in vodka making.
3. Draw a diagram on the method of vodka making.
4. Give the history of Smirnoff and Absolut. Give their unique characteristics.
5. Name the interesting facts about vodka.

9.7 KEY TERMS

- ABV
- Activated charcoal
- Bison Grass
- Continuous still
- Cubeb peppers
- De-mineralize
- Distillation
- Marry
- Oak
- Tsar

GIN

CHAPTER OUTLINE

LET'S DEFINE

'It is a flavoured beverage obtained by redistilling a neutral spirit with high alcoholic strength in the presence of juniper berries and other flavouring agents'.

Gin is a neutral spirit very similar to vodka, but flavoured with juniper berries and other herbs.

10.1 HISTORY

Gin has evolved its name either from the Dutch word *Jenever* or the French word *Genièvre*, both meaning 'juniper'.

The Italian monks can be accredited to have started making a crude distilled spirit flavoured with juniper berries. It was considered as a cure for one of most devastating pandemics in human history, namely, the 'Black Death'. The Black Death affected Europe between AD 1348 and AD 1350 and claimed over 50 million lives by the end of the 14th century. Unfortunately, gin was not a successful remedy for this plague.

As distillation processes evolved over a period of time, juniper was one of the many botanicals used for its virtue of perfumes, flavour and medicinal properties.

Gin, which is often served along with tonic water as a 'chaser', had medicinal properties to cure malaria. Tonic water that is flavoured with 'quinine' is a natural remedy to cure malaria, as doctors give dosage of quinine to prevent and cure malaria till this date.

Today, tonic water contains only a fraction of quinine added for flavouring and not for its medicinal purposes.

Dr Franciscus Sylvius is credited for the invention of gin. By the 17th century, many small distillers had popularized the distillation of malt spirit or wine with the addition of juniper berries along with other herbs and spices such as amuse, caraway, coriander etc., which were sold in pharmacies. These beverages were used to treat medical problems such as kidney ailments, stomach ailments, gall stones and gout.

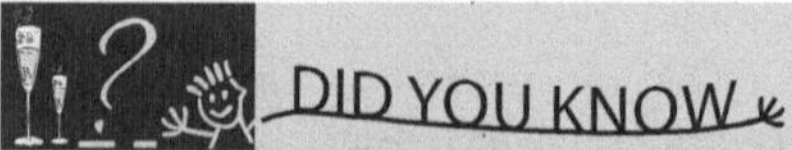

The British troops fighting against the Spanish in Holland noticed the calming effects of gin before going into battles and hence called it Dutch courage.

The history of gin is very rich. Another reference into the history books shows us that the popularity of gin grew by leaps and bounds in England due to government regulations. The government imposed huge import duties on foreign liquor at the same time allowed unlicensed gin production. The excess grains harvested that were not fit for beer making became an automatic choice for gin making by one and all in England leading to the *Gin Craze*. The Gin Craze was almost en epidemic in its own way, which was the cause for rampant alcoholism. This can be seen in *the beer street and gin lane* as illustrated by William Hogarth in his engravings. The gin act of 1751 forced distillers to sell only to licensed retailers, thereby bringing the local gin shops under the jurisdiction of local magistrates. This inevitably controlled alcoholism in the society by and large.

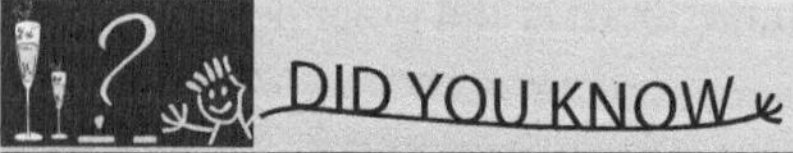

The American prohibition of alcohol lead to the famous 'Moonshine liquor' or 'Bathtub liquor'. It is named as such due to a relatively simple method where it was produced secretly during midnight (Moonshine) in every household's bathtub wherein the juniper berries would macerate, giving the liquor its unique characteristic.

10.2 TYPES OF GIN AND THE PRODUCTION PROCESS

Essentially, there are only two types of gin, namely: (1) Dutch/Hollands, Genèver or Schiedam gin, and (2) Dry—English or American gin, better known as London Dry Gin. Let us discuss in detail the difference between these two types of gins.

Holland Gin (Genèver or Schiedam Gin)

In the Netherlands, gin is made by following a few processes:

1. **Formation of the mash and fermentation:** A mash with equal quantities of barley malt, corn and rye are mashed, cooked and fermented into beer.
2. **Double distillation:** The resultant beer is distilled in a pot still, may be once or twice. The resultant distillate is still low in alcohol at approximately 50–55% ABV. The distillate is referred to as 'malt wine'.

The 'malt wine' is then mixed with juniper berries in another pot still and then redistilled to 96% ABV. Other botanicals are also added with the juniper berries. However, it should be noted that the quantities of these botanicals are limited and not added as generously as done in England or in the United States.

The process described here, produces a low proof 'gin' with a full body, malty aroma and flavour. Holland's or Genèver's cannot be mixed with other ingredients to make cocktails as their own definitive taste will over power any other ingredient. A dash of any popular bitter is always a preferred choice.

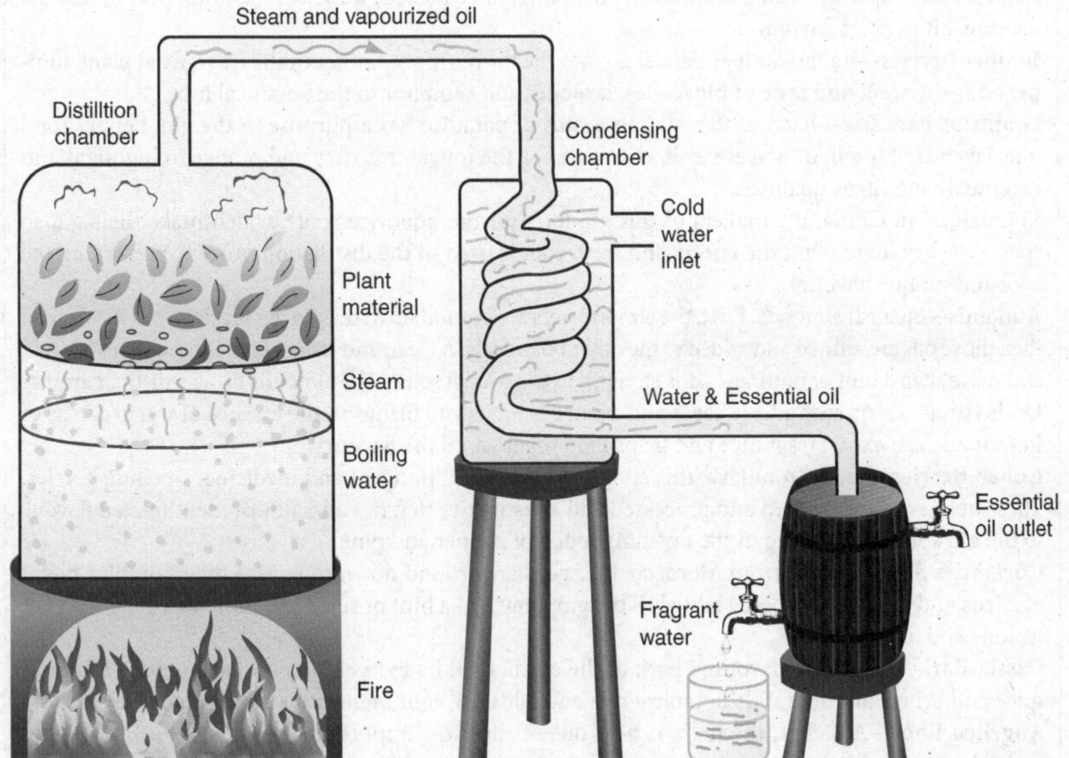

The distillation process—This diagram shows the vapours passing through the fragrant plant material absorbing the essential oils. When it is condensed, it results in a liquid, which is rich in fragrance, absorbed from the plant material.

Fruits and spices used in flavoring gin.

ABOUT FAMOUS FLAVORING AGENTS USED IN MAKING BOMBAY SAPHIRE

Lemon Peel—Spanish lemons in Bombay Sapphire, once picked, we select the finest peel to add the delicate, bittersweet flavour.

Juniper Berries—Italian juniper berries go into the flavouring. Another multi-fragranced plant, juniper adds the scent and taste of pinecones, lavender and camphor to the botanical mix.

Grains of Paradise—Each of the African grains of paradise has a purpose in the gin. Pepper for a bite, lavender for a light, sweet smell, chocolate for the touch of luxury and orange to highlight and accentuate the citrus qualities.

Liquorice—In China, the makers of this gin look for the liquorice roots, which make their gin so special. A key ingredient, the strong and fresh root is used in the distillation process, preserving the cool and unique flavours.

Almonds—Spanish almonds. First, the almond nuts are ground up to release the precious oils inside, and then those oils are refined and added to the other botanicals. A clean and strong taste is brought to the mix and more than a hint of nuttiness adds strength to the overall spirit. The almonds bring a distinct aroma.

Orris Root—Orris root adds a scent and smell of violets and brings in the essence of warm earths of Italy. It adds an exotic fragrance and helps bind together all the flavours.

Cubeb Berries—Fresh from Java, this climbing plant bears pungent and medicinal smelling berries. These berries when crushed and processed add a distinctive dry, hot and almost mentholated flavour to the gin spirit. They bring in the finishing touch of pepper and pine.

Coriander Seeds—Fresh from Morocco, the seeds are ground down to release their complex blend of citrus and spice before being added to the gin; they add a hint of spice and more of a suggestion of lemons and oranges.

Cassia Bark—Delicately flavoured bark of the cassia tree. Its light cinnamon flavour adds a hint of spice and brings out the subtle botanical mix and adds a unique element to the finish of the gin.

Angelica Root—Angelica, the herb, is now one of the most important ingredients in the gin. The ground root is added in perfect proportion to this spirit to help emphasize and complement the flavours of the botanicals. Its sweet, dry and pine kernel flavour is what helps hold the botanicals together and gives the gin such a superb taste.

(Information Courtesy: *Bombay Sapphire, Bacardi International Limited*).

English Gin (London Dry Gin)

Originally the term 'London Dry Gin' referred to the geographical location, that is, London or surrounding areas where this variety of gin was produced. However, today this term has been adopted by American distillers and distillers from other countries. The term 'dry' does not have much significance either, as all the types, namely, American, English and Dutch are equally 'dry', having equal ratio of alcohol to the residual sugar in the gin.

English and American gins differ from Dutch gins in many ways. This is due to the different production used. The process of making London Dry Gin is as follows:

1. **Making the mash and fermentation:** For making London Dry Gin, the mash is prepared from a formula made with 75% corn, 15% malted barley and 10% other grains is used. A sugary mash is created from these grains by cooking the grains in hot water to release the sugars. The mash is similar to the mash created to make whisky. Once the mash is ready, it is fermented.
2. **Double distillation:** After fermentation, the resultant beer or liquid is distilled in a column/patent still. The distillation method produces a distillate with approximately 95% ABV. This is reduced to 60% ABV by addition of distilled water.

The resultant spirit is placed in a pot still and redistilled after the addition of juniper berries and other flavouring agents. The dominant flavour is always juniper berries and the other flavouring agents are added in small quantities.

Examples of other flavouring agents are dried orange peel, dried lemon peel, anise, cassia, coriander seeds, bitter almonds, angelica roots, caraway seeds, fennel, liquorice and many more. The precise quantities and exact ingredients are a distiller's trade secret.

The other difference, from one distiller to the other, is the method of distillation after the addition of herbs and spices. Some distillers prefer to macerate the ingredient in the spirit and then distil the liquor, thereby the resulting distillate having congeners of all the flavouring agents.

Others use a unique method of tying the flavouring ingredients in wire gauze towards the top of the still, thereby infusing the flavour to the evaporating fumes of alcohol.

As for all liquors produced in the pot still, the 'heads' and 'tails' containing ethyl alcohol and burnt spirit respectively are let off. The 'heart' is collected which contains methyl alcohol and congeners (containing the essential oils of the flavouring agents).

The resulting distillate is at an alcoholic strength 75–85% ABV. This is then diluted to 40–45% ABV, according to the need of the distillers and is ready to be bottled and marketed. Gin is not aged and is stored in stainless steel vats. It is not bottled at once.

Other Varieties of Gin

Other than the two popular varieties mentioned, there are other varieties of gin that are essential to note.

Other than the most dominant variety of gin from the British Isles, that is, London Dry Gin, the other most successful variety is *Plymouth gin*. It is a distinctive gin that is heavier, more strongly flavoured gin than the London dry type.

Some distillers also produce *Old Tom Gin*, which is slightly sweetened mostly produced in Scotland. This gin is rarely available for sale today.

American Dry Gin

American gin is similar to the London Dry Gin. The only major difference is that this variety of gin is distilled at a higher alcoholic proof, thereby resulting in a gin not as heavy as the London dry variety.

American gin is either distilled or compounded. Compounded gin is made by combining the distilled spirits with the essential oils or extracts of the botanicals, predominantly juniper. The other methods of distillation are the same as the London dry Gin. Quality ingredients result in an overall good-quality products, only if the processes followed are monitored correctly. Therefore, a good-quality neutral sprit without any odours with good flavouring agent produces a great end product.

Fruit-flavoured gins

For the regular 'Gin-Aholic' a slight twist in the taste with and addition of complimenting fruit flavours to the gin is most desirable. Flavours such as orange, mint, pineapple and lemon are quite popular in England and America. However, it is vital that for a liquor to be called a 'gin', juniper berries should be the principal flavouring agent.

10.3 SERVICE OF GIN

Gin is often considered as an afternoon drink in summer for its cooling effect when had with tonic water or other cocktails. However, the most famous gin-based drink is the 'martini—shaken not stirred'. This punch line not only made James Bond stand out but also the martini cocktail. There are a number of gin-based cocktails such as gin Rickey, Gimlet, Alexander, Negroni and Gibson to name a few.

The Holland's or Genèver gins are usually served on their own due to their malty characteristics, or perhaps with a dash of bitters making it a fine aperitif.

10.4 BRANDS OF GIN

Some important brands of gins are listed in Table 10.1.

Table 10.1 Brands of Gin—Differentiated by Category

Category	Brand Name	Country of Origin
Budget	Aristocrat	USA
	Balfour Street Dry	USA
	Barton London Extra Dry	USA
	Booth's London Dry	England
	Burnett's London Dry	USA
	Fleischmann's Extra Dry	USA
	Glenmore London Dry	USA
	Gordon's London Dry	USA
	McCormick Dry	USA
	New Amsterdam Straight	USA
	Seagram's Extra Dry	USA
	Taaka Dry	USA
Premium	Beefeater	England
	Beefeater Wet	England
	Bombay Dry	England

Premium	Boodles London Dry	England
	Broker's London Dry	England
	Clearheart gin	USA
	Greenall's London Dry	England
	Iceberg London Dry	Canada
	Quintessential Dry	England
	Tanquerays London Dry	England
	Tanquerays Rangpur	England
	Tower of London	England
Super Premium	Aviation	USA
	Bafferts	England
	Bluecoat American	USA
	Bombay Sapphire	England
	Bulldog	England
	Cascade Mountain	USA
	Citadelle	France
	Damrak	Holland
	DH Krahn	USA
	Hendrick's	Scotland
	Juniper Green Organic	England
	Junipero	USA
	Mercury London Dry	England
	Martin Miller's London Dry	England
	Plymouth gin	England
	Quintessential	England
	Right gin	Sweden
	Tanquerays No. Ten	England
	Tru2 Organic	USA
	Van Gogh	Holland
	Zuidam	Holland
Ultra Premium	G'Vine (Grape flower base)	France
	Kensington London Dry	Scotland
	Oxley gin	England
	Leopold Bros. American Small Batch	USA
	Magellan	France
	Old Raj	England
	Right	Sweden
	The London gin No. 1 Original Blue gin	England

Photo 10.3 - *Bombay sapphire is a popular brand of gin. Bombay sapphire east is a newer version infused with two additional botanicals, crisp Thai lemongrass and spicy Vietnamese black peppercorn. - Image courtesy Bacardi International Limited.*

ABOUT BOMBAY SAPPHIRE

One of the world's greatest spirits is London Dry Gin. The Bombay Sapphire recipe is based on one of the earliest recorded recipes for a premium quality London Dry Gin, originally created in the northwest of England in 1761, the secret recipe has been passed down from generation to generation ever since. The 10 botanicals used to create Bombay Sapphire are depicted on every bottle, what is secret is the exact quantity of each botanical used to achieve the perfectly balanced taste which is Bombay Sapphire.

Name

Bombay Sapphire was inspired by the 182-carat 'Star of Bombay Sapphire' that now resides in the National Museum of History, Washington DC.

Queen Victoria

The portrait recognizes her status as an empress of India and reflects gin's British heritage and popularity during this era.

100% Neutral Grain Spirit

London Dry Gin must be prepared by a re-distillation of neutral grain spirit. Bombay Sapphire uses 100% wheat spirit that is the best carrier of botanicals.

Distillation

Traditional methods are used and the 'Gin Act', for London Dry Gin, of the 18th century demands the quality standards in production. Bombay Sapphire uses triple distilled grain spirit and the only four Caterhead stills in the world, with the oldest one in use dating back to 1831. A copper basket at the top of the still holds the 10 botanicals, the vapour of the 100% grain neutral spirit passes through these when heated and the oils from the botanicals are caught in the spirit vapour and is then condensed back into liquid. It then lands in the spirit safe and samples are taken before passing to the bottling tank.

10.5 IMPORTANT FACTS ABOUT GIN

1. Gin and vodka both have a neutral spirit base, but in essence differ as gin is flavoured with juniper berries.
2. American gin manufacturers often age their gin, imparting a yellow colour and are called, '*Golden Gin*'. However, this feature cannot be advertised.
3. Sloe gin is a type of a cordial and not a gin. It is a liqueur that is flavoured with Sloe Berries.
4. There is misconception that Dutch gin is aged. However, in reality this gin is coloured due to the addition of caramel colouring.

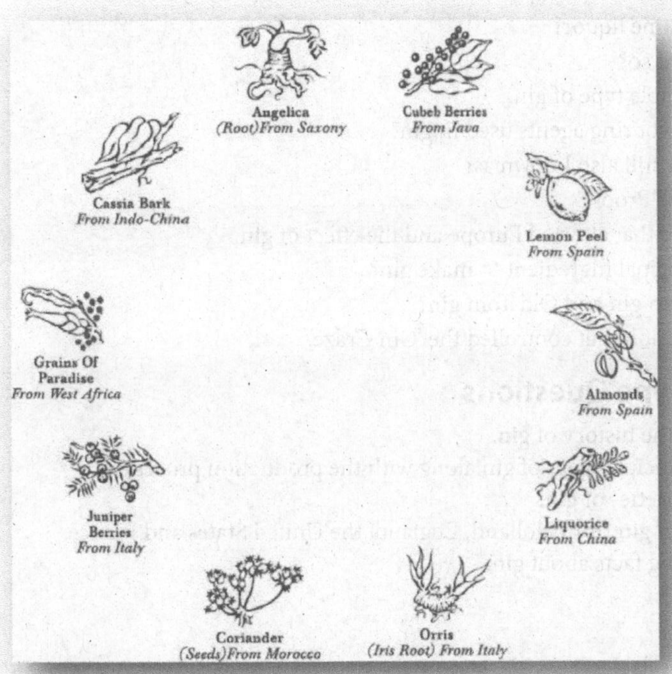

Image of the botanicals used to make the famous Bombay Saphire Gin
(Courtesy: *Bacardi International Limited*).

LET'S SUMMARIZE IN POINTS

- Gin is a flavoured beverage obtained by redistilling a neutral spirit with high alcoholic strength in the presence of juniper berries and other flavouring agents.
- Gin has evolved its name either from the Dutch word *Jenever* or the French word *Genièvre*, both meaning 'juniper'.
- Essentially, there are only two types of gin, namely, Dutch/Hollands, Genèver or Schiedam gin and Dry—English or American gin better known as London Dry Gin.
- Other than the most dominant variety of gin from the British Isles, that is, London Dry Gin, the other most successful variety is Plymouth gin. It is a distinctive gin that is heavier, more strongly flavoured gin than the London Dry type.
- Gin is often considered an afternoon drink in summer for its cooling effect when had with tonic water or other cocktails.
- There are a number of gin-based cocktails such as Gin Rickey, Gimlet, Alexander, Negroni and Gibson to name a few.

10.6 FAQs

Short-Answer Type Questions

1. What is Moonshine liquor?
2. Why gin is called so?
3. Name two principle type of gin.
4. What are the flavouring agents used in gin?
5. What is a patent still also known as?
6. Define the word, 'Proof'.
7. Name the plague that affected Europe and the effect of gin.
8. What is the principal ingredient to make gin?
9. What is Plymouth gin and Old Tom gin?
10. Name the legislation that controlled the 'Gin Craze'.

Long-Answer Type Questions

1. Discuss in detail the history of gin.
2. Name the two principle types of gin along with the production process.
3. Give the other varieties of gin.
4. Give five brands of gin from Holland, England, the United States and France.
5. Give the interesting facts about gin.

10.7 KEY TERMS

- American gin
- Chaser
- Genièvre
- Holland
- Juniper berries
- Malt wine
- Moonshine liquor/ Bathtub liquor
- Plymouth gin
- Quinine
- Redistilling

RUM

CHAPTER OUTLINE

LET'S DEFINE

'Rum is a potable spirit, which is suitably aged in wood obtained from the distillation of the fermented mash of sugarcane juice or molasses.'

Due to films, rum is often associated with pirates and the high seas. This famous beverage that accompanied sailors on the discovery of the West Indies and the Americas is still very popular. A famous white rum brand, namely Bacardi is the second-most consumed liquor after whisky in India.

11.1 HISTORY

Sugarcane, also known by its botanical name *Saccharum officinarum*, is the source for making rum.

History points to Alexander's journeys to India where sugarcane was first mentioned in 327 BC. However, it is better known that the Arabs brought this plant to Europe after AD 636. Crystallized sugar was very rare and hence expensive. It was Columbus, who is credited for bringing sugarcane from the

The evolution of the most famous brand of rum—'Bacardi' (Courtesy: *Bacardi International Limited*).

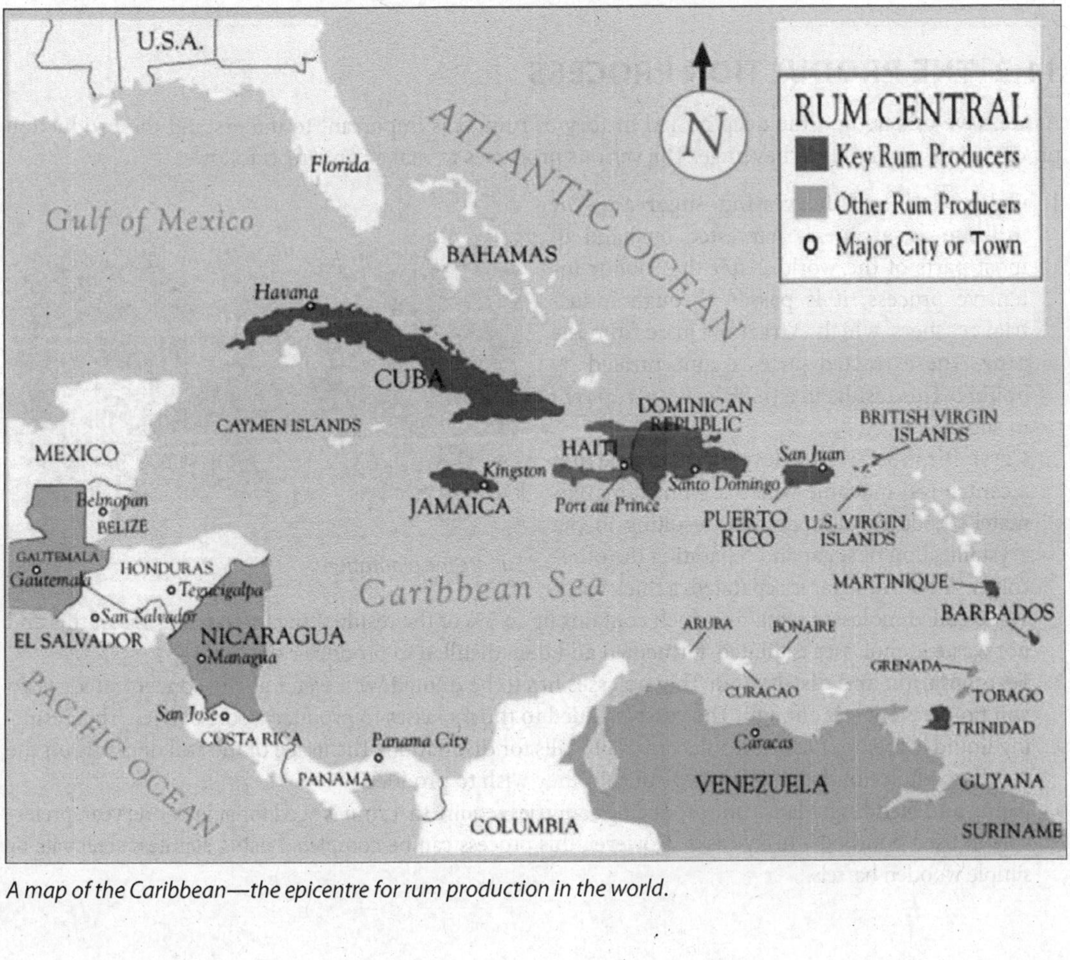

A map of the Caribbean—the epicentre for rum production in the world.

Canary Islands to the West Indies, where it prospered and lead to a reduction of cost of crystallized sugar. Even today Caribbean Islands account for a large supply of sugarcane to the western hemisphere.

It is no surprise that this lead to the distillation of molasses, a by-product of the sugar factory, making rum. From the definition of rum, we can understand that rum is made from sugarcane juice and molasses.

The origins of the name rum are varied. We shall discuss each category in detail. The first logic being that in the 16th century, pirates shortened the word 'saccharum' meaning sugar to call this beverage rum.

The second logical reasoning points to the English Navy. Admiral Vernon and his men in AD 1745 were suffering from scurvy. Not knowing what to do, he cut the men's daily nation of beer and replaced it with the West Indian beverage—rum. The scurvy problem was cured. The men were so pleased with their Admiral; they affectionately referred to him as 'Old Rummy' and the beverage to as rum in his honour. The third logic being that the word *rum* in the 18th century was a slang to describe things and events that were very good. Hence, the most honourable name for this beverage was christened.

Rum has been in production from molasses for over 300 years in the West Indies. Shippers from New England imported molasses to produce their own rum. This was then shipped to Africa where it was either sold or traded in exchange for slaves, who in turn worked in the sugarcane plantations in West Indies.

11.2 THE PRODUCTION PROCESS

As we have understood the deep rooted history of rum, it is important to understand the production process of this marvellous beverage. The various processes to make rum are as follows:

1. **Cultivation and harvesting sugarcane for milling:** Sugarcane is harvested by hand in most parts of the world. After this labour intensive process, it is passed through industrial crushers, which extract the juice from the cane. The extracted juice is concentrated by boiling. This results in a thick heavy syrup rich in sugar.
2. **Crystallization:** The thick syrup is pumped into a centrifugal machine where it whirls approximately 1,500 revolutions/min, resulting in the crystallization of sugar and separating the other solids. After the sugar is separated, a thick black syrup called molasses remains, which contains up to 5% of the residual sugar. To make use of this and not waste it, molasses is diluted, fermented and then distilled to produce rum.

Sugarcane plantations.

3. **Fermentation and distillation:** The molasses has to be diluted with water as the concentrated syrup will not ferment fast enough. The yeast is added to the molasses to produce a sort of beer. This resulting liquid is then put into pot stills or patent stills for distillation. The usage of the still depends on the distillers' choice of the resultant type of rum they wish to produce.
4. **Aging and blending:** Many rum-producing countries require that rum is aged for at least one year, preferably in used bourbon whisky casks. However, this process can be completed using stainless steel vats or simple wooden barrels.

The famous Bacardi Distillery (Courtesy: *Bacardi International Limited*).

The ageing process gives the rum its colour. Rum aged in oak casks becomes deep amber in colour, whereas rum aged in stainless steel vats remains colourless. After ageing, the rum is then blended with other rums differing in age to produce a distiller's master blend before bottling. The dark rums get their dark brown colour by the addition of molasses during the blending stage. This is the reason why most dark rum is sweeter than the light-bodied colourless rums.

There are various categories of rum, each following a different pattern of ageing and maturing. The details of which are discussed subsequently.

5. **Bottling:** After distillation, the rum is reduced to an alcoholic strength of 40% ABV before bottling. The aged liquor is then bottled into 1 lt–750 ml bottles, depending on the discretion of the manufacturers.

A Craftsman making a barrel (Courtesy: *Bacardi International Limited*).

Blending being done by a master blender at Bacardi Factory (top) and barrels being marked before aging (bottom) (Courtesy: *Bacardi International Limited*).

Bottling done at Bacardi Factory in Cuba (Courtesy: *Bacardi International Limited*).

11.3 TYPES OF RUM

Rum can be classified into four main types, each having a unique method of production:

1. **Dry light-bodied rum:** It is produced in Spanish-speaking countries, the best example being Puerto Rico, Dominican Republic, Brazil, Mexico and Venezuela.
2. **Medium-bodied rums:** It is produced in Haiti, Barbados and Trinidad known as *Demeraran* rums.

3. **Rich-bodied pungent rums:** It is produced in English-speaking islands or countries. Examples include Jamaica and Martinique.
4. **Light-bodied rums:** It is a pungently aromatic East Indian Batavia *Arak* rum from Java.

Region specific rums have made a mark on the world, for example, Jamaican rum or Puerto Rican rum. The word 'type' cannot be used in identifying rum, for example, only rum produced in Jamaica can be called as a Jamaican rum. Therefore, there cannot be Jamaican-type rum being produced in any other country.

Rums are mostly produced in the regions around the Caribbean Sea as sugarcane flourishes there, especially in the West Indies and the Northern countries of South America.

Different variants of rum (from left to right): Bacardi Gold Rum, Bacardi Black Rum (Dark Rum), Bacardi Reserva and Bacardi 8 (Aged Rum) and Bacardi Superior Rum. (Courtesy: *Bacardi International Limited.*)

The types of rum can be attributed to the country of origin. However, that does not mean Jamaica will produce only rich-bodied pungent rums, whereas Puerto Rico will produce only light-bodied rums. Countries can produce either of the rums, but are famous for their traditional types mentioned above.

Puerto Rican Rum

Let us first understand how this type is made:

1. First, the molasses is placed in large vats and then water is added along with the mash from the previous distillation.
2. Special yeast strains are added to a small amount of molasses. The yeast culture is then transferred on to the large vats. The fermentation process begins and takes between two and four days.
3. The resultant mash post fermentation contains 7% ABV. It is then transferred to a patent or continuous still where it is distilled to an alcoholic strength of 80% ABV. This distillate of high proof has lesser congeners, is light bodied and fairly neutral in flavour. The middle part of the distillation otherwise referred to as the hearts is used. However, the hearts are known as *Madilla* in Puerto Rico.
4. It is then transferred into oak barrels, which may be charred or un-charred if the colour is not required.
5. Puerto Rican law specifies rum to be aged for a minimum of one year and more than six years for special-aged rum. These are then filtered. These light-bodied, clear rums are referred to as 'white' or 'silver' rums.
6. Deeper coloured rums that are more flavoured called amber or gold are aged for a minimum of three years. Caramel is often added to impart colour to these rums.

The characteristic taste of white and gold label rums is dry with a slight flavour of molasses. Golden label rums, however, are slightly mellower and have a full-bodied taste. Puerto Rican producers also offer full-bodied rums in addition to their world famous light-bodied varieties. These rums are labelled either Red or Heavy dark.

Virgin Island Rum

The Virgin Islands purchased by the United States in 1917 were subjected to their US prohibition laws and had to confine their efforts to only buy rum until 1933. With certain amount of help from the US Government, the Virgin Islands rum industry was re-established. The Virgin Islands produce light-bodied rums, the best coming from the Island of Saint Croix. Most of this rum is consumed domestically by the US Mainland market itself.

Dermeraran Rum

Demeraran rum gets its name from the Demerara River located in Guyana, South America. Along the river, the sugarcane is grown to make the distilled spirit. Demerara rums are darker and full-bodied rums due to the character of the sugarcane and the soil, but not as pungent as the Jamaican rum.

Demerara rums are bottled between 40% and 43% ABV, but this rum is also available at 75% ABV. This high-proof variety is very popular in colder climates such as Alaska, where it is consumed in the form of *Grog*, that is, half hot water and half rum that helps warm the body in the extreme winters.

Jamaican Rum

This is the next variety of rum and is the most popular variety. Jamaican rum is a full-bodied variety and its production process is different from the Puerto Rican variety.

1. First, the *dunder*—that is the skimming from the previous distillation also known as the 'burned ale' is added to the molasses prior to fermentation. Natural yeast spores from the air settle on the surface and begin the fermentation process. This fermentation is natural, but it is slow and takes between 5–20 days depending on the climatic conditions and the amount of yeast spores in the air. This natural fermentation process develops larger amounts of congeners, adding to the overall flavour of Jamaican rum.
2. The fermented mash is the put into a pot still where it is distilled. The rum is distilled twice in a pot still. The resultant distillate is at an alcoholic strength of 80% ABV or lower and is very pungent and full-bodied.

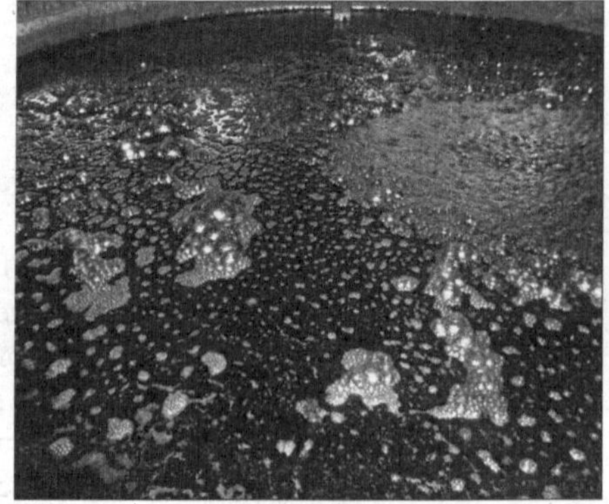

Dunder.

3. The distillate is colourless and is then aged in oak casks making it gain a golden colour. Jamaican rum is very high on congeners and is, therefore, aged for at least 5–7 years or more. However, the colour of Jamaican rums is due to the caramel added to the distillate. Darker rums from Jamaica having a *mahogany* colour are very popular, as they add colour to the drinks they chase or accompany.

Jamaican rums are diluted to 40% ABV before bottling and sometimes even 75% ABV. Traditional Jamaican rum is the most pungent of all alcoholic beverages. It has a unique buttery molasses aroma and flavour. Jamaica also produces light-bodied rums, but the full-bodied rums are the highlight of Jamaican rums.

Batavia Arak

The sugar factories near Batavia (formerly known as Jakarta) on the Java Island in Indonesia produce a rum called, 'Arak'. The specialty of this rum is attributed to the treatment given to the molasses and the quality of the river water used for making this highly aromatic rum. The rum also gets its distinct characteristics due to the natural uncultured yeast used, namely *Saccharomyces vordermanni* and to the specially cooked Javanese red rice cakes, which are placed in the fermenting tanks of molasses.

The Arak is aged for 3–4 years in the Java Island and is then shipped to Holland, where it is aged again for 4–6 years. After that, it is blended and bottled for sale. Arak is a brandy-like rum of great pungency. It is used and consumed just like all the other rums.

Indian Rum

Rum is a very popular beverage in India. Few dark types of rum from India have made a mark on the international market as well. The best example in 'Old Monk' brand of rum. It is highly popular in the domestic market and is also gaining popularity overseas markets.

A range of Bacardi flavoured rum (from left to right): Raspberry Rum, Limón Rum, Strawberry and Dragon fruit Rum, Apple Rum and Orange Rum. (Courtesy: *Bacardi International Limited.*)

Spiced and Flavoured Rums

Many rum manufacturers prefer to make spiced varieties of their rums, mostly out of their gold rum varieties. These have a characteristic taste. Mostly the spices used in the rum are cloves, cinnamon, cassia bark, star anise and many more, which is a closely guarded secret of each manufacturer. Flavoured rums too are gaining popularity. Some popular rum flavours are lemon, vanilla, coconut, mango, pineapple, passion fruit, raspberry and orange.

DID YOU KNOW

Backed by over a century of Bacardi tradition, Bacardi Oakheart has been crafted by the Maestros de Ron Bacardi, who throughout the production process, rely on their senses of sight, smell and taste to ensure that the quality and unique taste profile of Bacardi Oakheart meet exacting standards. Using their expert blending techniques, they have created the perfect base for the liquid, using rums that have been mellowed in specially selected charred American white oak barrels to impart a hint of smokiness, further enhanced by the addition of natural charred oak extract to give the rum woody notes. Finally, they add selected flavours and spices–honey essence for the light floral and delicate top notes; vanilla extracted from the finest

Bacardi Oakheart. (Courtesy: *Bacardi International Limited.*)

Madagascan vanilla beans, cinnamon and nutmeg selectively sourced for quality from Vietnam (cinnamon) and Indonesia (nutmeg) in South-East Asia. The result is a truly unique specialty rum: boldly spiced, velvety smooth and with a hint of smokiness.

On the nose, Bacardi Oakheart delivers the characteristics associated with walking into an aging warehouse, oak barrel staves with the essence of bourbon or brandy, a hint of smoke from the charring process, with background notes of dried fruits and a heavy delivery of sweet creamy butterscotch. After one sip, it is smooth at the front, slightly coats the tongue with a custard taste, maple and honey flavours and ends with a slightly peppery rum kick.

11.4 SERVICE OF RUM

In rum-producing countries, it is drunk straight or may be with water. However, rum is now synonymous with best cocktails served in most bars. This is due to the aroma and flavour that it compliments with most juices and mixers.

Many people consume rum with cola and it is the most preferred way of drinking it. 'Rum and cola' is called, 'Cuba Libre'.

Traditional *Cuba Libre*. (Courtesy: *Bacardi International Limited*.)

Cuba Libre in Spanish means *Free Cuba*. This drink was invented in Havana, Cuba, by the patriots during the Spanish-American War in around 1898–1902. Each brand such as Havana Club and Bacardi claim their rights over the invention of this popular cocktail, but all agree that it was invented during that period and in Cuba, hence suiting its name.

11.5 BRANDS OF RUM

Undoubtedly, the world's most famous brand of rum is Bacardi. Let us find out a few details about this brand.

ABOUT BACARDI*

Founded in 1862, Bacardi is the source of some of the world's great cocktails, The Mojito, Bacardi Daiquiri and the Cuba Libre, to name but a few.

In the 19th century, rum could be harsh and inconsistent, so Don Facundo Bacardi created the first rum that was refined and fit for sophisticated palates of the emerging middle class. Battling with personal and financial adversities, he eventually pioneered the techniques that would revolutionize the standards of the rum production. He bought a distillery located in Santiago de Cuba in 1862 which was the beginning to a worldwide phenomenon. The Bacardi logo is adopted from the fruit bats that lived in this distillery. Bacardi is the single largest privately owned liquor firm in the world. In 1960, the Fidel Castro regime established a law which confiscated all privately owned assets including bank accounts. This inevitably led to the Bacardi family moving out of Cuba and re-establishing itself to Puerto Rico and Mexico where they setup new distilleries. This is the reason behind Bacardi being labelled as a product of Puerto Rico, although it was founded on the Island of Cuba.

Bacardi rum has won over 190 awards internationally, plus the Royal Warrant from the Spanish Royal Family and has long been the world's favourite rum.

THE NAME

Bacardi is the legacy of Don Facundo Bacardi Masso. In 1862, both the name Bacardi and the logo Bat were registered. Synonymous with the name, the Bat appeared on every label of every product carrying the Bacardi family name. This has become one of the world's most well-known and loved marques.

INGREDIENTS

The key ingredient is the yeast, which defines rum's profile, a carefully isolated and cultured yeast strain (now known as La Levadura Bacardi) gave the lighter flavour due to its fast fermentation.

Don Facundo was the first rum producer to isolate a proprietary strain of yeast and use it repeatedly to give the rum the same flavour profile every time.

Evolution of the Bacardi Bat Label. (Courtesy: *Bacardi International Limited.*)

For sugar, molasses were chosen. The thick dark remains of the sugar refining process, was still sugar rich, but had more vitamins and minerals, which allowed for controlled fermentation. For water, naturally occurring spring water from the Sierra Maestra Mountains in Cuba was used.

DISTILLATION

Don Facundo pioneered the distillation of two separate rum bases, which would ultimately be blended together to make a lighter tasting rum. The deliberate ageing of the two rums creates smoothness, aroma and flavour.

Creating a secret blend of charcoals made from various tropical woods and coconut shells, a proprietary filter was formed for the rum bases, giving a unique balance, and as an unintentional side effect, one of the woods' removed the colour. The blending of the two rums produced perfectly balanced rum with a delicate flavour profile, which would become synonymous with sophisticated drinking.

Bacardi Superior has become the number one selling spirit in the world. Today, the company sells excessively of about 200 million bottles per year in over 200 countries.

**Courtesy*: Bacardi International Limited.

The world's most popular rums are listed in Table 11.1.

Table 11.1 Popular Brands of Rum

Brand	Country of Origin	Type
Appleton Estate White	Jamaica	Light Rum
Bacardi Superior	Santiago de Cuba	Light Rum
Barton White	Virgin Islands, USA	Light Rum
Castillo White	Puerto Rico	Light Rum
Myers Original Platinum	Jamaica	Light Rum
Ron Castillo White	Puerto Rico	Light Rum
Wray & Nephew	Jamaica	Light Rum
Clear Heart Rum	USA	Light Rum
Mount Gay	Barbados	Light Rum
Appleton Special Gold Rum	Jamaica	Gold Rum
Old Mill Gold	Virgin Islands, USA	Gold Rum
Bacardi Gold	Santiago de Cuba	Gold Rum
Ron Castillo Gold	Puerto Rico	Gold Rum
Totuga Gold	West Indies	Gold Rum
10 CANE	Trinidad	Gold Rum
Ron Matusalem Gran Reserva	Dominican Republic	Gold Rum
Mount Gay Eclipse	Jamaica	Gold Rum
Coruba Dark	Jamaica	Dark Rum
Cruzan Estate Dark (2 Years)	Saint Croix	Dark Rum
Angostura Dark 5 Year	Trinidad And Tobago	Dark Rum
Myers Dark	Jamaica	Dark Rum
Bacardi 8 Year	Santiago de Cuba	Dark Rum
Mount Gay Extra old	Jamaica	Dark Rum
Captain Morgan	Puerto Rico	Spiced Rum
Castillo	Puerto Rico	Spiced Rum

(*Continued*)

Table 11.1 Popular Brands of Rum (*Contd.*)

Brand	Country of Origin	Type
Admiral Nelson	USA	Spiced Rum
Montecristo	Guatelmala	Spiced Rum
Voodoo	Virgin Islands, USA	Spiced Rum
Bacardi—Apple, Coconut, Lemon, Melon, Oranage, Peach, Raspberry	Santiago de Cuba	Flavoured Rum
Malibu-Banana, Coconut, Mango, Pineapple	Jamaica	Flavoured Rum
Mount Gay—Mango, Vanilla	Jamaica	Flavoured Rum

There are very famous brands of rum that have become icons by themselves. Each brand has a unique story and history behind it. A few such popular rums along with their brief histories are as follows:

Captain Morgan Rum: One of the world's most famous Jamaican rums was earlier owned by the Seagram's company, but exchanged hands in 2008, and is presently controlled by the alcohol conglomerate Diageo. Captain Morgan is named after the 17th-century Welsh privateer of the Caribbean, Sir Henry Morgan. The slogan introduced on the bottle since 2011 is 'To Life, Love and Loot.' Captain Morgan rum is by volume the seventh largest rum manufacturer worldwide. It is labelled as a product of Puerto Rico, but the Sir Henry Morgan is a part of Jamaican history and heritage. Hence, the Captain Morgan rum produced by J. Wray and Nephew is labelled as a product of Jamaica.

Myers: One of the most famous Dark rums named after its founder Fred. L. Myers. Currently, this rum is produced by Diageo Pvt Ltd. This rum is a product of pure Jamaican molasses, which has been processed through both pot still and patent still distillation. It requires a minimum of two years ageing. While Myers rum is a blend of many rums some of which are aged for more than 50 years.

Old Monk: Old Monk is a vatted Indian dark rum that has been blended and aged for seven years. This rum has been appreciated world over bringing India to the forefront of rum production. Mohan Meakin Ltd is the owner of this brand.

Rum is one of the world's largest consumed liquors. Although this beverage found its humble beginnings as a peasant's beverage due to its harsh qualities, but it has evolved into one of the most highly regarded beverages of the world.

11.6 INTERESTING FACTS ABOUT RUM

1. Dark rum is extensively used in the preparation of many desserts, such as flambé, cakes, pastries and *Baba au Rhum*.
2. Some rums are bottled with a label of *Over Proof*, because they are bottled between 70– 80% ABV.
3. Admiral Nelson had his body preserved in a cask of rum after he lost his life during the Battle of Trafalgar.
4. Barbados serves a drink called *rum Sour* and it is served in a conch shell.
5. Tot-o-rum was a concoction given to the British Navy mixed with lime juice to cure scurvy.

LET'S SUMMARIZE IN POINTS

- Rum is a potable spirit, suitably aged in wood obtained from the distillation of the fermented mash of sugarcane juice or molasses.
- Rum originated in the Caribbean Islands.
- Puerto Rican rum, Demeraran rum, Jamaican rum, Batavia Arak and Indian rum are the five kinds of rum produced in the world.
- Spiced and flavoured rums are some very popular variants of rum.
- Rum can be consumed straight, mixed with a shooter or can even be served as a grog.

11.7 FAQs

Short-Answer Type Questions

1. What is *Dunder*?
2. When and where was the use of sugarcane documented?
3. Who is Admiral Vernon and how is he related to the history of rum?
4. What are the types of rum, name them?
5. Name the steps in the production of rum.
6. What is grog?
7. Where is the Demerara River located? Name three brands of Demeraran rums.
8. Name the famous rum-producing countries of the world.
9. What is over-proof rum? Where in the world is *Rum Sour* served and how?
10. What is the British Navy's association with rum?

Long-Answer Type Questions

1. Give the production process of rum in detail.
2. Discuss the specific differences between Jamaican rum, Puerto Rican rum and Demeraran rum.
3. What is Batavia Arak?
4. Give the history of rum in detail.
5. How are rums served?

11.8 KEY TERMS

- Batavia Arak
- Bourbon whisky Casks
- Caribbean
- Cuba Libre
- Demararan rum
- Dunder
- Heads
- Hearts
- Jamaican rum
- Madilla
- Molasses
- *Saccharum officinarum*
- *Saccharomyces Vodermani*
- Scurvy
- Slaves
- Sugarcane Plantation
- Tails
- Virgin Islands

Tequila

CHAPTER OUTLINE

LET'S DEFINE

'Tequila is a distilled spirit made from fermenting pulque, one kind of juice obtained from the blue Agave plant, which is extensively grown around the city of Tequila in the western Mexican state of Jalisco.'

The red volcanic soil in the regions is well suited to grow blue Agave plant that is the reason why 300 million plants are harvested each year.

Mexican law states that tequila can only be produced in the state of Jalisco and in the limited regions of the states of Guanajuato, Michoacán, Nayarit and Tamaulipas. Mexico has claimed international rights to the word 'Tequila'. Legal action is proposed by the Mexican Government against those who use this word to produce agave spirits in other countries.

12.1 HISTORY

Tequila is a descendent of an ancient beverage prepared by the Aztec tribes of North America. The Spaniards brought the art of distillation to Mexico in the early 1500s. Before that the Aztecs were preparing a fermented alcoholic beverage called 'pulque'. This beverage is a product of the mescal plant that belongs to the genus *Agave* (in Spanish referred to as 'Maguey').

Pulque has a heavy flavour resembling sour milk and is a preferred beverage among Mexicans for its cooling, wholesome and nutritional properties. It is freshly made and cannot be found far from the source of making.

The pulque when distilled makes 'Maguey' brandy known as 'Vino Mezcal'. The best Vino Mezcal is called 'Tequila', which comes from the valleys surrounding the town of Tequila in the state of Jalisco, Mexico.

Tequila was first produced in 16th century near the city of Tequila. The Spaniards in their conquest of North America ran out of their brandy. They began to distil Agave plant to produce North America's first indigenous spirit.

Don Cenobio Sauza, who was the first to export Tequila to United States, played pivotal role in the history of tequila. He was the founder of Sauza tequila. His grandson Don Francisco Javier gained international attention for insisting that 'there cannot be tequila where there are no agaves'. His insistence led to the practice that the name 'tequila' can be given to a distilled spirit only if it is made in the state of Jalisco, Mexico.

12.2 PRODUCTION PROCESS

As for all beverages a basic production process is followed. The process followed for making tequila is as follows:

Blue agave cactus plant used in making tequila.

1. **Harvesting:** The *Agave Tequileana* Weber blue variety is the best species of the mezcal plant used to make tequila. The plant takes 10–12 years to mature after that it is carefully harvested, removing the outer leaves, leaving behind the heart of the plant. This fruit resembles a pineapple, containing a sweet sap called 'Aguamiel' (*i.e.*, honey water). The hearts can weigh from anywhere between 75–100 kg.

   The agave plant has to be tended to with care, monitoring it constantly. This is an essential process because if the plant is harvested too soon there would not be enough sugars. If done too late the sugars would be used by the plant to grow into a 20–30-foot-high stem called *Quiote*. The heart of the blue agave plant called *Pinas*, which is used in making tequila.
2. **Pressing and fermentation:** The *Pinas* are placed in an oven for around 15–20 hours at 90°C, after that they are shredded; the juices (*Aguameil*) are pressed out and put into fermentation tanks.

   Next, the yeast is added and fermentation begins. This process takes 2–3 days. The yeast culture is a closely guarded secret of each distiller.

Tequila distilling still in Jalisco, Mexico.

3. **Distillation:** The fermented liquid is then distilled once in a pot still to produce and *ordinario*, which is cloudy or milky. This is then distilled for the second time to produce clear silver Tequila. Some distillers triple distil the Tequila. However, as per expert advice, this is a wrong practice, as it removes too many flavour elements from the liquor.
4. **Ageing:** After distillation, the Tequila is then put into barrels for ageing. Different types of Tequilas are produced and each aged differently. This is discussed in the next section.

12.3 TYPES OF TEQUILA

There are five broad categories of Tequila as follows:

1. **Blanco ('White') or Plata ('Silver'):** This is a white spirit un-aged and bottled immediately after distillation or aged less than two months in stainless steel tanks or neutral oak barrels.
2. **Joven ('Young') or Ovo ('Gold'):** A mixture of Blanco Tequila and Reposado tequila.
3. **Resposado ('Rested'):** This tequila is aged for a minimum of two months but less than a year in oak barrels of any size, resulting in richer and complex flavours. The oak is imported from the United States, France or Canada; some companies char the wood to impart a smoky flavour. Some distillers also use barrels that were previously used to age different kinds of alcohol, for example, scotch or wine.
4. **Añejo ('Aged' or 'Vintage'):** This is a fine variety, aged for a minimum of one year, but less than three years in small oak barrels. Añejos are often aged in oak barrels which were previously used to age Reposado. Many of the barrels used are imported from the US Bourbon Distilleries. The Jack Daniel's barrels are very popular for this purpose. This ageing process gives Tequila a dark colour and more complex flavours. After aging for at least a year, Añejo Tequilas can be removed from the oak barrels and stored in stainless steel vats to reduce evaporation under the hot Mexican sun.
5. **Extra Añejo ('Extra Aged Ultra Aged'):** Aged for a minimum of three years in oak barrels, this type was established in March, 2006.

Cazadores Tequila, a famous brand of Tequila (from left to right): Tequila Blanco, Tequila Reposado and Tequila Añejo. (Courtesy: *Bacardi International Limited.*)

DID YOU KNOW

The famous 'worm in the bottle' was a successful marketing trick used by tequila producers in the 1940s. The worm called 'Gusano' is not added to all the tequilas, but now only found in the Mezcals from the state of Oaxaca in Mexico. Some stories often state that if the worm or Gusano was alive in the bottle, then the tequila was potable. However, this is a misconception and all efforts are being made to market Tequila as premium liquor, such as 'Cognac' among the brandies.

12.4 SERVICE OF TEQUILA

Consumption of tequila is simple in Mexico, where it is consumed straight, without any *chasers*.

Worldwide the consumption of Tequila has become a tradition by itself. Made popular by many Hollywood movies, silver Tequila is always served with salt and wedge of lemon.

The salt is first placed on the hand (as shown in the photo here) and the Tequila in the shot glass is gulped down followed by the wedge of lemon, which has to be sucked on.

The logic behind this tradition that the salt prevents the Tequila from burning the throat and the lime compliments and brings out the flavour. Tequila is also consumed in wide range of cocktails the most famous being 'Tequila Sunrise', which discussed in detail in Chapter 28. The Anejo Tequila and Extra-Anejo types are preferably had by themselves or sometimes with orange juice.

The three essentials of a Tequila shot—A 60-ml shot of Tequila, a lemon wedge and a pinch of salt.

12.5 BRANDS OF TEQUILA

Some popular brands of tequila are listed in Table 12.1.

Table 12.1 Brands of Tequila

Brands	Type	Brands	Type
1800 Añejo	Añejo	Herradura Blanco	Silver
1800	Reposado	Herradura Gold Reposado	Reposado
1800	Silver	Herradura Reposado	Reposado
3 Amigos Tequila	Silver	Inocente Tequila	Silver
Camino	Silver	Jose Cuervo Black Medallion	Reposado
Corralejo Blanco Corralejo	Silver	Jose Cuervo Clasico Silver	Silver
Cuervo La Reserva	Gold	Jose Cuervo Especial Gold	Gold
Cuervo Tradicional Reposado	Reposado	Mi Tierra Añejo	Añejo
Cazadores Tequila	Blanco/Silver	Milagro Silver	Silver
Cazadores Tequila	Reposado	Monte Alban	Silver
Cazadores Tequila	Añejo	Montezuma Gold	Gold
El Jimador Blanco	Silver	Oro Tequila	Añejo
El Tesoro Reposado	Reposado	Pepe Lopez Gold	Gold

(*Continued*)

Table 12.1 Brands of Tequila (*Contd.*)

Brands	Type	Brands	Type
Sauza 100 Anos Reposado	Reposado	Scorpion Añejo	Añejo
Sauza Conmemorativo Añejo	Añejo	Two Fingers Gold	Gold
Sauza Extra Gold	Gold	Voodoo Tiki Anejo	Añejo
Sauza Hacienda Reposado	Reposado	Voodoo Tiki Cazadores	Gold
Sauza Silver	Silver	Voodoo Tiki Reposado	Reposado
Sauza Tres Generaciones Añejo	Añejo	Zafarrancho Gold	Gold
Sauza Tres Generaciones Plata	Silver	Zafarrancho Tequila	Silver
Sauza	Silver		

12.6 INTERSTING FACTS ABOUT TEQUILA

Tequila is often associated with fun and frolic. Over the years, there have been many misconceptions about tequila. Let us discuss a few in detail:

1. *Is Tequila made from Cactus juice?*
   The blue *Agave*, which is the source of Tequila, is in fact classified as a *succulent* botanically, and is a relative of the Amaryllis family.
2. *Is Mezcal a type of Tequila?*
   All Tequilas are Mezcals but all Mezcals are not Tequilas as per the Mexican law. A spirit made from other types of agave other than the blue Agave variety, and not produced in the designated state of Jalisco in Mexico is called Mezcal.
3. *Are tequila and mezcal hallucinogenic?*
   The myth originates because of the similarity; between the words 'Mezcal' and 'Mescaline'. Mescaline is an alkaloid that creates hallucinations in a variety of cactus called *peyote*. Drinking too much tequila can cause hallucinations but solely due to alcohol as the intoxicant.

LET'S SUMMARIZE IN POINTS

- Tequila is a distilled spirit made from the fermenting pulque, a juice obtained from the blue Agave plant, which is extensively grown around the city of Tequila in the western Mexican state of Jalisco.
- The juice of the plant is fermented to produce pulque and is then double distilled to make *'Vino Mezcal'* and is called Tequila.
- The five categories of Tequila are Blanco, Joven, Reposado, Anejo and Extra-Anejo.
- Tequila is popularly served with a wedge of lime and a pinch of salt.

12.7 FAQs

Short-Answer Type Questions

1. What is Mezcal?
2. What is Pulque?
3. What is Maguey?
4. Differentiate a Mezcal and Tequila.
5. Where is tequila made?
6. Define Joven, Reposado, Anejo and Blanco.
7. Why is lime used while consuming tequila straight?
8. Who invented Tequila?
9. Name three brands of Tequila from each type.
10. How many years is Tequila aged for?

Long-Answer Type Questions

1. Discuss the history of Tequila in details.
2. Name the types of Tequila with details and suitable examples.
3. Give the detailed production process of Tequilas.
4. Explain the services of Tequila. Explain the relevance of the 'Gusano'.
5. Discuss a few facts of Tequila with example.

12.8 KEY TERMS

- Aguameil
- Anejo
- Gusano
- Jalisco State
- Maguey
- Mezcal plant
- Ordinario
- Pinas
- Pulque
- Quiote
- Tequila city
- Vino Mezcal

13 BRANDY

CHAPTER OUTLINE

LET'S DEFINE

'Brandy is a potable spirit often aged in wood, obtained by distilling wine or sometimes a fermented mash of fruits.' An alcoholic beverage with this description can be made in any part of the world.

PART I. THE BRANDIES OF FRANCE

French brandies are the most revered of all brandies in the world. We shall discuss the details to understand these precious beverages better.

13.1 HISTORY

Historical references show that even though the ancient civilizations knew the science of distillation, those were not applied to wine until the beginning of the AD 16th century. Apparently, there was an extensive wine trade between France, from the Port of the La Rochelle located on the Charente River all the way up to Holland. All the trade was via sea and the perils of war put a premium on shipping.

It was extremely difficult and expensive as casks of wine took up a lot of space, especially on small sailing vessels. There is an interesting story of a young and bright Dutch ship master who wanted to reduce his freight costs and decided to concentrate the wine. He devised a method that removed water from the wine, concentrating the wine and exporting *the soul of the wine* to Holland. His plan was to add the water back to this concentrate on reaching the destination. As he reached Holland with the concentrated wine, his Dutch friends tasted it and like it very much. They decided not to add the water to the concentrated wine again. They named this popular beverage *Brandewijn* meaning 'burnt wine', due to the fire or heat used in the process of concentration of the wine. Later the name was anglicized and now better known as brandy.

13.2 COGNAC

When we think of ultra luxury products such as Italian super cars in case of automobiles, the Burj Al Arab in case of hotels and in case of beverages it is none other than the universally accepted ultra luxurious beverage cognac.

All Cognacs are Brandies but all Brandies are not Cognacs. Cognac is a brandy made from the grapes of Charente and Charente Maritime regions of France. The ancient city of Cognac on the River Charente is a heartland of this brandy production, making the word 'cognac' one of the most popular French words in the world. As mentioned in Chapter 17, *terroir*, which comprises of climatic conditions, soil conditions, rainfall and other conditions, plays a vital role in producing the best-quality grapes. Cognac is considered a superior quality brandy due to the superior terroir conditions of the region. Hence, many countries have failed to produce a beverage of such high quality.

The Cognac district or *Charentais* have seven sub-divisions or *crus*. The last two are often ranked together (Table 13.1).

Table 13.1 Sub-division of the Cognac District with Ranking

Sub-division	Rank
Grande Champagne (Grande fine Champagne)	1ST CRU
Petite Champagne (Petite fine Champagne)	2ND CRU
Borderies	3RD CRU
Fins BOIS	4TH CRU
Bons BOIS	5TH CRU
BOIS Ordinaires and BOIS Commune	6TH CRU AND 7TH CRU, respectively

The Grande Champagne is a small district that is the epicentre of the cognac region. The town of cognac is located in this district around which the entire magic of cognac unwinds.

The Petite Champagne almost surrounds the whole Grande Champagne district. To the north of this region is the small district of Borderies. Completely surrounding these three sub-divisions is the largest sub-division (by area of cultivation), Fins Bois. Bons Bois is along this region and to its west are Bois Ordinaires and Bois Commune.

The entire soil conditions in this region are rich in chalk, essential to produce a good cognac. Farmers in the Cognac region own stills and produce cognac under strict government regulations.

Due to the immense prestige value globally for this beverage, the farms are inspected by French authorities namely the AOC (*Appellation d'Origine Contrôlée*).

Grape Varieties for Making Cognac

Only white grape varieties are used to make cognac. In 1936, the French law classified the specific white grape varieties that are supposed to be used to produce the wines that are distilled to make cognac. The primary grape variety is Saint Emillion, also known as Ugni Blanc. The grapes popularity is due to the grapes characteristic to produce wines low in alcohol (*i.e.*, 8% ABV) and high in acidity. Although these wines may be unpleasant to drink, but they produce the best cognacs. The other grape varieties permitted are Folle Blanche and Colombard grapes.

Production Process

1. **Picking the grapes and making the wine:** The grapes are picked, pressed and allowed to ferment with the skin, pulp and pips to give the distinct characteristics to the cognac. The method of making wine is the same as discussed in Chapter 18 (French Wine—Vinification process).
2. **Racking—removing the lees:** Racking is performed to remove the sediments from the wine before distillation. This process is called 'removing the lees'. Some distillers prefer to leave some part of the lees to give more flavour and aroma to the cognac.
3. **Distillation—twice in a pot still:** The wine is now put into a copper pot still for distillation. Patent stills are not permitted by law. The pot stills or alembics made of copper are used as they are non-reactive with the acidic wine.

   Distillation is done by the use of charcoal fire or wood fire. The conversion of the wine to *Eau de Vie de Charente* is accomplished in two operations, the Première Chauffe and the Bonne Chauffe.

   The first part of the distillate vapours called the heads are collected back separately as they are not portable and added back to the première chauffe. The heart of the distillate called *Broullis* better known as *La Bonne Chauffe* is collected for the second distillation. The alcohol content of the Broullis is 24–32% ABV. After the hearts, the residual burnt vapours called the *Tails* are also collected separately and are added back to the première chauffe containing a new lot of wine.

   When enough Broullis have been collected the second distillation process begins. Similar to the first distillation the heads and tails are collected separately and the heart or middle range vapours are condensed and collected with an alcoholic strength of 70% ABV to become cognac.

   All the processes are regulated, which is the key to traditional cognac production. From the beginning of November, the alembics are fired and work continuously for 5–6 months 24 hours a day. All the distillation must be completed by 30th April each year.

4. **Ageing:** Right after distillation, the cognac is colourless and has a sharp but fruity coppery nose and taste. The coppery character called *Gout de Cuivre* passes after ageing in oak for a year.

   Cognac is aged in limousine oak obtained from the forests near Limoges. After one year of maturation, the cognacs are transferred to older casks to prevent excess tannin transfers from the new wooden casks. The cooperage (the wooden barrels) should stand for 40–50 years and hence the quality of the wood is examined with much care.

   Every year, considerable amount of alcohol is lost due to evaporation during ageing. This loss or *Angel's Share* is considered very good for the overall character of the cognac. During this stage, the colourless cognac is transformed into a bright amber-coloured liquor, which is rich in taste and aroma.
5. **Blending/coupage and bottling:** This process is done months before bottling. The various cognacs are put into large vats and brought down to an alcoholic strength of 40–43% ABV, by the addition of diluted cognac or distilled water. Caramel is often added to give a uniform golden colour to the cognac. Wooden fans similar to aeroplane propellers mix the entire contents of the vat from the bottom. This helps in *marrying* the blends together after which the contents are bottled.
6. **Labelling:** There are two basic systems of classifying cognac, which are as follows:
   (i) **Star system:** The Hennessey firm claims to have originated this system. Wine makers, being very superstitious, initiated this system. The legend is that, in 1811 when a comet appeared in the sky, a superb brandy was produced, which was labelled with a star. The following year produced an equally great cognac and was labelled with two stars. Fortunately, this system did not continue beyond 'five stars' despite the shippers acquiring a habit to put stars on their labels. Now the French law has specified that a 'three star' cognac should be aged in wood for a minimum of two and half years.
   (ii) **The letter system:** This system defines the quality of cognac based on different letters of the English alphabet and is practiced for better-quality cognacs (Table 13.2). The letters do not represent French words but English words because of the significance of cognac sales in the English market.

Table 13.2 The Letter System of Classifying Cognacs

Letter	Meaning
C	Cognac
E	Extra or Special
F	Fine
O	Old
P	Pale
S	Superior
V	Very
X	Extra

These words are used on the label on the discretion of the producers. For example, a bottle with the letter VO or VSOP not only signifies 'Very Old' or 'Very Superior Old Pale' but also means the cognac is a 'Reserve' and has been aged for a minimum of four and a half years in wood. VSOP cognacs are usually aged for 7–10 years.

Some producers have abandoned both the systems and identify their cognacs by proprietary name or by the district of origin. As per French law, the 'Extra', 'Napoleon' and 'Vieille Reserve' require the cognac to be aged for six and a half years in wood.

Napoleon Cognacs or brandies sometimes claim to be 80–104 years old. Unfortunately, this is a ploy for the unknowing buyer and most of the time, as these are just marketing strategies of the cognac producers.

Cognac ages in wood for up to 50 years and as expected the cost and risk of this is very high. Hence, the prices of these cognacs are also expensive. Once a cognac is bottled the ageing process stops. Even if a bottle is 100-years old, the age of the cognac is only considered as to the amount of time it was aged in wood. The best cognacs are aged between 25–40 years.

Important Cognac Notes

What is Fine Champagne?

Fine Champagne on the label refers to cognac that has been made from the grapes harvested from the Grande Champagne and Petite Champagne sub-regions of Cognac. This is one of the finest and best qualities of cognac.

What is Fine?

Fine is a cognac. In France, every restaurant includes among its list of brandies a *Fine de la maison*, which is a bar brandy. This may be a cognac but one cannot confuse this for a *Fine Champagne* cognac.

Cognac Tasting

Some connoisseurs say, 'a cognac has to be first *sipped from the nose*'. This is not in the literal sense, but a good cognac has a great bouquet and aroma, which should be savoured before sipping. As the alcohol content is high, the nose should be put on the rim of the glass and not inside the glass, to get a good aroma. This is also a reason why connoisseurs prefer smaller tulip glasses to broader and larger snifters. After *nosing* the cognac, a few drops should be placed on the tongue for tasting. A good cognac is light and not over powering.

The wonderful characteristic of a fine cognac is displayed in the glass in which it had been poured. The glass retains the wonderful aroma even after an hour or two.

***Note*:** Once a bottle of cognac is opened, it is recommended that it should be consumed before six months.

Brands of Cognac

Baron Otard VS—This blend of the finest growths from the Cognac region is aged in French oak barrels producing discreet touches of tannin. The balanced roundness of the Baron Otard VS does not need years of ageing to release its intense and fruity aromas of vine flowers. On the nose, it is not only virile, but also delicate and slightly floral. The initial taste on the palate is full but never aggressive, with a predominance of balance and elegance. It comes draped in golden robes.

Baron Otard VSOP—Baron Otard VSOP is mainly blended from the major Cognac growths, the Grande and Petite Champagne. This elegant Cognac comes with relatively powerful aromas, lots of finesse and a good length on the palate. The nose is rich in floral aromas, backed by the fragrance of lime trees, and touches of pear, tobacco and a hint of vanilla. On the palate, it is round and mellow, with subtle, sugary and fruity flavours enhanced by hints of spices, which presents itself in a natural deep golden colour.

Baron Otard, a famous brand of cognac (from left to right): Fine VS, VSOP Cognac, XO Gold and Extra 1795. (Courtesy: *Bacardi International Limited.*)

Baron Otard XO Gold—The personality of the Baron Otard XO Gold is expressed through the perfect balance of the blending of the finest growths. On the nose, its roundness reveals arich harmony of aromas of dawn woodland, with hints of hazelnut and leather enhanced by touches of honey. On the palate, the flavours are complex, combining all the finesse of the fruity aromas (plum and hazelnut) with the sweetness of just a hint of honey, enhanced by the remarkable length of the 'rancio'. Its long stay in red oak barrels has unblushingly given an amber hue to its natural colour.

Baron Otard Extra 1795—A generous blend of Grande *Champagne Eaux-de-Vie*, aged in the unique cellars of the Château. Baron Otard Extra 1795 is the result of all the experience, patience and tradition of Baron Otard Cognacs. Baron Otard Extra 1795 offers a rich and complex bouquet of dried fruit (plum, grape and hazelnut), orange peel and cigar box. This profusion of aromas further explodes on the palate providing incomparable pleasure; thanks to the mellowness of the old *Champagne Eaux-de-Vie*. Its gold and ruby colour is the sure sign of its long years of maturing. Some popular brands of cognacs are listed in Table 13.3.

Table 13.3 Famous Brands of Cognac

Type	Brand Name
XO Cognac	Hennessy XO Extra Old
	Camus XO Borderies
	Courvoisier XO Impérial
	Martell XO Extra Old
	Rémy Martin XO Excellence
	Baron Otard
	Prunier 20 Years Old
	Tesseron Lot N°53 XO Perfection
	Maxime Trijol XO Grande Champagne
VSOP Cognac	Rémy Martin VSOP Fine Champagne
	Hennessy VSOP Fine de
	Courvoisier VSOP Exclusif
	Martell VSOP Medaillon Old Fine Champagne
	Camus VSOP Elegance
VS Cognac	Hennessy Pure White
	Rémy Martin VS Petite Champagne
	Conjure
	Hennessy VS Very Special
	ABK6 VS Premium Single Estate

13.3 ARMAGNAC

The other exceptional brandy second only to Cognac is Armagnac. This brandy is produced in the region of *Gers* South, East of Bordeaux in the heart of Gascony. The centre of the trade is in the city of Condom. Armagnac is produced in three sub-regions. They are as follows:

1. **Bas–Armagnac:** The most westerly area,
2. **Tenareze:** In the centre, and
3. **Haut Armagnac:** To the east.

These three regions have been identified by the AOC authorities, which is the highest governing authority of wine and brandy in France. Any label having the word 'Armagnac' on the bottle should be certified by this authority.

Grapes Used for Armagnac

Specific white grape varieties are used to make Armagnac for quality control purposes, similar to the practice followed in the manufacture of cognac. The specified grape variety predominately used is Saint Emillion (also known as Ugni Blanc). Other grape varieties used are Colombard, Meslier, Jurancon and some others. The grapes are almost similar to the one grown in the Cognac Region, but the soil in Armagnac is not as chalky. This makes the difference to overall quality of the brandy.

Production Process

The method of distilling Armagnac is almost the same as cognac but with a few differences. The few points to be considered are as follows:

1. The original and re-distillation process is continuous, whereas in the case of cognac, it is done in two separate batch operations. This is done in a unique still known as the Armagnac still. It is a combination of the pot still and the patent still, which is depicted in Figure 13.1.
2. Armagnac casks are made from black oak from the Monlezun Forest, instead of limousine oak used in Cognac. Armagnac is labelled and regulated in a similar way as done for cognac. The age requirements are the same, such as three stars, VSOP and so on. *Hors d' Age* is more than 10-years old.

Armagnac has a pungent bouquet, but a dry and surprising smooth taste.

Brands of Armagnac

Some popular brands of armagnac are Janneau-Grande Armagnac, Saint Vivant, Cles Des Ducs Armagnac, and Larressingle, etc.

13.4 MARC

This type of brandy is available in all parts of France, but notably in Burgundy. Brandy that is made from grape pomace of the wine press is called *Eaux-de-Vie de Marc* (pronounced as *mar*). They have a straw-like woody character appreciated by some people.

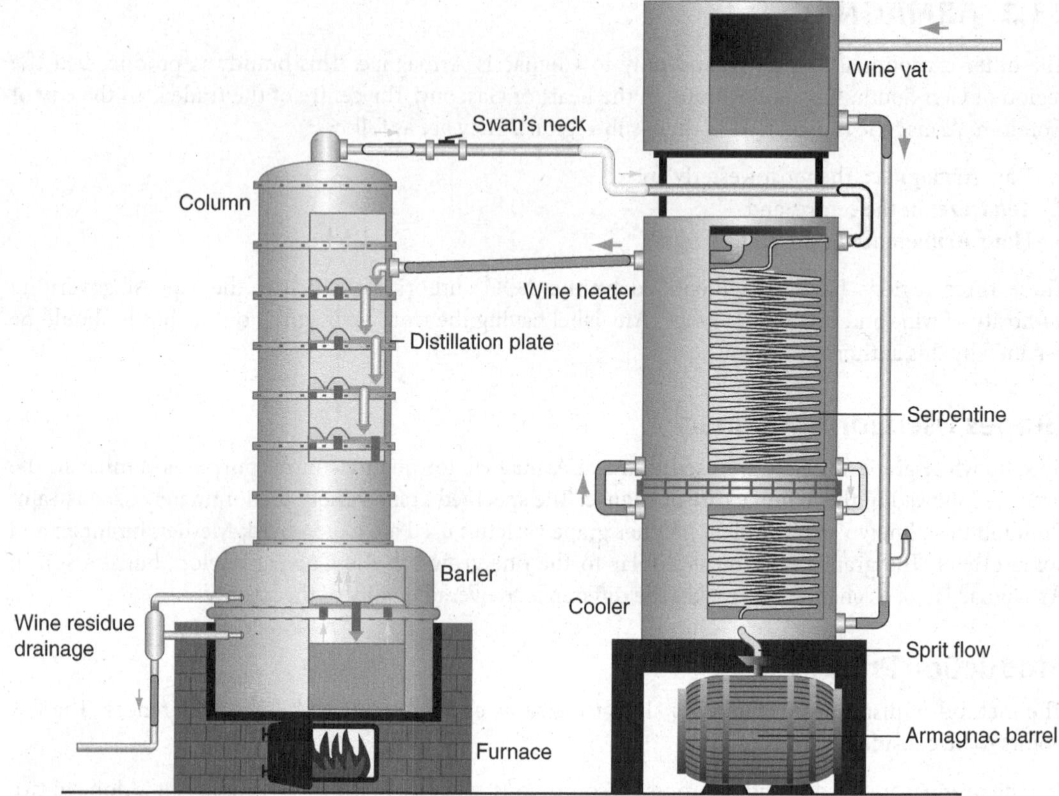

Figure 13.1 An Armagnac still.

PART II. BRANDIES FROM OTHER LANDS

13.5 CALIFORNIAN BRANDY

'California Brandy' is a term controlled by the Government of California and used only for brandy made only from Californian grapes. Californian brandy is produced from Thompson Seedless and Flame Tokay grape varieties. Ugni Blanc, Colombard and Folle Blanche are used at times.

Californian distillers prefer to use a patent or continuous still to traditional pot stills, which are preferred in France. Californian distillers prefer the clean and uniform distillate high in aroma and congeners. Only a fraction of Californian distillers use the pot stills, the resultant brandy is used to enhance other blends.

Californian brandies are supposed to be aged in oak casks procured from Tennessee and Arkansas for two years by law. Most brandies are aged for a minimum of four years. Some eight-year-old brandies are available both as straights and as blends.

13.6 GERMAN BRANDY

Blended from specially selected distillates of various distilleries across Germany and matured in oak wood casks. It has a fine aroma and bouquet with a mellow taste.

13.7 GREEK BRANDY

Greek brandy is gaining popularity with its fine flavour and sweet taste due to the caramel added for colour. Cyprus is a separate country producing good brandies, but it is always linked to Greece from where it gets it Greek heritage.

13.8 ISRAELI BRANDY

Israeli brandy has come into prominence due to its great taste and also affordability. From ancient times, wines were made that regions, but only after Israel has become a state that it products are reaching international shores.

13.9 INDIAN BRANDY

Indian brandy has a very large market. Due to the sweet taste attributed to the addition of caramel to give it colour, it has a wide appeal in the Indian market. Indian brandies are yet to make their place on the international market, but they have a large domestic demand.

13.10 ITALIAN BRANDY

Italian brandy, popularly known as *Grappa*, is a brandy made from grape pomace. It is usually un-aged and sharp in taste. Its popularity is growing as an after-dinner drink across the globe.

13.11 MEXICAN BRANDY

Mexican brandy has shockingly dethroned tequila and rum, becoming the most consumed beverage in Mexico. Many brandies are made in the Spanish style following the *Solera* blending system used in making 'sherry'. Some brandies use pot still distillation and are aged in limousine oak.

13.12 PERUVIAN BRANDY

Pisco is the brandy of Peru, taking it name from the port in South Peru. This brandy is produced from Muscat wines from the Ica Valley, near the town Pisco. Pisco punch, which is very sour, is the most popular cocktail in Peru, which is also famous in Chile. It is a very delightful drink.

13.13 SPANISH BRANDY

Spanish brandy is distilled from the famous sherry wine. This brandy has a distinctive flavour and aroma, which is very different from cognac and Armagnac. It is a brandy sweeter than other with an earthy character.

PART III. FRUIT BRANDIES

As we have learnt that apple juice can make cider. Similarly other fruits can be the source to make brandy. There are three broad categories for making brandy from fruits. First, brandies made from apple and pears; second, brandies made from stoned-fruits, such as cherries, plums and apricot and third, brandies made from berries such as strawberries, raspberries, blackberries and elder berries. These brandies come from Switzerland, France, Germany, Hungary, Israel, Yugoslavia and the United States. Let us understand in detail from Table 13.4 as to which fruit produce which brandy.

Table 13.4 Different Types of Fruit Brandies

Fruit	Brandy Name
Apple	Apple brandy Applejack Calvados
Apricot	Apricot brandy Barack Palinka (from Hungary)
Cherry	Kirch Kirchwasser (from Switzerland, France and Germany)
Elderberry	Elderberry brandy
Pear	Pear brandy Eua de vie de Poire
Pineapple	Pineapple brandy
Plum	Slivovitz (from Central Europe) Mirabelle Quetsch Prunelle Pflumli
Raspberry	Framboise
Strawberry	Fraise

13.14 APPLE BRANDY—CALVADOS AND APPLE JACK

The United States of America and France are two countries that extensively produce apple brandy. It is called Applejack in the United States and Calvados in France, from the region of Calvados in Normandy, which is the epicentre for apple production for France. Calvados is also made in Brittany and Maine regions of France.

The best Calvados, with the appellations *Calvados Du Pays D' Auge* is distilled only in pot stills. Other ordinary French apple brandies are called *Eaux-de-Vie-d-Cidre de Normandie or de Bretagne* or *du Maine.*

Calvados du Pays d' Auge is double distilled in a pot still, similar to the way cognac is made. The distillate spirits are collected at an alcoholic strength of 70% ABV. Then, they are aged in limousine oak barrels, where they pick up colour as they mature. Calvados can be aged for 40 years and becomes as good as a cognac.

The labelling of Calvados is similar to cognac and Armagnac and is bottled at 40% ABV. Applejack from the United States is made in a similar way to Calvados. The US laws specify the minimum aging for Applejack as two years in wood. However, most of them are aged for a longer period. Applejack is blended with neutral spirits before bottling at 40% ABV. Applejack also known as Apple Brandy.

13.15 PEAR BRANDY

Pear brandy or *Eau-de-Vie de Poire* is made both in France and in Switzerland. It is distilled from the Williams pear. Pear brandy is un-aged and colourless with a distinct aroma.

13.16 OTHER FRUIT BRANDIES

After apple brandies, the second-most popular type of brandies are made from cherries and plums. As illustrated in Table 13.4, the brandies show their place of origin where they are distilled and consumed. There are brandies that have such exquisite aromas, that they are immediately bottled or stored in glass-lined vats or casks.

Some of the fruits used in making fruit brandies. (Courtesy: *Mohammed Hadi.*)

13.17 SERVICE OF BRANDY

Most brandies are consumed as an after-dinner beverage. They are preferred neat by most connoisseurs or with a little warm water. Brandy is also excellent in coffee. Fruit brandies, on the other hand, are a chef's delight and are used for flambé and for making famous cold desserts such as cakes puddings and ice creams.

We should note that in formal French classical menu setting, when palate cleanser is called for, calvados is often served. This is said to aid in digestion.

Tasting Notes of Otard Cognac Range

BARON OTARD Signature

A Smooth Style

Roundness

Unlike other cognac companies, Château de Cognac benefits from natural humid cellars which give the Eaux-de-Vie their roundness and mellowness.

Balance

BARON OTARD Castle has also dry cellars, enabling the Cellar Master to juggle with these completely different ageing conditions. The result is the carefully balance taste of the *eau-de-vie*.

Baron Otard Cognac, famous XO Cognac. (Courtesy: *Bacardi International Limited.*)

Length

From the VSOP to the EXTRA, BARON OTARD uses very long ageing periods, far longer than the minimum required, and uses mostly Grande Champagne especially for the XO quality. This policy has the advantage of giving BARON OTARD cognacs an exceptionally long finish on the palate.

Delicacy

BARON OTARD only uses 4 crus to compose blends with incomparable delicacy.

Floral Notes

This is the main characteristic of the two Champagnes, especially at the beginning of ageing.

BARON OTARD VS

Identity

This blend of the finest growths is aged in French oak barrels producing discreet touches of tannin.

Baron Otard VS

Tasting Notes

The balanced roundness of Baron Otard VS releases the intense, fruity aromas of vine flowers. The initial taste on the palate is full but balance and elegance predominate. The colour is golden yellow.

For Maximum Enjoyment

This is ideal for cocktails and aperitifs. BARON OTARD VS can be used in a wide variety of mixtures. Try it with tonic, on the rocks, with orange juice or a splash of soda.

BARON OTARD VSOP

Identity

This elegant cognac comes with full-bodied aromas, great finesse and a good length on the palate.

Baron Otard VSOP

Tasting Notes

The nose is rich in floral notes, backed by touches of linden tree leaves, pear, tobacco and a hint of vanilla. On the palate, it is round and mellow, with subtle, fruity flavours enhanced by a hint of spices. It has an opulent deep golden colour.

For Maximum Enjoyment

BARON OTARD VSOP can be enjoyed as an aperitif with 5 or 6 cl of tonic added to 2 cl of cognac with several ice cubes. As an after-dinner drink, serve it neat at room temperature. Try it also in signature cocktails like the BARON SOUR.

BARON OTARD XO GOLD

Identity

The personality of the Baron Otard XO Gold is expressed through the perfect balance of the blend of the finest growths.

Tasting Notes

On the nose, its roundness reveals a rich harmony of aromas of dawn woodland, with hints of leather. Baron Otard XO Gold combines the smoothness of fruity flavours (plum, hazelnuts) with the softness of honey, enhanced by a touch of violet. Years of maturing of the finest eaux-de-vie in the dim cellars of the chateau have given it a rich amber colour, with vermilion reflections, the sure sign of a cognac of great distinction.

For Maximum Enjoyment

Baron Otard XO Gold will deliver the best of its flavour neat, as an after-dinner drink, to appreciate its exceptional length on the palate. Try also Baron Otard Perfect Serve.

BARON OTARD EXTRA 1795

Identity

A generous blend of Grande Champagne *Eaux-de-Vie*, aged in the unique cellars of the chateau. Baron Otard Extra 1795 is the result of all the experience, patience and savoir-faire of Baron Otard Cellar Master.

Tasting Notes

Baron Otard Extra 1795 offers a rich, complex bouquet of dried fruits (prunes and grapes), orange peel and cigar box. This profusion of aromas has a long finish with an extraordinarily rich taste due to the mellowness of the old Grande Champagne *Eaux-de-Vie*. Its gold and ruby colour is the sign of its long years of maturing.

For Maximum Enjoyment

As with any exceptional cognac, this rare blend is to be enjoyed neat.

Most brandies are consumed as an after-dinner beverage. They are preferred neat by most connoisseurs or with a little warm water. Brandy is also excellent in coffee. Fruit brandies, on the other hand, are a chef's delight and are used for flambé and for making famous cold desserts such as cakes puddings and ice creams.

We should note that in formal French classical menu setting, when palate cleanser is called for, calvados is often served. This is said to aid in digestion.

13.18 INTERESTING FACTS ABOUT BRANDY

1. Brandy was the largest consumed beverage until the 1880s. Due to the *Phylloxera* epidemic, grapes were scarce and hence adversely impacted production. This was the sole reason for whisky gaining popularity in the world. Else, brandy would be still the undisputed king of spirits.
2. Brandy sold from the Cognac Region of France is the most revered spirit till date.
3. Cognac bottles are unique many resembling perfume bottles.
4. Brandy is best consumed warm, with some warm water or even warmed by the hand holding it, unlike most other beverages, which are recommended to be served at either room temperature or chilled.

LET'S SUMMARIZE IN POINTS

- Brandy is a spirit that is made by distilling wine made from grapes or a fermented mash of fruits.
- Cognac is considered the best brandy in the world. It is made from the grapes grown in the Cognac region of France. It has two basic systems for classification—star and letter system.
- Armagnac is the second-best brandy in the world after cognac. It is made in the Armagnac still.
- Marc is a French brandy made from grape pomace.
- The other famous brandies of the world are Californian, German, Greek, Italian, Indian, Mexican, Peruvian, Spanish and Israeli brandies.
- Brandy can also be produced from fruits, such as plums, apples, apricots and cherries.

13.19 FAQs

Short-Answer Type Questions

1. What are the grape varieties used to make Cognac?
2. List down the sub-regions of Cognac.
3. What are the various brandies of France?
4. Differentiate between marc and grappa.
5. Differentiate between fine and fine Champagne.
6. What are fruits used in making fruit brandies?
7. Describe Armagnac regions.
8. List the grapes used in making Armagnac.
9. List five brands of Cognac and Armagnac.
10. List the other brandies of the world with a brief note on their distinct characteristics.

Long-Answer Type Questions

1. What is the production process of Cognac and Armagnac?
2. List five differences between Cognac and Armagnac.
3. Describe the labelling system used in the Cognac region.
4. What is an Armagnac still? Illustrate with a diagram.

5. Write short notes on:
   (i) Applejack
   (ii) Pear brandy
   (iii) Other fruit brandies

13.20 KEY TERMS

- ABV
- Angel's Share
- Broullis/la Bonne Chaffe
- Connoisseurs
- Eau de Vie
- Gout de Cuivre
- Grappa
- Marrying
- Phylloxera
- Pisco
- Première chauffe
- Racking
- Removing the lees
- Sherry
- Solera
- Tails
- Vielle Reserve

Whisky

CHAPTER OUTLINE

- **14.1** HISTORY
- **14.2** SCOTCH WHISKY
- **14.3** IRISH WHISKEY
- **14.4** AMERICAN WHISKY
- **14.5** FAQs
- **14.6** KEY TERMS

LET'S DEFINE

'Whisky is a spirit suitably aged in wood, usually oak, obtained from the distillation of a fermented mash of grain.'

Whisky is one of the most omnipresent liquors across the world. In fact, it is the most consumed spirit in India, constituting more than 50% of all the liquor consumed domestically in India.

14.1 HISTORY

It was inevitable that human would use the product most easily available to them after they discovered the science of distillation. Hence, the places that witnessed the abundance of grain were the distillers of whisky.

The word *whisky* comes from the Celtic word *uisgebeatha* or *uisegebaugh* pronounced as [*whis-geh-baw*], the Scottish and Irish words for 'water of life'. The Scots and the Irish both have their own tales to tell and claim the rights over the invention of whisky. The English found the Celtic words too difficult and hence named this spirit *whisky*.

The Canadians and Scottish use the same spelling, that is, 'whisky' without an 'e'. While the Irish spell it as 'whiskey' with an 'e'. The United States used to use the 'e' but now omits it in the *Standards of Identity*; however, it permits its use in traditional text.

Further on we shall discuss the different whiskies of the world in detail.

14.2 SCOTCH WHISKY

'Scotch' is one of the most popular words, especially in India. This whisky, made famous by the British, has left a lingering desire in every individual across the world. Today, Scotch whisky holds a high regard in the minds of beverage enthusiasts and most homes across the world who keep a bottle of Scotch in their 'treasure chest' to open for an occasion.

Scotch whisky was being made in Scotland for many years. In 1814, a law was introduced; this prohibited people from making whisky on small scale and allowed distillation to be done with a minimum of 500 gallons capacity. This ensured no whisky was made in home and farms, allowing quality control norms to be implemented. The British Government continued to tax whisky throughout the 19th century. Illicit distillation was prevalent in Britain up to 1823.

Scotch whiskies are either malt whiskies, grain whiskies or a blend of both.

Scotch-producing Regions

Four principal regions that produce malt whisky in Scotland are as follows (Figure 14.1):

1. The Highlands,
2. The Lowlands,
3. Campbeltown and
4. Islay (pronounced as '*I-lay*').

Let us understand the individual characteristics of the whisky of each sub-regions of Scotland.

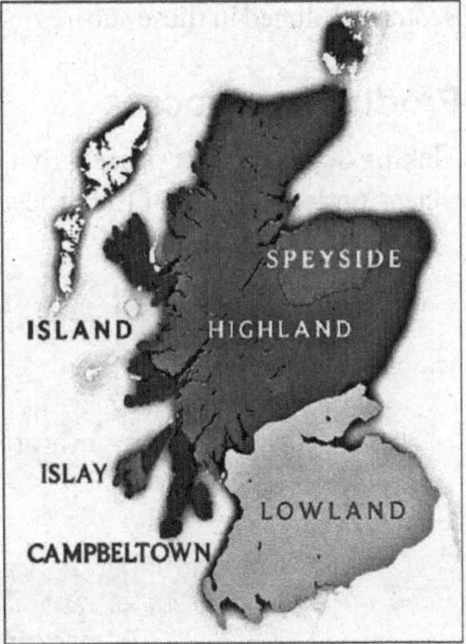

Figure 14.1 Map of Scotland.

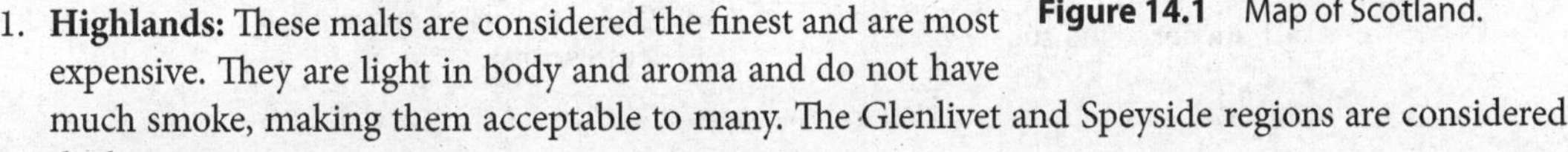

1. **Highlands:** These malts are considered the finest and are most expensive. They are light in body and aroma and do not have much smoke, making them acceptable to many. The Glenlivet and Speyside regions are considered the best.
   a. **Aberfeldy:** Aberfeldy produces a distinctly heather-honeyed whisky, which forms the core character of all of our blends. Today, the original distillery is also home to Dewar's World of Whisky, the world-class five-star brand centre that draws thousands of Scotch enthusiasts from around the globe every year.
2. **Lowlands:** These too are light, but less smoky. Almost all the grain whisky distillers are in the lowlands.

   Some of the brands and their tasting notes from this region are as follows:

   a. **Auchentoshan**—One of the principal malts from the lowlands. It has fresh aroma and lightly sweet. Well-balanced and aged for 12 years.
   b. **Bladnoch**—It has a very delicate aroma with a distinct lemony character, but a bigger sweet palate.

3. **Campbeltown**—They are very full in body and quite smoky in character. Some of the brands are Springbank, Glen Scotia, Scotia Royale, Longrow, Royal Culross, Old court.
4. **Islay**—Islay malts are generally full-bodied smoky and pungent.

   Some of the brands and their tasting notes from this region are as follows:

   a. **Ardbeg**—It is among the most intense of Islay single malts. Found in several bottles, the finest being the one by the distillery established in 1815.
   b. **Laphroaig**—It is the best-known single-malt Scotch from Islay. In addition to its seaweed character, it has fullness and oiliness in body.

Aberfeldy, a famous brand of Highland single malt whisky.

The above-listed characteristics are the general qualities of malted Scotch produced in these sub-regions, but there are always exceptions.

Production Process

Making Scotch is a set process that has been standardized and perfected over the years. Figure 14.2 gives a clear understanding of the procedure.

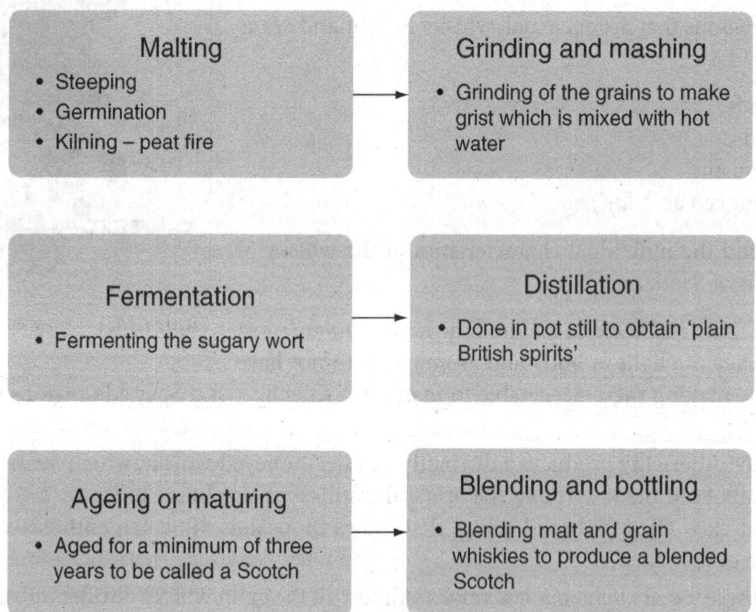

Figure 14.2 The Process of Making Scotch Whisky.

1. **Malting:** As we had studied the process of malting barley, in Chapter 5, a similar process is followed to malt barley, which is used in making whisky. The main difference is the *kilning* process, where the germinated barley is *kilned* over peat smoke. The timing of kilning is the most important and has to

be done perfectly. If done too soon, it will result in less soluble sugars in the grain, and if done too late, it would result in the germination of the seed to form a plant leaving no soluble sugars.

'Peat' is a type of charcoal obtained from a vegetable source. The smoke of this type of charcoal gives Scotch its peculiar flavour. Each distillery has its own secret procedure for making their distinct Scotch. Kilning with peat smoke makes a great difference.

Most Scotch distillers rely on specialized industrial units called *maltings* to produce their malt. The *maltings* produce malt according to the requirements of their clients who own distilleries. Some companies such as Diageo, who own a great deal of Scottish distilleries, have created their own *malting* units to meet their own requirements.

Rye grain, wheat grain and barley grain used for making whisky.

2. **Grinding and mashing:** Once the malt is dry, it is put though grinders to make coarse flour, which is called '*grist*'.

   The powdered 'grist' is then mixed with warm water at 75°C approximately to extract the sugars and mix it into the water to produce a sweet liquid called '*wort*'. The wort is separated from the sediments of barley that are used as cattle feed. This is then cooled to 15–20°C and sent to the fermentation tanks.
3. **Fermentation:** In order to produce alcohol fermentation is an essential step. The yeast culture is added and the wort is allowed to ferment in stainless steel tanks. The following chemical equation occurs in the tanks.

   The yeast acts on the sugar to produce alcohol, carbon dioxide and heat. The process results in a beer with 8% ABV. The process of making beer and whisky till this step are the same. The difference

Interesting Facts

Equation

The following chemical equations summarize the fermentation of sucrose, whose chemical formula is $C_{12}H_{22}O_{11}$. One mole of sucrose is converted into two moles of ethanol and two moles of carbon dioxide:

$$C_{12}H_{22}O_{11} + H_2O + \text{invertase} \rightarrow 2\,C_6H_{12}O_6$$

$$C_6H_{12}O_6 + \text{zymase} \rightarrow 2C_2H_5OH + 2CO_2$$

C_2H_5OH is the chemical formula for ethanol.

being that in beer manufacture, *hops* are added post this stage, whereas to make whisky, this liquid is sent to the distillation stills.

4. **Distillation:** In the production of Scotch whisky, the wash is distilled twice in a pot still. First, the wash is put into the first pot still also known as the *wash still*. The resultant distillate is low in alcoholic strength, which is known as *low wines*. The low wines are then redistilled in the second pot still. The first part called *fore shots* and the last pat is called *feints* are collected separately. The middle part, which is the useful part, is then collected referred to as the *hearts*.

   This procedure is followed as the fore shots contain methanol, which is not potable, and the *feints* contain impurities, which will impair the flavour of the spirit when matured.

   The spirit obtained has an alcoholic strength of 70% ABV, which is then matured or aged.

Table 14.1 Cask Sizes of Various Whiskies

Name	Capacity in Gallon
Pin	4–5
Firkin	9
Kilderkin	16
Barrel	36
Hogshead	54
Puncheon	72
Butt	108

5. **Maturing or ageing:** The distilled spirits are called *plain British spirits* before maturation/aging and whisky after maturation/aging. The casks used are generally made of American white oak wood varying in size. The typical cask sizes are shown in Table 14.1.

   The different sizes of barrels are used as per convenience. They may be brand new, old—used by wine makers, which are very popular with malt whisky distillers. For example, barrels used to age sherry, when used to mature whisky, impart sweeter taste. Figure 14.3 depicts different parts of a barrel.

Dewar's warehouse for ageing Scotch whisky in the Highland region of Scotland.

For ageing, the whisky is barrelled between 60–65% ABV by diluting it with water. The law stipulates that Scotch has to be aged in wood for a minimum of three years. However, practically all Scotch malts remain in the casks for a minimum of five years. The blends with higher percentages of malt whiskies to grain whiskies are aged for a longer period of time. Please note some brands have different ages on their various brand labels. This does not indicate that it is the same whisky with different level of ageing, but the whisky indicating longest ageing on its label was a fuller-bodied whisky to begin with and needed more time to mature and mellow. For example, the Johnnie Walker brand of whiskies has a range starting with the eight-year-old Red label, the 12-year-old Black Label and the finest of them the Blue Label. The blue label whisky is a different distillate that is more full-bodied, hence ageing would mellow it down.

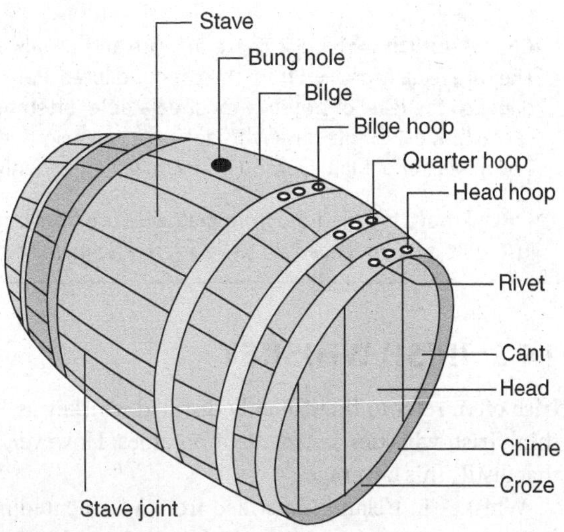

Figure 14.3 Parts of a Barrel.

6. **Blending and bottling:** Scotch whiskies were either straight malts or straight grain whiskies till 1853. When a few distilleries began the practice of blending malt whiskies with grain whiskies, it produced a whisky popularly called as *blended Scotch*.

   The blending is done after the whiskies have been aged for a minimum of four years. A master blender then examines them, and then fixes a proportion of each malt to be used from Highland, Lowland, Campbelltown and Islay to make the master blend. A proportion of grain whisky is also added.

   This blend is then rested in vats for them to marry, stirring them occasionally. It is then returned to sherry or oak casks before bottling or shipping. Blending is an essential process and from the above we can understand its value. It is the master blender's exceptional skill to produce the same blended product for a brand year after year. A Scotch can be a blend of as many as 40 malt whiskies and up to five grain whiskies.

   Hence, we can say that the blender's role is the key in producing a great Scotch whisky. The overall product is also influenced by other factors such as water, peat smoke, climate conditions and the traditional distillation and maturing procedures.

Interesting Facts

For better understanding, a few terms have been highlighted to gain more insight into the different types of Scotch whiskies.

Single malt: The term *single malt* has a very precise meaning, and it indicates that all whisky in the bottle was made in the same distillery. It is made exclusively from malted barley, not from any other grain, sugar or fermentable material.

Cask strength whiskies: These are rare and usually only the very best whiskies are bottled in this way. They are usually bottled from the cask undiluted. Rather than diluting, the distiller is inviting the drinker to dilute to the level of potency most palatable (often no dilution is necessary, such is the quality of single-cask whiskies). Single-cask whiskies are usually bottled by specialist independent bottlers, such as Duncan Taylor, Master of Malt, Gordon & MacPhail and Cadenhead are among others.

Vatted malt: It is blended from malt whiskies from different distilleries. If a whisky is labelled 'pure malt' or just 'malt' it is almost certain to be a vatted whisky. This is also sometimes labelled as 'blended malt' whisky.

14.3 IRISH WHISKEY

Irish often refer to their illicitly distilled whiskey as *Poteen*. Hence, it is not surprising that most people think Irish whiskies are made of potatoes. However, this is untrue. In fact, *Poteen* refers to the pot still that distils this beverage.

Whiskey in Ireland is distilled from a fermented mash of grain such as corn, rye, wheat, oats, malted and un-malted barley, similar to the mash used in Scotland.

The malted barley used is dried in a kiln with a solid floor. Peat smoke is not allowed to come in contact with the grain, even if it is used. Today, smokeless anthracite is used. The malt is not exposed to smoke unlike its Scottish counterpart.

Irish whiskey is made by distilling the liquor thrice. The Scottish distillers use the pot still twice, whereas the Irish go one step further to redistill the distillate of the second still to obtain a stronger distillate. Some Irish distillers use the patent still to distil their grain whiskies. These are then blended with the distillates of the pot still to produce a light-bodied whisky, which is generally exported.

As per law, Irish whiskey must be aged for five years in wood; however, they are usually aged for 7–8 years before bottling and shipping. Irish whisky has its own distinct identity. It is a smooth medium-bodied whiskey with a clean and distinct aroma. It is popularly used in Irish coffee.

Interesting Facts

Difference between Irish whisky and Scotch whisky

1. Scotch is made from home-grown barley as well as cereal grown in other countries, whereas Irish whiskey is made only from home-grown barley. Scotch is made only from malted barley whereas Irish whiskey uses both malted and un-malted barley.
2. Scots pot stills are smaller than Irish pot stills.
3. Scotch is distilled twice whereas Irish whiskey is distilled thrice. Scotch uses only peat during kilning to impart the peculiar flavour whereas Irish whiskey follows no such standard.
4. Scotch is matured minimum for three years whereas Irish whiskey is matured minimum for five years.
5. Scotch is made only by pot still method of distillation whereas Irish whiskey utilizes both pot and patent still method of distillation.
6. Scots and Canadians spell it as "Whisky", while the Irish and Americans spell it as "Whiskey".

14.4 AMERICAN WHISKY

American whiskies are famous for their own aroma and flavour. American whiskies have a long history and are being distilled since the 18th century, due to the easy availability of rye and corn. The settlers found corn to be the most viable source to distil their whiskies.

Whiskey has played a pivotal role in American history. Post Independence, the new American government levied an excise tax on whiskey in order to earn revenues. This did not go down well with the distillers, especially the ones in the 'western' communities. There were riots and President Washington sent a force of militia to quell the situation. It is of tremendous significance to the US Federal Government and is still known as the whiskey rebellion. This taxation policy led to many Scottish and Irish farmer–distillers to shift further into the Indian territory, making them invisible to the tax collector. This inevitably led them to a proper water source in Indiana and Kentucky.

The first whiskey distilled in Kentucky is generally attributed to the Reverend Elijah Craig at Georgetown, in Bourbon County. The grain used was corn (maize), and was popularly known as Bourbon County whiskey. Bourbon has remained the name for whiskies made from corn mash.

The distilleries are strategically located in areas with the right quality of water for whiskey production. The areas are rich in springs that pass the water through limestone rocks. This imparts the desired taste to the American whiskey. Today, establishing a distillery is not location specific in the United States. This is due to the advancement in water technology, which helps the distillery to obtain the exact quality of water through mineral adjustments.

Grain Whisky Production

Most American grain whiskies and grain whiskies from the other parts of the world follow the same production procedure. The various steps involved are listed as follows:

1. **Rick Burning**—First, the grain is inspected and cleaned of all the dust at the distillery. To make Jack Daniel's, the grains are subjected to 'Rick Burning' which imparts a distinctive smoky characteristic to the grains and finally into the whiskey.
2. **Grinding**—It is then put into grinders to make it into a *meal.*
3. **Cooking**—The meal is cooked to release the starch from the tough cellular coating. Then, the malt is added, which helps convert the starch to soluble sugars.
4. **Fermentation**—Pure cultured yeast is propagated in large vats. This process of fermentation is very similar to the one followed in making Scotch whisky. After the wort has cooled, the cultured yeast is added to it and fermentation begins. This process takes 7–14 days and results in a beer.

Rick burning at the Jack Daniel Distillery, USA.

5. **Distillation**—The resultant beer is put into patent stills. This results in a whisky high in alcohol with 80% ABV. It is then diluted to an alcoholic strength of 50–55% ABV.
6. **Maturation or Ageing**—The distillate is placed in charred white oak barrels to age in bonded warehouses. We are aware that a portion of alcohol is generally lost in the ageing process, as it escapes from pores of the wood. This is the reason that Scotch whisky, rum and brandy are barrelled between 65% and 75% ABV, to compensate for the loss of alcohol due to humid conditions.
7. **Charcoal Mellowing**—This is quite a unique step in the making of an American whiskey. The whiskey is dripped through at least 10 feet of charcoal, giving it a unique flavour. This art was perfected by

the Jack Daniel Distillery to produce one of the best whiskies in the world. This unique step takes out all the unwanted odours resulting in a whisky ready to undergo the maturation process. This is one of the major reasons for putting American whiskies at par, if not ahead, of all the other whiskies of the world.

On the other hand, American whiskies are barrelled between 50% and 55% ABV. Surprisingly, as they mature, the alcoholic strength increases because of the warm and dry conditions that they are stored in. During ageing, more water is lost compare to alcohol, which leads to an increase in the alcoholic strength of whiskey.

The fermentation tank at the Jack Daniel Distillery, USA.

Sweet and Sour Mash

The sweet and sour mash process is predominantly followed in making American whiskey. There are two types of yeasting process, one being the sweet mash or yeast mash process and second being the sour mash process, which is primarily used in making Bourbon whiskey.

Sweet mash means that it is produced by adding all the freshly developed cultured yeast to the mash and the *stillage* is not added (stillage is the liquid which is left after the alcohol has been distilled; this is usually added to adjust the acidity). The mash is allowed to ferment for 36–50 hours.

Sour mash means that at least one quarter of mash has to be *stillage*, along with the fresh mash. This sour mash is fermented taking 72–90 hours. It offers a favourable pH for yeast growth and prevents bacterial contamination. Sweet mash is more difficult to control and must be done at approximately 35°C to end quickly and avoid contamination.

The distillation still at the Jack Daniel Distillery, USA.

Types of American Whiskies

There are three main types of whiskies produced in America, namely, straights, blends and light whiskies.

1. **Straight whiskey:** It has to be distilled with an alcoholic strength not exceeding 80% ABV, aged in new, charred white oak barrels for at least two years and reduced to an overall alcoholic strength

The unique charcoal mellowing process of American whiskey followed at the Jack Daniel Distillery, USA. Image shows the whiskey being passed through the charcoal.

The famous barrel house at the Jack Daniel Distillery, USA which is used for maturing their famous whiskey.

Sour mash fermentation at the Jack Daniel Distillery, USA.

Jack Daniel's is the most famous brand of American whiskey (from left to right): Jack Daniel's Tennessee Honey, Jack Daniel's Old No.7 Tennessee, Gentleman Jack and Jack Daniel's Single Barrel whiskey.

of 40% ABV before bottling. All the criteria are under federal regulations, which also specify that they have to be made from 51% of a grain. Straights include Bourbon, Tennessee, rye, corn and wheat whiskies. Straight Bourbons are whiskies made from a mash comprising 51% corn, whereas a straight Tennessee must be distilled in Tennessee containing 51% of any grain (corn is generally used). This is

ABOUT JACK DANIEL'S

Jack Daniel's is a brand of sour mash Tennessee whiskey that is the highest selling American whiskey in the world. It is known for its square bottles and black label. It is produced in Lynchburg, Tennessee, by the Jack Daniel's Distillery, which has been owned by the Brown–Forman Corporation since 1956. Despite being the location of a major operational distillery, Jack Daniel's home county of Moore is a dry county, so the product is not available for consumption at stores or restaurants within the county, although the distillery does sell commemorative bottles of whiskey.

The Famous Barrel House at the Jack Daniel Distillery and (on the right) the Jack Daniel's iconic Old No. 7 whiskey.

a Bourbon-type whiskey, but is very full-bodied, as it is treated with maple wood charcoal to remove the lighter flavours. Straight whiskies may be mixed, but they have to be of the same distilling period from the same distillery to retain the 'Straight Whiskey' label. Two-thirds of American distilled whiskies consumed in the United States are straight whiskies.

2. **Blended whiskey:** When full-bodied straight whiskies are mixed with grain spirits or light whiskies to produce a well-balanced, harmonious and consistent whiskey called a blended whiskey. It is a very challenging task for the blender to produce the same product year after year.

   To be a blended whiskey, at least 20% must be a straight whiskey. The balance can be a neutral spirit, a grain spirit or light whiskies. Grain sprits are neutral and have been aged in reused oak barrels to impart some amount of flavour and mellowness.
3. **Light whiskey:** It is a whiskey distilled in the United States with an alcoholic strength between 80–95% ABV stored in charred oak casks. These charred oak casks are re-used, which help develop the colour and flavour to these light spirits.

   As we are aware, a spirit that is distilled at a higher alcoholic strength contains less congeners, which imparts flavour. The light whiskies are distilled with such a high alcoholic strength that if they are not aged in the reused cooperage, they would be very similar to neutral spirits.

Thus, these are the broad categories of American whiskies. Straight American whiskies have dominated the markets, leaving less space for the blended whiskies. The light whiskies have not been as widely accepted and are predominantly used to create American blended whiskies.

The very famous barrel house of Jack Daniel at Lynchburg, USA.

Canadian Whisky

Canadian whisky is a distinct product of Canada, manufactured according to Canadian law containing spirits aged for minimum of three years before bottling and labelled as 'Blended Canadian whisky'.

As per Canadian law, Canadian whisky must be produced from cereal grains only. Canadian regulations do not interfere with grain formulas, distilling proofs or ageing cooperage etc. and leave the art to the expertise of the distillers.

Canadian whiskies in many references quoted it as a rye whisky which it is not. Corn, wheat, rye, malted barley are the grains that are generally used. None of them exceeds 50% of the mash. Canadian whiskies are light-bodied whiskies with delicate flavour. This is obtained by distilling the mash to an alcoholic strength ranging from 70–90% ABV, ageing it in wood. Most Canadian whiskies are aged for 6–7 years. However, if they are aged for less than four years, it has to be indicated on the label.

Japanese Whisky

The Japanese beverage industry that dedicated itself to sake (Japanese rice beverage), *umeshu* (Japanese plum wine made by infusion) and *umechu* (a Japanese medicinal wine) is now emerging as a great whisky-producing country. This is mainly attributed to the domestic demand after the Second World War. Today, producing whisky, liqueurs and brandies have become a part of Japanese culture.

The Japanese whisky distillers began with an attempt to duplicate Scotch whisky, but have made their own distinct product. These whiskies are made from malted barley (a small portion of which is cured in peat), millet, corn, Indian corn and rice in varied proportions, according to their secretly guarded formulas. The production process is similar to the methods used in the West, but the main difference is in the saccharification process where in *Koji* enzyme is used, to convert the starch to sugar (for details please refer to Chapter 6).

Japanese whiskies are distilled at an alcoholic strength of 65% ABV for full-bodied varieties and 90% ABV for light-bodied varieties. They are then aged in used charcoal barrels before blending. Post blending the whiskies, they are aged for several years. Japanese authorities regulate ageing and handling of whisky.

Whisky production has also emerged in Australia, Germany, Holland and Denmark. Each one has its own distinct character. Whiskies produced in India are very few.

Brands of Whisky

Some popular brands of whiskies are listed in Table 14.2.

Table 14.2 Various Brands of Whiskies

Type	Origin	Brands
Single Malt Scotch	Scotland	**Campbeltown**—Glengyle, Springbank **Highlands**—Aberfeldy, Ancnoc, Balblair, Ben Nevis, Dalmore, Edradour, Glencadam, Glen Garioch, Glenglassaugh, Glengoyne, Glenmorangie, Glen Moray, Loch Lomond, Old Pulteney, Speyburn, Speyside, Tomatin, Tullibardine **Other Notable Speyside Malts**—Aberlour, Ardmore, Balvenie, Benriach, Benromach, Glenfarclas, Glenfiddich, Glen Grant, Glenlivet, Glenrothes, Macallan, Tomintoul **Islay**—Ardbeg, Bowmore, Bruichladdich, Bunnahabhain, Kilchoman, Laphroaig, Smokehead **Lowlands**—Auchentoshan, Bladnoch, Daftmill
Blended Scotch	Scotland	**Regular:** Ballantine's, Dewar's White Label, Famouse Grouse, J&B, Cutty Sark, Jw Red Label, Something Special, Teacher's, White and Mackay **Premium:** Dewar's 18, Jw Black Label, Chivas Regal, Haig Dimple, Dewar's 12, Ballantine 12 Year Old, White and Mackay 21 Year Old, Grant's Rare 12 Year old **Deluxe:** Chivas Royal Salute, Dewar's Signature, Jw Blue Label, Jw Swing, Ballantine's 30 Year, Bell's 12 Year Old, Dimple 15 Year Old, Black and White Select
Irish Whiskey	Ireland	Dunphy, Murphy, John Jameson, Old Bushmill, Old Bushmill's Black Bush, Paddy, Power's Gold Label, Hewitts, Midleton
Bourbon	USA	Ancient Age, Early Times, Jim Beam, Old Crow, Old Grandad, Maker's Mark, Wilde Turkey
Tennessee Whisky	USA	Jack Daniel's Old No. 7 Black Label, Jack Daniel's Green Label, George Dicker's Old No. 12, George Dicker's Old No. 8, Elm Motlow
Canadian Whisky	Canada	Canadian Club, Crown Royal, Schenley Ofc, Seagram Vo, Canadian Mist, Black Velvet, Lord Calvert, Windsor Supreme
Indian Whisky	India	Solan No. 1, Mcdowell's Single Malt, Moghul Monarch
Rye Whisky	USA	Heaven Hill, Four Roses, Jim Beam, Catoctin Creek and Wigle
Japanese Whisky	Japan	Yamazaki—Owned by Suntory Distilleries Nikka—Owned by Asahi Breweries Fuji-Gotemba—Owned by Kirin Distilleries Karuizawa—Owned by Mercian Distilleries-A Part of Kirin Distilleries

About Dewar's

Dewar's whisky which is a very popular brand of whisky.

John Dewar, a pioneer of whisky blending, built a thriving Scottish business on a fine reputation for quality. Born in 1805 to a humble farming family, he was raised in Perthshire County near the small town of Aberfeldy (where the distillery is located today) in the heart of Scotland. He rejected a traditional life in farming and started his own wine and spirits business in 1846. By the time of his death, in 1880, he had built a successful Scottish business, highly respected for its excellent blended whiskies. Of his 10 children, two would take over the business, transforming it into a success story—perhaps beyond even his wildest dreams. Each Dewar's blended Scotch whisky is carefully crafted from up to 40 different single malt and grain whiskies. The entire process takes time and requires many years of expertise. At Aberfeldy, the experienced craftsmen take a number of steps that help to distinguish Dewar's whisky. First, the traditional fermentation process is prolonged to ensure that the final whisky is rich in fruity flavours and aromas. Then, the still men carefully select the finest part of the distillation (known as 'the heart') and place it into oak casks to mature for at least three years in awarehouse in Scotland. While in the bourbon and sherry casks, the heart gently shapes and its rich flavours are fully developed. The Dewar's master blender chooses the very best individual whiskies from the many distilleries throughout Scotland to complement Aberfeldy Single Malt Scotch Whisky—the heart and foundation of each Dewar's blend. It is the master blender's job to ensure each blends perfect balance, so that no single flavour dominates and all of the whiskies blend together in perfect harmony. Dewar's unique double-ageing process is the extra step taken to give Dewar's 12 Year Old, Dewar's 18 Year Old and Dewar's Signature their remarkable smoothness and depth of character. Pioneered over 100 years ago by Dewar's master blender A.J. Cameron, it is a process that involves returning the newly made blend—the point at which most whisky makers would simply bottle it up—back to vintage oak casks to mature for an extended period of time. This extra step creates a smoother blend, with a long and lingering finish. The outstanding results are well worth the extra time and effort.

Dewar's White Label—Created in 1899 through the innovation and expertise of Dewar's first master blender, Dewar's White Label has become one of the world's most awarded Scotch whiskies. A blend up to 40 of Scotland's finest single malt and grain whiskies issued to make Dewar's White labeland each one is hand-picked to create this full, round and lively whisky.

Dewar's 12 Year Old—Using only whiskies that are 12 years or older, Dewar's 12 Year Old draws its rich flavour from a unique double-ageing process that gives it a superior, smooth and perfectly balanced profile. The whisky is returned to vintage oak casks, so it can mature a little more. This extra step is called, 'double-ageing'. It means the flavours are allowed to further develop in the cask, creating a smoother blend with a long and lingering finish.

Dewar's 18 Year Old—Dewar's 18 Year Old is created with a rare and special blend of whiskies using a time-honoured double-ageing process that lends refinement to this exceptional blend. Only Scotland's finest 18-year-old malt and grain whiskies are used to create the full, smooth and creamy blend of Dewar's 18 Year Old.

Dewar's Signature—Based on over 160 years of blending experience, Dewar's Signature is created using carefully selected single malt Scotch whiskies and a double-ageing process. Dewar's Signature uses a blend of the rarest of rare whiskies from across Scotland and is returned to vintage oak casks to age for a second time.

Dewar's 15 Year Old—Dewar's 15 Year Old is a blend of rare and exclusive whiskies at their peak of perfection, aged for a period of at least 15 years in Scotland, delicately created and specifically selected by Dewar's master blender to suit the sophisticated Asian palate. With a rich and golden colour, the aromas of vanilla and toffee develop to reveal floral notes and succulent exotic fruits on the nose. The complexity of Dewar's 15 Year Old increases with accents of herbal, citrus and green apple notes and, with the addition of water develop to create a delicate hint of coconut, revealing yet more fruity notes and exquisitely scented floral aromas. Exceptionally smooth in taste, this silky smooth and well-rounded blend displays a long and warming finish, with delicate fruity, floral and grassy flavours built upon on a sweet and malty base.

Traditionally, whisky is served in old-fashioned glasses as shown in the above photo. (Courtesy: *Libbey's International Limited.*)

Service of Whisky

Whisky is traditionally served in an old-fashioned glass. It is served either straight, on the rocks or with either water, soda or both.

Single malt Scotch is consumed with cold water to enjoy the explosion of its full taste and aroma. Blended Scotch is generally preferred with either water or soda, with or without ice.

American whiskies can be had in the same way. However, Jack Daniel's's Whisky, which is a Bourbon, has a unique combination with cola and is universally accepted as its best chaser. Whisky also makes traditional cocktails.

Whisky is an evergreen drink, which is referred 365 days of the year, summer or winter.

Interesting Facts about Whisky

1. The distilling process was originally applied to perfume then to wine and finally adapted to fermented mashes of cereals in countries where grapes were not plentiful such as Great Britain.
2. Most Indian whiskies are made from molasses. The standard formula used is: 1 part Indian whiskey = 1 bottle scotch + 100 bottles molasses whiskey. Some of the pure grain whiskies from India are Solan No. 1, McDowell's single malt, Moghul Monarch.
3. Whiskies do not mature in the bottle, so the 'age' of a whisky is the time between distillation and bottling. This reflects how much the cask has interacted with the whisky.
4. By the 1880s, Phylloxera had devastated the vineyards of France, wine and brandy had virtually disappeared from cellars everywhere. The Scots were quick to take advantage of the calamity replacing brandy as the preferred spirit of choice, as the French recovered slowly.

LET'S SUMMARIZE IN POINTS

- Whisky is made from the fermented mash of grains such as barley, wheat, rye and corn.
- Whisky production began in Scotland and Ireland, and then spread to the United States, Canada, Japan and many other regions across the world.
- Scotch whisky has an essential characteristic of being kilned in peat smoke and is aged for a minimum of three years. It is categorized as single malt, blended Scotch, cask strength whisky and vatted malts.
- Whiskies from Ireland have to be aged for a minimum of five years.
- Whiskies from other regions of the world, although having their own quality standards are not regulated by any governmental agency.
- Whisky is served straight, on the rocks or with water or soda.

14.5 FAQs

Short-Answer Type Questions

1. Define whisky.
2. Differentiate between *whisky* and *whiskey*.
3. Name the four Scotch producing regions of Scotland.
4. What is a single malt whisky?
5. What is peat?
6. What are vatted malts, cask strength whiskies and blended Scotch? Differentiate.
7. Name the various types of American whiskies.
8. What is rye whisky?
9. Give the three basic steps involved in malting.
10. Name five brands of single malt whiskies. Specify the sub-regions.

Long-Answer Type Questions

1. Give the difference between Scotch and Irish whisky.
2. Give a detailed explanation about whisky production.
3. Explain the production process of American whisky in detail.
4. Write short notes on:
   (i) Japanese whisky
   (ii) Canadian whisky
5. Explain grain whisky production in detail and the sweet and sour mash process.

14.6 KEY TERMS

- Bourbon
- Poteen
- Evergreen drink
- Rye whisky
- Feints
- Scotch whisky
- Foreshots
- Smoky character
- Grist
- Standards of identity
- Kilning
- Sucrose
- Maltings
- Tennessee
- Marry
- Uisge Beatha/Uisge Baugh
- Meal
- Umechu
- Peat
- Umeshu

EAU-DE-VIES AND OTHER SPIRITS

CHAPTER OUTLINE

One can only imagine human's growing desire to experiment with their food and beverage, which has lead to the discoveries of a whole array of spirits.

In this chapter, we shall see the various other such spirits that have been made in a particular region or nation due to the need or an abundance of that particular food grain or crop. The various spirits that are unique has been discussed in the following sections.

15.1 ANISE- AND LIQUORICE-FLAVOURED SPIRITS

Absinthe is the world's most famous yet the most misunderstood spirit. A poetic reference describes it as *The Green Muse*. It was wicked and was supposed to drive the drinker insane and sometimes even killing a few. In France, sale of *Absinthe* was prohibited before the First World War, as it was one of the most potent of all alcoholic beverages on the planet. *Absinthe* was generally shipped at an alcoholic strength of 68% ABV. The sale of *Absinthe* is prohibited in Switzerland (where it was invented), the United States, France and many other countries.

The *elixir* better known as absinthe contained aromatic plants, balm mint, hyssop, fennel, star anise and a high proof spirit. It was invented by Dr Ordinaire, a physician and a pharmacist, who was a French exile, living in Covet, Switzerland towards the end of the 18th century. In 1797, Henri-Louis Pernod acquired the recipe and even today, the names Pernod and *Absinthe* are taken in one breath.

Service: *Absinthe* service is discussed in Chapter 29 of this book.

An Absinthe bottle (left) and the service of Absinthe (right) over a cube of sugar using an Absinthe spoon.

Since the prohibition of *Absinthe* in many parts of the world, Pernod produces a substitute in France, which is an anise-flavoured spirit at 45% ABV similar in character and flavour to *Absinthe.* It has a light yellowish-green colour and a sharp pronounced aroma of liquorice. When mixed with water, it turns milky and finally a cloudy opalescent colour. This occurs due to the precipitation of the natural essential oils in the liquor when mixed with water.

There are many spirits flavoured with anise; however, none are absinthe, as they do not contain worm wood in the formula. This spirit is made in many countries and is called by local names. For example, in France it is called 'Pastis', in Spain it is 'Ojen', in Italy is 'Anesone', in Greece 'Ouzo' and 'Mastikha', in Israel, it is 'Arak', in Turkey it is 'Raki' and in the United States it is 'Herbsaint'.

They are usually mixed with water and rarely consumed neat. They are served as aperitifs and coolers.

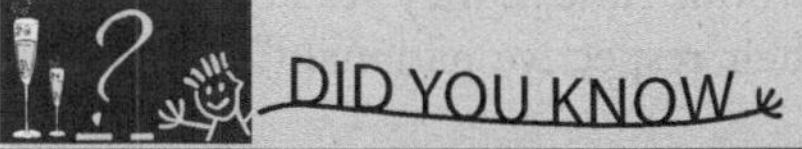

A drink made with equal parts (usually an ounce each) of absinthe and anisette, which is slightly sweet, is an excellent restorative in cases of sea sickness, air sickness and nausea.

15.2 AQUAVIT OR AKUAVIT

Aquavit literally translates to mean *water of life*. It is the national beverage of the Scandinavian countries and has been used to cure many ailments since the 1500s.

It is made from the fermented mash of either malted barley, grains or even potatoes depending on the availability and the time of year. The principal flavouring agent is the caraway seed. Aquavit is distilled as a neutral spirit at 95% ABV and then diluted with de-mineralized water to 60% ABV. In addition to caraway seeds, other herbs and botanicals such as coriander, fennel, cinnamon, anise and cardamom are used. They were initially added for their medicinal properties.

Aquavit is a colourless spirit bottled with an alcoholic strength of 40% ABV. Another version of aquavit is amber coloured at 45% ABV, with a predominant dill flavour in addition to caraway. Some compare aquavit to kummel because it has a strong caraway flavour. While aquavit is dry, kummel, on the other hand, is sweetened with sugar syrup and bottled with an alcoholic strength of 37.5–40% ABV. Chapter 16 discusses Kummel in detail.

Aquavit is always served ice cold. It is served in one ounce and not sipped but swallowed in one gulp similar to tequila. It is usually consumed neat with food, namely, appetizers such as caviar, smoked salmon or other smoked fish.

15.3 PIMM's

A bartender in a Pimm's restaurant in London's financial district is said to have invented this gin sling over a hundred years ago. It grew so popular that people would take it with them in bulk on their holidays. As time progressed, the supply could not keep up with the demand, and it was not long before the signature Pimm's No. 1 was bottled at 33.5% ABV. It was sweetened and flavoured with herbs, fruits and spices. Pimm's served over ice and chased with soda and a twist of lime is extremely popular and is a great thirst quencher.

15.4 OKOLEHAO

Okolehao, also known as 'oke' in Hawaii islands, is a fermented and distilled beverage made in the Islands of Hawaii. Oke is made from the roots of a local plant called *the Sacred Ti Plant*, whose botanical name is *Cordyline Australis*.

These roots are very high in a type of fructose called levulose. This beverage was first made by William Stevenson, an Australian, in 1790. After fermentation and distillation, Okolehao is not aged, but is filtered through charcoal to remove any odours and flavours. There are two varieties to this beverage, a crystal clear and a golden oke. It is bottled at 40% ABV.

Oke is consumed straight, on the rocks, in tall drinks and in highballs. It is also used to make signature Hawaiian cocktails, such as mohalo (meaning 'thank you' in Hawaiian tongue).

These were the most popular other spirits from around the world. Though they are not as popular as whisky, rum, gin or vodka, these beverages add value to their respective nationalities and local cultures.

LET'S SUMMARIZE IN POINTS

- *Eaux-de-Vies* refers to a spirit that has been made in a particular region or nation due to specific need or an abundance of the food grain or crop.
- Some examples are anise- or liquorice-flavoured spirits, Aquavit/Akuavit, Pimm's and Okolehao.

15.5 FAQs

Short-Answer Type Questions

1. What is an *Eau-de-Vie*?
2. What is Pimm's?
3. Name the inventor of Okolehao.
4. What is *Absinthe*? Briefly explain.
5. Why was *Absinthe* banned?

Long-Answer Type Questions

Write short notes on:

(i) Anise- and liquorice-flavoured spirits
(ii) Pimm's
(iii) Okolehao
(iv) Aquavit

15.6 KEY TERMS

- Aquavit/Akuavit
- Eau-de-Vie
- Elixir
- Okolehao
- Opalscent
- Pimm's
- Ti plant

LIQUEURS

CHAPTER OUTLINE

LET'S DEFINE

'A liqueur is a neutral spirit that has been flavoured with fruit, herbs, nuts, spices and flowers or cream and bottled with added sugar.'

16.1 HISTORY

Making liqueurs can be dated back to the medieval times or even before. The origin of liqueurs, such as most European herb-based spirits was for medicinal purposes. Hence, it is not surprising that monks have been preparing herb-based liqueurs since the 15th century, such as Chartreuse and Benedictine, which are held in high regard even till this day.

While the ancient physicians discovered that nothing much could be done to infuse herbs in wines or beers for medicinal purposes. Hence, they started infusing distilled spirits with herbs and other spices that gave flavour. Liqueurs became a way for physicians, distillers and many others to create the finest beverages in the world.

Today, many liqueur manufacturers have created a benchmark that has been recognized across the worldwide, especially from France and Holland. Other countries have also made their mark, such as

Italy, which produces *Streak* and *Liquore Galliano*; Germany's *Kummel* and so on. In this chapter, we shall discuss the various types of liqueurs along with their countries of origin.

The term *liqueurs* is synonymous with the term *cordials*. The former being used in Europe and the latter in the United States to label their respective products of similar nature.

Liqueurs and cordials are different from other flavoured spirits, as they have to contain at least 2½% sugar by weight. Most liqueurs contain up to 35% of sugar. The sugar used is not necessarily obtained from sugarcane, but from a variety of sources, such as beet, maple, honey or even a combination of these.

16.2 PRODUCTION PROCESS

There are two basic methods for extracting the flavours from the flavouring agents in the production of liqueurs. One is a hot method and the other is a cold method. The method used depends on the nature of the flavouring agent; second, the discretion of the manufacturer to produce the desired end product.

Usually fruit flavours are extracted by the cold method whereas seeds, flowers and peels have their flavours extracted by the hot method. While there is no formula for doing this, to produce a good liqueur, it has to be subjected to several processes and only a well-trained eye can determine which process should be used to extract maximum flavours from each flavouring agent.

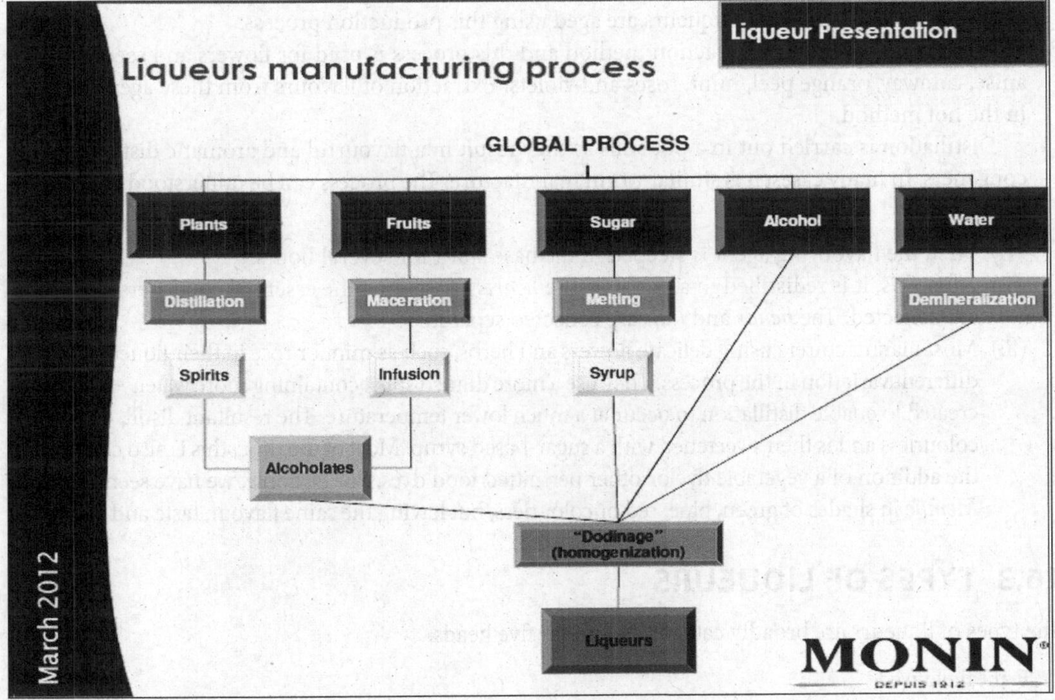

Figure 16.1 Liqueurs Production Process. (*Courtesy:* MONIN Liqueurs, France.)

1. **Infusion or maceration:** Infusion and maceration are both cold extraction methods. Usually, these are followed for flavours that are either sensitive or may spoil on heating. We can understand these two processes better through an example. *Infusion* is when crushed fruits are steeped in water. When the crushed fruits are steeped in alcohol (70% ABV), such as brandy, it is called *maceration*.

   Cold extraction can take even up to a year. Eventually, the water or brandy absorbs the aroma, flavour and colour of the fruit. It is to be noted, when stone fruits (fruits containing seeds) are used, they generally leave bitter oils that account for the almond undertones, which are found in liqueurs made from apricots or cherries.

   After maceration, the liquid is separated from the fruit mass and rested for a few days. The residual pulp is still rich in flavour and alcohol. To prevent wastage, this mass is placed in a still and distilled. This results in a flavourful and aromatic distillate that is mixed with the original maceration giving it more character. This is then sweetened with the desired level of sugar or other sweetening agents in syrup form. The final product is only aged sometimes.
2. **Percolation:** This is another example of cold extraction or brewing similar to making percolated coffee. The flavouring agents are usually herbs and leaves that are placed on the perforated plate at the top of the apparatus. Brandy or other base spirit is pumped from the bottom of the apparatus over the top allowing it to percolate through it, extracting and carrying down the flavour and aroma of the flavouring agent. This pumping and percolation is repeated continuously for weeks or evenly probably months until most of the flavour constituents have been obtained. The spirit-soaked flavouring agent is then distilled and then added back to the percolate. The whole flavourful spirit consisting of the distillate and the percolate is filtered and sweetened with a sugar-based syrup and often bottled at once. Only some herb-based liqueurs are aged using this production process.
3. **Distillation:** This is a hot extraction method and this process is used for flowers and seeds, such as anise, caraway, orange peel, mint, roses and violets. Extraction of flavours from these agents is faster in the hot method.

   Distillation is carried out in a pot stills as they result in a flavourful and aromatic distillate full of congeners. In many cases, it is similar to gin manufacture. The process can be understood by the steps listed below:

   (i) First, the flavouring agent is steeped in the base spirit for several hours.
   (ii) After this, it is redistilled in a pot still. The *hearts* containing the essential congeners and spirits are collected. The *heads* and *tails* are collected separately.
   (iii) Most manufacturers using delicate flowers and herbs, such as mint or rose in their liqueurs follow a different variation in the process. They use a more diluted spirit containing more water. A vacuum is created to enable distillation to occur at a much lower temperature. The resultant distillate is always colourless and is then sweetened with a sugar-based syrup. Most of the time, this is also coloured by the addition of a vegetable dye or other permitted food dyes. For example, we have seen *Crème de Menthe* in shades of green, blue, red or colourless, but having the same flavour, taste and aroma.

16.3 TYPES OF LIQUEURS

The types of liqueurs are broadly categorized under five heads.

1. Fruit flavoured,
2. Nuts/seeds or individual plant based,

3. Herb flavoured,
4. Liquor-based liqueurs, and
5. Cream liqueurs.

Fruit liqueurs get the colour and flavour from one fruit variety. Herb-based liqueurs often require one or more flavouring agents to balance them out. For example, honey is added along with herbs to *Drambuie* to get its distinct taste, flavour and aroma. Herb-based liqueurs are quite complex as sometimes over 50 different ingredients are added to make the distinctive liqueur. These liqueurs are made by monks; hence, they are at times referred to as *Monastery Liqueurs*.

Another distinctive characteristic is observed in cream liqueurs. Originally, it was developed in Ireland where fresh cream was mixed with Irish whisky and then stabilized, so that it did not need refrigeration. *Bailey's Irish Cream* made this type of liqueur world famous. Other famous traditional houses, such as Myers original Rum and Grand Marnier liqueurs have added cream-based liqueurs to their product line.

There are also a range of proprietary liqueurs that can be categorized under any of the above-mentioned heads. They have gained popularity by themselves as individual brands.

16.4 GENERIC LIQUEURS

Listed below are the generic liqueurs, manufactured by many producers under universally used names (Table 16.1). The list contains the names of the liqueurs with their principal flavouring agents. Since each producer uses their own formula, the taste and flavour vary with each brand producing the same type of liqueur.

When he founded his company in 1912, Georges Monin started to create spirits with an innovative and unique taste. Launched in 1920, MONIN Original is one of them, an exclusive lime peel liqueur which belongs to the classic old French signature liqueurs. Years later, he created a specific range for cocktail creators using his perfect knowledge of nature to give his liqueurs access to all the hidden secrets of fruits, flowers and spices. From the 'classic' aromas to the 'exotics', such as Violet or Lychee, MONIN offers 25 colourful flavours to brighten up signature drinks for guests as well as the shelves behind the bar. MONIN is one of the most popular liqueur companies in the world. Today, it has a wide range of generic liqueurs which it produces. Photographs of these liqueurs are displayed along with the appropriate descriptions in Table 16.1.

MONIN original is one of the famous and unique liqueurs in the world. (Courtesy: *MONIN Liqueurs, France.*)

(*Courtesy:* MONIN Liqueurs, France.)

Table 16.1 Generic Liqueurs

Liqueur Name	Base Spirit	Description
Advocat	Brandy	It is a Dutch specialty made in Holland with eggs, sugar and brandy. It is creamy with an eggnog flavour. Preferably, had as a bed-time drink, served with warm milk.
Amaretto	Neutral spirit	An Italian almond flavoured liqueur. The word 'Amaretto' means *slightly bitter* due to its bitter after taste. Served chilled or as a Frappé (on crushed ice) that is highly refreshing.
Anesone	Neural spirit	Anise- or liquorice-flavoured liqueur made in Italy and the United States.
Anisette	Neural spirit	A French sweetened liqueur flavoured with aniseed. It is generally had with chilled water or on the rocks.
Anis	Neural spirit	Spanish spelling of anisette when made in Spain and Latin American countries.
Apricot Liqueur	Neural spirit	Principal flavour is from apricots. Often shipped under a trade name *Apry*.
Blackberry Or Crème de Mure	Neural spirit	As the name suggests it is flavoured with blackberries with an addition of red wine or other fruit essences.
Butterscotch Schnapps	Neutral spirit	A liqueur made from butter and brown sugar and tastes like butterscotch candy.

Liqueur Name	Base Spirit	Description
Cherry Liqueur	Neural spirit	Flavoured with small, black cherries. 
Coconut Liqueur	Rum	Usually using a rum base with a coconut flavour. Often consumed in a cocktail. 
Crème d'Almond	Neural spirit	A pink liqueur flavoured with almonds and fruit stones similar to crème de Noyaux.
Coffee Liqueur	Neural spirit	Sold under many proprietary names. Flavoured with coffee. Used as a flavouring for cocktails and many cold desserts. 
Cranberry Liqueur	Neural spirit	Flavoured with cranberry juice
Crème de Bananes	Neural spirit	Flavoured with banana essence. 
Crème de Cerise	Neural spirit	A French name for cherry liqueur.
Crème de Noyaux	Neural spirit	Flavour obtained from fruit stones resulting in a bitter almond flavour.
Crème de Rose	Neural spirit	Flavoured with rose oil and a hint of vanilla.
Crème de Cassis	Neural spirit	Flavoured with black currant. 

(*Continued*)

Table 16.1 Generic Liqueurs (*Contd.*)

Liqueur Name	Base Spirit	Description
Crème de Cacao	Neural spirit	Flavour obtained from cacao and vanilla beans. The word *Chouao* often seen on these bottles indicates that the Cocoa comes from the *Chouao* region of Venezuela, considered to produce the finest cacao beans in the world. 
Crème de Menthe	Neural spirit	Flavoured with a variety of mint but predominantly pepper mint. As mentioned earlier it comes in various colours, even colourless. 
Crème de Vanille	Neural spirit	Flavoured with the finest Mexican vanilla beans. 
Crème de Violet	Neural spirit	Flavoured with oils extracted from violets and mixed with the essential oils from green oranges from the Island of Curaçao. 
Curaçao	Neural spirit or light rum	One of the most popular orange-flavoured liqueurs due to its sky blue colour. It is flavoured with the famous green oranges from the Island of Curaçao. It is also produced in orange and white colours. 
Ginger Liqueur	Neural spirit	Flavoured with ginger root.
Green Apple	Neutral spirit	Flavoured with green apples. Has a sweet and sour taste. 
Kummel	Neural spirit or vodka	Principally caraway seed flavoured.

Liqueur Name	Base Spirit	Description
Mandarin Liqueur or Orange Curaçao	Neural spirit	Flavour obtained from dried peels of mandarins also called tangerines. 
Maraschino	Neural spirit	Flavour obtained from the special Dalmatian marasca cherries.
Melon Verte or Midori	Neutral spirit	Melon verte is a french name for this green melon flavoured liqueur. Midori is another popular name used to describe it. Modori is a japanses word meaning 'green' referring to its bright green melon color. 
Menthe Verte	Neutral spirit	This is a unique green mint flavoured liqueur. Often used as a substitute for fresh green mint. 
Peach or Peche	Neural spirit	Flavour obtained from fresh and dried peaches. 
Pear Williams	Neural spirit	Made from fresh pears from France and Austria
Peppermint Schnapps	Neural spirit	A mint liqueur, less sweet compared to crème de menthe.
Prunelle	Neural spirit	Flavour obtained from black thorn or sloe plum.
Raspberry	Neural spirit	Flavour obtained from French raspberries 

(*Continued*)

Table 16.1 Generic Liqueurs (*Contd.*)

Liqueur Name	Base Spirit	Description
Rock 'n' rye	Rye Whisky	A rye whisky-based liqueur, including neutral spirit, rock candy syrup and sometimes fruits such as lemons, oranges and cherries.
Sambuca	Neural spirit	Flavoured with liquorice and the elder bush shrubs.
Sloe gin	Neural spirit	Flavour obtained from sloe berry.
Strawberry	Neural spirit	Flavour is obtained from strawberries. Often called crème de framboise.
Triple sec	Neural spirit	A colourless orange flavoured liqueur.
Wishniak	Neural spirit	A wild cherry liqueur from Israel, Russia, Poland and Czechoslovakia.
Watermelon	Neural spirit	A very refershing watermelon flavoured liqueur. Poupularly used in making tropical cocktails.

(Photographs Courtesy: MONIN Liqueurs, France.)

The names discussed here are generic and are used by all the manufacturers. Most of these have created a brand of their own with copyrights. For example, Kahlua is a coffee liqueur but all coffee liqueurs cannot be called Kahlua.

16.5 FAMOUS BRANDS

As we have understood generic liqueurs, we shall proceed to understand the famous liqueurs, their history and unique stories that have made them into household names.

Aurum: It is a liqueur made in the Abruzzi Mountains on the Adriatic Coast of Italy. *Aurum* means gold in Latin and is made from an eight-year-old brandy, bitter oranges, sugar and herbs. The golden colour is due to saffron. It is served like a cognac, not chilled but warmed by hand.

Benedictine: The world famous DOM Benedictine is the oldest liqueur in the world. It is still produced in the same place where the secret formula developed in 1510 AD.

Benedictine is a herbal liqueur produced in France. Its recipe is a well-guarded secret. Some references quote the beverage to contain over 27 different plants and spices on a base of brandy. Dom Bernado Vincelli from Benedictine Abbey of Fecamp, Normandy in France is credited to have invented this elixir. He was a monk who invented this beverage as a comfort drink for his fellow monks who felt unwell. DOM appears on every label and stands for the Latin words *Dio Optimo Maximo*, which means 'To God, Most Good, Most Great'.

Benedictine is produced after undergoing a series of operations, because not at all the flavours are distilled at once. They are distilled separately and then skilfully blended. After blending it is aged for up to four years.

Many producers have tried to make counterfeits but none have come close to making this *one of a kind* liqueur. There is another variation to Benedictine made by the same family-owned firm founded by Alexander le Grand in 1863. It is called B&B liqueur, DOM is a drier version of Benedictine with more brandy in the formula. This was preferred by many consumers, as most of them would add brandy to the original version themselves.

A bottle of Benedictine with DOM label. (Courtesy: *Bacardi International Limited.*)

Chartreuse: Chartreuse is a French liqueur made with alcohol and flavoured with 130 herb extracts. It is the most famous French liqueur made from the secret formula given to Les Pères Chartreux (the Charthusian fathers) of the convent of the Grand Chartreuse at Grenoble, France, in 1605 by the Marechal d' Estrées.

There are claims both by the Monastery and the French Government over the invention of this liqueur. According to tradition, Marshall to the French King Henry IV, Francois Hannibal d' Estrees, presented the Charthusian monks at Vanvert with an alchemical manuscript that contained a *recipe for long life* in 1605. Eventually, it was passed to the religious headquarters in Voiron near Grenoble. It is since then being produced as *Elixir Vegetal de la Grande Chartreuse.*

On the other hand, it is believed that, in 1903, a law was passed against the religious order in France, forcing the Charthusian fathers to leave their country. The clever fathers took their formula to Tarragon Spain and continued with the production. The Spanish bottles had two labels on them; one was the original from France and the second read *Liqueur fabrique a'Tarragon Pas Les Pères Chartreux*. Due to the failure of the French Government to duplicate the formula, the production company was bankrupt in France. Some local businessmen bought almost all the shares that were trading at almost nothing and sent it to the Charthusian fathers as a gift. Regaining control of their company, the fathers returned to France but still illegally. The French Government despite knowing of their whereabouts decided not to prosecute them. Production resumed in 1929. However, in 1935 the original distillery was destroyed with the heavy downpour of rain. The French Government sent soldiers to relocate and rebuild this distillery in Voiron, not the original site on the mountain side but next to the railroads where the distillery had its own store house.

There are two types of Chartreuse—*Yellow* (40–43% ABV) and *Green* (55% ABV) made as per their traditional formula. Both are plant liqueurs having a spicy, aromatic flavour made with a brandy base. The green chartreuse is drier and more flavourful than its yellow counterpart.

Campari: A bitter Italian Aperitif made with a unique blend of herbs and spices with orange being the dominant flavour. Gaspare Campari, in 1860, developed this secret recipe in the town of Novara, Italy, near

Milan. Campari is often served on the rocks or along with soda. One needs to develop a palate to enjoy this iconic brilliant red colour beverage, as it is quite bitter in taste. Famous cocktails, such as Negroni and Americano use this as an ingredient.

Chocolat Suisse: It is a chocolate-flavoured liqueur with square pieces of chocolate floating in the bottle making it a unique Swiss liqueur.

Cointreau: it is a brand of one the best orange-flavoured liqueurs produced in Angers, France. The Cointreau family produces only the orange liqueur under its family name and other flavours are produced under the *Reigner* label. It is preferred by many on the rocks or in frappes.

Danziger Goldwasser: The flavour obtained from orange peel, anise and various other spicy herbs and plants. It contains tiny foils of gold leaf that are harmless to the body. Some even consider consumption of gold leaf improves blood circulation to the vital organs of the body.

Drambuie: The story of Drambuie begins over 265 years ago in July 1746. Prince Charles Edward Stuart (also known as Bonnie Prince Charlie) was on the run, after defeat at the Battle of Culloden had ended his hopes of restoring the Stuarts to the throne of Great Britain.

The prince was pursued by the king's men across the Highlands and Islands of Western Scotland, bravely aided by many Highland Clans. Amongst them was Clan MacKinnon, it was their Chief John MacKinnon, who helped the prince escape to the Isle of Skye. To express the gratitude for his bravery, the prince gave John MacKinnon the secret recipe to his personal liqueur, a gift that the clan were to treasure down the generations. An extraordinary elixir that would, many years later, become known to the world as Drambuie.

In 1873, the recipe was passed on to John Ross of the Broadford Hotel on Skye, who started making it to serve in his hotel. One local person who has tasted it commented in Gaelic that it was 'the drink that satisfies'—*an dram buidheach*—shortened to 'Drambuie'. The name stuck, and in 1893, John's son James registered it as a trademark. Malcolm MacKinnon travelled from Skye to Edinburgh in 1900 to work in the wines and spirits business. He recognized the opportunity that the liqueur offered and in 1909 produced the first commercial bottling for his company MacBeth & Sons. By 1914, he had acquired the recipe and the trademark and established the Drambuie Liqueur Company.

Word began to spread about the Drambuie elixir, and it became the first liqueur to be introduced to the House of Lords in 1916. A year later, Buckingham Palace ordered a case for its cellars. The breakout of the First World War interrupted the rise of Drambuie's popularity commercially; however, it did gain favour amongst many army officers, becoming an officer's mess staple in the Highland regiments.

After the First World War, Drambuie began to exploit new international opportunities. As it gained a foothold in America, prohibition struck. Initially, this was a problem for Drambuie, with supplies no longer legally allowed to enter America. Many distillers and drink producers began to participate in the secretive Sub Rosa campaign, where pirates and smugglers were used to get Scottish spirits into America. In fact, there is a recorded instance of Drambuie being seized by the US Customs officers *en route* from Canada in 1931.

<u>Secret Recipe:</u> The exact recipe for Drambuie has been a closely guarded secret since it was brought to Scotland in 1745. The process by which it is made has remained largely unchanged over the years and remains a secret known only to a few in the company to this day. Herbs, spices and Scottish heather honey are carefully measured and blended by hand to that original recipe.

Drambuie's chief blender then creates the perfect Scotch whisky base. He uses a blend of grain and a selection of the finest Speyside and Highland malt whiskies which, renowned for their softness and smoothness, are the perfect complement to the subtle flavours of the secret elixir. Many of these malts are aged up to 15 years adding real depth to the whisky base.

Finally comes the craft of infusion, as the elixir is married into the whisky base to create the distinctive, complex flavour of Drambuie.

Dambuie. (Courtesy: *Drambuie, UK.*)

From the House of Drambuie: Apart from Drambuie Original which is a signature liqueur, there are other iconic liqueurs produced by the Drambuie Company, all of which have been mentioned below in the following.

Drambuie Original: Drambuie is an extraordinary blend of aged Scotch whisky, heather honey, spices and herbs. It is a unique spirit that offers drinkers an extraordinary taste experience. Drambuie is a bright, deep golden colour, with the aromas of aged malt whisky combined with a mix of floral and herbal overtones and rich honey. The flavour provides a kaleidoscopic taste sensation, a complex arrangement of herbal, spicy, sweet and honey notes. It's voluptuous, mellifluous and full bodied.

Drambuie 15: Drambuie 15 is a whisky connoisseur's expression of Drambuie drawn from the company's finest selection of 15 Year Old Speyside Malts. Selected for their soft complex fragrance and flavour, the rare Speyside Malts ideally complement and balance the herbs and spicy aromas of Drambuie's famed secret recipe.

Drambuie 15 (Courtesy: *Drambuie, U.K.*)

With a nose of Drambuie's aromatic citrus spice, fragrant grass and butterscotch notes, Drambuie 15 has a velvet soft mouthfeel with a tang of lemongrass and warming malty notes, berries and heather. A finish of shortbread, fresh herbs and the unmistakable long afterglow of the Drambuie elixir results in a refined, drier expression, perfect for sipping and savouring either neat or over ice.

Royal Legacy of 1745: Only 3,720 bottles have been produced, each at 46% ABV and signed by our chief blender. At its heart remains the prince's legacy — his secret elixir of exotic herbs and spices sourced from around the globe and unchanged for 260 years.

Today Drambuie's whisky blender has the luxury of hand picking a bespoke selection of Scotland's finest rare-aged malts to complement the elixir's distinctive flavour notes. The art of spirit infusion, perfected by Drambuie over the last century is taken to new heights, with cask infusion and small batch production guaranteeing unique product quality.

The Royal Legacy of 1745. (Courtesy: *Drambuie, U.K.*)

The Jacobite Collection: The Jacobite Collection is the rarest and most valuable member of the House of Drambuie. Only 150 presentation boxes have been released. The collection contains a hand-blown crystal decanter, which holds the rare blend of precious 45-year-old whiskies, infused with Drambuie's secret recipe of herbs and spices, every detail of the design has been created to capture the craft and heritage at the heart of Drambuie.

The Jacobite Collection (Courtesy: *Drambuie, U.K.*)

The solid wood presentation box contains a hand-etched crystal replica of a Spottiswoode 'Amen' glass, with a second large crystal stopper for the decanter. A letter-pressed hand-bound 32-page leather booklet, drafted by whisky writer Ian Buxton, tells the story of the Jacobite rebellion, Drambuie, its antique Jacobite glass collection and the details behind the Collection.

The teardrop lead crystal decanter takes inspiration from a mid-18th century design, with the engraving of the crown motif and intricate decorative scrollwork.

The product contains notes of vanilla, green apples and cut grass, blended with sweet honey and herbal notes, with suggestions of toffee, liquorice, fennel and cardamom. The result is a complex, sophisticated and multi-layered, before a light oaky finish with a gentle herbal glow.

Forbidden Fruit: It is a popular American liqueur made from a type of grape fruit called *Shaddock*, which is steeped in a fine brandy.

Fior d'alpe Isolabella: An Italian liqueur, spicy to taste, bottled with a herb sprig inside it. The liqueur is made with an excess of sugar that crystallizes the herb sprig and obtains its flavours from numerous herbs found in the Alps mountains, such as Wild Marjoram, hyssop, mint and thyme to name a few.

Gilka berliner Kummel: As the name suggests, it is a liqueur made in Germany. For over 100 years, it has been accepted as a new benchmark in making Kummel. The Bols Company takes pride in making this beverage since 1575 calling it 'Bols Kummel'. Highly impressed by the taste of this liqueur, a Russian czar took the recipe back and made Russia the principal manufacture and consumer of Kummel, which is a caraway seed and cumin seed flavoured liqueur. It is usually served with ice-cold water or on the rocks.

Grand Marnier: It is one of the finest Curaçao-based liqueurs and made on a cognac base flavoured with the peels of small, green Curaçao oranges. The peels are sun-dried to concentrate the flavours and are then shipped to France for maceration and distillation.

Irish Mist: A spicy liqueur made with heather honey and Irish whisky from Tulloch Mhor.

Jagermeister: It is a German liqueur made with a secret blend of over 50 herbs, fruits and spices. It is usually served as a shooter and hence gained a very notorious reputation (*e.g.*, The *Jaeger Bomb*). Although the recipe is a secret, some references indicate the use of cinnamon bark from Sri Lanka, orange peels from Australia, sandal from India and ginger roots from southern Asia among the other secret ingredients.

Kahlua: It is one of the world's favourite liqueurs flavoured with coffee. It is made in Mexico. Used in various cocktails, a dessert topping and for flavouring desserts such as Tiramisu.

Liqueur Creole Shrubb: It is produced by the Clement firm in Martinique. It is made from orange peels and rum, which is regarded as a traditional local recipe.

Liqueur Galliano: It was created in the late 1800s and was named after the Italian major Giuseppe Galliano. It is flavoured with herbs and flowers and is a golden, spicy and aromatic liqueur.

Parfait Amour: This means *perfect love* in French. It is a liqueur made with lemons, cloves, cinnamon, coriander seeds and violets. It is best served unmixed.

Pasha: This is a Turkish coffee liqueur.

Peter Heering: One of the finest cherry liqueurs of the world. It is from Copenhagen, Denmark and was formerly known as Cherry Heering.

Sabra: A liqueur made from a blend of Jaffa oranges and chocolate. It is a popular liqueur from Israel.

Southern Comfort: It has showcased the American liqueur making skills to the rest of the world. Legend has it that it was Louis Herron, a bartender in St Louis, who named it 'Southern Comfort', which suited the liqueur well. To a bourbon whisky, peach liqueur and fresh peaches are added. The liqueur and fruit mellow the whisky despite it having an alcoholic strength of 50% ABV.

Southern Comfort liqueur. (Courtesy: *Southern Comfort Properties, Inc.*)

Strega: It is an Italian spicy plant liqueur.

Tia Maria: This rum-based liqueur is a very famous and is made in Jamaica using the finest blue mountain coffee, which is considered one of the best coffees in the world.

Vandermint: it is a chocolate and mint-flavoured liqueur from Holland. It is preferred by many as an after diner drink consumed neat.

Vieille Cure: Is an aromatic plant liqueur blended with cognac and Armagnac and sometimes with brandies of Bordeaux. It is bottled both as a green and as a yellow-coloured liqueur.

The proprietary liqueurs, discussed here, have made their space and have become household names. Some have now become a part of the cultural history of a region and country. Many versions are made by their competitors, but almost none can match up to the original liqueur.

16.6 USING AND SERVING LIQUEURS

There are various ways to serve liqueurs, but each liqueur is consumed in its own unique way. Some of the popular methods of using and serving liqueurs are mentioned as follows:

1. It is served as a natural digest if and hence normally consumed as an after dinner beverage.
2. As flavouring agents for cocktails, due to their rich flavour and sweetness (which cuts the dry after-taste of spirits). In fact, it is considered that a liqueur improves a cocktails smoothness, palatability and texture.
3. Crème de menthe used in France is had in the form of highballs (highball is the name for a category of mixed drinks, composed of an alcoholic spirit base and a larger proportion of a non-alcoholic mixer).
4. Crème de cassis made from blackcurrant is mixed with French Vermouth, soda or even white wine.
5. Liqueurs and syrups are often used as flavouring agents in food. To flavour baked products, ice creams, in making sauces for puddings and other desserts in general.

16.7 SOME INTERESTING FACTS ABOUT LIQUEURS

1. Each liqueur has its own secret recipe.
2. Initially used as a medicinal cure. Due to their flavourful and aromatic qualities, liqueurs are popular drinks on their own or largely used in cocktails, as they do not dilute the alcoholic strength of the cocktail.
3. *Poire Prisonnière*—This is a unique liqueur made from pears grown in Alsace, France. The bottle contains a whole piece of pear. The unique production process starts when the fruit is in the bud stage. The bottles are tied to the tree, enabling the fruit to grow into the bottle. After that, the pear brandy is added into the bottle. The pear brandy is made from a Perry base. Some consider this a brandy, an *Eau-de-Vie* or a liqueur.

LET'S SUMMARIZE IN POINTS

- A liqueur is a neutral spirit that has been flavoured with fruit, herbs, nuts, spices and flowers or cream and bottled with added sugar.
- Production process of liqueurs:
  - Infusion and maceration,
  - Percolation, and
  - Distillation.
- The types of liqueurs are fruit flavoured, nuts/seeds or individual plant based, Herb-flavoured, Liquor-based liqueurs, Cream liqueurs.
- There are generic liqueurs made under various brands but the overall taste and flavour are similar.
- Many liqueur houses have patented and kept their recipes secret; hence, they are the only ones producing their distinct liqueurs. Benedictine and Chartreuse are best examples of this type.

16.8 FAQs

Short-Answer Type Questions

1. Define a liqueur.
2. What is percolation process?
3. What is infusion?
4. What is maceration?
5. What does the term 'Advocat' mean?

Long-Answer Type Questions

1. Explain in detail the liqueur-making process.
2. Explain what are Benedictine and Chartreuse with their history.
3. Name 10 proprietary liqueurs with a detailed explanation.
4. Give the method of using and serving liqueur.
5. Explain the types of liqueurs.

16.9 KEY TERMS

- Adriactic coast
- Gold leaf
- Heather honey
- Infusion
- Licorice
- Maceration
- Monastries
- Percolation
- Propriatary
- Tulloch Mhor

Viticulture and Vine Diseases

CHAPTER OUTLINE

LET'S DEFINE

'Viticulture is the science of cultivating grape vines, especially for the production of wine. It involves the study of the various events that occur in the vineyard. It is a branch of the science of horticulture.'

17.1 HISTORY

The grape vine is a plant that belongs to the genus *Vitis*. The vine plantations originated in Caucasus and the Middle East and spread to Europe evolving into the *Vitis Vinifera* vines that are used today. As a genus, *Vitis* is a plant that has adapted to more global climates than any other. From Russia to the desert regions of California and the temperate coasts to mid-European continental conditions, it has been cultivated successfully. *V. Vinifera* is considered apt for cultivation due to its grapes being more complete and of higher quality for wine making.

17.2 THE VINE

The plant that bears the grape, belongs to the botanical family of *Vitaceae*, the most important of them is *V. Vinifera*—from which is made more than 99% of the wine produced in the world—and whose origins are from Europe and Central Eastern Asia.

V. Vinifera is not the only species used for the production of wine. The other most common species suitable for the production of wine are *Vitis. Labrusca*, *Vitis Riparia* and *Vitis Rotundifolia*, all originating from the American continent. These species as opposed to *V. Vinifera* are resistant to the attacks of the devastating phylloxera. Hence, the plants of *V. Vinifera* are grafted on rootstocks of the American species—in particular *V. Riparia*—in order to contrast the devastating effects of this parasite.

17.3 THE VINEYARD

The term *terroir* refers to a group of vineyards (or even vines) from the same region, belonging to a specific appellation and sharing the same type of soil, weather conditions, grapes and wine making savoir-faire, which contribute to give its specific personality to the wine.

Site Selection

Other than the susceptibility of the vine to disease, there are other factors important while selecting a site for cultivating the grape vine. The factors can be described as follows:

1. **Soils:** To support plant growth, soils must contain water, air and nutrients. The soil should be well drained as under high rainfall conditions; poorly drained soils become waterlogged and can lead to

Grover Vineyards on the outer city limits of Bengaluru, India. (Courtesy: *Grover Vineyards Private Limited.*)

rapid plant death. The ideal soil for any perennial crop is a well-drained sandy loam with a well-drained sandy clay sub-soil located 18′–24′below the surface.

Grape vines can be cultivated in rocky soils, but the rock must be well fractured in order to allow for root penetration. Rocky sites should be well explored with appropriate equipment to determine soil depth. Sites with less than 3 feet of soil above bedrock should be avoided.

2. **Air drainage:** Air drainage involves selecting a site that is topographically higher than surrounding areas, which is an important factor and plays an important role in avoiding damage from spring frosts. Cold air is denser than warm air, it settles to low-lying areas, thereby damaging the crop. As warm air rises to the top, a vineyard located on higher slopes is less susceptible to spring frosts.
3. **Layout of the vineyard:** Aligning rows to run parallel with the prevailing wind during the growing season has several advantages. The benefits of aligning rows are as follows:
   (i) With a full canopy of leaves, a trellis will encounter tremendous stress from wind during late spring and summer storms and may help in preventing trellis wire breakage.
   (ii) Improved airflow through the vineyard reduces canopy-drying time after a rain and will reduce pressure from fungal diseases.
   (iii) Row orientation eases equipment operation. It takes far less time to transverse a vineyard with long rows as opposed to making many more row-end turns with short rows.
4. **Row spacing:** The distance between rows is a decision reached largely on the equipment available to a grower. In the east, rows have been traditionally spaced 9 feet apart, but in the west, ten-foot rows are a common practice. The growth patterns of a particular variety are imparted by a rootstock and soil type, which will impact vine size. In shallow soils, vines are typically placed more closely together than on deep alluvial soils. The following formula is used to determine the number of vines needed for a new site.

Row width × Distance between vines = x. 43,560 (square feet/acre) divided by x, is equal to the number of vines needed per acre.

Example: Rows 9 feet. apart, 8 feet. between vines. 9 × 8 = 72. 43,560/72 = 605 vines per acre.

A vineyard plantation at Grover Vineyards, Bengaluru, Karnataka, India. (Courtesy: *Grover Vineyards, Bengaluru*)

Site Preparation

Ideally, a site should be cleared from trees and brush 2–3 years before vines are planted. Perennial weed growth should be controlled by disking the field twice, prior to planting the grape vines a non-selective contact herbicide, such as glyphosate should then be applied twice during vine cultivation. A fall cover crop, such as annual rye grass or oats is commonly recommended to prevent soil erosion and to provide a source of additional organic matter to the new vineyard site.

1. **Irrigation:** Availability of high-quality irrigation water is essential. Ponds can be used, but a large, deep pond will be required to hold enough water for any length of time.

   In most cases, wells are used to provide supplemental irrigation in vineyards. As a rule, a well capacity of 5 gallons/min per planted acre is sufficient to supply ample water to mature vines. Drip irrigation systems are normally used to supply supplemental water in a commercial vineyard.
2. **Choosing varieties and rootstocks:** Before a vineyard is planted, prospective growers should have plans for how the grapes they grow will be utilized. If a winery is included in plans for the vineyard, extensive market research should be done to determine the line of products that will be offered at that facility.

   Grape varieties are categorized as either susceptible or tolerant to Pierce's disease. In sites where Pierce's disease is probable, growers may opt to plant tolerant varieties. As a general rule, the demand of tolerant varieties, such as 'Blanc du Bois' and 'Lenoir' is considerably less than for susceptible *vinifera* varieties and consequently revenues for the production of these varieties will be lower.
3. **Planting the vineyard:** New growers should consider a small planting in the first year to have a better idea on the amount of labour and materials that will be needed for a larger planting. It may be wise for prospective growers to plan on planting on a large scale over a period of years.
4. **Grape vine nutrition:** Maintaining a nutritional balance in the vineyard is essential to proper vine growth, productivity and optimal fruit quality. Soil sampling helps in understanding soil pH and initial nutritional needs and nutritional limitations. Elements such as potassium and phosphorus should be applied to a new site prior to planting. As vines mature, petiole (leaf stem) analysis is very helpful in predicting the vine requirements and needed fertilizer inputs.

A Cabernet Sauvignon grape variety being grown on a vine, which is just above the ground, allowing the warmth of the soil to build up grape sugars in the grape faster.

5. **Crop load management:** In order to remain a profitable enterprise, vineyards should be guided towards producing an average yield of 3.5–5.0 tons/acre. Notions that low yields necessarily constitute higher fruit quality should be dispelled. In other grape growing regions of the world, law prescribes sustainable grape yields.

17.4 GRAPE COMPOSITION

The Grape

The grape comprises of four parts, which are stalk, skin, pips and pulp (Figure 17.1).

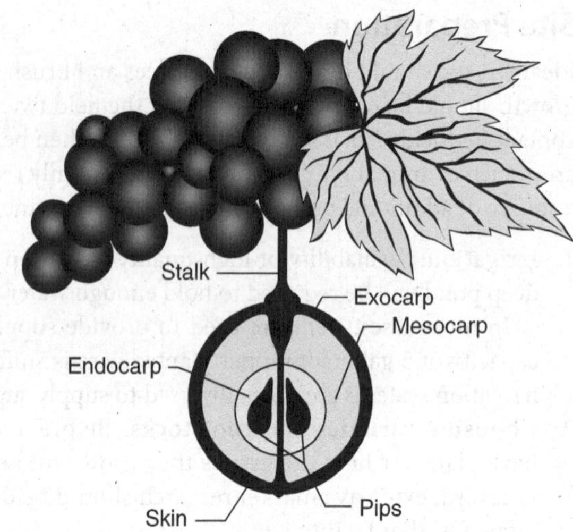

Figure 17.1 Image displaying the grape diagram.

The *stalk* is woody portion of the grape that connects the fruit to the vine. It is full of a substance called tannin, which is a preservative with a bitter flavour.

The *skin* covers the fruit and its function is to dust away wild yeasts and bacteria. The skin contains more tannin and, in black grapes, a colouring pigment.

The *pips* are the seeds of the grape. They contain bitter oils and are not desirable in production of white wine.

The *pulp* is the most important part of the grape while producing wine. Over 70% of the pulp is just water, but the remaining 30% contains most of the elements, including fruit sugars and acids, trace elements absorbed from the earth and pectin (a gelling agent). These elements give wine character, flavour and interest.

The juice of almost all grapes is pale in colour. White wines can be made from any colour of grapes. If black grapes are used in white wine production, the skins of the grape must be separated from the juice immediately after pressing and before the fermentation stage, so that no colour is picked up from the skins. Some examples of white wine made from black grapes are Champagne, Blanc de Noirs and white Zinfandel. All red wines extract their colour only from the skins of black grapes. Red wines, therefore, can only be made from black/red grapes.

17.5 GRAPE VARIETIES

At least seven varieties—Cabernet, Pinot Noir, Riesling, Sauvignon Blanc, Chardonnay, Gewürztraminer and Muscat—have tastes and smells distinct and memorable enough to form international categories of wine. Merlot, Syrah, Sémillon, Chenin Blanc, Pinots Blanc and Gris, Sylvaner, Nebbiolo, Sangiovese, Tempranillo also have distinct aromas. The following sections describe the white grape varieties and red grape varieties (Tables 17.1 and 17.2).

Red grapes (right) and white grapes (left) grown at Grover Vineyards, Bengaluru, India. (Courtesy: *Grover Vineyards Pvt. Ltd.*)

White Grape Varieties

Table 17.1 White Grape Varieties

Grape Variety	Description—Tasting Notes
Albarino	The Spanish name for Portugal's Alvarinho, emerging as excellently fresh and fragrant wine in Galicia.
Aligoté	Burgundy's second rank white grape. Crisp (often sharp) wine, needs drinking in 1–3 years. Perfect for mixing with cassis (blackcurrant liqueur) to make a *Kir*. Widely planted in Eastern Europe, especially Russia.
Arinto	White central Portuguese grape for crisp, fragrant dry white.
Blanc Fuméé	Also known as of Sauvignon Blanc, referring to its reputedly 'smoky' smell, particularly from the Loire (Sancerre and Pouilly). In California it is used for oak-aged Sauvignon and reversed to 'Fumé Blanc'. However, the smoke is from oak.
Bual	Makes top-quality sweet Madeira wines.
Chardonnay (Chard)	The white burgundy grape, or Champagne grape, and the best white grape of the New World. Partly because it is one of the easiest to grow and *vinify*. All regions are trying it, mostly aged in oak to reproduce the flavours of burgundy. Australia and California make classics. Those of Italy, Spain, New Zealand, South Africa, New York State, Chile, Hungary and the Midi are all coming on strong. It is called Morillon in Austria.
Chasselas	A prolific early-ripening grape with little aroma, mainly grown for eating. Best known as Fendant in Switzerland (where it is supreme), Gutedel in Germany.
Chenin Blanc	Great white grape of the middle Loire (Vouvray, Layon etc.). Wine can be dry or sweet (or very sweet), but always retains plenty of acidity, hence its long life and use in California, where it can make fine wine, but is rarely so used (*See also* Steen).
Clairette	A low-acid grape formerly widely used in the South of France as a vermouth base.
Colombard	Slightly fruity, nicely sharp grape, hugely popular in California, now gaining ground in South West France, South Africa and California etc.
Fendant	*See* Chasselas.
Folle Blanc	High acid/little flavour make this ideal for brandy. Called Gross plant in Brittany, Picpoul in Armagnac. Respectable in California.
Fumé Blanc	*See* Blanc Fumé.
Furmint	A grape of great character: the trade mark of Hungary both as the principal grape in Tokay and as vivid vigorous table wine with an apple flavour. Called Sipon in Slovenia. Some also grown in Austria.
Gewürztraminer [Also known as traminer (Gewürz)]	One of the most pungent grapes, distinctively spicy with aroma like rose petals and grapefruit. Wines are often rich and soft, even when fully dry. Best in Alsace; also good in Germany, Eastern Europe, Australia, California, Pacific North West and New Zealand.

(Continued)

Table 17.1 White Grape Varieties (*Contd.*)

Grape Variety	Description—Tasting Notes
Grauburgunder	*See* Pinot Gris.
Grechetto or Greco	Ancient grape of central and South Italy: vitality and style.
Grüner Veltliner	Austria's favourite (planted in almost half her vineyards). Around Vienna and in the Wachau and Wienviertel (also in Moravia) it can be delicious: light but dry and lively. The best age five years or so.
Italian Riesling	Grown in Northern Italy and Eastern Europe. Much inferior to Rhine Riesling with lower acidity, best in sweet wines. It is also known as *Welschriesling*, *Olaszrizling* (no longer legally labeled simply 'Riesling').
Kéknyelü	Low-yielding, flavourful grape giving one of Hungary's best whites. Has the potential for fieriness and spice. To be watched.
Kerner	The most successful of many recent German varieties, mostly made by crossing Riesling and Sylvaner, but in this case Riesling is crossed with a red variety, Trollinger. Early ripening and a flowery wine with good acidity. Popular in Pflaz, Rheinhessen etc.
Loureiro	The best and most fragrant Vinho Verde variety in Portugal.
Macabeo	The workhouse white grape of N Spain, widespread in Rioja (also known as Viura) and in Catalan cava country.
Malvasia	Known as Malmsey in Madeira, Malvasia in Italy, and Malvoisie in France. It is also known as Vermentino (especially in Corsica). It is also grown in Greece, Spain, Australia and Europe. It makes rich brown wines or soft whites, ageing magnificently with superb potential not often realized.
Marsanne	Principal white grapes (with Roussanne) of the Northern Rhone (e.g., used in Hermitage, St-Joseph, St-Péray). Also good in Australia, California. Soft full wines that age very well.
Müller-Thurgau (Müller-T)	Dominant in Germany's Rheinhessen and Pfalz and too common on the Mosel; a cross between Riesling and Sylvaner varieties. Ripens early to make soft aromatic wines for drinking young. Makes good sweet wines but usually dull, often coarse, dry ones.
Muscadelle	Adds aroma to many white Bordeaux, especially Sauternes.
Muscadet, also known as melon de Bourgogne	Makes light, very dry wines with a sea side tang round Nantes in Brittany. They should not be sharp, but faintly salty and very refreshing.
Muscat	It has many varieties but the best is Muscat Blanc à petits Granis. Universally grown, easily recognized, pungent grapes, mostly made into perfumed sweet wines, often fortified (as in France's *Vinsdoux Naturels*). Superb in Australia. Rarely made dry (e.g., Alsace).
Palomino	Makes all the best sherry but poor table wine.

Table 17.1 White Grape Varieties (*Contd.*)

Grape Variety	Description—Tasting Notes
Pedro Ximenez, also known as PX	Makes very strong fortified wines. Used in blending sweet sherries. Also grown in Argentina, the Canaries, Australia, California and South Africa.
Pinot Blanc	A cousin of Pinot noir variety and is not related to Chardonnay, but with a similar, milder character, light, fresh, fruity, not aromatic, not to be drunk young. For example, Good for Italian Spumanté. Grown in Alsace, North Italy, Southern Germany and Europe.
Pinot Gris	At best makes rather heavy, even 'thick', full bodied whites with a certain spicy style. Known (formerly) as Tokay in Alsace; Ruländer (sweet) or Grauburgunder (dry) in Germany; Tocai or Pinot Grigio in Italy and Slovenia but makes a much thinner wine.
Riesling	Germany's great grape, and at present the world's most under-rated. Wine of brilliant sweet and acid balance, either dry or sweet, flowery in youth but maturing to subtle oily scents and flavours. Unlike Chardonnay, it does not need high alcohol for character. Very good (usually dry) in Alsace (but absurdly nowhere else in France), Austria, Australia (widely grown), Pacific NW, Ontario, California, South Africa. Often called White-Johannisberg or Rhine-Riesling. Subject to *Nobel Rot*.
Ruländer	German name for pinot gris used for sweeter wines.
Sauvignon Blanc	Makes very distinctive aromatic grassy—gooseberry—sometimes rank – smelling wines; best in Sancerre. Blended with Semillon in Bordeaux. Can be austere or buxom. Pungent success in New Zealand, now planted everywhere. Also called Fumé Blanc or vice versa.
Scheurebe	Spicy-flavoured German Riesling crossed with Sylvaner, very successful in Pfalz, especially for Auslese. Can be weedy in dry wines.
Sémillon	Contributes the lusciousness to Sauternes; subject to 'noble rot' in the right conditions but increasingly important for Graves and dry white Bordeaux too. Grassy if not fully ripe, but can make soft dry wine of great aging potential. Formerly called 'Riesling' in part of Australia. Old Hunter Valley can be great wine.
Sercial	Makes the driest Madeira.
Cheval Blanc	French—made hybrid of French and American vines. Very hard and attractively fruity. Popular and reasonably successful in eastern states and England but banned by EC from 'quality' wines.
Steen	South Africa's most popular white grape: good lively fruity wine said to be the Chenin Blanc of the Loire.

(*Continued*)

Table 17.1 White Grape Varieties (*Contd.*)

Grape Variety	Description—Tasting Notes
Silvaner, also known as Sylvaner	Germany's former workhouse grape: wine rarely fine except in Franken where it is savoury and ages admirably, and in Rheinhessen and Pflaz, where it is enjoying a renaissance. Good in the Italian Tyrol and useful in Alsace. Very good as 'Johannisberg' in the Valais, Switzerland.
Tokay	*See* Pinot Gris. Also a table grape in California and supposedly a Hungarian grape.
Traminer	*See* Gewürztraminer.
Trebbiano	Important but mediocre grape of central Italy, used in Orvieto, Chianti, Soave etc. Also grown in France as Ugni Blanc, and Cognac as St Emilion. Mostly thin, neutral wine; really need blending.
Ugni Blanc	*See* Trebbiano.
Verdejo	The grape of Rueda in Castile, potentially fine and long lived.
Verdelho	Madeira grape making excellent medium sweet-wine; an Australia, fresh soft dry wine of great character.
Verdicchio	Gives its name to good dry wine in central-eastern Italy.
Vermentino vernaccia	Grape grown in central and Southern Italy and Sardinia for strong smooth lively wine, sometimes inclining towards sherry.
Viognier	Rare grape of the Rhone, grown at Condrieu for very fine fragrant wine. Much in vogue in the Midi, California etc., but still only a trickle. It is gaining in prominence in New World Wine market.
Weissburgunder	*See* Pinot Blanc.
Welschriesling	*See* Italian Riesling.

Red Grape Varieties

Table 17.2 Red Grape Varieties

Grape Variety	Description—Tasting Notes
Aleatico	Dark Muscut variety, also known as Aglianico, used the length of Western Italy for fragrant sweet wines.
Baga	The standard red of Bairrada in central Portugal. Dark, tannic and potentially very good.
Barbera	Most popular of many productive grapes of Northern Italy, especially Piedmont, giving dark, fruity, often sharp wine. Gaining prestige in California.
Brunello	South Tuscan form of Sangiovese, splendid at Montalcino.

Table 17.2 Red Grape Varieties (*Contd.*)

Grape Variety	Description—Tasting Notes
Cabernet Franc (also known as Bouchet)	The lesser of two sorts of Cab grown in Bordeaux but dominant (as *Bouchet*) in St-Emilion. The Cabernet of the Loire, making Chinon, Saumur etc., and rosé.
Cabernet Sauvignon	Grape of great character: spicy, herby, tannic, with characteristic 'blackcurrant' aroma. The first grape of the Médoc; also make most of the best Californian and Eastern Europe reds. Vies with Shiraz in Australia. Its wine almost always needs ageing; usually benefiting from blending with Merlot, Cabernet Franc and Syrah. It makes very aromatic rosé.
Cannonau	Grenache in its Sardinian manifestation; can be very fine, potent.
Carignan	By far the most common grape of France, covering thousands of acres. Prolific which dull but harmless wine. Best from old vines in Corbiéres. Also common in Africa, Spain and California.
Cinsaut	Common bulk-producing grape of France; in South Africa crossed with Pinot Noir to make Pinotage. Pale wine, but quality potential.
Dolcetto	Source of soft seductive dry red in Piedmont. Now high fashion (though low budget).
Gamay	The Beaujolais grape: light, very fragrant wines, at their best young. Makes even lighter wine on the Loire slopes, in central France, and in Switzerland and Savoie. Known as 'Napa Gamay' in California.
Gamay Beaujolais	Not Gamay, but a poor variety of Pinot Noir in California.
Grenache (also known as Garnacha, Alicante, Cannonau)	Useful grape for strong fruity but pale wine: good rosé and *Vin Doux Naturel*. Especially in Southern France, Spain, California. Old-vine versions are currently prized in Southern Australia. Usually blended, for example, used in *Chateauneuf-du-Pape*.
Grignolino	Makes one of the good everyday table wines of Piedmont.
Kadarka, also known as Gamza	Makes healthy, sound, agreeable reds in Hungary, Bulgaria etc.
Kékfrankos	Hungarian Blaufränkisch, said to be related to Gamay and producing similar light red wines.
Lambrusco	Productive grape of the lower Po Valley, giving quintessentially Italian, cheerful sweet and fizzy red.
Malbec (also known as Cot)	Minor in Bordeaux, major in Cahors (also known as Auxerrois) and especially Argentina. Dark, dense and tannic, capable of making a real-quality wine.
Merlot	Adaptable grape making the great fragrant and plumy wines of Pomerol and St-Emilion, an important element in Médoc reds. Soft and strong (and à la mode) in California, Washington, a useful adjunct in Australia, lighter but often good in Northern Italy, Switzerland, Slovenia, Argentina etc.

(*Continued*)

Table 17.2 Red Grape Varieties (*Contd.*)

Grape Variety	Description—Tasting Notes
Montepulciano	Confusingly, a major central-eastern Italian grape of high quality, as well as a town in Tuscany.
Mourvédre, also known as Mataro	Excellent dark aromatic tannic grape used mainly for blending in Provence and the Midi. Enjoying new interest in Southern Australia, California.
Nebbiolo, also known as Spanna and Chiavennasca	One of the Italy's best red grapes; makes Barolo, Barbaresco, Gattinara, Valtellina. Intense, nobly fruity and perfumed wine but very tannic, taking years to mature.
Perquita	Ubiquitous in Portugal for firm-flavoured reds. Often blended with Cabernet Sauvignon and also known as *Castelao Frances*.
Petit Verdot	Excellent but awkward Médoc grape now largely superseded.
Pinot Noir	The glory of Burgundy's Côte d'Or, white scent, flavour and texture unmatched anywhere. Less happy elsewhere; makes light wines rarely of much distinction in Germany, Switzerland, Austria and Hungary. The great challenge to California and Australia and South Africa. Shows exciting promise in California's Carneros and Central Coast, Oregon, Ontario, Yarra Valley, Adelaide Hills, Tasmania and New Zealand.
Pinotage	Singular South African grape Pinot Noir crossed with Cinsaut (Pinotage). Can be very fruity and age interestingly.
Saint-Laurent	Dark, smooth and full-flavoured Austrian specialty. Also a little in the Pfalz.
Sangiovese (Sangiovento)	The main red grape of Chianti and much of central Italy. *Brunello* is the Sangiovese-Grosso.
Saperavi	Makes good sharp very long-lived wine in Georgia, Ukraine etc. blends very well with Cabernet.
Spätburgunder	German for Pinot Noir, but a very pale shadow of burgundy.
Syrah or Petite Sirah, also known as Shiraz	The great Rhône red grape, giving tannic purple peppery wine which can mature superbly. Very important as Shiraz in Australia, increasingly successful in the Midi, South Africa and California. Has a growing fan club.
Tannet	Raspberry-perfumed, highly tannic force behind Madiran, Tursan and other firm structured reds from southwest France. Also for rosé.
Tempranillo	The pale aromatic fine Rioja grape, called Ull de Lebre in Catalonia, Cencibel in La Mancha. Early ripening.
Touriga Nacional	Top port and Douro grape, travelling further afield in Portugal for full-bodied reds.
Zinfandel	Fruity adaptable grape peculiar to California with blackberry like and sometimes metallic flavour. Can be gloriously lush, but also makes 'blush' white wine.

17.6 GRAPE VINE DISEASES

The major diseases that attack grape vines are described in Table 17.3.

Table 17.3 Grape Vine Diseases

Diseases	Description
Pierce's Disease	Pierce's disease (PD) is caused by a xylem-limited bacterium that clogs the vascular tissue of susceptible grape cultivars. The causal organism is a gram-positive, rod-shaped bacterium named *Xylella Fastidiosa*, which is indigenous to the Gulf Coast region of the United States. The grape strain does not appear to infect peach and the peach strain does not appear to cause symptoms in grape. Grape vines become infected when a sharpshooter that carries the bacterium feeds on tender tissue. Once a susceptible cultivar is infected, there is no known, approved method of treating the infection and the disease will most probably be fatal to the vine. Cultivars vary in the length of time it takes the pathogen to cause vine death. Tolerant cultivars appear to have internal mechanisms of suppressing bacterial numbers to the point that the vine can live and be productive even in the presence of the bacteria. Hence, removal of wild grape vines is imperative to disease management.
Black Rot 	A fungal disease of American origin that was spread to the Old World through the phylloxera resistant rootstock. Brown circular lesions appear on infected leaves and within a few days, black fruiting bodies are formed within the lesions. These leaf lesions then become the primary source of infection to developing fruit clusters. Infected berries shrivel, turn hard and black and are called mummies. Spring rains trigger the release of airborne aeciospores from mummies and subsequent infection of susceptible tissue takes place if temperature and duration of leaf wetness are conducive. Pycnidia form within lesions and produce pycnidiospores that are spread by rainfall. Leaf lesions are capable of producing spores and causing secondary infection approximately 5–7 days after they first appear. Control of black rot is based on properly timed applications of fungicides.

(*Continued*)

Table 17.3 Grape Vine Diseases (*Contd.*)

Diseases	Description
Powdery Mildew 	Powdery mildew (*Uncinula necator*) can infect all green tissue of the grape vine. Cluster infection at or shortly after bloom can lead to a reduction in set or cause berry damage leading to cracked, damaged fruit at harvest. Infection of the foliage can cause a reduction in vine growth, fruit yield and quality and a reduction in winter hardiness. Sulphur is an integral part of the powdery mildew control programme, use of this product is suggested in late spring and for post-harvest applications.
Downy Mildew 	Infection in the canopy can lead to premature defoliation and fruit or rachis infection can cause crop loss. Again, control of downy mildew is focused on the early to mid-season use of preventative fungicides. Downy mildew (*Plasmopara Viticola)* has a complicated life cycle, but inoculums come from previously infected leaves that overwinter on the ground. Extended leaf wetness during dark conditions is needed for primary infection that can result in unnoticeable subtle foliage lesions. Greatest pressure usually comes about with extended rainy periods in late spring or early summer. Again all green portions of the vine are susceptible to infection.
Phylloxera 	Grape phylloxera commonly just called, is a pest of commercial grape vines worldwide, originally native to eastern North America. These tiny, pale yellow sap-sucking insects, related to aphids, feed on the roots of grape vines. In *Vitis vinifera*, the resulting deformations ('nodosities' and 'tuberosities') and secondary fungal infections can girdle roots, gradually cutting off the flow of nutrients and water to the vine. Nymphs also form protective galls on the undersides of grape vine leaves and overwinter under the bark or on the vine roots; these leaf galls are not found on vines grown in California.

Table 17.3 Grape Vine Diseases (*Contd.*)

Diseases	Description
Botrytis Bunch Rot 	Many fungal and bacterial organisms, of which *Botrytis cinerea* is the most important, can infect grapes and result a bunch to rot. Wet weather favours infection and disease development, especially near harvest when canopies are dense and berries accumulate sugar. The fungus can quickly spread from berry-to-berry within ripening bunches and can develop readily on wounded or split berries. 'Cabernet Sauvignon' is the least susceptible wine grape grown in Oregon. 'Gewürztraminer' is less susceptible than 'Chardonnay', 'Pinot noir', and 'Riesling'. Bunches that are more tight or compact are at higher risk of the disease. Under certain environmental conditions, white grapes infected solely by *B. cinerea* may result in a special rot known as noble rot. These grapes are used to produce a very sweet wine. Young shoots and leaves may be infected in spring and develop brown, water-soaked areas. These areas generally girdle the shoot, causing it to wilt and die back rotted berries appear in late summer. The berry skin may slip off easily when rubbed. Characteristic tufts of grey fungal growth appear on the surface of infected berries.

17.7 WINE TASTING

1. Tasting wine is all about taking the time to think about what you are drinking.
2. A few minutes focus on a wine—to look at it, smell it and then taste it, enable you to experience all of its nuances and enjoy the complexity of wine entirely.
3. The process of wine tasting involves three important activities.
4. They are the logical ways of approaching a wine: by sight, smell and taste.

Wine tasting at Grover Vineyards by wine expert Michel Rolland. (Courtesy: *Grover Vineyards, Bengaluru.*)

1. **Look (observe)—in the glass:**
   (i) An opportunity to assess the colour, texture, age and flavour of the wine.
   (ii) Look at the wine in your glass over a piece of paper or clean white table cloth to classify your wine as red/rose or white according to its colour. Moreover, study whether the wine is clear or cloudy.

2. **Smell—on the nose:** By smelling the wine in the glass, you can unravel the layers of flavour in the wine. Sniff the wine once or twice then swirl the one in the glass and sniff again. You will notice the release of aromas. The aromas indicate the character of the wine. The aromas may be as follows:
   (i) *Fruit Aromas:* Can indicate certain grape varieties. Sauvignon Blanc smells like gooseberry; Cabernet Sauvignon can give blackcurrant aromas.
   (ii) *Floral Aromas:* Can indicate certain grape varieties such as Gewürztraminer (roses) or Riesling.
   (iii) *Spicy Aromas:* Can indicate oak with vanilla, cinnamon and pepper.
   (iv) *Vegetal Aromas:* Can indicate the age and grape varieties, such as Pinot Noir, which has whiff of cabbage.
3. **Taste—on the palate:** Draw the wine in to your mouth. Roll it around the mouth and all over the tongue to get the feel of the wine. Draw some air to pass over the taste buds to find the real taste of the wine that you are drinking. The wine may indicate the following:
   (i) *Sweetness:* dry, medium or sweet.
   (ii) *Fruit character:* fruity, spicy, floral and vegetal.
   (iii) *Body:* light, medium or full.
   (iv) *Others:* tannins, acidity, oak.
4. **Tasting tips:**
   (i) Make sure that the wine is at the right temperature. If it is too warm or too cold your perceptions of its flavours may be altered.
   (ii) Make sure that you use uncut, clear glass, so that you can see the wine clearly.
   (iii) Swirl your glass to release the aroma of the wine before you smell it.
   (iv) Taste the wine before you consume any food to get an untainted perception of its flavours.
   (v) Start a tasting diary of wine you have enjoyed.
   (vi) Extend your perception of smells by taking note of the smells around you.

LET'S SUMMARIZE IN POINTS

- Viticulture is the science of cultivating grape vines, especially for the production of wine. It involves the study of the various events that occur in the vineyard. It is a branch of the science of horticulture.
- The grape vine is a plant that belongs to *Vitis* genus. The vine plantations originated in Caucasus and the Middle East and spread to Europe evolving into the *Vitis Vinifera.*
- Site selection involves—selecting the right soil, air drainage, layout and row spacing.
- Site preparation involves—Irrigation, choosing the right grape variety, Planting the vineyard, nutrition and crop load management.
- The grape comprises of stalk, skin, pulp and pips.
- Each grape variety has its unique characteristic quality.
- Vine diseases have been known to affect vineyards not only in a specific regions but also countries and continents.
- Wine is supposed to be observed, nosed and then tasted.

17.8 FAQs

Short-Answer Type Questions

1. Define viticulture.
2. Write a short note on the history of viticulture.
3. Give the factors involved in site selection.
4. What are the factors involved in site preparation?
5. Name five white grape varieties, red grape varieties and five vine diseases.

Long-Answer Type Questions

1. Give details on 10 red grape varieties.
2. Write a detailed note on:
   (i) Site selection
   (ii) Site preparation
3. Write a note on five vine diseases.
4. Give the detailed note on wine tasting.
5. Give a detailed note on 10 white grape varieties.

17.9 KEY TERMS

- Noble Rot
- Phylloxera
- Swirling the glass
- Terroir
- *Vitis Vinifera*

18 FRENCH WINES

CHAPTER OUTLINE

France is a country that showcases the best quality of fashion, merchandise and gastronomy and exports this to the world.

It is the foundation of the culinary industry giving us the classical courses from caviar, smoked salmon and the best cheese of the world. However, the best wines of the world are from France and this country is ranked the best in wine production.

France is a leading exporter and importer of wine. It is considered the world leader not only in terms of quantity of wine produced, but also the superior quality of wine. It is divided politically into 95 states that are further divided into communes or parishes, which are also called counties. Some of the states produce the most famous wines of the world, such as Gironde (red and white Bordeaux), the Côte d'Or (red or white Burgundy) and Marne (Champagne), which are the most famous. The other important states are Youne (producing Chablis), Bas-Rhine and Haut Rhine (Alsace wines), Rhône Beaujolais and other famous wines, such as Côte Rotie, Hermitage and Château-Neuf-du-Pape). The Saone-et-Loire (producing Pouilly-Fuissé and Macon) and others along the Loire River (which produce going from east to west, Pouilly-Fumé, Vouvry, Saumir, Anjon and Muscadet).

18.1 MAKING OF WINE—RED, WHITE AND ROSÉ

Let us follow the steps illustrated in Figure 18.1 to get a clear understanding on how wine is made in France.

Harvesting

The period between end of September and early October is the harvest season in France. During this time, the 'Vendangeurs' or 'Vintagers', who are men, women and sometimes children under the supervision of a foreman, identify the ripe and sound grapes to make the finest quality of wine. A well-planned and well-executed harvest will ensure the grapes reach the winery in its prime condition. This is easily achievable at a smaller scale; however, with large vineyards, the efficiency of the 'Vendageurs' plays a vital role in making a good wine.

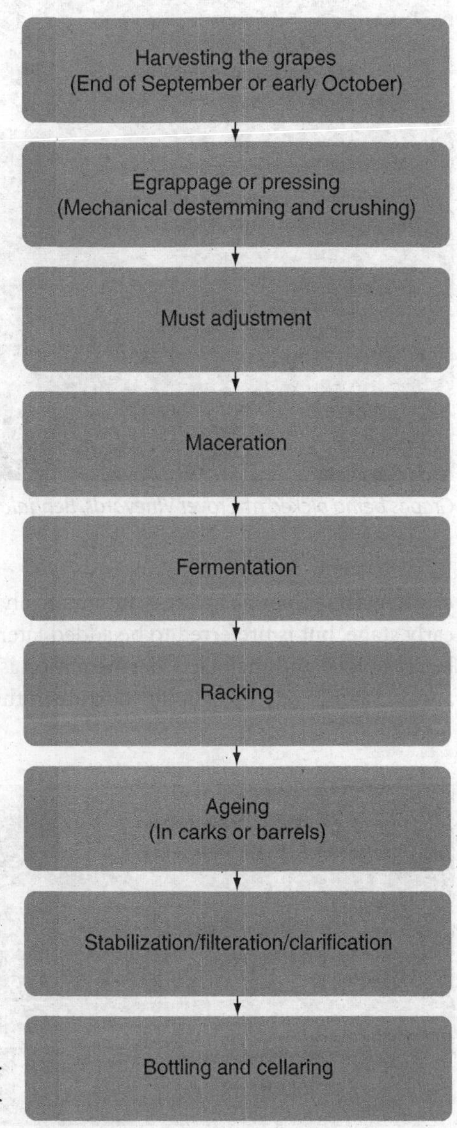

Figure 18.1 The Wine-making Process—Red, White and Rosé.

Egrappage

Egrappage refers to the steps where the grapes are passed through a mechanical device for de-stemming and crushing. Crushing is done to break the skin, so that the juices will run out freely. The skin is the protective layer; once cracked, it exposes the juice for the yeast to act and begin fermentation. Some wine makers destalk and crush the grapes manually.

Pressing and Stomping

Other than crushing the grapes, some wine makers use pressing as one option to extract the juice. The third method is wine stomping, which is an old-fashioned way of extracting the juice from the grapes. In this process, the grapes are pressed manually by foot. In France, the harvest season is often celebration and now this procedure of stomping by bare feet, which is called 'Special Boots', is now just a tradition and not practiced to make wine, as it is highly labour intensive.

Must Adjustment

After the grapes are crushed, modern manufacturers often check a few parameters before starting fermentation. The following are a few additives that are essential to create a well-balanced wine.

1. **Sulphur dioxide:** This helps to control the growth of wild yeasts. It also helps to reduce the oxidations of the must, juice or wine. Large wineries have a sulphur dioxide (SO_2) container and a pump mounted on the

Grapes being picked at Grover Vineyards, Bengaluru. (Courtesy: *Grover Vineyards Pvt Ltd.*)

crusher. The sulphur dioxide is automatically added when the grapes are going through the crusher in the early stage, but is preferred to be added later in the wine-making cycle. They believe white wine retains better colour and malolactic fermentation is easier to complete without sulphur dioxide. However, it is always safer to add the sulphur dioxide in the initial stage.

Grapes-being destemmed manually (left) and grapes being crushed at a winery (right). (Courtesy: *Grover Vineyards Pvt Ltd.*)

2. **Yeast nutrients:** Yeast requires nitrogen, oxygen, vitamins, minerals and other materials to produce new cells. Some grape varieties lack to meet the needs of the yeast, such as Chardonnay, which is difficult to ferment naturally. In such cases, yeast nutrients are essential, but excessive quantities of this could produce undesirable odour in the wine.
3. **Acid:** Tartaric, malic and citric acids are present in the grapes and other organic acids in the wine. Where a wine is high or low on acids, it can be out of balance. Because of this, wine makers add tartaric acid before fermentation, to balance the wine.
4. **Sugar addition:** This process of adding extra grape sugar (fructose) to the must when it is low on sugar is called 'chaptalization'. This is done so that after fermentation, the desired quantity of alcoholic strength is achieved in the wine. Thus, these are the various parameters that are checked and balanced, if required to produce a balanced wine.

Wine being aged in barrels at grover vineyards, Bengaluru. (photograph courtesy-grover vineyards: Bengaluru).

Maceration (Vital Step to Differentiate Red/White and Rosé Wines)

The wine-making process differs from this step, to make either red, white or rosé wines. The grape juice, which is now called 'must', is colourless. The colour in red wine is imparted by the inner layer of the red skin. The juice does not extract the pigments directly, but the fermentation process that renders alcohol and heat dissolves the pigments in the skin, to make a red wine.

Maceration is the process in which the grape skins and pips (seeds) are left in the must and fermented. This process is done to give the wine the red colour, body and tannin. Tannins are complex compounds that give stability and longevity to the wine.

If this is done for a day, the must gains a pinkish colour to it. If the skins are separated from the must at this time, they make rosé wines. While white wines are made by drawing off the free run juice immediately after crushing, not exposing it to the skins and pips. White wines can be made from both red and white grapes, but red wines have to be made using red grapes.

Fermentation

Fermentation takes place in a closed stainless steel vat to avoid oxidation of the wine leading to spoilage. The wine yeast *Saccharomyces* is naturally present on the skin but most winemakers use a cultured yeast from propagated strains to import a unique character to their wine. Due to the high levels of sugar, fermentation begins almost immediately. The vat of the fermenting liquid begins to bubble, most often referred to a 'boiling'. This boiling effect is due to the carbon dioxide, which is produced as the yeast acts on the sugar to produce alcohol. The fermentation process is completed when the wine reaches an alcoholic strength of 14% ABV as the yeast then dies. Sometimes there is sugar that is left and is called,

DID YOU KNOW

Yeast reproduces rapidly in the presence of oxygen, often doubling in an hour. This initial rapid growth is called exponential growth phase, leading to an enormous yeast population of approximately 10 million cells/ml of juice within 24 hours. In the presence of oxygen, yeast multiplies rapidly but produces very little ethyl alcohol. However, with little oxygen, the yeast reproduces slower but produces more alcohol. Hence, most wine manufacturers prefer to have oxygen released initially for the yeast to multiply and then control the oxygen to convert the grape sugars to alcohol in a more dependable way.

'residual sugar', creating some sweet dessert wines, such as sauternes. Fermentation process takes about 7–10 days for red wines and 15–18 days for white wines, as it is done at a lower temperature to retain the fruity characteristics of the grape.

Racking

The first racking is done soon after fermentation. Racking is the process in which the wine is allowed to rest as the sediments or larger particles settle to the base of the container. Next, the sediments called, 'the lees' are drawn off and collected separately. This procedure results in a wine, which is clear in appearance. This procedure is often done three to four times, depending on the discretion of the winemaker.

Ageing

The 'racked' wine is put into clean 'sulphured barriques' of 225 ltr. capacity and placed in the cellar for ageing. During the first few months due to evaporation, there will be a loss of leaving 'air space' (called ullage) into which bacteria are prone to penetrate and make the precious wine into vinegar. To prevent this from happening, the wine in the casks is topped up, twice a week during first two months and twice a month subsequently. This ageing process also results in settling of the remaining sediments, primarily compressing of cream of tartar, dead yeast cells, colouring and other proteins collectively known as 'lees'. As it is not good for a new wine to remain in contact with the lees for long, it is racked. 'Racking' is done three times in a year, namely, in March or April, second in June when the vin flowers and then in October. As the wine matures, it breathes through the pores of the wooden cask and its development continues. When the wines are left in the cask, they undergo 'malolactic fermentation', which is when the malic acid is converted into a softer lactic acid.

Wine being aged in barrels at Grover Vineyards, Bengaluru. (Photograph Courtesy: Grover Vineyards Bengaluru.)

Stabilization/Filtration and Clarification

After ageing, the wine, especially red wine, needs to be clear and free of sediments or floating particles. Most winemakers prefer not to filter their wines, fearing that it would lose its characteristics. However, many use clarification by adding various clarifying agents to the wine. The clarifying agents used in a wine are also referred to as fining agents.

Vinegar bacteria (*Acetobacter* spp.) are found in the vineyard, on the grapes, in the cellar, on the equipment, in the wood of used wine barrels and in the wine. *Acetobacter spp*. are the bugs that convert the precious wine into acetic acid (vinegar). Sometimes very small amount of acetic acid in a red wine makes a positive contribution to the aroma, but when acetic acid exceeds 0.04%, it adds an unfavourable burning after-taste, which decreases the wine quality. In a warm cellar and with sufficient presence of air, acidification can progress rapidly and fine wine can be spoilt in a short time. Along with the acetic acid, vinegar bacteria also produce ethyl acetate, which has a strong aromatic smell like finger nail polish remover. This odour is easily identified and a smallest hint of ethyl acetate suggests wine spoilage.

1. The process is done by first taking a small amount of albuminous material that maybe gelatin, isinglass, egg white or egg albumen and mixed with a small quantity of wine and poured into the cask.
2. The albuminous matter coagulates the solids in the wine, forming a heavy film and slowly settling at the bottom of the cask. It leaves a bright and clear wine that is ready to be bottled.
3. The fining process is usually done twice and takes up to four weeks to complete. After this, it is filtered to ensure clarity before bottling.

Before we move on to the next process, let us understand the characteristics of the various clarifying agents in detail.

Clarifying Agents

The characteristics, preparation and use of several common wine-fining materials are outlined as follows. These materials are inexpensive and easy for home winemakers to use. The characteristics and use of several wine-fining materials are shown in Table 18.1.

Table 18.1 Characteristics and Use of Wine-fining Materials

Material	Purpose	Typical Dose
AAA Carbon	To remove odours (H2S)	1 g/gal
AAA Carbon	To completely strip wine for blending	4 g/gal
KB Carbon	To remove unwanted colour	1/2 g/gal
Bentonite	To remove protein from white wine	2 g/gal
Bentonite	To general clarification	1 g/gal
Casein	To remove browning	1/4 g/gal
Casein	To remove bitter taste	1/2 g/gal
Casein	To remove excess oak	1/2 g/gal

(*Continued*)

Table 18.1 Characteristics and Use of Wine-fining Materials (*Contd.*)

Material	Purpose	Typical Dose
Gelatin	To reduce tannin in red wine	1/2 g/gal
Gelatin	To clarify white wine	1/8 g/gal
Gelatin	To remove bitter taste in white wine	1/4 g/gal
Egg whites	To reduce tannin in red wine	1 to 6 eggs per barrel
Egg whites	To clarify red wine	1/2 to 2 eggs per barrel
PVPP	To remove browning	1/2 g/gal
PVPP	To remove excess colour	3/4 g/gal
PVPP	To remove oxidized taste	1/2 g/gal
PVPP	To remove bitter taste	1/2 g/gal
Sparkolloid	To clarify white wine	1/2 g/gal
Sparkolloid	As topping over bentonite	1/4 g/gal

Albumin (Egg White)

Egg whites are often used to reduce astringency by removing small quantities of phenolic materials from red wines. They have been used to fine French Burgundy and Bordeaux wines for hundreds of years, and this inexpensive protein material is still used for fining high-quality red wines. Egg whites are also used to 'polish' or clarify red wines to give added brilliance. They should not be used to clarify cloudy wines. They are not beneficial when used in cloudy wines, and excessive protein can cause additional problems.

The whites from one to four eggs are the usual quantities used for a barrel (60 gallons) of wine. This is roughly equivalent to 1/2–2 ml of egg albumin/gallon of wine. A small pinch of table salt should be added to a cup or so of warm water. The egg white should be separated from the yoke carefully. One part egg white should be mixed with two parts salt water. The mixture should be stirred thoroughly before being added to the wine, but the mixture should not be beaten to a stiff froth. Add the egg white mixture to the wine slowly and stir continuously. The wine should be racked in a week or so.

Bentonite

Bentonite is an extremely fine, clay-like material. It has a negative electrical charge and it is used to remove positively charged particles from wine. It is most commonly used to remove excess protein from both white and blush wines. It is also used for clarification fining of white and blush wines and is sometimes effective in clearing hazy fruit wines.

A normal dose is 1–2 g of dry bentonite/gallon of wine. However, it is often used at dose levels that range from 1/2 to 4 g/gallon. Bentonite can strip desirable aromas from wine when used in excessive amounts (more than 2 g/gallon), so bench testing should always be done. It should be mixed with water and allowed to stand for 24 hours before being added to the wine.

Bentonite can be mixed easily in a blender. Put the required amount of hot water in the blender, turn the blender on and slowly add the dry powder. When the mixture is cool, place it in a refrigerator and allow it to hydrate for at least 24 hours. Add the hydrated mixture to the wine slowly and stir continuously. Bentonite is a popular fining material, but it has a major disadvantage. It produces large quantities of lees, which are light and fluffy. Wine is difficult to rack off the bentonite lees, since they are so light.

Carbon (Charcoal)

Carbon is a fine, black and lightweight powder used to remove unwanted colour and odours from wine. Although a common commercial fining material, finely ground carbon is difficult to handle since it flies easily. This material can be extremely dirty and sometimes home winemakers have difficulty obtaining carbons in small quantities because of the handling problem.

Casein

'A half pint of skimmed milk to five gallons of wine' is a traditional fining treatment for white wine. Milk contains casein, which is still a popular fining material for white and blush wines. Casein is a protein and is used to remove phenolic materials including tannin, excessive oak character and some bitter flavours from wine.

Gelatin

Gelatin is a popular protein-fining material and is often used to reduce the bitterness and astringency of red wines. It removes a quantity of tannin roughly equal to its own weight. Sometimes, white wines have a slightly bitter finish and this bitterness can be reduced by fining with a small quantity of gelatin. Gelatins are also used to clarify white and blush wines and Kieselsol is used to precipitate any excess gelatin residue.

Isinglass

Isinglass is a protein material made from the air bladders of Sturgeon fish. The commercial, granular form of isinglass is called 'Biofine,' which is much easier to use than the dried, sheet material. Isinglass is used to clarify quality white wines. Some winemakers feel this material can improve wine flavours and aromas. Small quantities of isinglass are often added to sparkling wines to help the riddling process.

Typical doses of isinglass range from 0.05 to 0.3 g of dry isinglass/gallon of wine. A nominal dose for white table wines is about 0.1 g/gallon of wine. Make a solution by dissolving isinglass in a small quantity of low-pH wine. Use about 100 ml of wine for each gram of granular isinglass and stir this solution into the wine thoroughly.

Kieselsol

Kieselsol is a heavy, liquid silica colloid. Nalco 1072 is the material that is most often used in the U.S. wine industry. The material reacts with protein in the wine and precipitates out quickly. Kieselsol is sometimes used to remove excess protein material from white and blush wines.

Centrifuging is very costly; however, as the particles of all sizes can be removed this way, it easily replaces several rackings in winery operations and it can make clarification simpler. It involves spinning the wine in a vessel at such a high speed that the particles migrate to the bottom of the vessel and are easily separated from the clear wine. It also enables the winemakers to combine fining and clarifying in a single step.

Mechanized bottling at a winery—the wine is sealed immediately, after which the label and excise duty stamp stickers are put on the bottle.

Bottling and Cellaring

After filtration and fining, the clear and bright wine is ready to be bottled and corked. Most wine manufacturers prefer using glass bottles and corks made of oak wood, as this is porous and allows the wine to 'breathe', a necessary step helping the wine to mature. After the cask is opened and its contents bottled, the wine takes time to settle. Much like any of us, who take time to settle down in a new place or job and get accustomed after some time, the wine too is initially not accustomed to change of environment from the cask to the bottle and this period, in wine trade, is referred to as 'bottle sickness'. It usually takes several months for the wine to adapt itself, slowly developing with time to its prime. However, a wine varies in its shelf life, as per its vintage. Less successful vintages reach their peak in 5–10 years, while the better vintages can take up to 30–40 years to reach their prime. A wine should be consumed and if left unconsumed, there are chances that the wine may die, having lost its colour, bouquet, body and flavour making it completely lifeless. Normally, an older wine will have a greater amount of residual deposit in the bottle and it will be more delicate. The sediment does not affect the quality of the wine but it proves the age of the wine.

Thus, we have understood in detail the various steps involved in making a quality wine from France.

18.2 WINE LAWS—APPELLATION CONTRÔLÉE

Wine production in France can be dated back to the Roman occupation; however, only in the 1930s, the France government brought about the regulatory wine laws to maintain quality checks and maintain authenticity and standards in wine production.

The 'Champagne Wars' (in 1911) lead to the first delimitative laws to be established, as the vignerous who were making their wines from grapes exclusively grown in the Champagne region revolted against certain merchants who imported their grapes at a lower price from a neighbouring region and sold them a cut cheaper. This revolt resulted in laws that clearly fixed the boundaries for the sparkling wine to be made from grapes grown only in the Champagne region for them to be legally entitled to the name 'Champagne'.

Since then, the laws have fixed the geographical boundaries for each wine- or brandy-producing region. The laws have gone a step further to set physical limits of the world famous vineyard to the maximum quantity of quality wine; it can produce of a given vintage year. This setting of a quantity assures the maintenance of the quality standards of the wine produced in that vineyard.

Under this law called 'Appellation of d'Origin Contrôlée' (A.O.C), the production of each vineyard is controlled. This government body controls wine production from the grass root level, *i.e.,* the vineyards report to the local authorities who in turn report to the central command located in Paris. The wines that are produced under this system carry on the bottle's label a phrase—*Appellation of d'Origin Contrôlée,* which is the French government's guarantee of origin and quality. There are various critical quality control measures defined by an official body called the *Institute National des Appellation of d'Origin des Vines et Eaux-du-Vie* (I.N.A.O) whose members belong to either the French civil service or the French wine industry.

The Controls of A.O.C

There are various controls established by this esteemed body. Some of the points pertaining to district boundaries are according to the following characteristics:

1. Nature of soil.
2. Grape varieties.
3. Maximum quantity of wine/acre allowed to be produced.
4. Minimum alcohol content of the wine.
5. Viticulture methods.
6. Vinfication practices and methods followed.

Growers must follow all the regulations if they wish to label their wines with the name of the vineyard, the commune or the district. Technicians exercise controls to enforce these regulations. Due to these regulations, an A.O.C-certified wine is considered the best quality wine of not only France but also one of the finest on earth. The origins of the wines are directly proportionate to the stringency of the regulations.

Some wines bear a label with the letters V.D.Q.S, which stands for '*Vins Délimités de Qualité Supérieure*'. This is the second highest grading of a wine in France from a special region. The regulations are similar to A.O.C specifications that these wines have been harvested from strictly defined vineyards following traditional methods.

V.D.Q.S wines are grouped into seven general places, where reds, whites and rosés are produced. The other sub-categories of the wines in France are '*Vine des Pays*' and '*Vin des Table*'. These are not regulations or wine laws but generally refer to domestic wines and table wines, respectively.

Each wine produced in a particular region of France is unique and often attempts are made to imitate these iconic wines from their respective vineyards by most wine-producing countries. Thus, to understand French wines in detail, it is important to understand each geographical sub-region separately and in detail.

Now, we shall discuss each region as per their importance and impact on the wine industry.

Regions of France

The regions of France are illustrated in Figure 18.2; some of the important regions are discussed in the following sections.

Figure 18.2 Regions of France. (*Courtesy*: allfranceinfo .com)

18.3 BORDEUAX

Bordeaux district (Gironde) comes first to mind in reference to French wines. Bordeaux is famous for producing the great red wines of France. This region is credited with making three distinct varieties of wines namely Clarets, clean and dry Graves and golden Sauternes.

History of Bordeuax

History of wine is as old as humans themselves; the first mention of these marvellous wines dates back to 50 BC. At the time, Bordeaux (known as Burdigala) was the chief town commercial centre. Later in the fourth century, it became the capital of Aquitanica Secunda. It was as famous then as it is now, and praised by Columella, a famous Roman writer of the first century.

Later in 1152, Henry of Anjou acquired the Sénéchassée of Bordeaux by marrying Eleanor of Aquitaine. Two years later, he became King Henry II of England and for 300 years Gascony belonged to the English crown. This is the reason why Bordeaux wines are still so popular on the British Isles.

A famous poet sang about the charms and virtues of the claret produced in Bordeaux during the Roman times. It is believed to have been made in the famous vineyard of Château Ausone.

LET'S DEFINE

Claret: A claret is the term that the Britishers use to describe a red wine from the Bordeaux. 'Claret' is not a legal term in France, but understood and even used due to the importance of Britain as an important export market for France.

Soil Conditions of Bordeuax

Bordeaux wine region has soil mainly consisting of gravel, limestone or sand with clay subsoil. A more agriculturally poor soil is difficult to find, but surprisingly this type of soil conditions are most favourable for the grape vine to flourish. This soil conditions are not only favourable for the grape varieties grown in Bordeaux but also for all other varieties grown in all famous viticultural regions of the world.

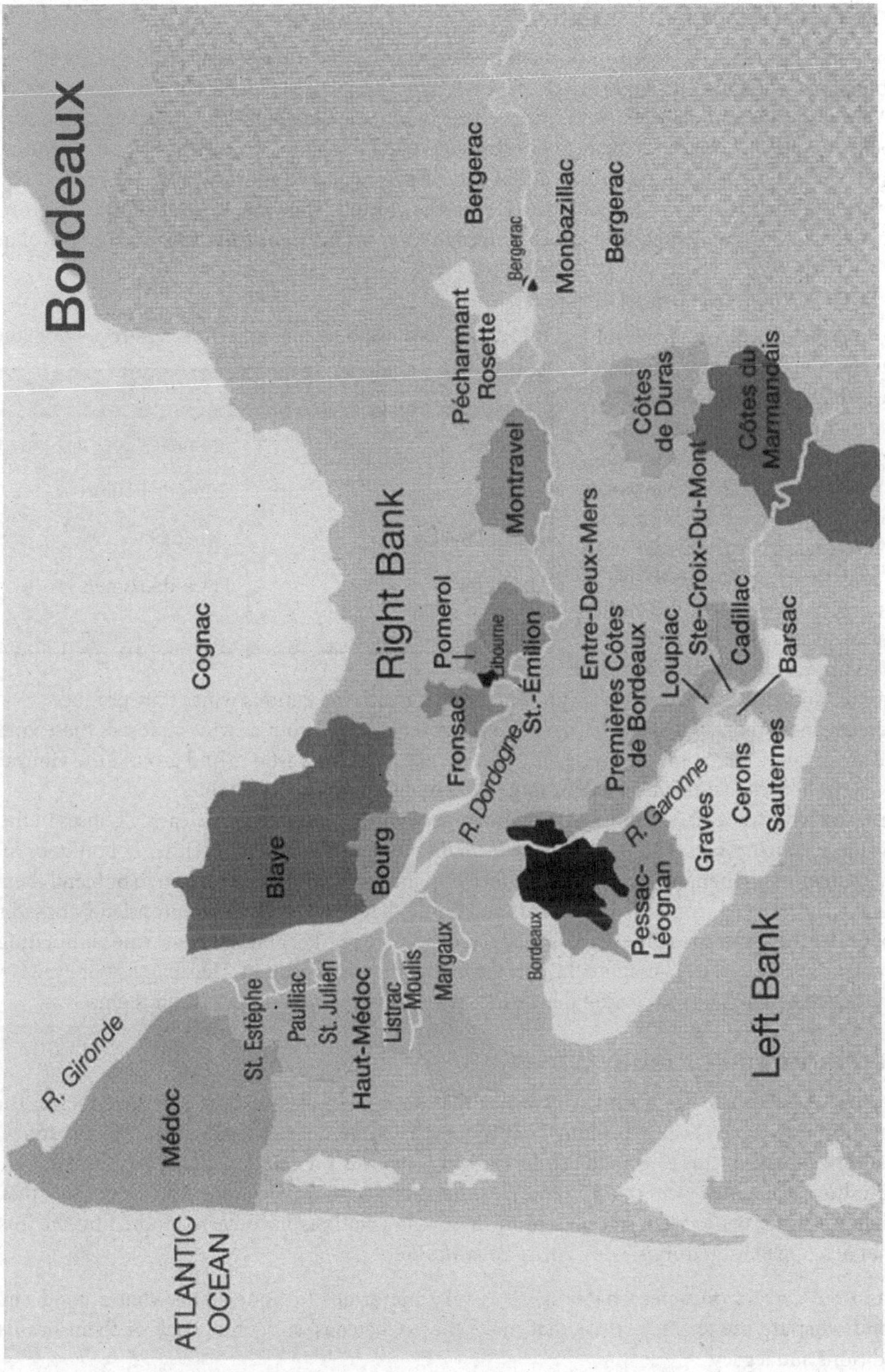

Bordeaux
ATLANTIC OCEAN
R. Gironde
Médoc
St. Estèphe
Pauillac
St. Julien
Haut-Médoc
Listrac
Moulis
Margaux
Blaye
Bourg
Cognac
Right Bank
R. Dordogne
Fronsac
Pomerol
Libourne
St.-Émilion
Montravel
Pécharmant
Rosette
Bergerac
Bergerac
Monbazillac
Bergerac
Côtes de Duras
Côtes du Marmandais
Entre-Deux-Mers
Premières Côtes de Bordeaux
Loupiac
Ste-Croix-Du-Mont
Cadillac
Barsac
Sauternes
Cerons
Graves
R. Garonne
Pessac-Léognan
Bordeaux
Left Bank

Grape Varieties of Bordeuax

The principle grape variety used to produce the famous Clarets from Médoc and grapes sub-regions is Cabernet Sauvignon. The other grape varieties that compliment Cabernet Sauvignon are Merlot, Petit Verdoh and Carmenére. However, in Pomerol and Saint Emilion, the principle grape variety is Merlot. As Grave and Sauternes make good white wines, it is essential to note that they use Sémillon and Sauvignon Blanc grapes. It is to be noted that the vine is cultivated in Bordeaux and pruned regularly to prevent it from growing wild, keeping it close to the ground. The vines are not allowed to grow more than two to three feet in height, to channel to strength derived from the soil to produce grapes of quality.

Sub-regions of Bordeuax

Bordeaux is divided into five main sub-regions and four other lesser significant regions, which are listed in Table 18.2.

Table 18.2 Main Sub-regions and Other Sub-regions of Bordeuax

Main Sub-regions	Other Sub-regions
Médoc	Premières Côte de Bordeaux
Graves	Côtes de Bourg
Saint-Emillon	Côte de Blay
Pomerol	Entre-deux-mers
Sauternes	

Before the state of France started managing the affairs of wine making, almost all the administrative works to overlook and supervise wine production were done by the local Parish Priest and the church. The Parish is the geographical, political and earlier a religious subdivision of the land.

Let us understand from Table 18.3 the features and characteristics of the sub-regions along with the famous wines they produce.

There are more than 30,000 vineyards in Bordeaux region that produce wines. Most of these vineyards are called Château, which means castle, but they do not have any castle in and around the vineyard but are just farm houses that maybe small or large, which make and store the wine.

Bordeaux wine trade has established itself many generations ago, evolving clearing houses in the form of wine merchants/brokers who buy the wine from different vineyard owners either in bottles or in casks for larger quantities. Then, these merchants either ship the wines as they receive them or blend them with the wines they received from other vineyards and bottle them under their own proprietary brand name, but not under the Château's name. If all the vineyards were to market and sell their wine eliminating their wine merchants, we can well imagine the confusion that it would result in. Hence, most vineyard owners rely on the wine merchants to market their wine and only very few vineyards do it themselves.

Understanding Bordeuax Wines

The region of Bordeaux has a set list of wines that have been classified as per their merit. The first classification was done at an exposium in 1855. At that time, 57 red wines from Médoc and 1 from Graves were chosen in this esteemed list. In 1955, this list was revised and 12 Clarets were added from Saint Emilion, 2 of which were rated 'A' and the other 10 rated 'B'. In 1959, the list was revised; this time, 13 red and 8 white wines were selected. Both these classifications have been adopted by the 'Institute National des Appellation d'orgine des *Vinset Eaux-de-Vie*'.

1. **Classified clarets (famous Châteaus):** It is very important to understand what a good vineyard is and what are the characteristics that make these Chateaus' so iconic. Each of them has its own traditions and legacy.

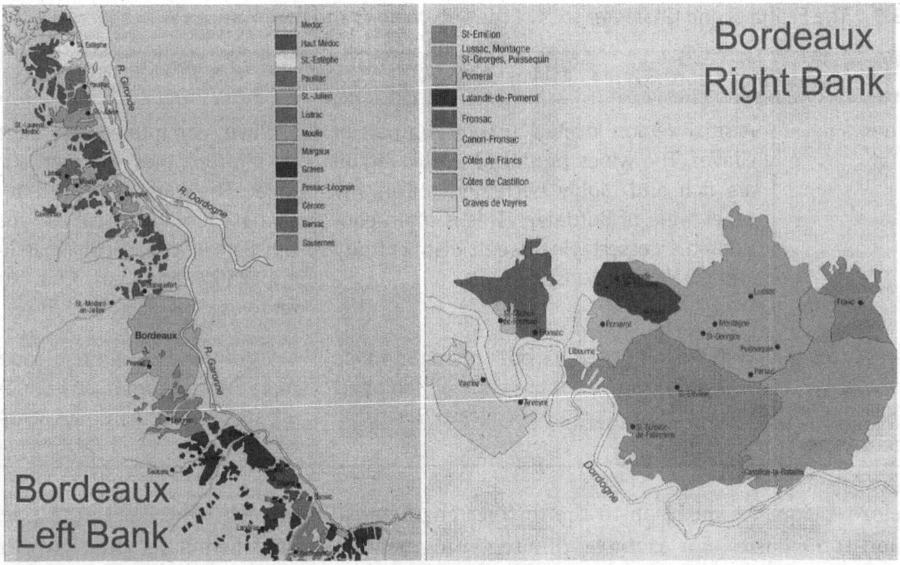

Bordeaux Region, France. (Courtesy: *allfranceinfo.com*)

Table 18.3 The Features and Characteristics of the Sub-regions and their Famous Wines

Sub-region	Features of the Region	Famous Wine Communes
Médoc	It is the most important district in Bordeaux that lies between the Gironde River on the east and the Atlantic Ocean on the west and is divided into Médoc and Haut-Médoc.	It is famous for red wine produced in its 53 communes. Four most important communes are Pauillac, Saint Julien, Margaux and Saint Estéphe, which are all located in Haut-Médoc.
Graves	Due to the pebbly and gravel soil this region has, it is called Graves. This sub-region is in the southwest part of Bordeaux. Most of it being plains, but a bit hilly toward the south. These are fuller-bodied and not as delicate as Médoc wines. These wines make up with their richness, where Médocsshowcase their finesse.	Most important wine communes are Pessac, Léognan and Martillac. Best examples being Château La Mission, Haut Brion, Pape Clêment, Haut Bailly, Bouscaut, Smith-Haut-Lafitte and Domaine de Chevalier.
Saint Emilion and Pomerol	Saint Emilion and Pomerol are in the eastern part of the Bordeaux and north of the Dordogne River around the town of Lilborne. The main grape being used is Merlot, which produces wines that are fruity and scented and mature earlier than Médoc wines. Famous wines produced from Pomerol are Petit-village, La Fleur Petrus, Nenin and Tratanoy, and famous wines produced from Saint-Emillion are Château Figeac, Canon, Pavie and Clos Fourtet.	Pomerol is a single commune located northwest of Saint-Emillion, which is famous for many vineyards despite being small geographically.

(*Continued*)

Table 18.3 The Features and Characteristics of the Sub-regions and their Famous Wines (*Contd.*)

Sub-region	Features of the Region	Famous Wine Communes
Sauternes	A small region located in southern part of Graves. The wines produced in this region are rich and highly perfumed unlike any other wine of Bordeaux. This is often considered a dessert wine due its distinct fruity and floral characteristics.	Its five communes are Sauternes, Barsac, Bommes, Fargues and Preignac. The wines produced from any of these regions are called Sauternes, but Barsac in particular has its own appellation and many Châteaus prefer to use this instead.
Premières Côte de Bordeaux, Bourg, Blaye, and Entre-deux-mers	These regions produce both good red wines and white wines, but are generally shipped as a Bordeaux Blancs or Bordeaux Rouge.	Most of these wines are blended into more famous commercial wines. Only a fraction of small Châteaus make it on their own.

Therefore, before we move on to the distinct characteristics of each wine label, it is essential to understand some basics. For example, differentiating between a classified claret (first growth) and a *cru bourgeois* (second growth) is easy; however, differentiating between a second and a third growths is very difficult.

Most of the classified 61 vineyards produce excellent wines differing only in certain bouquets (nose), body and the flavours apparent only to a connoisseur, but go unnoticed to a layperson. However, certain wines are just different and are quite distinct. For example, the wines of *Pauillac (Médoc), Château Lafite Rothchild, Château Latour, Château Mouton Rothchild* have more body as compared to wines from *Margaux*, such as *Château Margaux* that have finesse and delicacy, while the red wines of the Graves namely *Château Haut Brion* and *Château La Mission Haut Brion* are fuller than the *Médoc* wines mentioned. The fruitiest wines of this region are from Pomerol—*Château Petrusand* from Saint Emilion—*Château Ausone* and *Château cheval Blanc.*

Most of the basic regions and their most famous wines have been mentioned above, but understanding each classic first-growth wine is essential, which are listed in Table 18.4.

Table 18.4 Classic First-growth Wines Along with the Description

Château	Description
Château Lafite Rothchild	It is one of the most famous wine-producing houses in the world. It belonged to a gentleman known as Jean de Lafite; however, in 1868, Baron James de Rothchild acquired it at an auction for 165,000 pounds. Till today, the firm is owned by his heirs. In a good year, the wine has a deep colour, a soft and delicacy of flavour and a violet bouquet.
Château Margaux	The wines of this region are fully fragrant with a wonderful bouquet, full bodied and elegant. A limited quantity of wine is produced in this vineyard from Sémillion and Sauvignon Blanc grapes labelled Pavillon Blanc du Château Margaux. It has a very great history and has been exchanged by many hands. Today, a widow, named Madame André Mentzelopoulos, of a financier owns it.

Table 18.4 Classic First-growth Wines Along with the Description (*Contd.*)

Château	Description
Château Latour	The wine made from this region is a first-growth wine named after an ancient tower. Legends suggest that this is the last remains of the castle of Saint-Lambert, after which the English were driven out of Gascony. The English tales refer to a vast fortune left behind near the tower. Many searched below the ground but as we know, the real fortune was not under, but above the ground. *'Château Latour'* wines have more body and pronounced flavour than Château Lafite or Château Margaux.
Château Mouton Rothchild	The wine made from this region is a marvellous wine, which was classified as a second-growth wine; however, after a lot of effort from its owner Baron Philippe Rothchild, in 1973, this wine was and still is classified as a first-growth wine. Over the years Château Mouton Rothchild has equalled the prices of other four fist growths.
Château Haut Brion	Pronounced as *'O-Bree-Ohn'* the wine produced from this region is one of the first wines to be classified in 1855. These wines unlike the other first-growth wine are known for their deep colour, full-bodied aroma and flavour. The vineyard has been the property of Clarence Dillon.

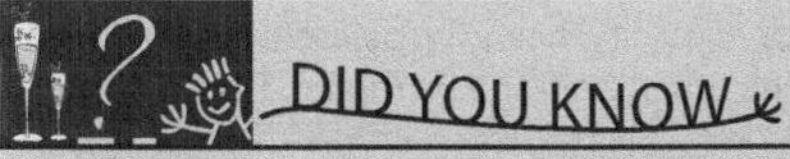

Today, *Château Ausone, Château Cheval*–Blanc from Saint-Emilion, *Château Petrus, L'evangile* and *Château Certan* from Pomerol are one of the greatest wines of Bordeaux. However, these were unclassified, despite them being in production during the classification in 1855. In fact, Cheval-Blanc and Petrus command a great price, equalling the great Médoc Clarets. Due to the high percentage of Merlot grapes, these wines have a deep colour, rich bouquet and are full bodied. They also mature faster than the wines made from Cabernet Sauvignon.

Apart from the first-growth wines, there are notable second-growth wines. In addition to these, there are third-, fourth- and fifth-growth wines, which are listed in Table 18.5.

2. **Famous white wines of Bordeuax:** *Graves*: The sub-region of Graves produces more white wines than the red wines. These wines are fresh, clean and dry having a pleasant and fruity bouquet of their own. Some famous labels of white wines are:

   - Château Olivier,
   - Château Carbonnieux,
   - Château Laville Haut Brion,
   - Château Bouscaut,

Table 18.5 Second-, Third-, Fourth- and Fifth-growth Wines

Second Growth*	Third Growth*	Fourth Growth*	Fifth Growth*
Château Léoville–Lascases	Palmer	Châteaus Prieuré–Lichine	Château Pontet–Canet
Léoville–Barton	Château Giscours	Talbot	Grand–Puy–Lacoste
Léoville–Poyferré	Kirwan	Beychevelle	Lynch–Bages
Lascombes	Calon-Ségur		Mouton–Baron–Philippe
Gruaud-Larose			Batailley
Ducru-Beaucaillou			
Rausan–Ségla			
Brane–Cantenac			
Montrose			
Pichon–Longueville–Comtesse de Lalande			
Cos d'Estournel			

*Wines grown in the Bordeaux region and sub-regions of France.

Note: Many people often consider the fifth-growth wines are inferior or poor in quality; however, please take note that these wines are amongst the 61 special wines that were classified amongst the other thousand on the list. They may not be a part of the first-growth variety but are still great wines.

- Château Haut Brion Blanc, and
- Château Domaine de Chevalier.

The ancient legends associated with *Château Carbonnieux* are common knowledge in France; to impress the Sultan of Turkey with the merits of French wine (as it was prohibited as per the holy Koran), Château Carbonnieux was sent to him labelled *mineral water from Carbonnioux*. He was impressed and the trade relations improved between the two states.

Sauternes: Sauternes wines are distinctly different, as they allow the grape to over-ripe before harvesting. Apparently, this practice was after the owner of a Château in this district namely 'Yquem' who went on a hunting trip. He was delayed and did not return on time and his men had no authority to start the work. He arrived four weeks late; by that time, the grapes had shrivelled and developed a mould, but he still made wine from them. Everyone was surprised by seeing the resulting highly perfumed wine that was rich and flavourful (see Table 18.6).

This mould that settles on the overripe grapes is called *Botrytis Cinerea*, while the French call it *Porriture Noble* meaning noble rottenness. While the grapes used are not rotten but overripe (rotten ones are disposed off). For obvious reasons, this labour-intensive work increases the cost of production. The *Porriture Noble* helps removing the water from the grapes and thereby concentrating

Table 18.6 First-growth Vineyards from Sauternes

Château	Description
Château D'Yquem	This wine produced from this region can be described as one of the most celebrated wines in the world. Therefore, it is not surprising that in 1859 the Grand Duke Constantine of Russia paid 20,000 gold francs for a *tun* (1,200 bottles), that is, about $3.50, which was an unheard price at the time. At Yquem, the usual proportion of grape is 80% Sémillon and 20% Sauvignon Blanc. The Sémillon is harvested after it is overripe and developed the *Porriture Noble*. The Sauvignon Blanc is harvested on time to provide acidity to the wine.
Château La-Tour Blanche	Please note that the words *La-Tour* are two words and often confused with the famous Château Latour (the Claret). The wine produced from this region is elegant and rich white wine.
Château Suduiraut	This Château borders Château d'Yquem formerly controlled by the King. However, today, its labels boast 'Ancient Cru Du Roy' meaning 'former property of the King'. The wine produced from this region is vigorous, rich in aroma and commands a high price.
Château Guiraut	The wine produced from this region was formerly called Bayle, which is known for its perfume and body along with delicacy of flavour.
Château Coutet and Climen	The vineyards situated in Barsac are first-growth vineyards and possess the typical firmness and elegant bouquet of Sauternes. They are rich Sauternes like the ones found in the other sub-communes of Sauternes.

all the sugars. This results in rich and sweet wines, which is now a characteristic of Sauternes. The casking of these wines is done with care, as they could easily have a secondary fermentation due to the high levels of residual sugars in the wine. To prevent this from occurring, the casks are exposed to sulphur dioxide, which sterilize the casks destroying any unwanted bacteria.

There are also second-growth vineyards from Sauternes, which are popular. Some examples are as follows.

Second-growth Vineyards from Sauternes

1. Château Filhot of Sauternes commune.
2. Château Myrat of Barsac commune.

Although these are classified as second-growth wines, they are excellent full-bodied wines with exceptional bouquet and flavour.

18.4 BURGUNDY

Burgundy is equally popular as Bordeaux for its fine red wines and white wines. These wines fetch a great price for their finesse.

History of Burgundy

History of wines from Burgundy dates back to Caesar's conquest of Gaul. The first grape vines were planted by the Roman legions that brought these grapes from nearby Italy. Due to the ideal conditions, soon these wines started competing with the ones from their motherland. However, this was not acceptable and in AD 96, Emperor Domitian ordered for uprooting the fields of grapes, replacing them with corns. Fortunately, this was not enforced whole heartedly and by AD 278, this order was withdrawn by Emperor Probus. Long before the region was named Burgundy, the church that controlled the development of quality wine was making famous wines such as Clos de Béze, Corton-Charlemagne Mersault and Moutrachet. Some of which are very popular even today.

Geography of Burgundy

The region of Burgundy is divided into sub-regions that are as follows:

1. **Côte d'Or:** Côte d'Or or golden slope is further divided into Côte de Nuits and Côte de Beaune.
2. **Côte Chalonnaise and Maconnais:** It lies in Saône-et-Loire.
3. **Beaujolais:** This lies in the state of Rhône (not to be confused with the wine-producing area called Côte du Rhône).
4. **The Northern:** The tip of the region beyond Côte d'Or lies in Chablis, which is a region that is famous for its excellent white wines.

Grape Varieties

The fine red wines are made from the Pinot Noir grapes, while the reputed white wines are made from Chardonnay. These grape varieties produce wines that are rich in quality but not in quantity. The other grape varieties used in making red wines are Gamay, which produces an enjoyable red wine from the soils of Mâcon, and Beaujolais, which are rich in clay and granite.

The other predominant white grape used in the region is Aligoté, which makes a simple and short-lived wine. Earlier Pinot Blanc was grown extensively but now is practically difficult to find.

Sub-regions of Burgundy

As we have listed down earlier the various sub-regions of Burgundy, it is important to understand the wines of each sub-region along with their qualities. We shall discuss first the regions producing the red wines and then proceed to the white wines.

1. **Red wines of Burgundy**

   (i) **Côtes de Nuits:** Côtes de Nuits produces red wines that have a great bouquet, are full bodied,

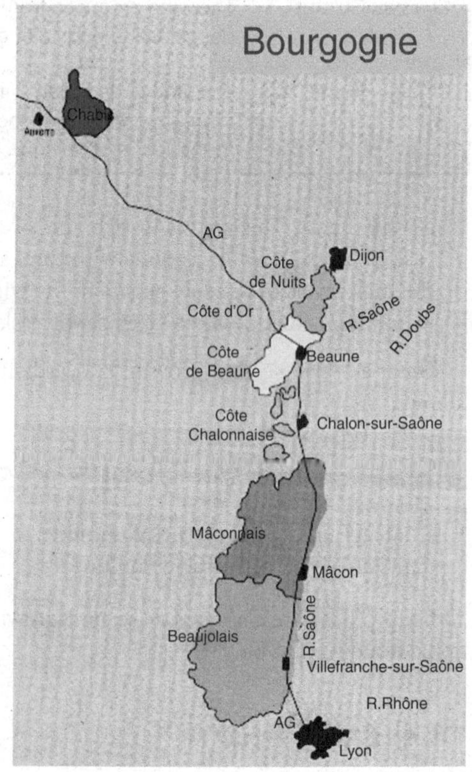

Burgundy or Bourgogne region, France. (Courtesy: *allfranceinfo.com*)

Vineyard ownership is very different in Burgundy than in any other region of France, having been duplicated to some extent only in Germany. The vineyards are very small in Burgundy, the largest being Clos de Vougeot, which is only 126 acres; the average being 25 acres. Each vineyard despite being small is owned by 3–6 owners depending on the rights of each, unlike Bordeaux vineyards that are extremely large but owned by a single person or firm. Burgundy vineyards such as Clos de Vougeot that has 66 owners, each cultivating their own grapes and vinifying them resulting in 66 different names produced; all of which are legally entitled to the Appellation Clos de Vougeot.

deep in colour and fruity, due to the Pinot Noir grapes used in the unique soil of the region. It has a unique way of naming their wines. In 1882, the commune of Musigny realized that if it combined the name of the commune with it most famous vineyard, it would increase sales, which was achieved. When Chambolle became Chambolle-Musigny, many others followed this practice, hence a double worded name is common to this sub-region, for example, Gevrey-Chambertin, Nuits-Saint-George, Aloxe-Corton and Puligny-Montrachet. Important Grand Cru vineyards of Côte de Nuits are listed in Table 18.7.

Table 18.7 Important Grand Cru Vineyards of Côte de Nuits

Vineyard	Description
Chambertin	Napoleon did not go to war without drinking his most precious wine, 'Chambertin'. However, before his conquest of Russia at the gate of Moscow, his supply ran out resulting in a regrettable retreat from Russia. Abbey of Bèze was gifted this 35-acres vineyard by Duc d'Amalgaire and since then it was called Clos de Bèze. A peasant named Bertin who owned a vineyard bordering Clos de Bèze using the same grape variety. His vineyard was known as Champ de Bertin (*Champ* is the French world for field), which was then contracted to Chambertin. Today, the area of Chambertin and Chambertin-Clos de Bèze is about 67 acres. Chambertin-Clos de Bèze can be labelled as either Chambertin-Clos de Bèze or Chambertin, but Chambertin cannot carry the label Chambertin-Clos de Bèze. Both these wines are well-rounded wines.
Les Musigny and Les Bonnes Mares	These two rival vineyards are located in the commune of Chambolle Musigny. Les Musigny is more famous of the two, but both are wines known for their finesse and elegancy.
Clos de Vougeot	The wines produced from this vineyard are fruity wines rich in body, bouquet, flavour and colour. They are graceful, elegant and rich in their character. The earliest records of this vineyard being owned by the Cistercian Abbey of Cîteaux, which dates back to AD 1110. Today, this Château is owned by the Confrérie des Chevalier du Tasterin who are 'the brotherhood of the gentleman of the tasting cup'. The great ceremonies of this brotherhood are held at this vineyard.

(*Continued*)

Table 18.7 Important Grand Cru Vineyards of Côte de Nuits (*Contd.*)

Vineyard	Description
Romanee Conti	The wines produced from this vineyard are considered to be the 'king' of Burgundy wines; it has great body, bouquet and flavour along with great character. These wines are rich and can live long.
Romanee, Romanee-Saint, Vivant and Latache	The commune that houses the greatest vineyards is Vosne Romanée. Only a connoisseur can make the difference between these fine wines, but all agree that these wines are fabulous with rich colour, a deep bouquet, flavour, body and elegance.
Les Grand Echezeaux and Echezeaux	These are in the communes of Flagey-Echézeaux, but are considered amongst the wines of neighbouring Vosne Romanée. These wines produced from these vineyards are softer on the palate than the famous wines of Vosne Romanée.
Clos de Tart, Clos de La Roche and Les Saint George	These three fine vineyards of *Côte de Nuits* have rich wines with brilliant colour, body and characters. The first two vineyards comprise 17 acres and 38 acres, respectively, which lie in the commune of Morey-Saint-Georges.

Note: The Appellation *Côte-de-Nuits-Villages* is restricted to the wines of five communes of Fixin, Brochon, Prissey, Comblanchien and Corgoloin.

(ii) **Côte de Beaune:** *Côte de Beaune* is the medieval city of Beaune is the epicentre of the Burgundy wine trade. The red wines of *Côte de Beaune* develop more rapidly and are ready for drinking sooner than their counterparts in *Côte de Nuits*. These are most pleasant wines with a fruity bouquet, which are mellower, having finesse and can be enjoyed all through the year (Table 18.8).

Table 18.8 Important Vineyards of *Côte de Beaune*

Vineyard	Description
Hospices de Beaune	The wine produced from this vineyard is a world famous wine of *Côte de Beaune*. Beaune's long history is preserved and the best monument representing it is Les Hospices de Beaune—a charitable hospital built in 1445, by Pore Eugene IV to care for the poor people of Beaune. A tax collector, Nicolas Rolin, and his wife, during the reign of Louis XI, donated the property and erected the building, donating vineyards to support this institution through its sales. For over four centuries, these wines were sold privately, but since 1859 they are sold at a festive public auction on the third Sunday of November. The auctioned wines generate enough money to support the hospital.
Le Corton, Le Clos du Roi, Les Bressandes and Les Pougets	The wine produced from *Le Cortonis* is the only *Grand Cru Red* wine from *Côte de Beaune*, usually a robust wine with a great body and characteristics comparable to the good wines of *Côte du Nuits*. The wines produced from *Le Clos du Roi* and *Les Bressandes* are also great wines but are more like Beaune wines in character, having a lovely colour and aroma. The wines produced from *Les Pougets Vineyards* are always fine with excellent colour, flavour and body.

Table 18.8 Important Vineyards of *Côte de Beaune* (*Contd.*)

Vineyard	Description
Les Feves and Les Greves	These vineyards comprise of 89 acres put together, *Les Fèves* with 10.5 acres and *Les Grèves* with 78.5 acres. They produce wines that are famous for their elegance and richness.
Les Rugiens and Les Epentos	The most famous Burgundy wine name is, without doubt, Pommard. It is better known than *Les Rugiens*, which is the 33 acres vineyard that produces this wine and that is the reason these wines carry the 'Pommard' on their label and demand a high price.

Note: The Appellation *Côte de Beaune-Villages* applies to only the red wine and is limited to 16 communes.

2. **White wines of Burgundy:** All the sub-regions of Burgundy produce white wine, some of which are exceptional and have created bench marks for white wines across the globe.

A few examples are Chablis from the state of Yonne considered the world best white wine by many. Mâcon produces crisp white wines including Pouilly Fuissé and Mâcon Blanc. Beaujolais too produces a good white wine called Beaujolais Blanc.

Chablis

Chablis is the most famous sub-region from northern Burgundy and it produces white wine. It produces a wine that is pale straw in colour and dry in taste. It has a distinct flinty quality (called *'Pierre-à-fusil'* or 'gun flint') similar to a sharp metallic taste. The fruity quality of this wine balanced with the flinty quality creates a refreshing and cooling wine.

The wine produced from this region is always preferred fresh and as an accompaniment for oyster—*Les Hûitres*. It is classified as per quality. Let us note them in ascending order of quality, which are as follows:

1. Chablis Grand Cru,
2. Chablis Premier Cru,
3. Chablis, and
4. Petite Chablis.

The best vineyards are located on the hillsides north of the village Chablis and make up a Grand Cru classification.

Cotes de Nuits

The white wines produced from this distinguished region are full of flavour and body. Some of the famous white wines are as follows:

1. Musigny Blanc produced by Compte George,
2. *Clos Blanc de Vougeot*, and
3. Nuit-Saint-Georges Blanc.

Table 18.9 The Greatest White Wines of Burgundy

Vineyard	Description
Corton Charlemagne	It lies in the commune of Aloxe–Corton named after the great Emperor. It is a Grand Cru Vineyard making both Grand Cru Whites and Reds.
Les Perrières, Les Genevrières and Les Charmes	These lie in the commune of Meursault. The wines produced from these regions are full-bodied and dry wines with an aroma of hazelnuts.
Chassagne Montrachet and Puligny Montrachet	At the southern end of Côte de Beaune lie these vineyards. Like some wines from *Côte de Nuits*, they have combined their names with the famous vineyard Le Montrachet to produce good quality wines.
Le Montrachet	The wine produced from this region is one of the great wines of the world. It is a full-bodied and robust wine, at the same time which is elegant and perfumed. This wine fetches prices equalling the best red wines of *Côte de Nuits*. Therefore, it is not surprising that it is called the *Chateau d' Yquem* of Burgundy.
Chevalier Montrachet and Le Bâtard Montrachet	The wines produced from these regions are similar to *Le Montrachet,* but with a bouquet and finesse. Care should be taken not to confuse Chevalier–Montrachet with Chassagne—Montrachet.

Côtes de Beaune

The greatest white wines of Burgundy are from the region of *Côtes de Beaune*. Some examples are listed in Table 18.9 with their details.

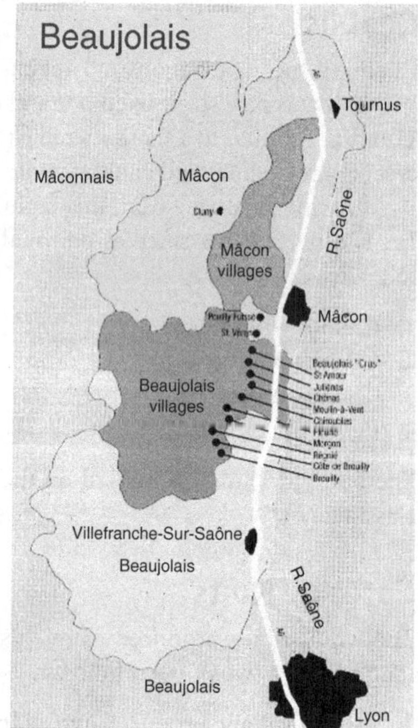

Beaujolais sub-region. (Courtesy: *allfrance info.com.*)

Côtes Chalonnaise

This region is also famous for its white wines but do not match the quality of the wines from *Côte de Beaune*. The four communes having appellations are Rully, Montagny, Mercurey and Givry; the first two communes produce white wines and the latter two communes produce red wines. In addition, Rully also produces sparkling wines.

Mâconnais and Beaujolais

Mâcon, as it is better known, is famous for its white wines, while Beaujolais (pronounced as 'bo-jo-lay') is better known for its red wines. The famous white wines produced from Mâcon are as follows:

1. *Pouilly Fuissé* (most famous wine from Mâcon),
2. *Pouilly Loche,* and
3. *Pouilly Vinzelles.*

Table 18.10 Classification of Beaujolais

Best Growth or 'Crus'	Second Classification	Third and Fourth Classifications
The first comprises of nine Crus (i) Brouilly, (ii) *Chénas*, (iii) Chiroubles, (iv) *Côte de Brouilly*, (v) Fleurie, (vi) Juliénas, (vii) Morgon, (viii) *Moulin-â-vent*, and (ix) Saint Amour.	The second is limited to 39 communes classified as Beaujolais Villages.	The third being Beaujolais Supérieur and the fourth is the Plain Beaujolais.

These wines are primarily made from Chardonnay grapes. Wines labelled Pinot–Chardonnay Mâcon use Pinot Blanc and Chardonnay grapes to make their wines. Beaujolais soil conditions bring out the best out of Gamay grape. Table 18.10 enumerate the classification of the wines of Beaujolais.

The wines of Beaujolais are brilliant, clear and having a light body. They are fresh and fruity wines. They are consumed young before they are two or three years old. They are often paired with white meat instead of following the set approach of white wine for white meat and red wine for red meat. This is due to these wines characteristics of being light and fruity.

Note: The region of Champagne is explained separately in Chapter 19.

18.5 ALSACE

Alsace is a region in France located to the northern most tip of France, sharing a border with Switzerland. The Rhine River, which flows through Germany and France, provided an excellent means of transportation and Alsace being in the centre, often exchanged hands. However, now it is an integral part of France. The most common grape variety used in this region is the Gewürztraminer, which is more common to German wines.

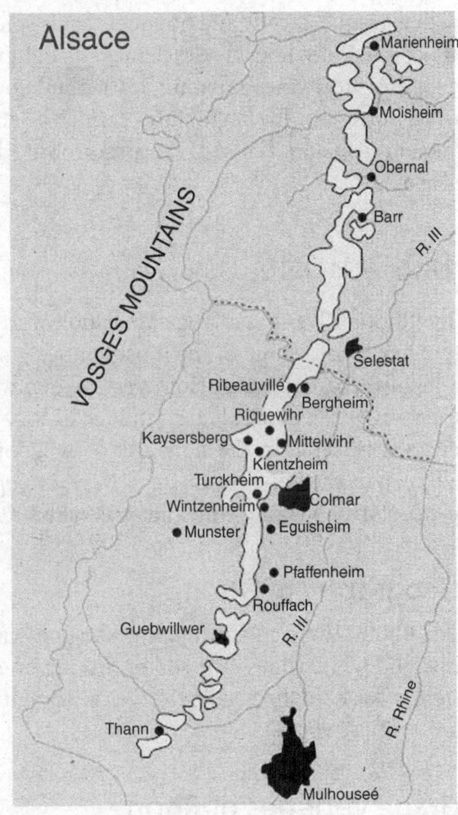

Alsace region, France. (Courtesy: *allfranceinfo.com*)

History of Alsace

We can credit the Romans for planting the grape vine in this region as well. However, today, the same vines are not found that were planted then. During the time when Germany controlled the region, the wine produced was more focused on quantity rather than quality. However, today, these wines command a high respect amongst the wine lovers.

Geography of Alsace

As mentioned, this region is located at the northern most part of France. It has popular vineyards that are part of many surrounding towns, like the other regions of France.

Grape Varieties of Alsace

There are certain grape varieties that are permitted as per the Appellation *Contrôlée Vin d' Alsace*. They are *Riesling, Pinot Blanc, Pinot Gris, Pinot Noir, Sylvaner, Muscat d' Alsace* and *Gewürztraminer*.

About wines—In Alsace, when the grape variety is mentioned, which is common practice for all Alsace wines, it has to be ensured that 100% of that grape variety is used. The Gewürztraminer makes a wine with a unique flavour and bouquet that is spicy with a dry finish while the Riesling makes a rich and dry wine. The Pinot noir in Alsace makes a light rosé wine.

All Alsace wines must be bottled in a green Alsace Flute that is a tall slim bottle. All wines have to be bottled in the region and cannot be shipped in casks. Some famous sparkling wines under the label of *Cremant d' Alsace* are also produced both as white and rosé sparkling wines (from *pinot noir* grapes).

18.6 RHÔNE

The Rhone River has a long association with the history of this region as it was an excellent means for transportation. Some of the most famous vineyards are situated in *Rhône. Côte Rôtie* (*roasted slopes*) is a highly regarded wine. However, the one wine most famous from this region (especially in India) is *Château Neuf du Pape*. It has a unique history and it is when Clement V—the Arch Bishop of Bordeaux—decided to settle in the holy city of Avignon, he built a palace outside the town that was known as Château of the Pope or '*Château Neuf du Pape*'. He was from Bordeaux so wines were dear to him and hence started making wine that was called '*Château Neuf du Pape*'.

Geography of Rhône

The Rhone River cuts through the region cutting into two parts, both of which produce excellent red, rosé and white wines. The soil of this region contains granite and shale in the northern part and round stones that hold the heat in the south. The entire region has a hot and long growing season that produces great robust wines.

Grape Varieties of Rhône

The principle grape variety is Syrah (It is unrelated to the Californian petite Syrah). Table 18.11 enumerates the details about the grape varieties grown in *Côte du Rhône*.

Table 18.11 The Grape Varieties Grown in Côte Du Rhône

White Grapes	Red Grapes
Viognier	Syrah
Roussanne	Grenache
Marsanne	Clairette
Picpoul	Bourboulenc
	Mourvèdre
	Cinsaut
	Carignan

Note: The Syrah is the only grape variety used in *Côte Rôtie* and Hermitage.

DID YOU KNOW

There are various shaped bottles used in France and Portugal. The shape of the bottle itself gives the wine its identity. Photo here shows the differentiation.

Different shaped bottles used in various regions of France and Portugal.
(Courtesy: *allfranceinfo.com.*)

Vineyards of Rhône

The famous wines from Rhône are called 'Rhône Reds', and have made this region famous. Table 18.12 provides us the details of the wines produced in the region.

Côtes du Rhône Villages are more recent appellations, applying to wines made from the best 17 communes amongst the other hundreds of Côtes du Rhône. For example, *Beaune de Venise* produces both dry and sweet red wines that are famous.

Tavel rosé: A famous rosé wine produced in the town of Tavel. Tavel rosé is a wine that has 'the best of both worlds' referring to its delightful dryness of a red wine and the freshness of a white wine. It has a coral coloured wine that is fresh and dry with a fruity bouquet and flavour. Rosé wines from Rhône are shipped in clear Flute bottles.

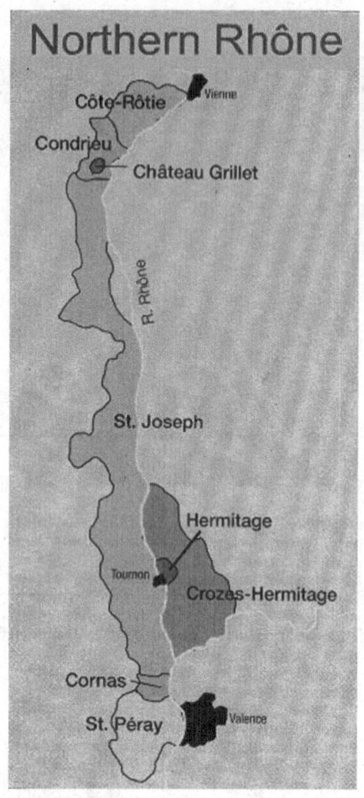

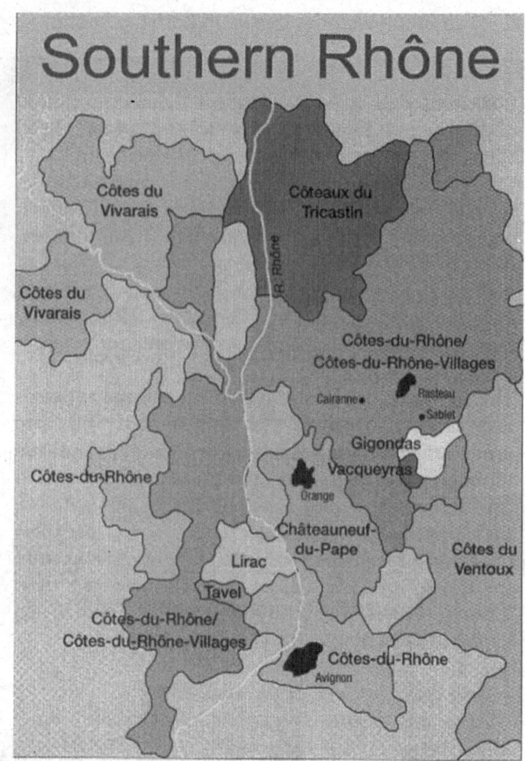

Rhone (north and south), France. (Courtesy: *allfranceinfo.com*)

Table 18.12 Vineyards of Rhône

Vineyard	Description
Châteauneuf, Du Pape	The wine produced from this region is a result of blending of over 13 different grape varieties. Some suggest that the perfect blend to make this wine from the following grapes: • Grenache and Cinsaut (for warmth and richness) – 20%. • Counoise and Picpoul (for bouquet and freshness) – 30%. • Mourvèdre and Syrah (for solidity, colour and flavour) – 40%. • Clairette and Bourboulenc (for finesse and fire) – 10%. This wine is slow to develop. The vineyard also produces a white wine that is not as famous as the red, but has a good body, flavour and character.
Côte Rôtie	The wine produced from this region is very deep in colour. It has a harshness that reduces as it is aged in wood before bottling. The youngest wine suitable for drinking from this vineyard is 12–15 years.

Vineyard	Description
Château Grillet	The white wines produced from this region are produced from Viognier grapes. The Château Grillet is pale in colour, medium bodied, rich in character and bouquet. It is an expensive wine as this is produced from one of the France's smallest Appellation Contrôlée areas.
Hermitage	The red wines produced from this vineyard are referred to as 'the manliest of wines' as they are full-bodied and deep coloured red wines, which are strong and flavourful and living up to the reputation of a classical 'Rhône Reds'. While the white wines are full and medium dry with a rich aroma.
Crozes Hermitage	Wines are produced in the eleven towns around the hillsides of Hermitage and have been in production since 1952. They are similar to Hermitage wines but not as rich in character.

Rhône wines (red and white) are bottled in bottles similar to the bottles used in Burgundy. Also having a similar character, these wines have often been confused; for example, Châteauneuf du Papeis often listed as a Burgundy.

18.7 LOIRE VALLEY

This region is very close to Paris and many in the social circles of Paris have always owned a Château or wanted to own one in this region. Hence, making the pleasant wines of this region is popular amongst Parisiennes (people from Paris).

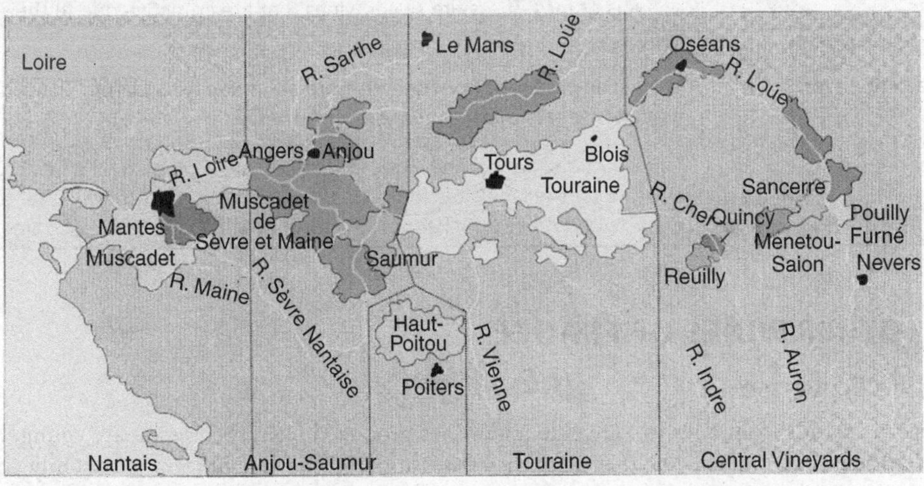

Loire, France. (Courtesy: *allfranceinfo.com*)

Famous Vineyards

Loire has famous wines to its credit such as Pouilly Fumé. The details of these wines are provided in Table 18.13.

Table 18.13 Famous Vineyards of Loire and the Characteristics of Their Wines

Vineyard	Description
Pouilly-Sur-Loire and Pouilly-Fume	The town of Pouilly-Sur-Loire is where these vineyards are located. They are planted with Sauvignon Blanc locally known as Blanc Fumé; hence, its name Pouilly Fumé. Pouilly Fumé has to be made from sauvignon Blanc grape only. This is a delicate, soft, dry white wine and has a slight smoky aroma to it. Pouilly-Sur-Loire is less delicate but better had when young. Please do not confuse Pouilly Fuissé of Burgundy with Pouilly Fumé as they are completely different.
Sancerre	Opposite of Pouilly-Sur-Loire is Sancerre. Also, made from the Sauvignon Blanc grape, this wine is very fruity and is more acidic.
Vouvray and Saumur	Vouvray produces both still and sparkling white wines. The premier wine is Chenin Blanc that grows well in the chalky soil of this region. The leading producers make their sparkling wines by *Méthode Champenoise*, using either Saumur or Touraine grapes and are labelled Crémant de Loire (from *Côteaux de Touraine*) and sparkling Vouvray is labelled *Vouvray Mousseux*.
Chenon and Bourgueil	These districts produce a wine similar to Beaujolais in style made from Cabernet Franc grapes. The wine is pleasing and recommended to be consumed when young and preferred chilled (like white wine).
Anjou	This vineyard is located near the city of Angers and it produces large amounts of white and rosé wines. *Rosé d' Anjou* is being very famous, which is predominantly made from Cabernet Franc, Cabernet Sauvignon, Gamay and Pineau d' Aunis grapes. These are sweet wines that are attractive due to their pink colour.
Côteaux du Layon	The wines produced from this vineyard are made with Chenin Blanc grapes that are sweet and make great dessert wines.
Muscadet	This is a light and gentle bone dry wine called Muscadet. When 'Sur lie' appears on the label, it is indicative of it being bottled shortly after it was made, without being racked. It is the most popular white wine of Loire.

18.8 OTHER WINES OF FRANCE

Cotes de Provence

This region extends from Nice to Marseille. The wines produced from this region are young, having a great aroma and bouquet. As they age, they lose some aroma but become soft. Only in 1977 did this region get its elevation to the Appellation Controleé status from previous V.D.A.S. category.

It is famous for both its white and red wines. Some areas are Cassis (famous for white), Bandol (famous for reds) and Bellet (produces red, white and rosé wines).

Midi

It is a huge plain that extends to the Spanish border of France. Famous for its sweet wines and large amounts of *Vin de Table* (table wines). Wines from this region have also been categorized under the V.D.Q.S status.

Jura

This region is located near Switzerland was famous for its wines; however, now, only *Rosé d' Arbois* and *Château Châlon* are famous. *Château Châlon* is an extraordinary wine that has approximately 16% ABV, ensuring it to have exceptional keeping qualities. This high alcoholic content is attributed to the yeast film (known as 'flor' in sherry making), which is formed during its ageing in casks. This gives the wine a large shelf life and a unique nutty flavour that some connoisseurs believe to be a delicacy.

There are other regions of France such as Beaune and Bergerac that produce sweet wines; the latter produces Monbazillac, which is often compared to Sauternes wines. This region has the world's utmost respect and has been and still is the world's best wine producer.

LET'S SUMMARIZE IN POINTS

- France is the largest producer of quality wines.
- The production process of white, red and rosé wines has been established in France. It has evolved over centuries to produce wines with finesse.
- France is governed by Wine Laws, namely, Appellation d' Origine Controlee.
- The Sub-regions of France are Bordeaux, Burgandy, Alsace, Rhone, Loire Valley, Cote De Provence, Midi and Jura. Champagne, Cognac and Armagnac are important regions of France, but are more famous for beverages other than wine.

18.9 FAQs

Short-Answer Type Questions

1. What is Egrappage?
2. Explain maceration.
3. Define racking and fining.
4. Name the various factors involved in must adjustment.
5. What is 'Lees'?
6. Explain the effects of Acetobacter.
7. What in cellaring?
8. Name the Wine Laws of France?
9. What are the specific controls of the AOC?

10. Who was Elenor of Aquitaine?
11. Name the sub-regions of Bordeaux.
12. Describe Sauternes wines? Name five classified growths from this region.
13. Name the grape varieties used in Bordeaux region.
14. Name five first-growth wines and five second-growth wines of Bordeaux.
15. Give the sub-regions of Burgundy.

Long-Answer Type Questions

1. Give the detailed production process of making wine.
2. Name and explain the characteristics of five first-growth wines of Bordeaux.
3. Explain all the Sauternes classified growths.
4. Explain red wines from Burgundy in detail.
5. Explain white wines from Burgundy in detail.
6. Explain the region of Alsace with grape varieties used, geography and characteristics of the wine.
7. What are Rhone reds? Describe five Rhone reds in detail.
8. Describe wines from Loire Valley.
9. What are the other regions of France that produce lesser famous wines?
10. Describe in detail the relationship among a commune, vineyard and a wine label.

18.10 KEY TERMS

- Acetobacter
- Bottling
- Fining
- Breathing of the wine
- Maceration
- Chaptalization
- Malolactic fermentation
- Chateau
- Must
- Claret
- Racking
- Clarification
- Stomping
- Cremant
- Sulphured Barriques
- Crus
- Terroir
- Egrappage
- Vineyard

19 CHAMPAGNE

CHAPTER OUTLINE

LET'S DEFINE

"Champagne is a sparkling wine with effervescence. The wine is made from grapes grown in the delimited Champagne region of France. It has to be made by the 'Méthode Champenoise'. All champagnes are sparkling wines but all sparkling wines are not champagnes".

Champagne is used in two references in the French language, *Le Champagne* and *La Champagne*. The former is the name used in reference to the sparkling wine and the latter refers to one of France's most precious wine-producing regions namely, Champagne.

People often associate champagne with celebration, birth, marriage and many other festive occasions.

19.1 HISTORY

History of champagne is associated with Dom Perignon (1639–1715), a blind Benedictine monk who put the bubbles into champagne, when he was treasurer and cellarer of Abbey of Hautvillers.

The carbon dioxide bubbles were formed naturally, when a secondary fermentation occurred in the bottle on the onset of the warm spring resulting in a sparkling wine. The residual sugars in the wine was a result of the cold winter which was responsible for halting or slowing down the primary fermentation process, hence resulting in a secondary fermentation.

Opening champagne signifies celebration.

Dom Perignon's brilliant contribution in blending different wines, possessing different qualities and making a fine sparkling wine is appreciated even today. As the secondary fermentation in the bottle left a large amount of sediment, it was very difficult to clarify this wine. Removing the sediment was time consuming and the sparkle was lost. It was earlier in the 19th century; the process of *Remuage* was developed and is in use even today.

19.2 WINE LAWS

The wine laws of France apply to the Champagne region with a single addition, which clearly defines and controls the method of making champagne—*Méthode Champenoise.* This regulation makes champagne one of the strictest quality-controlled regions of the world.

Vintage wines occur three to four times in a decade from the Champagne region of France. The bottles carrying them are specifically labelled with the years of the vintage. Some of them stand on their own merit whereas others are used for blending and enhancing other wines that are used to make champagne. Almost all vintages are *Brut* or very dry.

Appellation Controlee regulations have established that vintage champagnes must be matured for a minimum of three years in the bottle whereas non-vintage champagnes are matured for 1½ years in the bottle. Most producers age their best quality wines for a much longer period which are better known as *Tête d' Cuvee* wines.

Wine regions of the Champagne region of France.

19.3 GEOGRAPHY

The Marne River divides the Champagne region of France into two parts. To the north of the Marne River black grapes are grown, whereas to the south of the river white grapes are cultivated.

1. **Harvesting:** The vines are harvested a 100 days after they flower, which may start from the end of September to early October. The exact time is determined by CIVC (*Comite Interprofessionnel du Vin De Champagne)* through laboratory tests determining grape sugar content or the acidity in the grape.

   The ripe grapes are gathered in *panniers* (baskets). When a pannier is full, experienced sorters remove any defective grapes ensuring only the perfect ones reach the press. This selection process is called *Epluchage*. After *Epluchage* the grapes are placed in *Clayettes* or *Caques* (large baskets) and carried to the pressing houses.
2. **Pressing:** To avoid the colouration of the juice hydraulic presses that are wide and shallow are used. Each caque is weighed before being put into the press. One full load of the press is called 'marc'. From each marc, four pressings of juice are obtained in the following order:
   'Cuvée', 'Première Taille', 'Deuxième Taille', and *'Rabâche'.*

   While most reputed champagne houses use only Cuvee and Premiere Taille pressings only a few prefer to use Deuxieme Taille. The Rebache wine cannot be used for making champagne, but it is distilled and used in producing brandy.

DID YOU KNOW

Cuvee juice is obtained by pressing the marc twice whereas for obtaining the juice from the other three namely, Premiere Taille, Deuxieme Taille and Rebache pressure is applied only once. The Rebache juice is obtained from a smaller press.

3. **First fermentation:** The white wines start fermenting very rapidly and slow down during the second week. The entire fermentation process is complete within three weeks. The overall temperature maintained in the casks and stainless steel vessels is 21°C.

   The new wine is racked and chilled. The chilling causes the soluble tartarates to form insoluble bitartarates which when removed leave a clear and stable wine. The cellar master decides which blends are to be married in case of non-vintage years. Vintage years on the other hand are special by themselves and do not require blending.
4. **Secondary fermentation:** *Liqueur de Tirage* or *Dosage de Tirage* is added to the blend to ensure a uniform secondary fermentation, which is a combination of old wine, a small amount of sugar and special yeast. The additional sugar added varies each year in proportion to the residual sugars of the base wine. The wine is then bottled and corked.

   Nowadays, the bottles are capped using crown caps similar to the ones used on soft drink bottles, instead of the traditional corks which were secured with metal wires or clips known as *Agraffes*. The bottles are stacked on their sides in cellars. As the secondary fermentation begins, the yeast acts on the sugar to create carbon dioxide gas. As the carbon dioxide cannot escape from the sealed bottle, it combines with the wine to form the effervescence or sparkle; this is the main reason for

Champagne cork with the 'Agraffes'.

19.4 SOIL

Chalk in the soil is of utmost importance to create the characteristics necessary for good champagne. A thin top layer of earth covers porous, chalky subsoil, which allows excess water to drain retaining the required amount of water necessary for the growth of the vine.

19.5 GRAPE VARIETIES

The three specified grape varieties used for making champagne include two red grapes, *Pinot Noir* and *Pinot Meunier*, along with a white grape, Chardonnay. The *Chardonnay* adds freshness and lightness to the final blend, whereas the red grapes give full body and flavour. *Cote de Blanc* or *White Slope* is named so due to the growth of Chardonnay grape on this soil. The red grape varieties are grown on the *Montagne de Reims* vineyards and also in the valley of the Marne.

19.6 MÉTHODE CHAMPENOISE OR THE CHAMPAGNE METHOD

Figure 19.1 gives better understanding of the *Méthode Champenoise.*

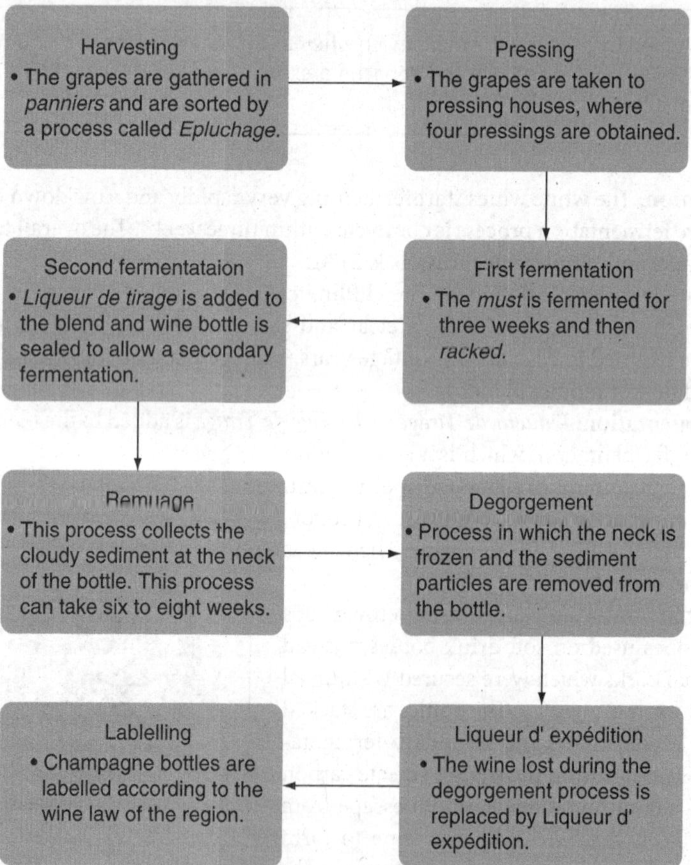

Figure 19.1 Flowchart explaining the Méthode Champenoise process.

champagne bottles being made with thicker quality glass that can bear at least 90 pounds of pressure per square inch. Earlier, there were many instances of bottles developing cracks or even exploding, but due to advanced bottling technology and precise measurement of sugar levels by a sacchrometer breakage has almost been eliminated.

DID YOU KNOW

Champagnes that produce smaller bubbles have a long-lasting effervescence than the ones that produce larger bubbles; hence, making the former more desirable. Champagne tulip glasses and Champagne flute glasses hold the effervescence longer than the Champagne saucer glasses.

5. **Remuage:** The secondary fermentation when complete leaves behind dead yeast cells in the bottle. These particles make the sparkling wine cloudy. As discussed earlier, the process of remuage was developed to achieve a clear and brilliant wine.

   This process is a long and tedious one in which the bottles are placed in specially built racks called *pupitres*. First the bottles are set at a 45° angle and over a period of a few weeks the angle is gradually increased until the bottles are standing perpendicular to the ground with their heads down (Figure 19.2). A worker (*remuer*) increases the angle by slightly shaking and turning the bottle, giving it a small jolt. This process is called 'riddling' or 'remuage' and is repeated every three days for each bottle. The operation takes 6–8 weeks with a sole objective to make the sediments settle at the neck of the bottle. The figure 19.2 shows a faster method completing the process in 21 days, but in most famous champagne houses the time taken can extend upto 8 weeks as mentioned. This process is very labour intensive and large champagne houses are developing machines to replace this manual system.

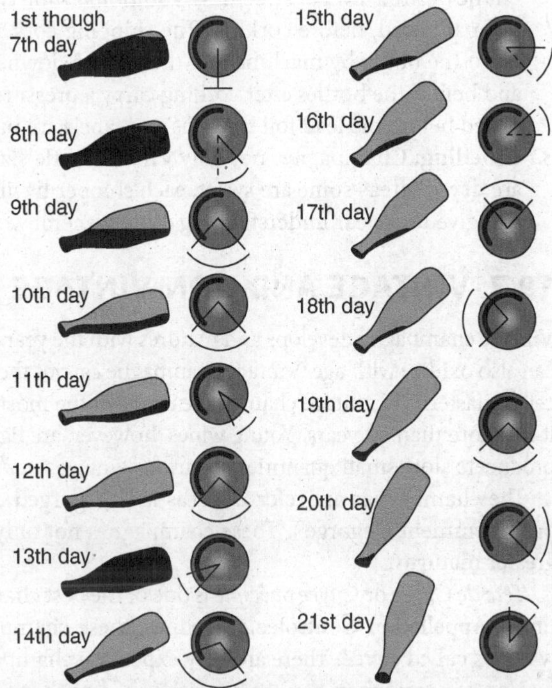

Figure 19.2 A diagrammatic representation of the Remuage process.

6. **Degorgement:** *Degorgement* is the process of removing the collected sediments from the neck of each sealed bottle. First, the neck of the bottle is dipped in a very cold brine or glycol solution that freezes or solidifies the sediments along with some wine located at the neck of each bottle. Next the skilled workman wearing protective gear and a leather apron tilts the bottle towards a shield and removes the wired cork or crown caps, making the frozen bit of sediment gush out along with some wine. The workman then pats the neck of the bottle and makes sure all the sediments are removed. After this the *Liqueur d'Expédition* is added.

Table 19.1 Labelling of Champagne Bottles

Term	Description	Sugar Level per Litre
Demi-sec	Sweet	33–50 g
Sec or Dry	Medium sweet	17–35 g
Extra Dry	Dry with a hint of sweetness	15–20 g
Brut	Very dry	Less than 15 g

7. **Liqueur d' expedition:** The wine that has been lost during *degorgement* has to be replaced. Depending on the desired level of sweetness, additional wine is added to the bottle in which the sugar levels have been adjusted, before corking. The shipping cork must carry the label of champagne, which is put on to the bottle by machine and then wired down. During *degorgement* some of the pressure is lost and hence, the bottles after corking carry a pressure of 75 pounds per square inch. The bottle is then rested before the lead foil capsules and labels are put on.
8. **Labelling:** Champagnes not only vary in bottle size but also in sweetness. Few types of champagne are dry whereas some are sweet, each shipper having their own description on the bottle. Table 19.1 will give us a clear understanding of the general words used on a champagne bottle.

19.7 VINTAGE AND NON-VINTAGE CHAMPAGNES

Vintage champagne develops and matures with the years if properly stored and left undisturbed, however it can also oxidize with age. Vintage champagne carries the vintage year on its label as per the discretion of the cellar master. Old vintage champagne is one of the most delicate of all wines and it is not advisable to keep it for more than 10 years. Young wines, however, are light, fresh and fruity. Many fine French champagne producers store small quantities of various vintages *undisgorged* in their cellars for their personal use.

The champagnes are referred to as late disgorged champagne labelled as RD ('Recently Disgorged' or 'Récemment Dégorgé'). These champagnes not only retain their qualities but are better as they have greater maturity.

Tête de Cuvee or *Cuvee Spéciale* is one of the best champagnes. Although it is not defined and regulated under Appellation Controlee guidelines, these champagnes are made from the first press of the marc which is called cuvee. There are very expensive champagnes bottled in replicas of antique bottles.

Non-vintage champagnes are produced with no date on the label and are less expensive. The quality is maintained by blending these wines of lesser years, with wines from a vintage year. Most champagne houses are judged by the non-vintage wine quality as they are more common than their vintage counterparts.

19.8 TYPES OF CHAMPAGNES

Blanc de Blancs: Pierre Tatinger is credited with making this light and delicate champagne. Instead of using the traditional proportions of 2/3rd red grapes and 1/3rd white grapes, he decided to use 100% Chardonnay to make his champagne. This champagne is marketed as *Blanc de Blancs* and is dry, elegant and quite expensive. Apart from Tatinger house, many others also produce this style of champagne.
Rose Champagne or Pink Champagne: This champagne is fast gaining popularity as it is fashionable. It is produced by adding red wine from the villages of Bouzy or Ambonnay from the Champagne district, either

before the first fermentation or just before the second fermentation. It is usually quite dry.

Cremant: Crémant champagne carries a pressure of 3–4 atmospheres as compared to a pressure of 5–6 atmospheres for a normal bottle of champagne. This champagne is characterized by a light foam. *Mumm's* exports a Crémant from the village of Cramant. French wine laws allow the word Crémant on Vins Mousseux, which are sparkling wines from other regions. Some examples are Crémant d'Alsace, Crémant de Loire and Crémant de Bourgogne. Although these are sparkling wines from their respective regions produced by *Méthode Champenoise*, they cannot be confused with the traditional champagne variants.

***Coteaux de Champenoise*:** It is an appellation under which the still wines from the Champagne region are shipped. They do not undergo a secondary fermentation in the bottle or any ageing due to which these cannot be called champagne. Famous houses such as Bollinger, Moet-Chandon and Laurent Perrier market these dry still wines.

Table 19.2 Bottle Sizes of Champagne Bottles

Name	Size
Split	187 ml
Half Bottle	375 ml
Bottle	750 ml
Magnum (2 bottles)	1.5 l
Jeroboam (4 bottles)	3 l
Methuselah (8 bottles)	6 l
Salmanazar (12 bottles)	9 l

19.9 BOTTLE SIZES

Table 19.2 enumerates different bottle sizes of champagne bottles. The bottle and the magnum sizes are the most practical to be used.

Interesting Facts

In Formula One racing, the official champagne opened at the award ceremony after the race is a Jeroboam size bottle from the famous G.H. Mumm House. It is believed that this ceremony brings in great luck to the driver and his team.

Various sizes of champagne bottles.

19.10 OTHER METHODS OF MAKING SPARKLING WINE

1. **Charmat method:** This is a method of making sparkling wine. In this method, the secondary fermentation takes place in large tanks or VATs before being bottled under pressure. This method is less labour intensive and requires to be aged for lesser number of years. Hence, the sparkling wines produced by this method are less costly. Sparkling wines produced in this bulk process cannot be labelled Champagne. This method follows a filtration process instead of remuage before bottling.
2. **Carbonation:** Another type of sparkling wine is produced by adding carbon dioxide to the wine, similar to the process followed for making soft drinks. It cannot be labelled champagne and must be labelled as carbonated wine. These sparkling wines, however, lose their effervescence much faster than the sparkling wines made by either *Méthode Champenoise* or the Charmat method.
3. **Transfer method:** The transfer method is very similar to the Champagne method. The major difference being that it eliminates the time consuming remuage and riddling procedure. Instead, the wine is put into tanks or VATs after the secondary fermentation is complete, then clarified and re-bottled (Figure 19.3).

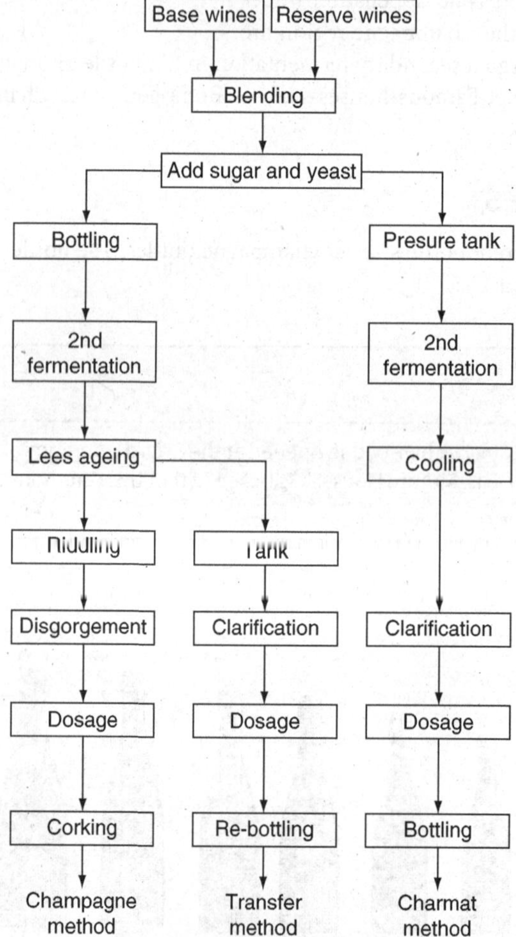

Figure 19.3 Flowchart differentiating between the various methods of carbonation.

Champagne wishes and Caviar dreams are some inspiring sentences used to express the finest products in human history. Hence, this expensive and most celebrated beverage is one of the most popular French words in the world.

19.11 BRANDS OF CHAMPAGNE

Table 19.3 enumerates the different brands of champagne.

Table 19.3 Brands of Champagne

Type	Brand
Non-vintage Champagne	• Krug Grande Cuvée • Gosset Grande Reserve • Moët et Chandon Nector Imperial Champagne • Moët et Chandon Brut Imperial
Vintage Champagne	• Joseph Perrier Joséphine 1990 Champagne • Perrier Joulet Belle Epoque 1996 Champagne • Nicolas Feuillâtes Cuvée Palmes D'Or 1996 Champagne • Dom Perignon 1996 Champagne
Rose Champagne	• Krug Rose • Joseph Perrier CuvéeRoyal Brut Rose Champagne • Moet et Chandon Brut Imperial Rose Champagne • Laurent Perrier Rose Brut Champagne

LET'S SUMMARIZE IN POINTS

- Champagne is a sparkling wine with effervescence. The wine is made from grapes grown in the delimited Champagne region of France. It has to be made by the *Méthode Champenoise.* All champagnes are sparkling wines but all sparkling wines are not champagnes.
- History of champagne is associated with Dom Perignon (1639–1715), a blind Benedictine monk who put the bubbles into champagne, when he was treasurer and cellarer of Abbe of Hauthvillers.
- Chalk in the soil is of utmost importance to create the characteristics necessary for good champagne.
- Pinot Noir and Pinot Meunier, along with a white grape, Chardonnay are the specified grape varieties used for making champagne.
- *Méthode Champenoise* is the approved method used for making champagne. There are other methods used for carbonation, but the resulting sparkling wine cannot be labelled champagne.
- The types of champagnes are Blanc de Blancs, Rose Champagne, Cremant and *Côteaux de Champenoise.*

19.12 FAQs

Short-Answer Type Questions

1. Define champagne.
2. What are the types of champagne?
3. What are the regions of champagne?
4. Give the grape varieties used to make champagne.
5. Name the method used to make champagne.
6. Give the wine laws governing the champagne regions.
7. Give the various bottle sizes used.
8. Name five brands of champagne along with their type.
9. Describe the terms used on champagne labels.
10. What are the other methods used to make sparkling wine?

Long-Answer Type Questions

1. Explain in detail the *Méthode Champenoise*.
2. Describe in detail the *terroir* along with the grape varieties used in making champagne.
3. Write a short note on vintage and non-vintage champagne.
4. Give the types of Champagne. Describe each type in detail.
5. Give the various bottle sizes of champagne specifying their exact volume.

19.13 KEY TERMS

- Agraffes
- Caviar
- Chalk
- Eplusage
- La Champagne
- Le Champagne
- *Méthode Champenoise*
- Monk
- Panniers
- Pupitres
- Remuage
- Remuer
- Riddling

Italian Wines

CHAPTER OUTLINE

The Romans, who ruled the world (the Eastern Hemisphere at that time), cultivated grapes and made great wines. Most of the leading wine-producing regions of France have traced their roots to the Romans who first planted their vineyards.

20.1 HISTORY

The Romans always referred to wines aged for 200 years and remained drinkable, calling them *Immortale Falernum*. To fulfil their desires, expert Roman wine makers tried to improve the art of storing wine. They travelled across the old world in search of an answer. From Greece, they adopted the technique of coating the casks used as barrels for aging with resin. This lined the barrels as they were porous. This helped but was not as effective. The next technique which they adopted was a new method of making wines high in alcoholic strength, concentrated to a jelly and served after being diluted with water.

The Romans went a step further by adding natural preservatives and spices such as sea water, aloes, resin, pitch, marble dust, perfumes and herbs.

After the fall of the Roman Empire, the church took over the cultivation of the vineyards and made wines as it was part of their culture. But by the 14th and 15th century, wine was very fashionable even if it meant to risk one's life through over indulgence. The renaissance is a great example of this practice.

Italy has and still is the vineyard of the world. The smallest plot of land too grows vines and has its own label. Italians drink wine from their early years, as it was safer to drink wine than typhoid infested water in early centuries. Now it is a common man's drink.

Vines in Italy were in abundance. Prior to the common market trade policies coming into effect, which brought about a lot of discipline amongst the growers, vines were allowed to grow on trees, poles, branches etc. Now through control, their yields have improved. But there were always great producers who had quality standards in place from before, but the law brought some uniformity.

20.2 ITALIAN WINE LAWS

The wine law of 1963, improved yield and brought strict government control over all the aspects of wine production. Its basic aim is to protect the name of origin, and the sources of the must and wine, and also to prevent malpractices, fraud and unfair practices. It is surprising to know that in Italy, Chaptalization (adding sugar to adjust the must) process is banned. This can be effectively controlled as the government distributes sugar in Italy.

The wine laws have three different levels, which are listed in Table 20.1.

Table 20.1 The Levels of Wine Law

Wine Law	Description
Vino da Tavola (table wine) or Vino Tipico (typical wine)	This is the simple grading, describing a simple wine with few restrictions on area, percentage of alcohol and are labelled with the name of the region, for example, 'Vino da Tavola di Piedmont'.
Denominazione di Origine Controllata (controlled denomination of origin)	This label is reserved for those wines that have met the standards of quality. First, the viticultural and production practices must meet approved standards and practices, which include soil type, geography of the area, the grape varieties used, planting methods and fertilizers used. Bottling specifications along with minimum alcoholic strength is also controlled. These are inspected at all times and their wines carry a DOC label.
Denominazione di Origine Controllata e Garantita (controlled and guaranteed denomination of origin)	This is the strictest classification of Italian wines. Apart from including all the DOC levels of standards and specifications, this includes many more criteria for control. The wine must be bottled with a government seal by the producer. A government inspector is allowed to test it at any given point from production to sale; the vessels from sale should not be more than 5 litres in capacity. The label of the bottles must have on it—the region of the wine, name of the producer, name of the bottler and place of bottling, with the net contents of the bottle with alcoholic percentage mentioned on it, which is controlled by the government.

Note: A DOC wine can only be upgraded to a DOCG wine if it meets the additional standard as required.

20.3 ITALIAN WINE LABELS

Italian wine labels apart from the DOC and DOCG specifications also carry a number of words, which are listed in Table 20.2.

Table 20.2 Italian Wine Labels

Italian Word	Meaning
Vecchio	Old—these wines are aged more than 'Superiore' wines but less than 'Riserva' wines.
Superiore	It is characterized by slight increase in alcoholic content and aged more than the others without this description.
Riserva Speciale	Aged longer than Riserva.
Riserva	This indicates long aging in casks, depending on DOC requirements.
Imbottigliato All'origine	Bottled at the estate or vineyard.
Classico	Most common word on many Italian wines. It is used to describe the wine's specific area of origin or bottling for example Chianti Classico.
Amaro	Tart, dry.
Secco	Dry
Abboccato	Semi-dry
Amabile	Semi-sweet
Dolce	Sweet
Bianco	White
Rosato	Rosé
Chiaretto	Light red
Rosso	Red
Nero	Deep red
Spumante	Sparkling

The above were descriptions about how to read an Italian wine label and what the words signifies. In addition to these labels, a few growers use a local seal guaranteeing authenticity. This practice is diminishing and is hardly practiced by Italian wine producers anymore.

All DOC wines have the place of origin mentioned on the label even if it is a famous brand such as Est! Est! Est!

20.4 GEOGRAPHY

Italy is a peninsula similar to India, most of which is covered with mountains. The north and west of Italy is covered by the Swiss Alps and to the east are the Venetian Alps. The soil is watered by the glacier fed rivers during the summer. But despite the snow, ice, erosion and avalanche, and other difficult weather conditions, the grape vines thrive due to the fertile soil and the Italian wine maker's interest and hard work.

The northern part of Italy is foggy and gets high rainfall whereas southern Italy has a Mediterranean climate, sunny and dry with a little rainfall.

Grape vines are abundant and grow in all of Italy. The varied climate conditions create different qualities of wine meeting the expectations of almost all taste buds.

The wine-producing regions of Italy.

20.5 GRAPE VARIETIES

Italy is abundant not only in the quantity of vines but the variety of grape vines used in the region. Table 20.3 explains the red grapes and the white grapes used in Italy.

Table 20.3 Red Grapes and White Grapes of Italy

Grape Type	Description
Red Grapes	
Nebbiolo	It is the noble grape of Italy, producing rich wines. Grown in regions of Piedmont and Northern Lombardy.
Barbera, Grignolino Dolcetto (pronounced as dol-chet-oh)	Grignolino and Dolcetta grapes produce softer and lighter wines as compared to the Barbera wines.
Sangiovese	This grape variety is grown in most regions of Italy, but they are the principle grape varieties of Chianti and Brunello di Montalcino.
Aglianico	Makes sturdy red wines in the region of Campania.
Cabernet Sauvignon, Merlot, Pinot Nero (Italian name for Pinot Noir)	All these grape varieties are grown in the southern region of Italy.
White Grapes	
Trebbiano	This is the grape variety that is cultivated extensively in Italy. This grape variety is used in Italy's signature wines such as Est! Est! Est! Lugna, Frascati and Lugna. It is used sometimes to balance Chianti.

Grape Type	Description
Cortese Bianco Verdicchio Moscatos	Cultivated in Piedmont region produces the famous Verdicchio wines. Produce dessert wines from Piedmont, Sicily and Sardinia.
Pinot Bianco (Pinot Blanc), Chardonnay, Pinot Grigio, Sauvignon Blanc, Riesling, Traminer, Tocai	These grape varieties are used in Italian wines. Mostly in the northern parts of Italy known as the Tre Venezie, which comprise of three regions namely, Friuli–Venezia Giulia, Trentino-Alto Adige, Veneto.

Due to its varied climatic conditions, from an extreme cold weather in the north to a warmer Mediterranean climate in the south, Italy produces a variety of wines differing from one region to the next.

20.6 PIEDMONT

Map of Piedmont, Italy.

A famous brand of spumante sparkling wine. (Courtesy: Bacardi International Limited)

Piedmont produces Italy's most rich red wines that are full bodied, full of flavour and age well. These wines have a great quality of resisting the perils of voyage. Piedmont is a name that is derived from *A Pie Del Monti* that translates to *at the foot of the mountains*. This is due to the location of this region, which is in Northern Italy bordering the Alpine glaciers.

Famous Red Wines

1. **Barolo:** It is a town and area with over 2,000 acres of vineyards. It has volcanic soil and is situated on porous rock. Barolo is the name given to the wine produced from this region. It is one of the finest wine Italy has to offer; a rich, full-bodied wine, ruby in colour turning brownish as it ages, having a

20.11 TUSCANY

Many people consider this region to be the wine heartland of Italy, the soil in this region being rich in iron; one makes distinctive wines, both white and red. This is due to the brilliant and most accepted wine of Italy, the Chianti being produced in this region. The Chianti area is subdivided into seven districts, around and between Florence. Wines produced in the central zone of this region may be called Chianti Classico.

The wine-producing regions of Tuscany, Italy.

Famous Red Wines

1. **Chianti:** This famous wine is regulated by DOC laws, regarding vinification processes. It is made from several grapes such as Sangiovese (ranging from 50–80%), the Canaiolo Nero (ranging from 10–30%), white Trebbiano Tuscano and Malvasia del Chianti (ranging from 10–30% of the must). The actual ratio varies as per the vintage of each year.

   Three types of Chiantis are produced, first, a wine light in colour and body that is best had young. Second, is a better quality Chianti, best after a year of aging after which it continues to it mellow. This Chianti type is produced in the largest quantity. The third is the best quality, which is aged for many years to develop roundness in taste.

   The first quality of Chiantis that are meant to be drunk young, a special process is used in Tuscany. A portion of the grapes that are harvested are dried under the sun making them raisins. This is added to the young wines causing a secondary fermentation; this makes the wine drinkable within six months of aging, with a slight sparkle. These young wines are called 'Chianti Governato' using designer bottles or Chiantiaginoa bottles. While the best quality Chianti is bottled in claret—bottles as they need to age.

Important features

Young Chianti—Sold within a year of harvest.
Chianti—11.5% minimum alcohol strength.
Chianti Classico—12% minimum alcohol strength.
Chianti Classico Riserva—12.5% minimum alcoholic strength and aged for minimum of three years.
We should note that both Chianti Classico and Chianti Classico Riserva are DOCG wines. The vineyards responsible for making these classical red wines have a reduced yield per hectare by regulation, to ensure higher quality.

2. **Montalcino:** A brilliant wine produced in the town of Montalcino 'Brunello di Montalcino' is made from the traditional Sangiovese Grosso Grape locally called Brunello. It must be aged for a minimum of four years in wood. Brunello di Montalcino Riserva must be aged for minimum of five years. This is a highly regarded DOCG wine.
3. **Montepulciano:** The wine 'Vino Nobile di Montepulciano' from the town of Montepulciano is a great wine aged for a minimum of two years. Riserva is aged for a minimum of three years, whereas Riserva Speciale is aged for a minimum of four years.

Famous White Wines

1. **Vino Bianco Toscano:** Earlier this wine was bottled as White Chianti or 'Chianti Bianco'. But with present regulations the Chianti label is to be used only to make red wines; hence, this white was renamed 'Vino Bianco Toscana' meaning 'White Tuscan wine' in Venetian.
2. **San Gimignano:** The town San Gimignano bordering the Chianti region produces 'Vernaccia di San Gimignano', a full-bodied white wine one of a kind. It is Italy's first DOC wine labelled in 1966 made from Vernaccia grapes.
3. **Vino Santo:** It is traditionally a white wine made from Muscat grapes, hence carrying its characteristics in totality. In some wine lists this rich, sweet wine is found in the dessert wine section.

20.12 MARCHES AND UMBRIA

The region of Marches faces the Adriatic Sea to the eastern side of the Italian Peninsula. The famous white wine Vérdicchio dei Castelli di Jesi is a distinguished wine from Marches which is a fine, crisp and dry white wine with a delicate bouquet and flavour. The red wines are also good, the well-known ones include Rosso Piceno and Rosso Conero.

The region of Umbria lies to the south west of Marches, which is the home of some beautiful cities such as Orvieto, Perugia and Assisi. The wines of Orvieto are both 'Seco' and 'Abboccato' (see Table 19.1). Both qualities of wine have a fresh fruity bouquet. The premium Orvieto wines are labelled Classico.

20.13 LATIUM

This region mainly produces white wines due to its favourable soil and climatic conditions, but red wines are also made. Vini dei Castelli Romani is the name given to the estates on the hills next to Rome, where the Romans built their country side villas. Frascati is a light white wine which is very famous. The others are the whites of Marino and Castelli Romani which are popularly available throughout Rome.

Est! Est! Est!

The most famous wine made in this region. It is a straw coloured fruity wine with a fresh bouquet. There is an ancient story associated with this wines peculiar name. The story is five centuries old, when Johannes de Fugger (a German Bishop) was on his way to Rome to pay his respects to his Holy Father. He had a practice to send his secretary to find suitable accommodation before his arrival. Where his secretary found a good Inn or hotel serving good food and wine he was supposed to write 'Est!' meaning 'It is!' on the Inn's board. This was an indication for the Bishop to halt his caravan. Apparently when the secretary reached Montefiascone he was so pleased with the wines he wrote 'Est! Est! Est! ' describing the over whelming pleasure he found on drinking this wine.

It is believed the Bishop never reached Rome and his burial site is found are Montefiascone till date. The modern day producers of Est! Est! Est! pay tribute to him every year by pouring one of their premium barrels on his tomb. Est! Est! Est! is a DOC wine and is very popular.

20.14 CAMPANIA AND BASILICATA

These two regions produce both red and white wines. Campania produces a famous 'Lacryma Christi', which is still producing white, red and rosé wines. However, the white wine is being most popular. Basilicata is a region located in the arch of Italy's 'boot'. (Refer map on p. 243). In the commune of Monte Vulture a young, pleasant and dry, red table wine is made namely Anglianico del Vulture. The 'Riserva' labelled version has to be aged for a minimum of five years making it a deep, rich and full-bodied wine having a long shelf life.

20.15 APULIA AND ABRUZZI

The Apulia region is the 'heel' of Italy's boot shape peninsula. The sun shines bright here resulting in more alcoholic wines. Apulia produces wine which equals, if not exceeds, the quantity of wines produced in Piedmont and in Lombardy put together. The DOC wines comprise only 2% of the total wines produced, it has to be noted that this region produces 18 DOC wines.

Abruzzi is to the north of Apulia, producing simple wine. Principle wines are Montepulciano d'Abruzzo, a red wine and Trebbiano d'Abruzzo, a white wine.

Note: 'Montepulciano' refers to a grape variety in Apulia and Abruzzi regions, while it is a town in Tuscany.

20.16 SICILY

When we think of this island region, Marsala, the famous fortified wine comes to mind.

1. **Marsala:** This is a fortified wine obtained from Catarratto, Grillo and Inzolia grapes. It is made in the provinces of Trapani, Palermo and Agrigento. This wine can be dry, semi-dry, sweet or very sweet. This wine has a acidic undertone due to the volcanic soil that is quite similar to Madeira.

   This region produces some good wines, such as Etna Bianco, Etna Rosso and Etna Rosato, named after the active Mount Etna located to the east, responsible for giving this region the rich volcanic soil. The descriptions of these wines are listed in the following sections.
2. **Etna Bianco:** A medium-bodied, straw coloured dry white wine from the slopes of Sicily around Mount Etna.
3. **Etna Rosso:** A red wine made from Nerello grape variety, which is full bodied.
4. **Etna Rosato:** Made from the same grapes as the Rosso but is a Rosé wine. It is lighter and fresher.

Many sweet dessert wines come from Sicily. The Moscato Passito di Pantelleria produced on the island of Pantelleria has an amber colour, rich bouquet and sweet flavour with 15% alcoholic strength.

20.17 SARDINIA

This region is famous for the cask, the vine and the olive; but Sardinia's dessert wines deserve their credit. Cannonau di Sardegna is a red wine—dry, semi-sweet or sweet—produced on the island. Monica di Sardegna is a lighter red wine.

Italian wines are as famous as their supercars. Italy is proud of its wine to such an extent that it retains the best for domestic consumption unlike the French who export the best to the world. This may be the reason French wines are held in higher regard. But that is an argument always open to debate. Today, with Italian cuisine evolving and spreading in its traditional essence, the wines too are gaining much popularity. So let us all marvel at these age-old creations.

LET'S SUMMARIZE IN POINTS

- The wine law of 1963, improved yield and brought strict government control over all the aspects of wine production. Its basic aim is to protect the name of origin, and the sources of the must and wine, and also to prevent malpractices, fraud and unfair practices. It is surprising to know that in Italy, Chaptalization (adding sugar to adjust the must) process is banned.
- There are three Italian wine laws namely, Vino de Tavola, Denominazione di Origine Controllata and Denominazione di Origine Controllata e Garantita.
- The regions of Italy are Piedmont, Lombardy, Veneto, Trentino-Alto Adige, Friuli–Venezia Giulia, Tuscany, Marches and Umbria, Latium, Campania and Basilicata, Apulia and Abuzzi, Sicily and Sardinia.
- The famous Italian grape varieties are Nebbiolo, Barbera, Grignolino, Dolcetto, Sangiovese, Aglianico, Merlot, Cabernet sauvignon, Trebbiano and Pinot Nero among others.
- Marsala is a famous fortified wine from Italy produced in the region of Sicily.

20.18 FAQs

Short-Answer Type Questions

1. Name the Italian wine laws.
2. Name five red grape varieties from Italy.
3. Name five white grape varieties from Italy.
4. Name 10 terms used on the Italian wine labels with their meaning.
5. What are the geographical conditions of the wine producing regions of Italy?

Long-Answer Type Questions

1. Write a detailed note on the wine-producing regions of Italy.
2. Give the details of the Italian wine laws.
3. Write a note on five most famous red wines and white wines of Italy.
4. Explain—Marsala and Asti-Spumanté.
5. Write detailed notes on the following:
   (i) Chianti
   (ii) Barbera
   (iii) Sicily
   (iv) Est! Est! Est!
   (v) Barbaresco
   (vi) Barolo

20.19 KEY TERMS

- Frizzante
- Spumante

21 German Wines

CHAPTER OUTLINE

Germany has been producing wine from the Roman Era. The vineyards are mainly located in the state of Rhineland-Palatinate, accounting for over 60% of the wines produced in Germany.

Germany is famous for all the types of wines, namely dry, semi-sweet, sweet, white wines, rose wines, red wines and sparkling wines known as Sekt. Eiswein is another famous wine of Germany, which shall be discussed later on in this chapter.

21.1 HISTORY

The history of German viticulture is very deeply intermingled with German history itself. The vines were brought by the Romans to this region and records can be traced back up to 800 BC. They were planted along the Rhine River, and were quite popular with the Romans of Caesars time.

During the 18th century most of the wine shipped to England was labelled *Hochheimer*. The English shortened it to *Hocks* or *Hock* as it is popularly known today referring to Rhine wine. This description is not used for the wines of Moselle or Franconia.

The monasteries of Germany have played a pivotal role in developing viticulture. The Benedictine monks in 853 AD erected the Chapel of Saint John, from where Johannisberg takes its name. The Castle Schloss on this hill produces exceptionally fine Rhine wines.

21.2 WINE LAWS

In July 1971, the German government introduced a new wine law which aligned all the older laws and strictly controlled all the different types of wine. The wine laws with the necessary description are enumerated in Table 21.1.

Table 21.1 The Wine Laws with the Necessary Description

Wine Law	Description
Deutscher Tafelwein	It is an ordinary wine which has to be made from certain grape varieties that are grown in Tafelwein region of Germany. The subdivisions of this region are Rhein/Mosel, Oberrhein, Bayern and Neckar. The name of the bottler (*Abfuller*) and the brand name must appear on the label; however, it is not compulsory for the vineyard name to be mentioned on the label.
Deutscher Landwein	These are dry and simple wines having more body than wines of Tafelwein region.
Qualitatswein and Qualitats-wein Mit Pradikat (*quality wine with distinction*)	These are wines which are made from specific grapes from one of the eleven permitted regions. Each of these regions is called *Gebeit* and the wine must have the characteristics of the grapes produced in that region. The sub region is called *Bereich whereas* the sub-district is called *Grosslage* which comprises of many *Lages,* referring to the individual vineyards. The name of the region, Bereich and Grosslage is always mentioned on the label of the wines under this wine law. If a specific grape variety is mentioned on the label, 85% of the grape variety is used in producing the wine.
Qualitatswein Bestimmter Anbaugebiete (*quality wine of specified region*)	A quality wine bears the control number assigned by the tasting panel. It can be labelled by Gebeit (region), Bereich (district), Grosslage (sub district) or Lage (vineyard). The label has to bear the name of the village where the vineyards are located.

Three Stages of German Wines Quality Control Process

1. During the harvest, a vine grower must specify the type of wine they intend to produce, such as Spatlese and Auslese. The quality of the grape varieties used along with the quality of the must is also controlled by the government.
2. The resulting wine is produced and analysed by the designated wine laboratory.
3. The final stage of testing is done by a panel of wine experts who judge the colour, clarity, bouquet and flavour of the wine. An official certification number is mentioned on all the Qualitatswein Bestimmter Anbaugebiete and Qualitatswein Mit Pradikat labels. Sealed samples of each certified wine is retained in case of any customer query or dispute.

21.3 TYPES OF WINE

Qualitatswein Bestimmter Anbaugebiete and Tafelwein wines undergo *Chaptalization* (addition of sugar) to increase the alcoholic strength of the wine. Qualitatswein Mit Pradikat wines cannot be chapitalized. Qualitatswein Mit Pradikat wines include Kabinett, Spatlese, Auslese, Beerenauslese, Trockenbeerenauslese and Eiswein (Table 21.2).

Table 21.2 Types of German Wines with Their Description

Type of Wine	Description
Kabinett	These wines must be made from grapes whose average percentage of sugar by weight is 18–19% to yield a wine with 10% alcoholic strength depending upon the method of vinification, the grape variety used and the region of origin.
Spatlese	These wines must be made from fully ripened grapes. The average percent of sugar by weight should be 20%. This can vary according to the grape variety used. For example, the Riesling produces a must with 19% sugar level. These Riesling wines are produced in the region of Ahr, Mosel and Mittelrhein.
Auslese	The grapes gathered for making the wine are selectively handpicked for their ripeness. The minimum percentage of the sugar in the must should be 22% depending on the region.
Beerenauslese	The grapes for this wine are also handpicked for its ripeness. The minimum sugar levels in the must should be 28–29% depending on the region of cultivation.
Trokenbeerenauslese	These are made from overripe grapes which have shrunken, resembling raisins. The minimum sugar levels in the must should be 35% with no exception to region.
Eiswein	This is a unique wine and a distinct Pradikat wine. It should have a 28–29% sugar level, similar to the Beerenauslese. The main distinctive feature is that these wines are made from frozen grapes. The ideal temperature for harvesting is –8°C and it is crushed before thawing.

Despite the high sugar levels, the wine is allowed to ferment completely. The characteristic sweet taste to these wines is due to the addition of the must (unfermented grape juice). The must used has to be of the same quality or higher. The sweetness balances the high levels of acidity common to most German wines.

Note: 'Troken' refers to the extremely dry wines which are preferred with food rather than by themselves, whereas 'Halbtroken' refers to wines which are semi-dry, between the Kabinett and Troken wines.

21.4 SOIL

The soil conditions across Germany are quite harsh and it is very difficult to cultivate anything else apart from the vine. The land is very uneven and rocky, high on slate or calcium carbonate. Towards the earlier half to the middle of the 20th century, the hilly landscapes were levelled; hence the tedious hand picking was replaced by mechanized picking, making things easier and affordable.

21.5 GRAPE VARIETIES

The Riesling varieties clone species called Müller-Thurgau grape variety produces the highest amount of wines in Germany at 27% of the total. It produces a light bodied, highly aromatic wine. The Riesling however stands at a close second with 20% of all the plantings.

The Sylvaner grape variety is grown in the regions of Rheinhessen, Rheinpfalz, Baden, Nahe and Franconia. The Gewurztraminer is a popular variety grown mainly in Baden, producing an aromatic spicy wine.

Germany is famous for its wonderful white wines rather than the red wines which are quite ordinary.

21.6 PRODUCTION PROCESS OF WINE

The process of making wine in Germany depicted in Figure 21.1.

1. **Harvesting:** The selective picking of the grapes plays a very important role in the quality of the wine produced. The summer sun plays an important role, more the sun-shines, merrier the vine growers. In summer if the vines receive over hundred days of sunshine it will produce a wine of high quality. If the sun does not shine adequately, the grapes are left on the vine to ripen and then sorted to produce wines such as Spatlese, Auslese, Trockenbeerenauslese and Beerenauslese.
2. **Test the must for sugar levels:** Earlier on we have discussed the various styles of wine produced in Germany; each style should have a specified sugar percentage.

   Often the Noble Rot or *Edelfaule* in German which is a mould that forms on the skin of the grape, reducing moisture and concentrating the grape. When this naturally occurs in a particular year, it produces great Beerenauslese wine. If the mould shrivels the grapes, it produces a very dry wine namely the Trockenbeerenauslese, which is quite expensive.
3. **Pressing:** The grapes are crushed to make the must then sent to the next step for fermentation.
4. **Fermentation:** This process is common for making wines from all regions. (Refer Chapter 17 for more details.)
5. **Minimal aging and bottling:** The wines are generally aged for an average period of six to eight months, in stainless steel VATs. There are a few exceptions, as the wineries in Moselle age the wines in casks.

   After this the wines are bottled immediately.

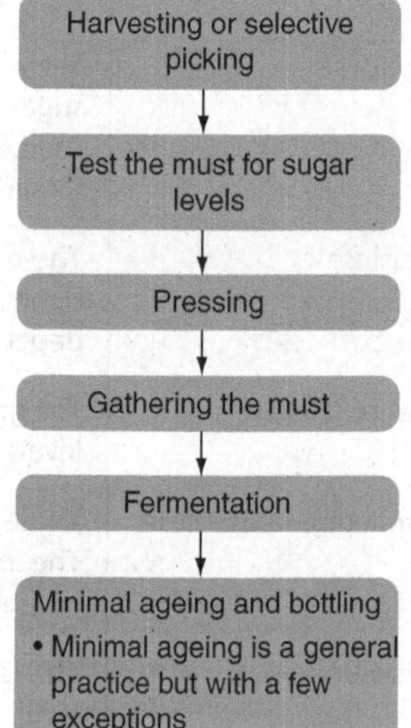

Figure 21.1 The Process of Making Wines in Germany.

21.7 WINE-PRODUCING REGIONS IN GERMANY

The wine regions of Germany are discussed as follows in the order of their significance and popularity in the world.

1. **Rheingau:** This wine region located on the right bank of the Rhine River and is one of the most famous wine regions of the world. Although, the region is small when compared to the others, it produces the most famous wines.

The famous wine labels are Eltville, Erback, Geisenheim, Hallgarten, Hattenhein, Hochheim, Winkle, Rudesheim, Oestrich, Kiedrich and Johannisberg.

The most famous vineyards of this region are Steinberger (the single largest government owned vineyard), Erbacher Marcobrnn and Schloss Johannisberg. These wines have a fruity bouquet, flavour and a distinct character. They are the best quality wines comparable to any of the fine wines of the world, having the longest shelf life of all the German wines of the world.

2. **Rheinhessen:** This is Germany's second largest wine producing region. The wines are full bodied and softer than the wines of Rheingau.

   The main villages producing fine wines from this region are: Bigen, Bodenheim, Dienheim, Laubenheim, Mettenheim, Nackenheim, Nierstein, Oppenheim and Worms.

   The region of Worms is home to Liebfrauenkirche ('Church of Our Beloved Lady') from where the most German wine—Liebfraumilch derived its name. Liebfraumilch is not a region or a vineyard but a collective name for wines from the Rhine. Since 1982, Liebfraumilch is the name given to wines only with a Qualitatswein classification from Nahe, Rheinhessen or Rheinpfalz. The region name has to be specified on the label.

   Liebfraumilch is a wine of consistent quality. Many shippers use fine wines from Rheinhessen to enhance their labels to distinguish them. Some famous examples are Seagull, Blue Nun, Hans Christof, Madrigal and Wedding Veil.

3. **Nahe:** Nahe is a small stream that lies between Moselle and the Rheine. This region produces a wine that is not as rich and heavy bodied as the Rhines and not as light as the Moselles but a wine which is in between both. The best known villages of the Nahe are Schloss Bockelheim, Norheim and Rudesheim (which is different from the Rudesheim produced in Rheingau).

4. **Rheinpfalz:** This is the largest wine-producing region of Germany. This area produces quite a few good white wines and almost 25% of all red wines from Germany. The Upper Palatinate produces the largest amount of table wines of Germany having an earthy flavour and full body.

   The Mittel-Haardt area in the Palatinate produces the best quality wines from this region having more Rieslingplantations than Rheingau.

   The best known labels are: Bad Durkheim, Deidesheim, Edenkoben, Forst, Hambach, Mussbach and Kallstadt to name a few.

5. **Moselle:** This is a very famous wine region. The wines have a lightness, fruity bouquet, elegance and dryness that is extremely pleasing. They are very low in alcohol averaging between 8–10% ABV. The exquisite quality of these wines is attributed to the effervescence, almost similar to sparkling wines. These wines are best enjoyed young, as their sparkle disappears on aging.

   The vineyard owners really work hard on the slopes of this region as they have to arrange slate from the base of the hill and carry them to the top of the hill. This is done to retain the sun's heat during the cold winter nights, allowing the vine roots to grow.

One of the most famous vineyards from Moselle is the 'Doctor at Bernkastel'. In the 14th century, legend has it that the Arch Bishop of Trier fell ill with a fever. The doctors did not know what to do for him but his follower, Ritter Von Holstein, helped him with his similar experience. He served the Bishop the finest wine from Bernkastel which cured him. Since that day this vineyard is popularly known as, 'Doctor's Vineyard'.

Map of the wine-producing regions in Germany.

Moselle wines can be differentiated from Rhine wines in two ways. First, Moselle wine bottles are always dark brown, whereas Rhine wine bottles are always green. Secondly, the name of the township mentioned on the Rhine bottles as a rule always ends with *heim* being the last letters, whereas there is no such defined rule for Moselle wines.

Mittel Moselleis a very high priced wine and commands the same fame as the *Doctor at Bernkastel.* The villages that produce excellent wines are Bernkastell, Dhrone, Erden, Graach, Crov, Piesport, Trittenheim, Wehlen and Zell.

The wines Mosele, Saar and Ruwer are quite similar, unlike the wines of Rhengau and Rheinhessen whose characteristics are distinct and more pronounced.

4. **Baden:** After the Second World War in 1950, this region was replanted with modern grape varieties, with the advent of technology and advanced vineyard management; today this region is a prominent wine producer. Twenty percent of the grapes grown are red grapes, the most prominent being Pinot Noir or Spat Burgunder which produces Weissherbst, a famous rose wine of this region. The remaining eighty percent are white grapes, the Müller-Thurgau, Pinot gris, Rulander Reisling and Gutedal are few examples.

   Krichgau, the central part of Baden, produces 78% of the wines of the region. It has four *Breiches* (sub-regions) namely Ortenau, Kaiserstuhe–Tuniberg, Briesgau and Markgrafelerland.

   Almost all the wines of Baden are marketed under *Bereiche* of 'Grosslagen' labels produced by large co-operatives. A few examples of famous vineyards are Badidches Frankenland, Badisches Bergstrasse and Bodensee.

21.8 OTHER WINE REGIONS IN GERMANY

1. **Wuttenberg:** Wuttenberg is a region which borders Baden wherein wine making is dominated by co-operatives. More than 50% of the grapes grown are red, such as Spatburgunder (also known as Pinot Noir in other parts of the world), Portugieser, Schwarz–Riesling (also known as the Pinot Meunier in other regions) and the most widely used Trollinger. The white grapes include Sylvaner, Kerner, Rulander and Wisburgunder producing the most elegant wines. Riesling is the most predominantly grown white grape of the region.
2. **Franconia:** Wines from this region are robust and largely made from Sylvaner and Müller-Thurgau grapes which possess more body and have a longer shelf life.
3. **Sekt:** This is a type of sparkling wine, which is produced in Germany, and is labelled as *Sekt.* Surprisingly, Germany is the largest producer and consumer of sparkling wines. The annual production of Germany is 30% more than the Champagne region of France.

   Sekt is made either by the Tank Process or the Charmat method (discussed in detail in the Chapter on Champagne). The base wines used to make Sekt is not always from Germany, but can be traced back to France–Loire Valley, or even Italy. Only the sparkling wines labelled Rheingau Sekt or Sparkling Moselle use German wines. Sekts varies from Brut to Extra-Dry (better known as Troken).

   Many people believe that only a famous wine is a good wine. However, excellent, pleasant wines with a simple township name on the label, such as Bernkastel, Piesport, Brauneberg, Rudesheim, Hockheim or with a generic name, such as Liebfraumilch are also considered as great wines.

   German wines, particularly the ones from smaller vineyards, are excellent when drunk young, but the finer wine styles, such as Ausles, Beerenauslese and Trockenbeerenauslese are best when matured.

LET'S SUMMARIZE IN POINTS

- The vines were brought to Germany by the Romans and can be traced up to 800 BC. They were planted along the Rhine River.
- The wine laws of Germany have four tiers.
- The types of German wine are Kabinett, Spatlese, Auslese, Beerenauslese, Trockenbeerenauslese and Eiswein.
- After the Second World War, most of the wine regions of Germany had to be replanted.
- The wine producing regions of Germany are Rheingau, Rheinhessen, Nahe, Rheinpfalz, Moselle and Baden.

21.9 FAQs

Short-Answer Type Questions

1. What is Sekt?
2. Name the wine laws of Germany.
3. What is Hochheimer?
4. What are the types of wine in Germany?
5. What is Edelfaule?

Long-Answer Type Questions

1. Describe in detail the types of wine.
2. Describe the production process of making German wine.
3. Describe in detail the wine laws of Germany.
4. Discuss the wine producing regions of Germany in order of their significance and popularity.
5. Describe Moselle and Baden.

21.10 KEY TERMS

- Beriech
- Lage
- Edelfaule
- Palatinate
- Gebeit
- Sekt
- Grosslage
- Troken
- Hoccheimer/Hock

22 SPANISH WINES

CHAPTER OUTLINE

Spain has its own share in the world of wines. They are the makers of some of the finest wines and fortified wines of the world, namely Sherry.

22.1 HISTORY

The ruins of Pompeii (the city of *Pompeii* is a partially buried Roman town-city near modern Naples in the Italian region of Campania, in the territory of the commune of Pompeii) clearly point to the wine trade between the Romans and the Iberians (the inhabitants of the Iberian Peninsula which is modern-day Spain). Around AD 900, the pot still was discovered under the Moor occupation of this region. In fact, this important discovery led to the pot still distillation and eventually the creation of fortified wines.

22.2 SPANISH WINE LAWS

The Spanish wine laws have five terms. They are listed in Table 22.1 starting from the lowest label moving to the highest label.

Table 22.1 The Spanish Wine Laws

Wine Law	Description
Vino de Mesa (VDM)	This is the lowest classification, comprising of table wines made from the unclassified vineyards.
Vinos de la Tierra (VDT)	This classification is equivalent to France's Vin de Pays. The labels of these wines carries the names of the 'Communid Autonoma' geographical regions which are larger. Andalucia, Castilla La Mancha and Levante are source examples from this brand.
Vino de Calidad Producido en Region Determinada (VCPRD)	This is equivalent to France's VDQS classification. (Vin de Limite Qualité Supérieure)
Denominaciôn de Origen (DO)	The first is classification deals with quality wine regions of Spain, regulated by Consejo. Regulators are responsible for marketing these wines.
Denominaciôn de Origen Calificada (DOC)	This is a classification, which deals with those quality wine regions producing consistent quality, a step above the DO classification.

Before we move on to discuss the generic wines from Spain, we have to mention Sherry, which made Spanish wines come to the forefront of the world of wine.

I FORTIFIED WINES OF SPAIN

22.3 SHERRY

LET'S DEFINE

'Fortification is the process of adding distilled spirit, normally a grape brandy, to a wine to enhance its quality and flavour.'

History of Sherry

Jerez is a region of Spain which is responsible for the creation of this splendid wine. It has been in the centre of the viticulture process dating back to 200 BC, introduced by the Phoenicians. As mentioned before, in AD 711, distillation was introduced leading to fortification of wine. Wines similar to Sherry have been made in southern Iran's city of Shiraz, but its name was not derived from there. The present name 'Jerez de la Frontera' has been given by King Don Juan I, during his regime in AD 1380. The invention of Sherry, though, is just four centuries old. There was an enterprising merchant who was quite distressed as to why their wines were not gaining their due popularity in England. Later, they did realize that if they Anglicise the names, it would gain popularity. There was no offence to the English, but certain people had their own preferences that have to be accepted by all. Hence, as the original word Jerez (pronounced as 'he-rehz') was anglicized and it became *Jerries*, then *Sherries* and finally Sherry. The city of Jerez de la Frontera is where the Sherry-producing vineyards are located. The grand 'bodegas' or warehouses were used to keep huge amount of reserves of wine which make Sherry, in Jerez, Sanlucar de Barrameda and Puerto de Santa Maria.

Interesting Facts!

Spain, which is located on the Iberian Peninsula, has been inhabited by the people of more than 13 ancient Kingdoms. Spain is a single country with regional diversity. For example, the Catalans from Barcelona speak a different language and maintain different customs from the Castilian of Madrid. Spain is quite similar to India, but not as culturally diverse.

Geography

Jerez de la Frontera is in the province of Andalucia, the most southern part of Spain. The Sherry district comprises of vineyards distributed in a triangular area of 50,000 acres. In this region, the driest Sherry to the sweetest are produced.

Map of wine-producing regions in Spain. (Courtesy: *Consejo Regulador Jeres-Xeres-Sherry, Manzanilla- Sanlucar de Barrameda y Vinagre de Jeres, in Jeres de la Frontera, Spain.*)

Soil Conditions

Around Jerez, primarily three types of soil are found. These are as follows:

1. **Barros:** It is reddish clay, containing iron and found in the south of Jerez.
2. **Albariza:** This type of soil is rich in chalk, lime and magnesium. It is the best soil for Sherry production. This soil is in the north of Jerez where the best Sherries comes from.
3. **Arenas:** It is found in the sea shore and is a sandy type of soil.

Soil conditions for growing grapes for making Sherry. (Courtesy: *Consejo Regulador Jeres-Xeres-Sherry, Manzanilla-Sanlucar de Barrameda y Vinagre de Jeres, in Jeres de la Frontera, Spain.*)

The Albariza soil is best for growing the Palomino variety of grape. By law 40% of all grapes, which make Sherry, must come from this soil. Whereas the Barros and Arenas types soils are meant for Pedro Ximinez (PX) and Moscatel grapes.

Pedro Ximinez grapes. (Courtesy: *Consejo Regulador Jeres-Xeres-Sherry, Manzanilla- Sanlucar de Barrameda y Vinagre de Jeres, in Jeres de la Frontera, Spain.*)

Grape Varieties

Palomino is the finest grape used for making Sherry comprising of 90% of all grapes grown in Jerez region. The other important grape variety used is the Pedro Ximinez (PX) and Moscatel used for making very sweet wines and for blending other Sherries.

All the traditional varieties had been grafted onto American Phylloxera-resistant root stocks, as all the vines were destroyed due to the vine disease towards the end of the 19th century.

Sherry Production Process

The production process of Sherry has been depicted in Figure 22.1 and described as follows:

1. **Gathering the grapes:** The grapes are harvested with the help of sharp knives and by hand beginning from the final week of August to the first week of September. The vintage festival ('Fiesta de la Vendimia') marks the official commencement of the vintage.
2. **Sunning and drying:** Before being pressed a few grape varieties such as Palomino are sunned and dried for 12–24 hours, solely depending on the quality of the wine desired. The Pedro Ximinez grapes and Moscatel grapes are dried for 2–3 weeks to become raisins.

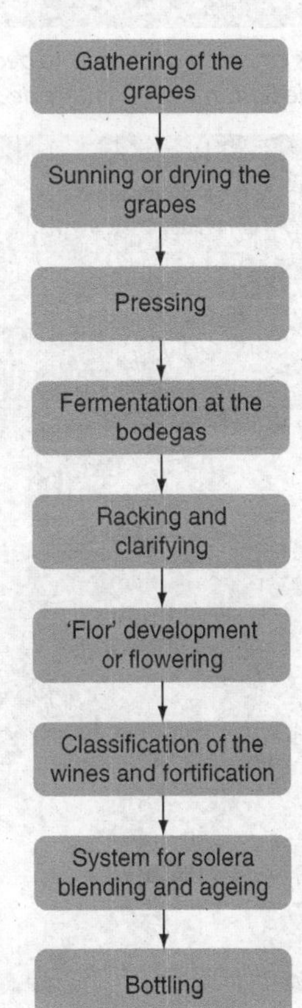

Figure 22.1 Production process of Sherry.

DID YOU KNOW

The festivities of 'Fiesta de la Vendimia' are celebrated for four days. This is a festival with fireworks, amusement and a whole lot of happiness. The first press of the wine is ceremoniously done during this festival known as 'Te Deum'.

Four treaders press and tread the 'first' press before the image of San Ginésde la Jara on the steps of the church.

The grapes covered under mats to become raisins. (Courtesy: Consejo Regulador Jeres-Xeres-Sherry, Manzanilla-Sanlucar de Barrameda y Vinagre de Jeres, in Jeres de la Frontera, Spain.)

The pressing of the grapes. (Courtesy: *Consejo Regulador Jeres-Xeres-Sherry, Manzanilla- Sanlucar de Barrameda y Vinagre de Jeres, in Jeres de la Frontera, Spain.)*

3. **Pressing:** Traditionally, pressing the grapes used to be done manually by treaders. They would gather the grapes in 'lagares' (wooden pressing troughs) which were 2 ft deep and approximately covering an area of 18 sq. ft. The 'lagar' has a seven food screw pole in the centre. The treaders (the men who press the grapes by foot) wear special hobnail shoes to press the grapes until they become pulp and the juice is collected in 'butts' ('Butts are 132 gallon casks). The remaining pulp is then sprinkled with gypsum (calcium sulphate) to ensure that tartaric acid balance in the wine. Then the pulp is gathered towards the screw pole at the centre of the 'lagar'. An 80 ft woven grass ribbon is used to gather the pulp, and then squeezed by rotatory tugging. This releases the residual juice which would otherwise remain in the pulp.
4. **Fermentation at the bodegas:** The Must called 'Musto' is collected in the 'butts' specially made of American white oak, as it has a porous and ideal grain for making Sherry. The 'butts' are shipped to the shipper's 'bodegas' located in Jerez, Sanlucar de Barrameda and Puerto de Santa Maria to ferment into wine. The fermentation process starts with a lot of gusto, bubbling and boiling as the yeast acts on the must to produce wine. This process takes about one to two week for most of the sugars to convert into alcohol. The wine is left to ferment in these 'butts' for six to eight weeks ending in December.

Fermentation tanks. (Courtesy: *Consejo Regulador Jeres-Xeres-Sherry, Manzanilla- Sanlucar de Barrameda y Vinagre de Jeres, in Jeres de la Frontera, Spain.*)

5. **Racking and clarifying:** As the wine is left to ferment, the larger sediments settle at the bottom of the cask, and are then racked into new 'butts'. The new 'butts' are filled only two-third, for allowing the 'flor' to develop on the sugar of the wine.
6. **'Flor' development or flowering:** The 'flor' is a natural yeast film which develops on the surface of the wine. This 'flor' is specially developed by Sherry makers for its characteristic aroma, flavour, freshness and nuttiness. The 'flor' can be from a few millimetres to over a quarter of an inch thick.
7. **Classification of the wines and fortification:** Sherry wine is very different in nature. Despite the production area, the process is the same, no two 'butts' of Sherry will be the same. Due to this unpredictable and unique nature of the wine, classifying each wine, is an important step. The development of 'flor' also plays a vital role, giving each 'butt' of the wine a different characteristic. The thick flor layer results in a pale coloured and lighter Fino-type wine, whereas the wine with a thin flor layer have a deeper colour and fuller body. The types of wines which are classified to further be blended to make sherry are as follows:

Flor development or flowering. (Courtesy: *Consejo Regulador Jeres-Xeres-Sherry, Manzanilla- Sanlucar de Barrameda y Vinagre de Jeres, in Jeres de la Frontera, Spain.*)

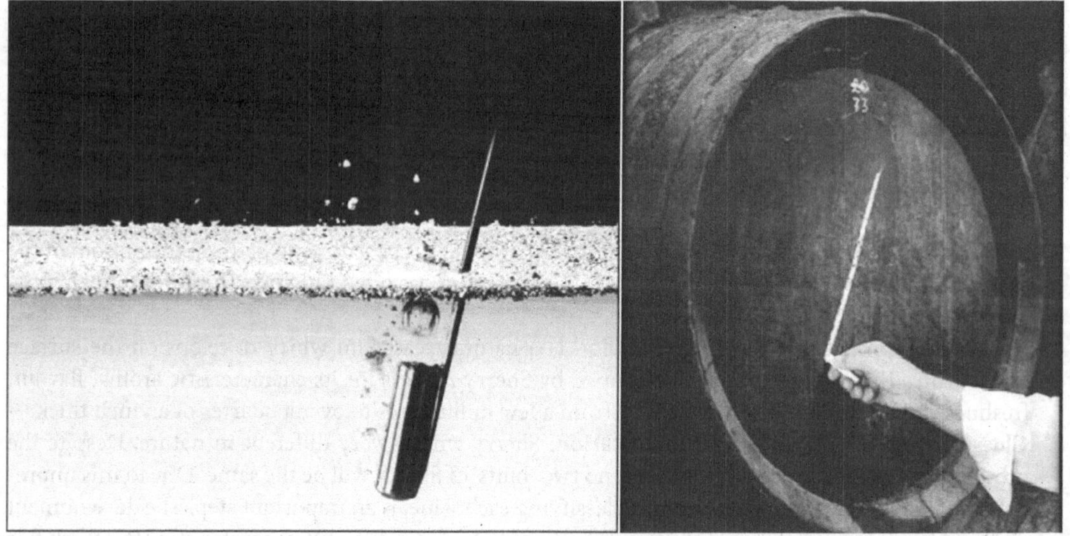

Wine being examined before classification (left), and a bodega master classifying the quality of each wine with a particular stroke (right). (Courtesy: *Consejo Regulador Jeres-Xeres-Sherry, Manzanilla- Sanlucar de Barrameda y Vinagre de Jeres, in Jeres de la Frontera, Spain.*)

The types of wines which are classified to further be blended to make sherry are as follows:

- Raya (/) – The palest and finest wines which are made into Finos.
- Dos Rayas (//) – Slightly heavier wines than the Raya, which are needed to make Olorosso.
- Tres Rayas (///) – Low quality wines, which will be distilled.
- Cuarto Rayas (////) – Ordinary wines used for seasoning or clearing the casks.

The word 'Raya' means stroke (/). This is an evolved system in which the 'bodega' master classifies each wine by taste and marks each butt with either one 'raya'(or stroke), two, three or four depending on its quality. The first 'raya' undergoes more scrutiny and is further subdivided into four more 'palmers' or sub-strokes. For example, (\\\/).

After the classification is complete, the sherry is fortified. Fortification is the process in which grape brandy is added to the sherry to increase the alcoholic strength. This is done by adding the distilled spirit or brandy with a mature sherry to make a 'half and half' blend known as *Mitad y Mitad*. This *Mitad y Mitad* is mixed with young wines in proper proportions. This is followed as a direct addition of brandy may not blend well, leading to its spoilage.

Once classified and fortified, the Sherries are ready for the Solera system.

8. **The Solera system for blending and ageing:** The Solera system is the main feature of the Sherry-making process (Figure 22.2). This system has been in place beginning from the early half of the 19th century.

   Solera is derived from the word 'suelo' meaning 'ground'. This is in reference to the butts nearest to the ground. The Sherry producers realized that the wines were different from the others, and hence, they required a process that would provide their wines with an average age and ensure a consistent volume of product being produced in every vintage year.

The Solera system. (Courtesy: *Consejo Regulador Jeres-Xeres-Sherry, Manzanilla- Sanlucar de Barrameda y Vinagre de Jeres, in Jeres de la Frontera, Spain.*)

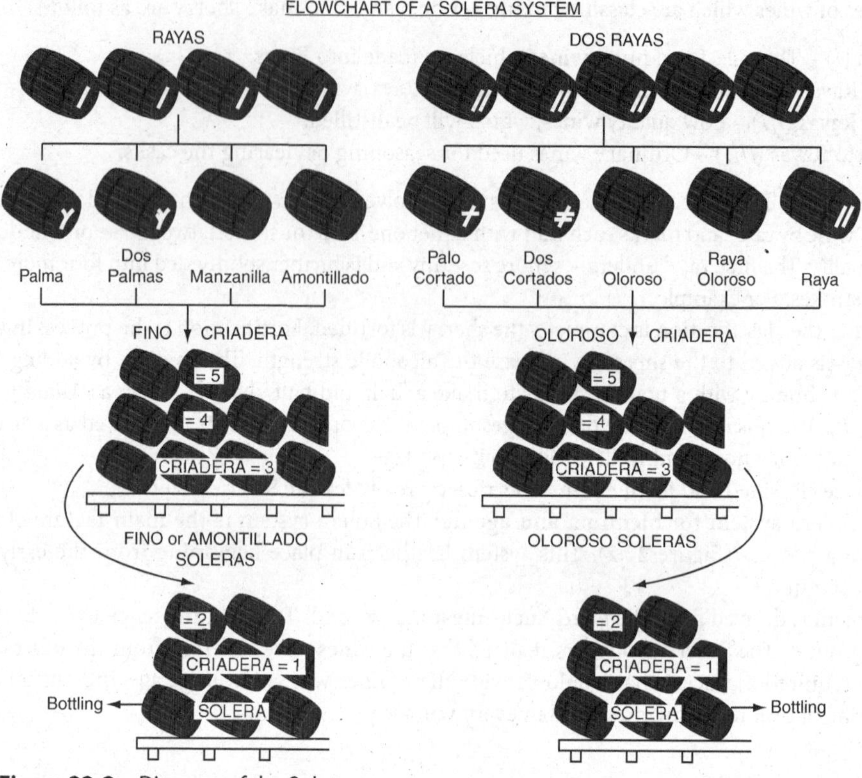

Figure 22.2 Diagram of the Solera system.

Working

The system works by first arranging a number of casks/butts of fine quality wine as the first tier (the lowest level). In the following year, a second tier is placed above the first, and a year after that a third tier is placed. All the tiers above the first tier are called 'Craideras'. The average Solera would have up to 6 'Craideras', but some goes up to even 12. Once the producer establishes the level of tiers they would like to keep, only then does the process being of selling the wine from the first 'base' level, but not more than one-third of each cask/butt in any given year. This drawn-off level is then replenished by the wine from the next tier, that is, the first 'Craideras'. The first 'Craideras' are replenished by the level above them and so on. The final *Craideras* are replenished with new wine which is the youngest.

Bottling of Sherry. (Courtesy: *Consejo Regulador Jeres-Xeres-Sherry, Manzanilla- Sanlucar de Barrameda y Vinagre de Jeres, in Jeres de la Frontera, Spain.)*

By the time this new wine, starting from the top, reaches the bottom tier, it would have been in the system for a minimum 7–10 years, if not more. This method of fractional blending produces the same type of Sherry every year, maintaining the standards and quality.

Sherry is always a wine, and vintage Sherry is a non-existing term. The year written on the bottle refers to the year in which the Solera was established, and not the year in which the wine was bottled.

9. **Fining:** This is the process of adding fining or clarifying agents to the wine to remove small sediments from the wine. The preferred fining agent is egg white with a little bit of wine. Some Sherries are refrigerated and then filtered, removing excess tartarates and stabilizing the wine.
10. **Bottling:** The Sherry after fining is bottled. After bottling the Sherry does not age, and can be consumed immediately.

Types of Sherry

All producers make the same general types of Sherry; however, they offer various qualities of each type. The qualities of each type of Sherry are illustrated in Table 22.2.

Table 22.2 Qualities of Each Type of Sherry

Type	Description
Fino ('fine' in Spanish)	It is the driest and palest of the traditional varieties of Sherry. It has a slight pungency.
Manzanilla	A very fine, very dry and medium bodied wine, developed in the 'bodegas' of Sanlucar de Barrameda, where the salt air of the Atlantic Ocean influences the wine's fragrance and lightness; however, if the same wine is moved to Jerez, the same Manzanilla turns into a Fino.
Manzanilla Pasada	This is a type of Manzanilla that has undergone extended ageing or has been partially oxidized giving it a richer, nuttier flavour.
Amontillado	This is a Sherry that is darker than a Fino but lighter than an Olorosso. This is because the wine is then exposed to oxygen. This is a fairly dry wine but some producers make their Amontillados less dry or mildly sweet.
Olorosso	Olorosso means 'scented' in Spanish. This type of Sherry is aged longer than a Fino or an Amontillado. This is a deep golden wine, which is full bodied, dry and rich with a nutty flavour. It has the highest alcohol strength than all the sherries at 20% ABV. 'Amoroso' was a term formerly used to describe a sweet and velvety Olorosso.
Paolo Cortado	It is a variety of Sherry that is initially aged like an Amontillado Sherry, but develops a characteristic closer to an Olorosso.
Cream	This is a richer and very sweet, full bodied wine with a golden colour.
Sweet Sherries or Jerez Dulce	Produced from dried Pedro Ximinez (PX) grapes or Moscatel grapes. This is also called Brown, as this wine is full bodied and sweet having a dark brown colour.

Courtesy: Consejo ReguladorJeres-Xeres-Sherry, Manzanilla- Sanlucar de Barrameda y Vinagre de Jeres, in Jeres de la Frontera, Spain.

Different varieties of sherry (from left to right): Manzanilla, Fino, Amontillado, Olorosso, Medium, Cream and Pedro Ximinez. (Courtesy: *Consejo Regulador Jeres-Xeres-Sherry, Manzanilla-Sanlucar de Barrameda y Vinagre de Jeres, in Jeres de la Frontera, Spain.*)

The Pedro Ximinez grape was brought by Peter Siemens from Germany. His name was Hispanicized and he was called Pedro Ximinez. The main use of this grape variety is to add richness and softness to rich Olorosso and brown Sherries.

Service of Sherry

Sherry is a wine, but served in a Sherry Copita glass. Sherries can be consumed as aperitifs, between the meal drinks, or even as a dessert wine.

The various types of Sherries have different characteristics and use. Sherry is served in the same way as wine. The sole difference being the alcoholic strength being higher in a Sherry makes it less susceptible to spoilage. Hence, it can be easily taken on a journey or a long distance picnic.

Sherry served in a Sherry Copita glass.

Brands of Sherry

1. Croft
2. Savory and James
3. Tio Pepe
4. Sandeman
5. Duff Gordon
6. John Harvey and Sons
7. Domecq La Ina

22.4 OTHER FORTIFIED WINES OF SPAIN

Malaga

It is an important wine region for many centuries producing excellent sweet wines, located on the Mediterranean coast. Various types of Malaga are made ranging from medium sweet to very sweet. It has an alcoholic strength of 14–23% ABV.

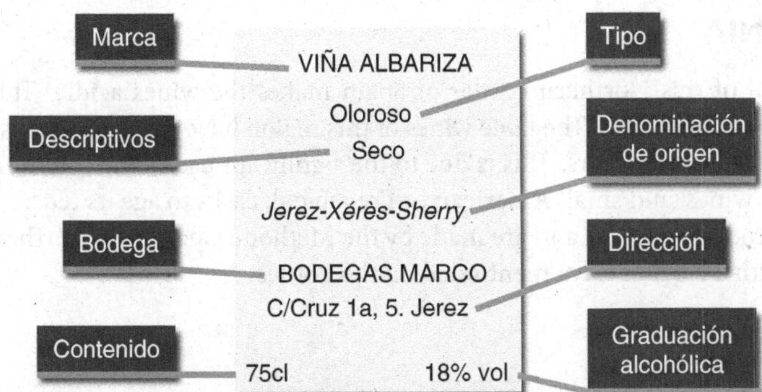

Figure 22.3 A standard Sherry label. (Courtesy: *Consejo Regulador Jeres-Xeres-Sherry, Manzanilla- Sanlucar de Barrameda y Vinagre de Jeres, in Jeres de la Frontera, Spain.*)

The grapes are often sun-dried before crushing, making a sweet wine. Pedro Ximinez and Muscat are two principle grape varieties used.

Tarragona

The famous city of Barcelona is the capital of this region, which produces very interesting fortified wines. Tarragona Port, a sweet red wine which is famous from this region, is made on the same lines as wine made in Portugal.

The most famous Moscatel wines of Spain are produced in a region to the northern part of Tarragona called Penedés region. The wines from this region are light golden in colour, have a pronounced Muscat flavour, and are very rich and soft. They have an alcoholic strength of 16–18% ABV, which is a rule.

II TABLE WINES FROM SPAIN

Annually Spain produces over a billion gallons of wine which is responsible for employing over 20% of Spain's population. Apart from the famous region of Jerez, there are 27 other controlled regions, producing mostly table wines. The most import of these regions is Rioja, Catalonia and Valdepeñas.

22.5 RIOJA

The term 'Rioja' is pronounced as 'Ri-o-ha' it is the most valued Spanish table wine. Rioja region has three wine-producing districts, which are listed as follows:

1. **Rioja Alta**—It has the highest elevation and produces wines of high acidity.
2. **Rioja Alavesa**—It has an abundance of sunshine that helps on producing fruity wines.
3. **Rioja Baja**—It is the hottest of the three regions and has a Mediterranean climate, producing wines of high alcohol.

Rioja wines are generally a blend of all three districts. These wines have to meet all the regulations set by the *Consejo Regulador*. The wines labelled *Reserva* must be aged for a minimum of two years in cask and one year in bottle. Whereas older *Gran Reserva* wines have to spend two years in cask and four years in bottle or three years in cask and two years in bottle. The older Reservas are aged for many years allowing the bouquet to develop.

22.6 CATALONIA

The rich granite soil of this Northern corner of Spain makes the wines acidic. This region produces excellent still and sparkling wines. The table wines of this region have gained immense popularity in the world market over the last few years. This is due to the significant use of the cold fermentation method to produce its white wines, and small American or French oak casks to age its reds.

Sparkling wines too are popular and are made by the Méthode Champenoise. They are distinguished from champagne with a label of Cava mentioned on the bottles.

22.7 VALDEPEÑAS

Around Madrid in Central Spain bordering Andalucia, delicate red and white wines are produced. White Valdepeñas are dry, full bodied, and flavourful wines. The reds are more like dark rosé wines, high in alcohol and fruity. These wines are best enjoyed young, and are often shipped under brand names, rather than region names.

LET'S SUMMARIZE IN POINTS

- Spain is famous for its wines especially Sherry—a premium fortified wine.
- It is governed by a five-tier wine law system.
- Sherry is made in the Jerez region of Spain. The original name of Jerez has been anglicized to Sherry.
- Sherry-producing regions around Jerez enjoy varied soil conditions.
- Palomino is the finest grape is used for making Sherry. It comprises of 90% of all grapes grown in this region.
- Sherry is blended in the unique Solera system.
- The various types of Sherry are Fino, Manzanilla, Manzanilla Pasada, Amontillado, Olorosso, Cream, Palo Cortado and Jerez Dulce.
- Sherry is consumed as an aperitif and in between meals. It is served in Sherry Copita glasses.
- The other fortified wines from Spain are Malaga and Tarragona.

22.8 FAQs

Short-Answer Type Questions

1. Where is Sherry produced?
2. Name the grape varieties used in making Sherry.
3. Name the various types of Sherry.
4. What glassware is used for serving Sherry?
5. Name three types of fortified wines from Spain.

Long-Answer Type Questions

1. Give the production process of Sherry.
2. Describe the Solera system in detail.
3. Give the types of Sherry with a detailed explanation.
4. Discuss the geography, soil conditions and grape varieties used in Sherry production.
5. Describe the history of Sherry. Explain the Spanish wine laws in detail.

22.9 KEY TERMS

- Bodegas
- Butts
- Cava
- CousejoRegulador
- Flor
- Lagres
- Musto
- PX
- Pompeii
- Raya
- Solera

PORTUGUESE WINES

23

CHAPTER OUTLINE

Portugal was influenced by the English to produce port wine from their existing table wines. The British Isles are one of the largest markets of port wine. In fact, the locals prefer table wines to the fortified Port. Due to the overall popularity of port wines, fortified wines have become the face of the Portuguese wine trade. Let us discuss the fortified wines of Portugal first, and then move on to the other table wines of this region.

23.1 PORT WINE

This is a sweet, aromatic and flavourful fortified wine made in Portugal.

LET'S DEFINE

Port – 'A fortified wine produced in the delimited Douro region and exported through the Bar of Oporto' as per the Anglo–Portuguese Treaty of 1916.

23.2 HISTORY

Grapes are being grown in stony soil conditions. (Courtesy: *Graham's Port Bottles, Portugal.*)

The name of this popular beverage is derived from the name of its country of origin, Portugal. Portugal is so called, because from the ancient Roman times, this region had a very busy harbour at the mouth of the Douro River. Part of the ancient region of Lusitania, Cale was the ancient name of the settlement in this region and it being a port, the Romans called it 'Portus Cale' meaning 'the port of Cale'. This name was modernized to present day name of Portugal, renaming the port to Oporto. The history of port, however, has not been so peaceful, and been laden with many wars. The wine trade between England and Portugal was established during the early part of the 18th century. In 1703, Queen Anne's armed forces were at war with France. It was during this time that the queen decided to reduce ties with France primarily starting off with the wine trade. She found a solution by establishing a commercial treaty with Don Pedro II in exchange for English woollens into Portugal. Port wines would enjoy a preferential duty over all other wines coming into England.

The port wines were very harsh and sharp and hence not very popular. The English wine merchants experimented and found that by fortifying the wine before all the sugars have been fermented, it had a characteristic flavour and aroma, which suited the English palate. The extra alcohol in the wine complimented the English weather too, gaining popularity overnight.

23.3 GRAPE VARIETIES

There are many grape varieties grown in Douro Valley; however, only two varieties are used to make Porto or Vinho do Porto (Table 23.1).

Table 23.1 Grape Varieties of Douro Valley

Grape Variety	Characteristics
'Plantes Nobles', such as Mourisco, Touriga and Bastardo.	Juice lacks flavour and colour. It is light bodied and gives the wine character and finesse.
Tinta Francisco, Tinta Cao and Souzao.	Contribute the colour and balance out the must.

While the above-mentioned varieties are mainly used for making red port wine, White Porto uses Rabigato, Moscatel Branco, Malvasia, Fina and Verdelho.

Many countries such as the United States and India produce fortified wines and label them as port. For example, Goan Port Wine. The Instituto do Vinho do Porto, which is the controlling body of Portuguese port wine, has legally established that the fortified wines produced and bottled in Portugal must be labelled 'Porto' or 'Vinho do Porto'.

23.4 PRODUCTION PROCESS OF PORTO OR VINHO DO PORT

The production process of port wine is depicted in Figure 23.1 and described in the following sections.

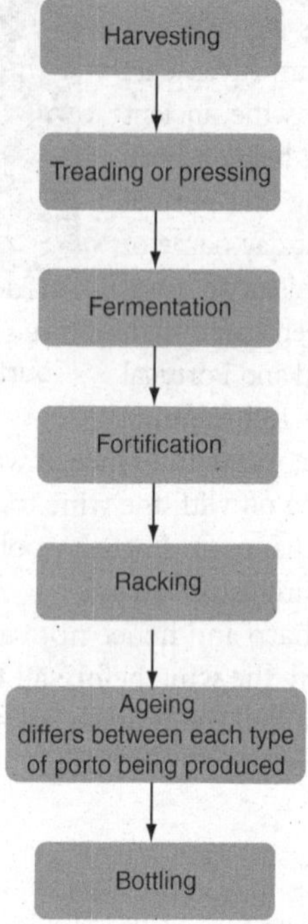

Figure 23.1 The Production Process of Port Wine.

Harvesting

The vintage begins at the end of September or beginning of October, depending on the weather. The grapes are usually handpicked and carried down the slopes on oxen-drawn carts.

The manual picking process. (Courtesy: *Graham's Port Bottles, Portugal.*)

Unique step of selection of grapes by hand is done especially at Graham's Port Winery—one of the primary reasons for its wines being of the highest standards and quality. (Courtesy: *Graham's Port Bottles, Portugal.*)

Treading or Mechanized Pressing

Due to mechanized pressing gaining more momentum, the earlier method of treading by using special boots is reduced to a tradition. A festival is celebrated during the harvest season and a small batch is treaded as per tradition which may become wine.

The famous treading process. (Courtesy: *Graham's Port Bottles, Portugal.*)

Mechanized pressing being done at Graham's Port Bottles Winery. (Courtesy: *Graham's Port Bottles, Portugal.*)

Fermentation

Fermentation begins immediately after pressing. The process is allowed to continue for 2–3 days. During the fermentation process, the sugar levels are constantly measured with a *mustimeter*. When the wine reaches the desired sugar levels, it is run off into casks. The remaining balance of the fermented must, consisting of the pulp, is distilled to make brandy to fortify the wines.

It has to be noted that the wine is constantly circulated during fermentation, to increase the skin contact with the wine, which was easily accomplished by treading the grapes.

Fortification

The casks in which the fermented wines, rich in residual sugars, are collected are prefilled with sufficient grape brandy. The brandy is made from the local wines of the district, which increases the Porto's alcoholic strength to 20% ABV. This stops the fermentation process and the remaining sugars in the wine add to the sweet taste, which is the characteristic of a classical Porto. The level of the residual sugars is usually 8%.

Racking

After the wine is fortified, it is racked after keeping it for a year at the *Quintas* (the vineyards where the vines are grown).

Ageing

After racking, the wine is sent to Oporto for storage. Earlier, sailboats called *Rabelos* were used to transport the casks down the Douro River to Oporto. Now it is done by truck or rail. The wines are stored with care and later it is decided whether to ship them as Vintage, Tawny or Ruby Port.

Bottling

The last step is bottling. The wine is supposed to be stored in an upright position to minimize the exposure to the air, which seeps in through the porous cask. Some of the wines age in the bottle, reaching their prime in 8–10 years.

23.5 TYPES OF PORT

Vintage Port

This is a very good quality of wine, which is a result of a great vintage year, with optimum rain, sun and soil conditions. It is bottled within two years after harvesting. It is quite rare and only occurs once in three years. This rich full wine needs to be rested in the bottle for 8–10 years. During this period, a heavy deposit is formed, consisting of tannins, colouring agents and tartarates. This forms a leafy crust in the bottle. Utmost care must be taken, not to disturb the bottle, as the deposit will then make the wine gets cloudy. The wine must be decanted before being consumed.

Vintage Porto has a deep ruby colour, the fruitiest bouquet and the most body of all styles of Porto. This type of wine is quite harsh until it matures. This has to be bottled in Portugal only. The bottling date and the vintage date must be mentioned on the label and the cask.

Ruby and Tawny Ports

These types of port wines mature in wood unlike the Vintage Port, which matures in the bottle. These are blended port wines, which are a blend of over 30 wines at times.

'Ruby Port' is a bright ruby-coloured blend of young Portos that have been aged for sometime in wood. It is very fruity, with pronounced sweetness in the wine. It has to be aged for a minimum of three years before bottling. It is consumed just after bottling.

'Tawny port' is a blend of matured Portos. It also has to be aged for three years by law, but is aged for a longer period.

Fining

These wines, as they age in wood, form a crust in the cask, comprising of sediments. To avoid the wines from becoming dull and loosing character, they are clarified twice a year. The better quality wines use egg whites, which help in settling the finer particles to the bottom of the cask, which can then be racked into other casks. Each time the wine undergoes fining, it loses colour; hence, the older the wine the more number of times it is clarified and is paler in colour. The paleness of the wine is called tawniness, as it loses its ruby-red colour and becomes drier. Most tawny Portos do not have any age statements on the label.

Late Bottled Vintage

This is a product of a single good year, which is not blended and remains in the cask. It is a type of tawny port. The wine matures faster than a Vintage Port, as it is done in a cask and not in a bottle. Late bottled vintage (LBV) are racked repeated, hence do not require decanting.

White Porto

This is a white wine version of the Porto. White grapes are exclusively used and matured in wood. This is a soft, dry and a flavourful wine. It is consumed on its own; however, sometimes used to blend young tawny wines to make them pale and soft earlier.

Crusted Porto

This wine is a classic and a close relative of Vintage Porto, but is a wine of a single year. It does not match up in quality compared to its counterpart Vintage Porto, though it deposits a crust and is similar in character.

Service: Port is usually an after-dinner drink. The only exception is being White Porto, which is preferred as an aperitif by the French. Port is often enjoyed with cigars, coffee or cheese. It is also used to flavour sauces and other desserts in the Kitchen.

Brands of Port

1. Cockburn
2. Fonseca
3. Croft
4. Sandeman
5. Delaforce
6. Dows

GRAHAM'S 1970 VINTAGE PORT

Quinta dos Malvedos, one of the Douro's greatest vineyard properties, has always been the heart of Graham's Vintage Port, where most of the grapes are sourced. Over time, Quinta da Vila Velha and Quinta do Vale de Malhadas (both privately owned by a member of the Symington family), as well as Quinta das Lages, have contributed to the Graham's unique style. The latest acquisition, Quinta do Tua, perfectly complements Malvedos and adds a further dimension to Graham's Ports.

Courtesy: *Graham's Port Bottles, Portugal.*

Table 23.2 About Graham's 1970 Vintage Port

The Viticultural Year	Tasting Notes	Food Pairing Suggestion Serving
A wet winter with a cold and dry March. Warm weather in April was ideal for flowering. Spring and summer were calm and settled. Rain fell in late August and early September. Harvesting started at Malvedos on 21 September. Good weather throughout the vintage.	Excellent deep red garnet colour at the heart of the glass. On the nose, a rich intensity of caramelized fruit and coffee. On the palate, this wine is in perfect harmony, round and soft yet with 'grip'. Great length on the palate.	Graham's 1970 Vintage Port is delicious after any meal, pairing wonderfully with cheese or simply to be enjoyed in the company of good friends.

GRAHAM'S 20 YEARS OLD TAWNY PORT

Time-honoured skills, craftsmanship and dedication are handed down from generation to generation at Graham's in the form of three unique arts—the art of blending, the art of cooperage and the art of ageing—to produce an extraordinary selection of Tawny Ports.

The perfect balance: Graham's '20-Years Old' is the Master Blender's quest for perfection and capturing the perfect balance between young and aged port wines. A port wine is perfected for more than 20 years, to delight those in the quest for excellence.

Courtesy: *Graham's Port Bottles, Portugal.*

Table 23.3 About Graham's 20 Year Old Tawny Port

Reviews and Awards	Tasting Notes	Food Pairing Suggestion Serving
Like all Graham's premium ports, its Aged Tawnies have a strong history of accolades. Since 2000, Graham's 20-Years Old Tawny has been awarded: • Two gold medals and four silver medals at the International Wine Challenge. • One gold and four silver medals at the International Wine & Spirits Challenge • Two gold medals at the Decanter World Wine Awards.	Graham's 20 Years Old Tawny has an amber and golden tawny colour. On the nose, it shows an excellent bouquet with a characteristic 'nutty' character and delicious mature fruit with hints of orange peel, exquisitely mellowed by careful ageing. Rich, softly sweet and smooth on the palate, it is perfectly balanced, with a long and elegant finish.	Graham's 20-Years Old Tawny should be enjoyed slightly chilled and pairs extremely well with nuts, dried fruits and fruitcake and also with vanilla ice cream or crème brûlée.

GRAHAM'S SIX GRAPES

Six Grapes Reserve is one of Graham's original port blends. The distinctive depiction of grapes on the label has always been used on the barrels to identify the 'Six Grapes' blend. Only grapes from first-class vineyards are used for producing brand of wine. Six Grapes is a true expression of Graham's house style in terms of great richness and complexity.

Six Grapes is a big-hearted wine. It is fruity and robust and of superb quality. It is blended to be as similar as possible to a young vintage port. It has often been referred to as 'the everyday port for the vintage port drinker'. Unique in the port trade, Graham's selects its 'proprietary blend' ahead of its more commercial styles. All other port shippers make a lighter style 'Reserve' blend out of lots that remain after they have bottled their LBV's.

Courtesy: *Graham's Port Bottles, Portugal.*

Table 23.4 About Graham's Six Grapes

Reviews and Awards	Tasting Notes	Food Pairing Suggestion and Serving
Silver Medal: International Wine Challenge, 2010. **Silver Medal:** International Wine Challenge, 2008. **Silver Medal:** International Wine & Spirit Competition, 2007.	Dark red colour with a seductive rich perfume of ripe plums and cherries. On the palate, complex with a good structure and a long lingering finish.	Graham's 'Six Grapes' is delicious when served at the end of a meal, for example, with rich, nutty or chocolate desserts, as well as strong cheeses.

(Continued)

Table 23.4 About Graham's Six Grapes (*Contd.*)

Reviews and Awards	Tasting Notes	Food Pairing Suggestion and Serving
Gold Medal: International Wine Challenge, 2006. *'Intense spice aroma dances on the nose. The fresh fruit palate has a firm tannin backbone, but it is the balance of this wine that is truly impeccable.'* **Gold Medal:** International Wine & Spirit Competition, 2003. **Gold Medal:** International Wine & Spirit Competition, 1999.		

23.6 MADEIRA

Madeira is an island, a part of Portugal in the Atlantic Ocean. The wine from Madeira is produced in a variety of styles ranging from sweet wines, which are excellent with desserts, to drier wines, which make great aperitifs.

23.7 HISTORY OF MADEIRA

The Islands of Madeira have a long wine-making history dating back several centuries. It was a port very famous for ships bound for the East Indies or to the New World. Before this, it is said that the Island of Madeira was discovered by Prince Henry with Captain Zarco in 1418 or 1420. It was named Madeira meaning 'Wooded Island', as it had dense forests. It was uninhabited and Captain Zarco found that the soil could not be tilled due to the heavy forest cover. To solve this problem with ease, he torched the forest. The forest fire burnt all the timber for over seven years. This resulted in rich volcanic soil, ideal for viticulture purposes. By the end of the 15th century, Madeira was colonized by the Portuguese and was producing excellent wines. These wines were transported by the docking ships to India, America and Europe. During this sea voyage, the wines were exposed to excessive heat and movement, which transformed the wine into a wonderful 'baked' wine. To prevent this wine from spoiling, the wines were fortified to endure this journey. Today, the wines are not exposed to the voyages. Therefore, to maintain the characteristic baked taste, they are subjected to the 'Estufas' or 'hot houses'.

23.8 GRAPE VARIETIES

The principle grape varieties grown on the steep slopes and rocky landscapes of this island are Sercial, Verdelho, Bual and Malvasia. These are pressed separately and the must is stored separately in larger vineyards. However, smaller vineyards press a variety of wines that give a deep-coloured must from the use of more black grapes.

23.9 PRODUCTION PROCESS OF MADEIRA

The production process of Madeira wine is depicted in Figure 23.2 and described in the following sections.

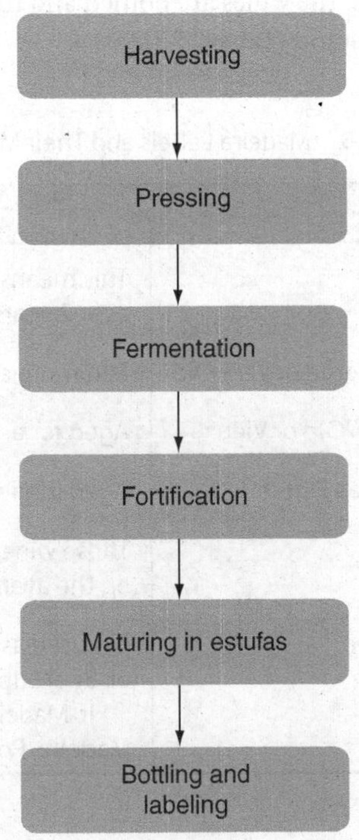

Figure 23.2 The Production Process of Madeira Wine.

Harvesting

The ripened grapes are harvested by hand, as the steep slopes prevent even the wheel barrows from being used. Therefore, all the grapes have to be carried in baskets on the head or shoulders. Both land and water are scarce. Most of the land is cultivated under the old feudal system of small tenant farmers called 'caseiros'. The landowners often collect as much as half of the produce as rent. On the other hand, water is as scarce and is given to each farmer at a particular time and day. Though this system sounds very impractical, it is in fact very efficient.

Pressing

The ripe grapes once picked are put into large wooden 'lagares', to be trodded on by workmen and then transported in a goatskin bag by foot, to the shippers lodges. However, now modern mechanized pressing and trucks have replaced the old methods.

Fermentation and Fortification

The must obtained ferments in 2–4 weeks. The dry wines are allowed to ferment till completion, whereas the sweeter wines are halted by the addition of grape brandy. The wine is now called 'Vinho Claro'.

Maturation in Estufas

History showed us how on the hot sea voyages this wine got its peculiar characteristics. Now that peculiar maturation process takes place on the island, in the *Estufas* or *hothouses*. The Estufas vary in temperature from 30°C–50°C according to the length the wine needs to be matured. The general practice is low temperature with long time span or high temperature with a shorter time span. The wines enter this system with a purple colour, but are obtained with an amber colour. The wine obtained from the Estufas is called *Vinho Estufado*. All the Estufas are very expensive to maintain and the wines too lose a considerable amount of alcohol. This system is regulated by government authorities. After this is completed, the *Vinho Estufado* is then rested for a period of time before racking. After which it becomes *Vinho Trasfugado*, the *Vinho Trasfugado* is additionally fortified to obtain an alcoholic strength of 20% ABV and now known as *Vinho Generoso*. This wine is blended with other similar wines and matured for a number of years.

Bottling and Labelling

After this, the wines are bottled and then labelled. Madeira labels carry a few words, which are essential to understand (Table 23.5).

Table 23.5 Madeira Labels and Their Meaning

Term	Meaning
Vintage	This means the wine is from a noble variety, spending 20 years in the cask and over 2 years in the bottle.
Old Reserve or Very Old	Minimum age of 10 years.
Reserve/Old or Vieux	Aged for a minimum of 5 years.
Choice as Finest	Aged for a minimum of 3 years.
Soleras	These wines follow the Solera blending process and have a vintage date based on the average age of all the wines.
Superior	It is used as an add-on to the variety of grapes. For example, 'Superior Malmsey' or 'Bual Superior'. If Madeiras have to be exported, they must carry a label of 'Produced in Madeira, Portugal'.

23.10 TYPES OF MADEIRA

There are four main types of Madeira in correspondence to the grape varieties mentioned earlier. All the Madeira is a reflection of the rich volcanic soil. The types are as follows:

1. **Sercial:** This is the driest type of Madeira. It is pale/golden in colour with a refreshing aftertaste. It is a good aperitif and can also be enjoyed on other occasions.
2. **Verdelho:** It is a medium-bodied golden wine, which is quite dry, enjoyed as a digestif.
3. **Bual or boal:** It is bright golden wine, slightly less sweet than Malmsey. It is a fine dessert wine.
4. **Malmsey:** This is full-bodied, soft textured and fragrant Madeira. It is brown in colour and the sweetest of them all.

Madeira is one of the long-lived wines and can be even 100 years old. They improve with age unlike any other wine. The phylloxera vine disease devastated the vineyards of Madeira over a century ago; as a result the old Madeira is difficult to obtain today. The ones that are available today are used in improving the new Soleras.

Brands of Madeira

1. Sandeman
2. Ferraz

3. Leacock
4. Lomelino
5. Henriques & Henriques.

23.11 TABLES WINES OF PORTUGAL

Although Port and Madeira define Portuguese wines, we should not forget the other fine wines from this country. Majority of these wines are red and made from Perquita grape.

Map of Portugal and Spain.

Bucelas and Colares

Bucelas is a town, north of Lisbon, making a pleasant, fresh and dry white wine. It has a straw yellow colour and an aromatic bouquet. It uses the Arinto grape variety, while Colares is a small town on the west of Lisbon. The vineyards use the Ramisco grape, which produces a ruby-red wine, clean and full bodied.

Dao

It is named after the Dao River that flows through this region. The red wines of this region are ruby-red in colour having a rich bouquet, a woody flavour and smooth taste. They have to be aged for a minimum of two years before bottling. The older mature wines are called *Vinho Madura*. The red wines are considered the best table wines of Portugal and are labelled *Garafiera*.

Dao also produces white wines, which are characterized by a woody aftertaste, having a full body and dryness.

Vinho Verde

This is the simplest and most pleasant wine of Portugal. *Vinho Verde* literally means 'green wine', but actually signifies young wine, which is opposite to *Vinho Maduro*. This can be a white, red or rose wine. It is a refreshingly light, acidic and aromatic wine with an alcohol content of 8–11% ABV. This is a wine, which is gulped like beer, but not sipped, as it is very refreshing. The grapes of such type are rich in malic acid and provides the malolactic fermentation, which gives the wine its flavour and aroma. Usually at any dinner, the ratio of serving is one bottle per person or even more.

Rose Wines

Portuguese rose wines are usually sparkling, but still varieties are also very popular. These wines are clean sound, moderately sweet and are served chilled with any food.

Portugal has been established as a major wine producer in the world. The only variety not gaining much popularity from Portugal is sparkling wine.

LET'S SUMMARIZE IN POINTS

- Portugal was influenced by the English to produce port wine from their existing table wines.
- This market demand helped enhance the overall quality of wines produced in Portugal.
- Port is a fortified aromatic and flavourful wine from Portugal.
- The various types of port are Vintage Port, Ruby or Tawny Port, LBV, White Port and Crusted Porto.
- Madeira is an island off the coast of Portugal, which produces a unique fortified wine. It uses the Estufas system to produce a wine that is rich in aroma and flavour.
- Types of Madeira are Sercial, Verdelho, Bual and Malmsey.

23.12 FAQs

Short-Answer Type Questions

1. What is a port wine?
2. What are Estufas?
3. Name the different types of Ports.
4. What is Madeira? Where is it made?
5. What are the types of Madeiras?

Long-Answer Type Questions

1. Describe the Estufa system.
2. Describe the production process of Port.
3. Describe the production process of Madeira.
4. Describe in detail the types of Ports.
5. Describe in detail the types of Madeiras.

23.13 KEY TERMS

- Estufas
- Fining
- LBV
- Mustimeter
- Portus Cale
- Quintas
- Rabelos
- Treading

NEW WORLD WINES

CHAPTER OUTLINE

Until now, we have discussed and understood wines from France, Italy, Spain, Portugal and Germany. These vineyards are very old; some have been in use since the Roman times. Due to this rich history, wine making has been an established art and science.

There are countries, which have started making wines in recent years as compared to the *Old World.* These countries are collectively referred to as the *New World.* In the wine trade, wines from these countries are called *New World Wines.* The New World not only comprises of countries from the west but also from the east.

Countries such as Australia, New Zealand, India, China, South Africa, Chile and the United States are making wines that make an impact on the wine trade. These wines are being marketed aggressively and are eating into the market share of Old World wines. Although the general opinion is that the New World is yet to match up in quality to the classical high quality Old World wines of France, Italy or Spain. Let us discuss each country in detail.

24.1 AUSTRALIA

History

Many pioneers are responsible for establishing and developing wine making in Australia. Grape cultivation began with Captain Arthur Phillips who brought vine cuttings to New South Wales in 1788, which he had founded. He brought these cuttings from Rio de Janeiro and Cape of Good Hope, which were docking ports in his journey to Australia. Unfortunately, his vineyards were attacked by fungus.

Apart from him, three others introduced and developed the art and science of wine making in Australia. Gregory Blaxland was the first in 1816. He planted a red grape variety, which he brought from the Cape of Good Hope, on his farm at Parramatta Valley. By 1827, vineyards in Penrith in New South Wales were producing 20,000 gallons of wine. This was due to the contributions of John Macarthur and his two sons. James Busby is often referred to as the father of viticulture in Australia. First, he is responsible for writing and educating a lot of the locals on planting wines and making wine. Secondly, he is responsible for collecting and planting 678 varieties of wine from France, England and Spain in Australia. He also set up the country's agricultural institute.

In the 1800s, many vineyards were planted across Southern Australia. The first development was in Hunter Valley–New South Wales, followed by South Australia and then Victoria. The Australian wine industry has witnessed exponential growth in the last 2–3 decades. This can be attributed to changes in local demand along with an improvement in technology, thereby resulting in better quality of wines.

Australian wines are fresh and light making them gain popularity.

Australian Wine Regions

The wine-producing regions of Australia are located in the southern part of the continent, spreading across 2,500 miles. The wine-producing regions are discussed in the following sections.

South Australia

This area is responsible for producing 60% of all Australian wines. The Barossa Valley is the best known area in Australia for wine making. It has a large influence of the German settlers, who planted the vineyards. Coonawarra is also a famous area of this region, which produces red wines of high quality. The Riverland district is one of the largest wine-producing areas, producing most of Australia's bulk wine.

New South Wales

Hunter Valley located in this region is a very famous premium wine; however, it accounts for only 1% of all Australia's wine production. The Murrumbidgee irrigation area (MIA) or *Riverina* supplies about 20% of Australia's vintage.

Victoria

Victoria has come to the forefront recently. The Yarra Valley has been known for smaller, limited production wineries. The north eastern part of Victoria, however, is famous for its fortified port wines.

Western Australia

The west coast of Australia gets a lot of sunshine, thereby producing grapes high on sugar and low on acid. Hence, the wines of this region are rich in alcohol and due to the cool climate, they carry a distinct flavour.

Tasmania

This is an island off the coast of Australia. It is quite smaller than the mainland, but enjoys a European climate as it is away from the Equator. The wines here are quite famous, using Rhine Riesling and Cabernet Sauvignon grape varieties.

Export quality wines and brandies are inspected by the Department of Customs and Excise as well as inspectors appointed by the Australian Wine and Brandy Corporation who ensure the highest possible quality.

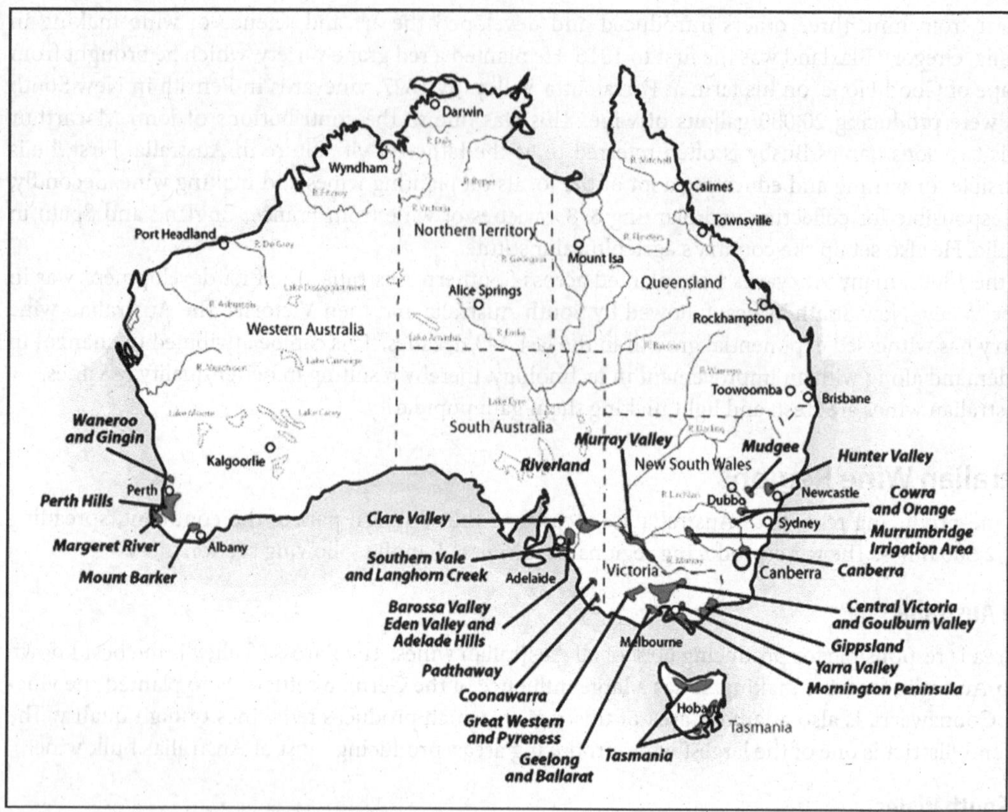

The wine-producing regions of Australia.

Australian Grape Varieties

Australian grape varieties define the characteristics of each wine (Table 24.1). The wine labels carrying a specific grape variety must ensure that 80% of these grapes are used to make the wine.

Table 24.1 Australian Grape Varieties

Grape Varieties	Specification
Red Grapes	
Shiraz	Over 20,000 acres of vineyards in Australia grow this variety, virtually in almost all the districts. Many wineries make this as a principle wine, but sometimes it is used to blend other varieties.
Cabernet Sauvignon	It is Australia's most famous grape variety. The Coonawarra vineyards are quite famous for this variety of grape.
Merlot and Pinot Noir	These are mostly used for blending and are not as popular in Australia.
Grenache	This is a primary grape variety used to make bulk wines.

Grape Varieties	Specification
White Grapes	
Semillon	This is a variety producing wines that are full bodied and dry. They are popularly known as *the poor man's Chardonnay*.
Rhine Riesling	This famous grape makes great fruity wines low in acidity when grown in warmer areas and good balanced acidity when grown in cooler climates. When picked late, it produces sweet wines.
Chardonnay	This is a premium variety grape, producing refreshing full-bodied wine when aged in wood. The younger wines are lighter but equally refreshing.
Gewürztraminer, Chenin Blanc and Sauvignon Blanc	These grapes are used to make Australia's white table wines.
Doradilo, Palomino and Pedro Ximenez	These grape varieties are primarily used for making fortified wines.

Due to the low taxes on alcohol and increased usage of technology, wine has become very affordable in Australia. Its good quality and affordable pricing has made it one of the fastest emerging wine-producing countries of the world. The Australians know their wines are one of the most important New World wine regions along with the United States.

24.2 NEW ZEALAND

History

The history of New Zealand wine production can be traced back to Australia in the 1800s. James Busby, a Britisher, who had established vineyards in Australia, is New Zealand's first wine maker.

Romeo Bragato, a graduate of Italy's School of Viticulture in Conegliano, was the first official head of the department of agriculture of New Zealand in 1902. The wine industry was facing a tough challenge with wine diseases, such as *Phylloxera* and *Mildew*.

Efforts to find resistant varieties led to the use of hybrid varieties and *Lubruscana* varieties instead of the original *Vinifera* variety. This led to only a few vineyards and wineries being able to sustain themselves, whereas the others perished.

Now, the *Vinifera* variety having been reintroduced in the 1980s has helped New Zealand to re-establish itself as a premiere wine region.

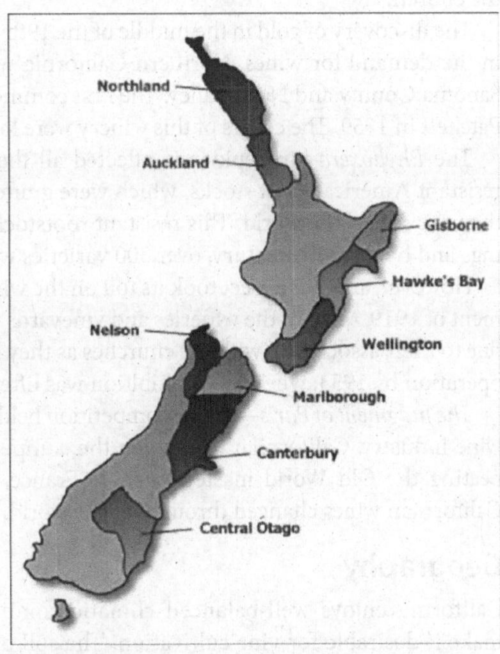

The wine-producing regions of New Zealand.

New Zealand's Wine Regions

New Zealand comprises of two Islands, North and South. Both the islands produce great quality wines. After surveying the Island, it was discovered that Marlborough, a region located towards the northern part of the South Island, had highest sunshine, a temperate climate with limited rainfall, ideal for making crisp white wines.

The North Island is also famous for its wines from Auckland.

Grape Varieties and Wines

The white grape varieties famous in New Zealand are Riesling, Sylvaner, Chardonnay, Gewürztraminer, Rhine Riesling and Sauvignon Blanc, which account for 80% of all the vineyard plantings from New Zealand. The red grapes account for only 20% of the vines used; the grape varieties used are Cabernet Sauvignon, Shiraz, Pinotage and Pinot Noir.

New Zealand is an emerging competitor, as the producer of finest wines of the world.

24.3 THE UNITED STATES OF AMERICA

When we refer to wines from the United States, we are immediately drawn to Californian wines. California's wine production accounts for almost 90% of all the wines produced in the United States. The region is two-thirds the size of France, hence producing wines in very large volumes.

History

Spanish missionaries are responsible for planting the vines in the 18th century to produce wines for the masses. The vines were brought from Mexico and were called *Mission grapes* due to its association with the church.

The discovery of gold in the middle of the 19th century saw an influx of people. This lead to an increase in the demand for wines. Northern California was the heart of viticulture and vinification, namely in Sanoma County and Napa Valley. The first commercial winery was founded in the Napa County by John Patchett in 1959. The cellars of this winery were located in the region, which is now part of the city limits.

The *Phylloxera* vine epidemic affected all the wine-producing countries of the world. Due to the resistant American root stocks, which were grafted, the wine industry was able to rebound much faster than the rest of the world. This resistant rootstock enabled American viticulturists to expand the plantings and by the 20th century, over 300 varieties were being produced.

However, another aspect took its toll on the wine industry, namely the prohibition part of the amendment of 1919. Most of the wineries and vineyards were ordered to shut down. The one that survived were due to their association with the churches as they supplied sacramental wines. Only 140 wineries were in operation by 1933, when the prohibition was lifted.

The Judgment of Paris—a wine competition held in Paris in 1976 changed the fortunes of the Californian wine industry. Californian wines won the competition both in the red wine and white wine categories, beating the Old World masters such as France, Germany, Italy and Spain. Hence, the perception of Californian wines changed throughout the world. Now, it is a highly regarded wine across the globe.

Geography

California enjoys well-balanced climatic conditions. Good amount of sunshine and ideal rainfall make it desirable for vine cultivation. The soil of this region varies immensely to such an extent that vineyards differentiate between the same vine varieties grown on different soils. This is to enable blending of these wines.

Wine Regions

The wine regions of California are divided into four main areas, namely:

1. **North Coast:** This large area covers most of the region and is located north of San Francisco bay. The famous Napa Valley and Sanoma County are located in this region.
2. **Central Coast:** This is the area south west of San Francisco bay down to Santa Barbara County. The famous wines of this region include Santa Clara valley AVA (American Viticultural Area), San Lucas AVA, Paro Robles AVA and Livermore Valley AVA.
3. **South Coast:** The southern part of California, south of Los Angeles going till the Mexican border. This region includes Temecula Valley AVA, Antelope Valley AVA, Leone Valley AVA and Ramona Valley AVA.
4. **Central Valley:** This is also a region including the Sierra foothills AVA. Lodi AVA is a notable sub-region.

Wine-producing regions of California.

Californian Grape Varieties

Amongst the several hundred grape varieties grown, there are seven leading grape varieties. Prominent grape varieties are Cabernet Sauvignon, Chardonnay, Merlot, Pinot Noir, Sauvignon Blanc, Syrah and Zinfandel.

The other red grape varieties are Barbera, Cabernet Franc, Malbec, Petite Syrah, Petite Verdot and Sangiovese. Important white grape varieties include Chenin Blanc, French Colombard, Marsanne, Pinot Blanc, Pinot Gris, Riesling and Viognier.

Thompson Seedless, Tokay, White Malaga and Muscat of Alexandria grape varieties are used in making table wines and dessert wines in California and hence do not feature in the following sections.

Wines of California

California produces wines of all styles including sparkling, dessert and fortified wines. Unlike the Old World wines, Californian wines (along with other New World wines from Australia, New Zealand and Chile) prefer making fresher, fruitier wines. Californian wines are fruitier and high in alcohol with 13% ABV being the average.

This can be attributed to the ample amount of sunshine that this area receives. Californian wines are classified based on the grape variety used. The characters of each wine can be understood from Table 24.2.

Table 24.2 Wines of California

Grape Varieties	Specification
Red Wines–Red Grapes	
Cabernet Sauvignon	A fine red wine made from the principle *claret* grape of Bordeaux. It is very sharp, but gains depth as it matures.
Merlot	It tastes like the Cabernet Sauvignon, but is less tannic. Merlot ages more rapidly than other grape varieties.
Zinfandel	It has a spicy berry-like aroma and taste.
Pinot Noir	A wine made from a grape difficult to cultivate in California. It produces an excellent wine if cultivated.
Gamay–Beaujolais	A medium-bodied wine with a fruity aroma, but not similar to the French Beaujolais.
Petite Syrah	A wine which is tannic with a deep red colour and a spicy taste.
Barbera	A dark full-bodied pleasant wine. The grape originated in Piedmont region of Italy.
White Wines–White Grapes	
Chardonnay	A full-bodied dry wine usually aged in wood from Bourbon county, which produces whisky. This imparts to the wine a refreshing vanilla aftertaste.
Riesling	A fruity wine with a distinct perfume and sweetness. This grape has its origins in Germany and Alsace. When the grapes are picked late, they result in a rich, exquisite and expensive sweet wine.
Sauvignon Blanc	This is a wine that is aged in wood like the Chardonnay. It is a medium-bodied wine.
Chenin Blanc	This is a fragrant wine, which can range from being dry to semi-sweet.
Gewürztraminer	A sweet and spicy wine having an aromatic bouquet and distinct characteristic.
Rose Wine	
Cabernet Rose	It has a distinct flavour.
California Rose	It is a generic wine, which is light and sweet, refreshing in the summer.
Gamay Rose	A delicate rose wine with a fruity taste and character.
Pinot Noir Rose	It has a pale tea rose colour and a delicate flavour.
Zinfandel Rose	It has a deeper colour than the other rose grape varieties.

California also produces fortified wines and sparkling wines. Although they are a mirror image of the Old World wines, some believe that they have to improve on quality to give them stiff competition globally.

24.4 SOUTH AFRICA

South Africa ranks ninth amongst the wine-producing regions of the world. Although the vineyards were planted almost three centuries ago, the wineries were established in the 1900s. Hence, their wines are fruity and distinct in character, and included among the New World wines.

Wine Laws

In 1973, a system was put in place to guarantee the origin and grape variety used in a wine and mentioned on the label. A simple seal of *W.O—Wines of Origin*—appears on the label if it contains 80% of wine from the area on the label and made from specified grape varieties.

The highest is *W.O.S—Wines of Origin Superior.* Gold seal is a guarantee of the finest quality of wine. There are various factors considered when a wine is certified with a gold seal.

Grape Varieties

The predominant grape variety is the Pinotage (a cross between the Hermitage and Pinot Noir grape varieties). The other red grape varieties grown are Cabernet Sauvignon, Hermitage (also known as Cinsaut), Shiraz and Gamay.

The white grapes are Chenin Blanc, Palomino, Colombard, Gewurztraminer and Riesling. The white grapes are vinified in the German style and sweet wines are often produced.

Wine Regions

There are three main regions, which are sub-divided into nine smaller districts, along with eight other districts located outside the three main regions. Table 24.3 shows us the regional classification in South Africa.

Table 24.3 Regional Classification of the Wine-producing Areas in South Africa

Regions	Subregion/District	Wards
Brede River Valley	Worcester	Nuy, Goudini, Slanghoek, Scherperhevval and Aan de Doorns.
	Robertson	McGregor, Gorce, Vinkrivier, Eilandia, Riverside, Mooirivier and Boesmansrivier
	Swellendam	Bonnievale
	Tulbagh	
Borberg	Paarl	Franschhoek and Riebeeckberg
Coastal	Stellenbosch	Simonsberg and Stellenbosch
	Durbanville	
	Swatland	
	Constantia	

Wines

All types of wines are produced in South Africa. The coastal region is famous for producing Sherry and Port-styled fortified wines. The most famous red wines are produced in Paarl, Stellenbosch, Durbanville and Constantia.

White wines are refreshing, the best coming from Paarl, Stellenbosch and Tulbagh.

The South African wine industry adopted regulations for the permitted amounts of residual sugars in the wines. The wine laws are made on the lines of their German counterparts, but sugar levels are measured in addition to the other specifications.

South Africa produces excellent wines having emerged with its own distinctive characteristics.

24.5 ARGENTINA AND CHILE

Argentina is the largest producer of wine in the western hemisphere ranking fifth in the world. The average yield per acre is double than Californian vineyards.

As compared to Argentina, Chile is a small country both in size and population. However, they produce South America's finest wines, as it has been blessed with ideal climatic and soil conditions for growing vines.

Both these regions produce excellent quality wines. The predominant grape varieties used in Argentina are Chardonnay, Semillon, Pinot Blanc, Riesling and Trebbiano. Pedro Ximinez and Muscat are used to produce fortified wines. Chile uses, Semillon, Pinot Blanc and Chardonnay for whites and Cabernet Sauvignon, Cabernet Franc, Petit Verdot and Malbec for its red wines. Chilean wines are readily acceptable, as their quality is high and prices are reasonable. Argentinean wines are classically soft, non-acidic and well matured as per their local preference. Due to expanded exports of wine, the Argentinean wineries are modifying their wines to produce fresher, drier wines, as preferred in Europe and the United States.

24.6 INDIA

India is fast emerging as the wine capital of Asia, overtaking its neighbours not only in quantity, but in quality as well. The Indian wine Industry is located predominantly in the areas around Nasik in Maharashtra, called the Sahyadri Valley and the areas around Bangalore and Mysore in the Southern states of Karnataka. Grover Vineyards has been pioneering the wine Industry in India. We shall discuss the details of Indian wine through the Grover's Brand.

Nandi Hills—The Region

Forty kilometres towards north of Bangalore, in the state of Karnataka, lies a region that has only recently come to the attention of the rest of the world. Today, it has risen triumphantly as a rich wine-producing area which was once known as Tipu Sultan's, and later as the British summer retreat. Nandi Hills is a picturesque region dotted with sloping green hillsides and miles of forestland, inhabited with incredibly beautiful wild life. In this paradisiacal landscape, stand our vineyards.

The region offers travellers tranquil surroundings, a rich history, beautiful vistas and allows them to train their binoculars over the spectacular Asian Paradise Flycatchers, Bulbuls, Blue-capped Rock Thrush, Tawny Eagles, Puff-throated Babblers, etc.

Spread over 410 acres and nestled on the foothills of the Nandi Hills are the Grover Vineyards, credited with starting the Premium Indian wine industry and slowly transforming India's reputation as a maker of exciting wines to a producer of world-class, award winning wines.

The vineyards are covered with lush grapes, strung from trellises, covering every available space on the soil in the valley. It flourishes with Cabernet Sauvignon, Shiraz, Viognier and Sauvignon Blanc grapes.

The climate of the Nandi Hills is unique. Temperatures vary from 23–29°C in summers and 11–21°C in winters. The vine-growing season, which is the longest in India, (thanks to the natural protection of the Nandi Hills against the monsoon) enables the grapes to reach perfect maturity. Moderate rain strike, sunny days and cool nights create a unique temperate microclimate. In addition, the diverse well-drained rich limestone soils of the region give to the wines their distinctive, terroir-driven earthiness with depth, richness and aromatic complexity.

ABOUT THE FOUNDERS OF GROVER VINEYARDS

Kanwal Grover is an unconventional man. He decided at the age of 60, when normally people think of getting retired, to transform his passion for wine into a lifetime dedication. He had the vision as well as the talent to achieve his dream.

Accepting the immense challenge of growing French grape varieties in India for the first time, Kanwal Grover, together with George Vesselle took the onerous task of creating the first premium wine estate in India.

The founder Kanwal Grover (left), and his son Kapil Grover (right).

Kapil Grover, Kanwal's son is today the owner of India's greatest family-owned wine estate. Keeping in mind the importance of respect for tradition, Kapil knew how to modernize and expand the winery. Like his father who initiated viticulture in India, he is also an innovator.

While extending the vineyard from 100 acres to 400 acres, Kapil always kept in mind his father's philosophy—no compromise on quality. Today, the winery produces 1,200,000 bottles. About 30% of Grover Vineyards production is exported to more than 20 countries and is appreciated in some of the world's best restaurants.

Grovers White Wines

Kanwal Grover at the cellar of the Grover vineyard. (Courtesy: *Grover vineyard Pvt. Ltd.*)

Known for their distinctive taste and quality, Grover Vineyards white wines, Sauvignon Blanc and Viognier are the result of a combination of a unique soil, climate and people. Tasting astoundingly fresh, our whites reflect our traditional way of wine making.

From the vineyards to the cellar, great importance is given to meticulous grape selection to ensure the use of the best-quality grapes. After going through the sorting table where teams carefully remove the unwanted berries, the grapes are fully de-stemmed enabling to get only the best fruits.

The next step is called, 'pressing,' when the juice is separated from the skins. In case of white wine, grapes are pressed quickly in order to separate juice from the skin, seeds and other solids. Essentially, white wine is allowed a very little skin contact, as by doing so unwanted colour (which comes from the skin of the grape, not the juice) and tannins cannot trickle into the wine. The juice produced thus goes through stabilization and clarification.

Temperature stabilization is done by cooling the juice between 10°–15°C for 24 hours; conditions that are more suitable for the white wine fermentation. Yeasts are added to induce the alcoholic fermentation. The action of the yeasts is to transform the sugar naturally contained in the grape juice into alcohol.

Once the fermentation is completed, the clarification process begins. Clarification is done by transferring the fermented juice from one tank to another, in order to remove the natural deposit or lees. This process is called racking. Whites normally go through 5–6 rackings until the wine is totally cleared. Before bottling, one filtration is done to ensure the optimum quality of the wines in the glass. The white wines are now ready to be bottled.

Grover's Red Wines

Selection of wines from Grover Vineyards.

Known for its distinctive taste and quality, Grover Vineyard's red wines, Cabernet Shiraz, is the result of a combination of a unique soil, climate and people. Concentrated, powerful and delicate, at the same time, Cabernet Shiraz reflects Grover's traditional way of wine making.

The wine-making process of red wine is fairly different than the making of white wine.

From the vineyards to cellar, great importance is given to meticulous grape selection to ensure the use of the best-quality grapes. After going through the sorting table, where teams carefully removes the unwanted berries, the grapes are fully de-stemmed enabling to get only the best fruits.

Red grapes are delicately crushed then sent to the tank without pressing. The juice is left in contact with its skins and seeds to garner colour, tannins and flavours. The juice produced thus goes through stabilization and clarification.

Temperature stabilization is done by cooling the juice at 22°C for 24 hours, conditions that are more suitable for the red wine fermentation. Yeasts are added to induce the alcoholic fermentation, which starts at 22°C and finish at 27°C. The action of the yeasts is to transform the sugar naturally contained in the grape juice into alcohol.

Once fermentation is completed, the maceration process begins. We leave the wine in contact with the pomace (skin and seeds) for 20 days in order to extract more colour and tannins.

During fermentation and maceration, regular pumping over are done to ensure the optimum extraction of colour as well as tannins.

Clarification is done by transferring the fermented juice from one tank to another in order to remove the natural deposit or lees. This process is called racking. Grover's red normally goes through 8–10 rackings, until the wine is totally cleared. The next step is blending, which is carried out by selecting wines made out from different varieties according to the winemaker's aspirations. Before bottling, one filtration is done to ensure the optimum quality of Grover's wines in the glass. The red wine is now ready to be bottled.

Grover's has pioneered in the wine industry and we had seen the picturesque vineyards in the earlier chapters of the book (*See* French Wine—Production Process of Wine).

The wine market in India is growing and its wines are gaining popularity amongst other New World wines as well.

Interesting Facts—Canadian wine

Health Benefits of Organic Wine

The health benefits of organic wine cannot be adequately underscored. Some of the main benefits that recommend organic wine as a part of nutrient dense lifestyle are as follows:

1. Organic wines have large amounts of resveratrol, a compound found in red grapes shown to be beneficial to health by lowering cholesterol and preventing cell oxidation.
2. Studies have shown that grapes sprayed with fungicides commonly used on conventional vineyards had 80% less resveratrol, which rubs these grapes of their beneficial health benefits.
3. Originally grown grapes have been found to contain significantly more vitamin C, iron, magnesium and phosphorus and significantly less nitrates than conventionally grown grapes.
4. There are indications of a higher level of nutritionally significant minerals with lower amount of heavy metals in organically grown grapes.

Ice Wine–Golden Elixir

Canada is the world's largest manufacturer of ice wine and makes much more than all the other countries put together.

Ice-wine, called the 'Golden Elixir' because of its rich golden colour and described as 'a rare gift from a magical Canadian winter', is being introduced into retail outlets for the first time in India.

Ice wine's versatility is phenomenal:

1. It can be sipped as a dessert wine or experimented with for pairing with different menus.
2. It is a tastier, healthier alternative to calorie-loaded dessert.

3. It can be sipped as an aperitif or as a digestif.
4. It can be used as a liqueur at the end of a sumptuous meal.

Vintners Quality Alliance (VQA)

Look for the VQA logo on Canadian bottles of ice wine. The VQA is a standards committee that ensures the production of ice wine that is tested for top quality. Ice wine is always served chilled in champagne flutes or slender wine glasses.

Ice Wine: Extreme Wine Making

Ice wine is unique to Canada and is produced under stringent government controls. The grapes are manually harvested usually at the dead of a winter's night when they have naturally frozen on the vines at a temperature of –8°C and below. They are then crushed in special crushers to separate the water content (crystallized into ice) from the pure concentrated grape juice. One grape yields just one drop of concentrate luscious ice wine. Considering the extreme production process, ice wine is a luxurious commodity and hence expensive.

Canadian Pinot Noir Ice Wine. (Courtesy: *Summer Hill Pyramid Winery*)

LET'S SUMMARIZE IN POINTS

- The New World Wine regions comprise of Australia, New Zealand, the United States, South Africa, Argentina, Chile and India. Canada is also an emerging wine producer.
- Australian wine regions are South Australia, New South Wales, Victoria, Western Australia and Tasmania.
- New Zealand is a great wine-producing country. The North and South Islands are both famous for their wines.
- Wine growing regions in the United States are two-thirds the size of France. The vines are grown in Californian sub-regions of North Coast, Central Coast, South Coast and Central Valley.
- South Africa produces table wines, fortified wines and distinct dessert wines.
- Argentinean, Chilean and Indian wines have their own distinct characteristics and aromas. These countries are emerging wine producers.

24.7 FAQs

Short-Answer Type Questions

1. Name the wine regions in Australia.
2. Give the grape varieties grown in Australia.
3. Give the soil conditions favouring New Zealand's wine production.
4. Name the wine regions of the United States.
5. Give the geography and soil conditions of California. Elaborate on the grape varieties grown.

Long-Answer Type Questions

1. What was the main feature of the Paris Wine Show, which played a major role in boosting the morale of New World Wine producers? Explain.
2. Describe grape varieties grown in California.
3. What are the wine laws followed in South Africa?
4. Write about the regions in South Africa.
5. Give details on Argentinean, Chilean and Indian wines.

24.8 KEY TERMS

- AVA
- Golden Elixir
- Grover Vineyards
- Ice Wine
- New World
- Old World
- VQA

Aromatized Wines Aperitifs and Bitters

CHAPTER OUTLINE

LET'S DEFINE

'Aromatized wines are also known as aperitifs in many countries. It is a fortified wine in which herbs, roots, barks, flowers, seeds and other flavouring agents are steeped, enhancing the natural flavour of the wine.'

In the previous chapters, we have already studied about the three types of wines, namely, still, sparkling and fortified wines. Aromatized wine is the fourth type of wine. These wines include Vermouth, Byrrh, Dubonnet, Carpano, Fernet Branca, Unicum and many others.

The word, 'aperitif' comes from the Latin word *aperio,* which means *to open*. Hence, it is easy to understand that these are consumed before a meal, to 'open up' the appetite for the meal.

25.1 HISTORY

Noilly Prat brand of vermouth that is very popular and owned by Bacardi International Limited. (Courtesy: *Bacardi International Limited.*)

The concept of drinking a small amount of liquor before a meal dates back to the ancient Egyptians. The records, however, show that in 1786, Antonio Benedetto Carpano from Turin invented *Vermouth.* In the 1800s, Joseph Noilly Prat from Lyon, France invented a drier version of the *Vermouth.* Vermouth was later popularized and marketed by other companies, such as Martini, Cinzano, Dolin and many others.

In 1846, Joseph Dubonnet, a wine chemist, invented a drink in order to increase the reach of Quinine—a malaria fighting drug. This drink was named 'Dubonnet'. Dubonnet was famous among the French Legionnaires (soldiers) who made great use of this aperitif in the mosquito-infested areas of North Africa. Dubonnet was also popularized by Joseph Dubonnet's wife, who was very fond of it and served it at her parties.

DID YOU KNOW

An 'aperitif' is an alcoholic beverage served before the meal to stimulate the appetite. Some examples are Vermouth, Cremant, Champagne, Sherry and any dry, light white wine.

A 'digestif' is an alcoholic beverage served after a meal to aid in digestion. When these are served after a coffee they are called 'Pousse-café'. Digestifs are consumed straight, that is, without any chaser. Some bitters are also considered to act as digestifs. Fruit Brandies, Grappa, Chartreuse, Ouzo and Aquavit are some examples of digestifs. Sherry, Port and Madeira can also be served as digestifs.

25.2 VERMOUTH

Vermouth became popular in the 1900s, when it was used in making a popular cocktail called *Martini.* There are two versions of vermouth, dry vermouth and sweet vermouth. Dry vermouth originated in France and sweet vermouth originated in Italy. Vermouth is generally bottled at 17% ABV. Surprisingly, the highest per capita consumption of vermouth in the world is in Argentina.

Dry Vermouth

Dry vermouth or French vermouth is a pale dry and light-bodied aperitif with a complex aroma. It is flavoured with 50 different types of herbs, roots, seeds and flowers. Some of them include angelica root, gentian, wormwood, rose leaves, marjoram, orange peel bitter, chamomile, nutmeg, coriander seeds, cloves, quinine bark and cinnamon. This aromatized wine is a very dry wine made from Picpoul and Clairette grapes. These are very special types of grape varieties, as the wines made from these grapes become very dry as they mature. The sugar content is not more than 4% in dry vermouth and is bottled at an alcoholic strength of 10% ABV.

There are three ways in which the dryness of this wine is balanced. First, the grape variety Grenache is added along with Clairette and Picpoul grapes. Grenache grapes give sweetness to the wine, as the grape has high levels of sugar. Second, this wine is fortified with a grape brandy to increase the alcoholic strength, in order to prevent the secondary fermentation and increase the shelf life of this wine. Third, Mistelle mixed with alcohol is added to the wine, in place of sugar. Grenache and Muscat grapes are used to make Mistelle as they are high in sugar. The alcohol is mixed with this sweet grape juice to stop fermentation. As the sugar does not ferment, the Mistelle remains sweet, balancing the dryness of the vermouth. Dry vermouth is aged for 3–4 years in oak casks.

Sweet Vermouth

Sweet vermouth or Italian vermouth is a red coloured mildly bitter and slightly sweet. Sweet vermouth usually contains 10–15% of sugar. This style of vermouth is much sweeter in taste as compared to its French counterparts. They are also referred to as *Rosso*. Quinine is the most important herb added to this aromatized wine, which gives it a slightly bitter taste. Quinine, obtained from the bark of the cinchona tree, is known for its medicinal properties for curing malaria. This wine is infused with many other kinds of herbs and roots for at least a year to give it a characteristic sweet taste and distinct flavour.

Many sweet Italian wines like *Moscato di Canelli* and wines from *Apulia* are blended to produce sweet vermouth. Once the basic wine is aged along with the herbs, they are fortified and filtered. Caramel is also sometimes added to red-coloured sweet vermouths to give it a brownish tinge.

Brands of Vermouth

The various brands of Vermouth are enumerated in Table 25.1.

Table 25.1 Brands of Vermouth

Brand	Type
Carpano	*Punt e Mes* is a deep-red-coloured sweet vermouth, and *Latinica* is a dry vermouth produced under this Brand.
Ricca Donna Boissiere Gallo Garcia	These are Italian brands of vermouth.
Cinzano	It is an Italian Brand of vermouth, they also produce rose vermouths.
Bianco	It is a sweet pale Italian vermouth.
Martini and Rossi	These are famous for making Rosso vermouths, they also produce rose vermouths.
Noilly Prat	This is brand from France and is known for its dry vermouth.
Dolin	This is a French vermouth.
Dubonnet	This is a very famous vermouth from France.
Vya and Imbue	These are vermouths from USA.

25.3 BYRRH

Byrrh was first produced by the Violet brothers in the 19th century in the cellars of Thuir, Pyrenees Orientales in Catalonia, Spain. Byrrh is a red wine-based aperitif with an alcoholic content of 17% ABV. It was first used as a revitalizing tonic. The Carrignan and Grenache grape varieties are used in making Byrrh. Dry wines from Roussillon are also used in the production of this aperitif.

It is served at 16°C and goes well with crème de cassis liqueur or lemon zest. Byrrh Rare Assemblage is an intense full-bodied wine. It is aged in oak barrels for 8–10 years. It is deep red in colour with a subtle quinine flavour.

There are different stages involved in making Byrrh. Matured wines from the wine coops of the Languedoc–Roussillon are infused with 10 different spices to give it a unique flavour. After infusing, they are chilled, filtered and bottled.

Martini brand of vermouth that is very popular and owned by Bacardi International Limited. (Courtesy: Bacardi International Limited)

25.4 DUBONNET

It is a fortified and aromatized wine from France flavoured with herbs, spices and a hint of quinine. It is produced in two styles: Dubonnet Blanc, which is white Dubonnet made from fortified white wine, and Dubonnet rouge, which is a sweet red wine-based aperitif.

25.5 BITTERS

Bitters, as the name suggests, taste bitter. They consist of bitter and aromatic essential oils of fruits, plants, seeds, flowers, leaves, barks, roots and stems.

Most bitters are a well-guarded secret made by proprietary concerns handing over the recipes from one generation to the next. Bitters vary in their qualities. Some can only be used as an additional flavouring agent in cocktails and cuisine. The best example is Angostura bitters made in Trinidad (West Indies). Others include Peychauds from New Orleans and Underberg from Germany.

ANGOSTURA BITTERS

The legend begins with Johann Gottlieb Benjamin Siegert. Originally from Germany, Johann Siegert, a doctor of medicine, left his homeland in 1820, the call of adventure ringing in his ears. He was bound for Venezuela, to join with Simon Bolivar in his fight against the Spanish throne. Then, Bolivar appointed him as Surgeon General of the Military Hospital in the town of Angostura.

Dr Siegert had seen soldiers battered by the enemy from without and within, by severe fevers and internal stomach disorders. He was determined to extract a cure from nature itself and after four years of researching and analysing the qualities of tropical herbs and plants, in 1824, he finally arrived at a unique blend of herbs that he called 'Amargo Aromatico' or aromatic bitters. From these humble beginnings, an international industry was soon to rise.

It was a period of great maritime activity in the Caribbean. The town of Angostura on the banks of the Orinoco River was an important trading post. Ships came into this port from all over the world, their sailors often complaining of seasickness. From the residents, they soon learned of the restorative qualities of Dr Siegert's remedies and of Angostura® aromatic bitters; they began their continuing trip around the world. Dr Siegert was encouraged to think of producing his bitters on a commercial scale.

In 1830, Dr Siegert exported his unique aromatic bitters to England and Trinidad. By 1850, he had resigned his commission in the Venezuelan Army, to concentrate on the manufacture of his bitters, since by then demand had leapt ahead of supply.

By the time Dr Siegert died in 1870, his reputation and the reputation of his Angostura® aromatic bitters were internationally established.

Dr J.G.B. Siegert & Hijo, a partnership with his son, Carlos Siegert, was established in 1867 by Dr Siegert. Two years after the death of Dr Siegert, the name was changed to Dr J.G.B. Siegert & Hijos, to include younger brother, Alfredo Siegert.

Don Carlos, as Carlos became known, recognized that he was in possession of the secret to a unique product. Bon vivant, impeccable in his dress and manners, he was among the first advertisers.

He exhibited his product in London in 1862 and sampled it. It became the magic ingredient, to be used in exotic concoctions. He exhibited the product in Paris in 1867 and in Vienna in 1873. He visited Philadelphia, the United States in 1876 and Australia in 1879.

The hallmark of Angostura® aromatic bitters was firmly established.

Home to Trinidad

Venezuela was not as politically stable as Simon Bolivar had promised. There was internal strife and dictator followed dictator. Carlos and Alfredo decided to leave and chose the nearby island of Trinidad as their country of adoption.

In the 1870s, Dr Siegert's descendants moved to Trinidad and Tobago; since then, all productions have originated from the twin-island state. In Trinidad, Carlos and Alfredo were joined by their youngest brother, Luis, and together they set up business once again.

Angostura® aromatic bitters made the brothers remarkably prosperous.

In 1903, Carlos Siegert died, which was followed after two years of the death of Luis, making Alfredo the sole owner of the secret formula for Angostura® aromatic bitters.

Angostura® Bitters in two different forms Angostura Orange Bitters (left) and Angostura Bitters original recipe (right). (Courtesy: *Angostura Bitters*)

In 1904, Alfredo was appointed purveyor of Angostura® aromatic bitters to the King of Prussia and in 1907 to the King Alfonso XIII of Spain. He went public with the company and named it Angostura Bitters (Dr J.G.B. Siegert & Sons) Limited. Three years later, the company was appointed purveyor of Angostura® aromatic bitters to King George V.

Alfredo speculated in several business projects and lost heavily great sums of money and the House of Angostura passed into the hands of its creditors.

It continues to be distilled in Trinidad, using the secret recipe from 1824 – the same blend of herbs and spices.

- It has retained its original formulation – one of the few remaining trade secrets.
- Distributed to over 140 countries across the world.
- An international brand that has over the centuries continued to flavour the world.

(Courtesy: Angostura Bitters.)

The other varieties of bitters are consumed as aperitifs and digestifs. Some great examples are Fernet Branca and Unicum from Italy. Campari is a very popular bitter from Italy where a premix of 'Campari-soda' is bottled and sold everywhere. It has been discussed in detail in the chapter on liqueurs.

25.6 UNDERBERG

This is red digestif bitter produced in Germany, made of aromatic herbs from 43 countries. The exact recipe is a well-guarded secret of the Underberg family. This drink is associated with its 20 ml portion sized bottle; the wine bottle is protected by its characteristic straw paper sleeve with the Underberg label glued on it.

25.7 FERNET BRANCA

This is a type of bitter with a base of grape brandy, usually coloured with caramel. The recipe varies according to the brand that produces it. In general, it usually contains chamomile, cardamom, aloe and saffron. It is usually served as a digestif. It is bottled at 45% ABV. Fernet Branca may be served straight or on the rocks, sometimes used in cocktails as well.

25.8 UNICUM

Unicum is a Hungarian herbal bitter, consumed as an aperitif or a digestif. It is made with 40 herbs and spices and aged in oak casks. It is the national drink of Hungary.

Apart from the aromatized wines and aperitifs covered in this chapter, there are many other kinds of aromatized wines, aperitifs and bitters found across the world in countries such as Argentina, Spain, Portugal, USA, South Africa and Australia. The ones mentioned above are of most significance and hence covered above.

LET'S SUMMARIZE IN POINTS

- Aromatized wines are also known as aperitifs, which is fortified wine flavoured with roots, herbs, barks, flowers, seeds and other flavouring agents to enhance the natural flavour of the wine.
- Some famous aromatized wines are Vermouth, Byrrh, Dubonnet, Underberg, Fernet Branca, Unicum and others.
- Bitters are a variety of aperitifs and digestifs, which are famous either on their own or used to flavour other cocktails.

25.9 FAQs

Short-Answer Type Questions

1. What is a bitter?
2. What is an aperitif?
3. What is a digestif?
4. Define aromatized wines.
5. Name any five aromatized wines.

Long-Answer Type Questions

1. Write short notes on Fernet Branca, Unicum, Dubonnet and bitters.
2. Write a detailed note on Vermouth.
3. Byrrh is …. Complete the sentence, discussing the details of this aperitif.
4. Discuss all the service styles used for aperitifs, bitters and digestifs.
5. Discuss the history and importance of aromatized wines.

25.10 KEY TERMS

- Aperitif
- Digestif
- Quinine
- Wormwood

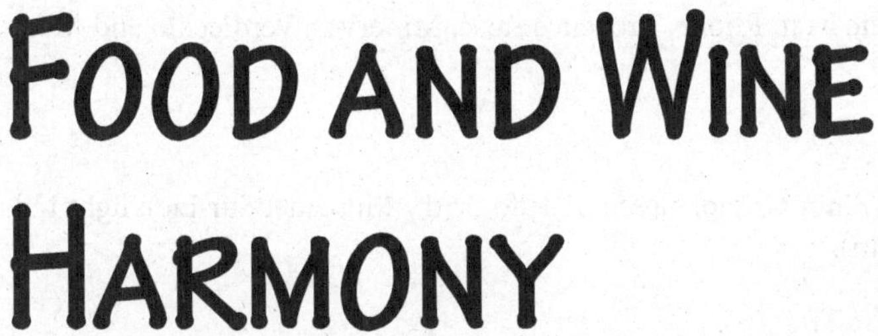

Food and Wine Harmony

CHAPTER OUTLINE

Critics are at last beginning to discuss this long neglected (or at least avoided) field of human endeavour. It is a fertile ground for experiment. Few combinations can be dismissed outright as 'wrong', but generations of tradition and error have produced certain working conventions that certainly do no harm.

The following are the ideas intended to help you make quick decisions. Any of the groups of recommended wines could be extended at will. In general, I have stuck to wines that are widely available, at the same time trying to ring the changes, so that the same wines do not come up time and time again, as they tend to do in real life. Remember that in a restaurant, that is truly regional (Proveçal, Basque, Tuscan, Catalan, Austrian etc.), there is a ready-made answer that the wine of the region should be considered.

26.1 BEFORE THE MEAL APERITIFS

The conventional aperitif wines are either sparkling (epitomized by Champagne) or fortified (epitomized by Sherry in Britain, Port in France, Vermouth in Italy etc.). A glass of white or rosé (or in France, red) table wine before eating is presently in vogue. It calls for something light and stimulating, fairly dry, but not acid, with a degree of character; rather Riesling or Chenin Blanc than Chardonnay.

Warning: Avoid peanuts; they destroy wine flavours. Olives are also too piquant for most wines; they need Sherry or a martini. Eat almonds, pistachios or walnuts, plain crisps or cheese straws instead.

26.2 FIRST COURSE

Aioli

A thirstquencher is needed for this garlic heat. Rhône, Provence Rosé, Minerva's, Verdicchio and Marc are recommended.

Antipasto in Italy

Dry or medium white: Italian (Arneis, Pinot Grigio, Greco di Tufo or try Muscadet Sur Lie); light red (Dolcetto, Franciacorta or Young Chianti).

Artichoke Vinaigrette

Young Red: Bordeaux, Côtes du Rhône, or a rather blunt white, or one from Greece. *Hollandaise* full bodied, slightly crisp, dry white: PouillyFuissé, Pfalz Spätlese or a Carneros or YarraValley Chardonnay.

Asparagus

A difficult flavour for wine, so the wine needs plenty of its own. Sémillon beats Chardonnay, especially from Australia. Alsace Pinot Gris, even dry Muscat can be good, or Jurançon Sec or try similarly flavoured Cabernet Franc.

Avocado with Prawns, Crab Etc.

Dry to medium or slightly sharp white: Rheingau or PfalzKabinett, Sancerre, Pinot Grigio; Sonoma or Australian Chard or Sauvignon, Cape Steen or Dry Rosé. Vinaigrettelight red, Italian Enferd'Arvier or Manzanilla Sherry.

Bisques

Dry white with plenty of body: Pinot Gris, Chardonnay. Fino or Dry Amontillado Sherry or Montilla. West Australian Semillon.

Boudin (Blood Sausage)

Local Sauvignon or Chenin, especially from the Loire.

Bouillabaisse

Herby Dry White, Roussette de Savoie, Provence or Corsica rosé, Cassis, Verdicchio or California Blanc Fumé.

Caesar Salad

California (Central coast) Chardonnay.

Carpaccio, Beef

It seems to work well with the flavours of most wines, including reds. Top Tuscan Vino Da Tavola is appropriate, but fine Chardonnays are good. So is vintage Champagne (*see also* Carpaccio under Section 26.3), Salmon Chardonnay or Champagne.

Caviar

Iced vodka. Full bodied champagne (e.g., Bollinger or Krug).

Ceviche

Australian Riesling or Verdelho, New Zealand Sauvignon Blanc.

Charcuterie

Young Beaujolais-Villages or Bordeaux Blanc, Loire reds such as Bourgueil, Swiss or Oregon Pinot Noir.

Cheese Fondue

Dry white: Valais Fendant or any other Swiss Chasselas, GrünerVeltliner, Alsace Riesling or Pinot Gris.

Chowders

Big-scale white, not necessarily bone dry: Pinot Gris, Rhine Spätlese, Australian Semillon or fino Sherry, dry Madeira or Marsala.

Consommé

Medium-dry Amontillado Sherry or Sercial Madeira.

Crostini

Morellino di Scansano, Montepulciano d'Abruzzo, Valpolicella.

Crudités

Light red or rosé: Côte du Rhône, Minerva's, Chianti Okanagan, Pinot Noir or Fino Sherry.

Dim Sum

Classically, tea: Oolong or BoLei. For fun, *fried Dim Sum*: Pinot Grigio or Riesling; *steamed*: light red (Bardolino or Beaujolais-Villages).

Eggs (*See also* Soufflés)

These present difficulties: they clash with most wines and spoil good ones. Try straightforward, not too oaky Chardonnay.

Escargots

Rhône reds, such as Gigondas or Vacqueyras or St Véran. In the Midi, Petits-Gris goes with local white or red. In Alsace, Pinot Blanc or Muscat.

Fish Terrine

Pfalz Riesling Spätlese, Trocken, Chablis, Washington Sémillon, Clare Valley Riesling, Sonoma Chardonnay or Fino Sherry.

Foie Gras

In Bordeaux, they drink Sauternes. Others prefer a late-harvest Riesling (including New World) or Gewürz. Tokay is the new choice. Old dry Amontillado can be sublime, not a Chardonnay.

Gazpacho

A glass of Fino before and after this cold soup.

Goat's Cheese—Grilled or Fried (Warm Salad)

Chilled Chinon, Saumur-Champigny or Provence Rosé else strong red: Château Musar, Greek and Turkish.

Grapefruit

If you must start a meal with grapefruit, try contrasting with port, Madeira or sweet Sherry with (or in) it.

Gravlax

Aquavit, Iced sake, Grand Cru Chablis or California, Washington or Margaret River Chardonnay, Mosel Spätlese (not Trocken).

Guacamole

California Chardonnay, Riesling Kabinett or Mexican beer.

Haddock, Smoked, Mousseoff

A wonderful dish for showing off any stylish full-bodied white, including Grand Cru Chablis or New Zealand Chardonnay.

Ham, Raw or Cured (*See also* Prosciutto)

Alsace Grand Cru, Pinot Gris or good and crisp Italian Colli White.

Herrings, Raw or Pickled

Dutch Gin (young, not aged) or Scandinavian Akvavit and cold beer. If wine is an essential, try Muscadet.

Hors d'oeuvres (*See also* Antipasto)

Clean, fruity, sharp white-Sancerre or any Sauvignon, GrünerVeltliner, Vinho Verde, Cape Steen or young, light red Bordeaux, Rhône or Corbiéres or Fino Sherry.

Humus

Pungent, spicy dry white (*e.g.*, Gewürztraminer or Retsina).

Mackerel (Smoked)

It is an oily wine-destroyer. Manzanilla Sherry or Schnapps, peppered or Bison Grass Vodka. A good lager.

Mayonnaise

Adds richness that calls for a contrasting bite in the wine. Côte Chalonnaise whites (*e.g.*, Rully) are good. Try New Zealand Sauvignon Blanc, Verdicchio or a Spätlese Trocken from the Pfalz.

Melon

Strong sweet wine (if any): Port, Bual Madeira, Muscat de Frontignan or dry, perfumed Viognier or Australian Marsanne.

Minestrone

Red: Grignolino, Chianti, Zinfandel, Rhône Syrah etc. or Fino.

Mushrooms à la Grecque

Greek Verdea or Mantinia, or any hefty dry white or fresh young red.

Omelettes

See Eggs.

Oyster Stew

California, Long Island or Australian Chardonnay.

Oysters

White: Non-vintage Champagne, Chablis or (better) Chablis Premier Cru, Muscadet, white Graves, Sancerre. Guinness or perhaps Scotch and water.

Pasta

Red or white according to the sauce or trimmings:

Cream Sauce: Orvieto, Frascati, Alto Adige Chardonnay.
Meat Sauce: Montepulciano d'Abruzzo, Salice Salentino and Merlot.
Pesto (Basil) Sauce: *Barbera*, Sicilian Torbato and New Zealand Sauvignon Blanc.
Seafood Sauce (*e.g.*, Vongole): Verdicchio, Soave and Palomino and Sauvignon Blanc.
Tomato Sauce: *Barbera*, S Italian red, Zinfandel and South Australian Grenache.

Pâté

According to constituents and quality:

Chicken Livers: Call for pungent white (Alsace Pinot Gris or Marsanne), a smooth red like light Pomerol or Volnay or even Amontillado Sherry.

With Simple Pâté: A dry white: Good Vin de Pays, Graves, Fumé Blanc.

With Duck Pâté: Châteauneuf-du-Pape, Cornas, Chianti Classico or Franciaacorta.

Pimentos, Roasted

New Zealand Sauvignon, Spanish Chardonnay or Valdepenas.

Pizza

Any dry Italian red or Rioja, Australian Shiraz or California Sangiovese. Corbiéres, Coteaux d'Aix-en-Provence.

Prawns or Shrimps

Fine dry white: Burgundy, Graves, New Zealand Chard, Washington Riesling—even fine mature Champagne.

Indian, Thai or Chinese Style: Rich Australian Hunter Valley Chardonnay. ('Cocktail sauce' kills wine, and I suspect, in time, people.)

Prosciutto (also with Melon, Pears or Figs)

Full-bodied dry or medium white: Orvieto, Gambellara, Palomino, Fendant or GrünerVeltliner, Alsace or California Gewürztraminer, Australian Sémillon or Jurançon Sec.

Quiches

Dry white with body: Alsace, Graves, a Sauvignon or dry Rheingau; or try young red (Beaujolais Villages, Chilean Pinot Noir), according to the ingredients. Never a fine-wine dish.

Ravioli

With Wild Mushrooms: Dolcetto or Nebbiolo d'Alba, Oregon Pinot Noir.

Saffron Sauces (*e.g.*, on Fish)

Pungent or full-bodied white (especially Chardonnay) or Provence rosé.

Salade Nicoise

Very dry, not too light or flowery white or rosé: Proveçal, Rhône or Corsican; Catalan white, Fernao Pires, California Sauvignon Blanc.

Salads

As a first course, especially with blue cheese dressing, any dry and appetizing white wine. After a main course: No wine.

Note: Vinegar in salad dressing destroys the flavour of wine. If you want salad at a meal with fine wine, dress the salad with a little lemon juice instead of vinegar.

Salami

Very tasty red or rosé: Barbera, top Valpolicella, young Zinfandel, Tavel or Ajaccio Rosé, Vacqueyras, young Bordeaux or Chilean Cabernet Sauvignon.

Salmon (Smoked)

A dry but pungent white: Fino Sherry, Alsace Pinot Gris, Chablis Grand Cru, Pouilly-Fumé, Pfalz Riesling Spätlese, Vintage Champagne. Lighter red or Vodka, Schnapps or Akvavit.

Seafood Salad

Fresh Italian Chardonnay or Pinot Grigio. Australian Verdelho or Clear Riesling.

Shark's Fin Soup

Add a teaspoon of Cognac. Sip Amontillado.

Soufflés

Dishes as shown, These deserve wines:

Fish: Dry White: Burgundy, Bordeaux, Alsace, Chardonnay etc.

Cheese: Red Burgundy or Bordeaux, Cabernet Sauvignon etc.

Spinach: (Tougher on wine) Mâcon-Villages, St-Véran and Valpolicella.

Taramasalata

A rustic southern white with personality; not necessarily Retsina. The Fino Sherry works well. Try Arbois or white Rioja. The blend supermarket version goes well with fine delicate whites or Champagne.

Terrine

As for Pâté, or equivalent red: Mercurey, St-Amour or Beaujolais-Villages, fairly young St-Emilion, California Syrah or Sangiovese, Bulgarian or Chilean Cabernet.

Thai-style Dishes (Seasoned with Lemon Grass, Coconut Milk, Ginger etc.)

Riesling Spätlese (Pfalz or Austrian), Gewürz or pungent Sauvignon.

Tortilla

Rioja Crianza.

Trout, Smoked

Sancerre, California or New Zealand Fumé Blanc. Rully or Bourgogne Aligoté.

Vegetable Terrine

Not a great help to fine wines, but California, Chilean or South African Chardonnays make a fashionable marriage.

26.3 FISH

Abalone

Dry or medium white: Sauvignon Blanc, Côte de Beaune Blanc, Pinot Grigio or Muscadet Sur Lie.

Anchovies

A robust wine: Red, white or rosé—try Rioja.

Bass (Striped or Sea)

Weissburgunder from Baden or Pfalz. Viognier for any fine/delicate white (*e.g.*, Coonawarra dry Riesling or Chablis).

Beurre Blanc

A top-notch Muscadet Sur Lie, a Sauvignon/Sémillon blend or a Rheingau Charta wine.

Carpaccio of Salmon or Tuna

Puligny–Montrachet, Condrieu or Australian Chardonnay.

Cod

Good neutral background for fine dry/medium whites: Chablis, Meursault, Corton-Charlemagne, Cru Classé Graves, Dry Vouvray; German Kabinett or Dry Spätlese or a good light red (*e.g.*, Beaune).

Coquilles St Jacques

See Scallops.

Crab, Cioppino

Sauvignon Blanc, but West Coast friends say Zinfandel.

Cold with salad Alsace Riesling or Muscat, dry California of Australian Riesling or Viognier from Condrieu.

Softshell Chardonnay or top quality German Riesling Spätlese.

Chinese, Baked with Ginger and Onion

Hungarian Furmint, Gewürz.
With black bean sauce: Big Barossa Shiraz or Syrah.

Eel (Jellied)

Non-vintage Champagne or a nice cup of (Ceylon) tea.
Smoked Strong/Sharp Wine: Fino Sherry, Bourgogne Aligoté or Schnapps.

Fish and Chips, Fritto Misto (or Tempura)

Chablis white Bordeaux, Sauvignon Blanc Arneis, fino, Montilla, Koshu, tea etc.

Fish Pie (with Creamy Sauce)

Napa Chardonnay, Pinot Gris d'Alsace.

Haddock

Rich dry white: Meursault, California or New Zealand Chard or Marsanne.

Hake

Sauvignon Blanc or any freshly fruity white: Pacherenc, Tuscan or White Navarra.

Herrings

Need a white with some acidity to cut their richness. Bourgogne Aligoté, dry Sauvignon Blanc or Cider.

Kedgeree

Full white, still or sparkling: Mâcon–Villages or Champagne.

Kippers

A good cup of tea, preferably Ceylon tea (add milk, but no sugar).

Lamproi à la Bordelaise

Five-year-old St-Emilion or Fronsac.

Lobster, Richly Sauced

Vintage Champagne, fine white Burgundy, Cru Classé Graves, California Chard, Australian Riesling or Pfalz Spätlese.

Salad white: New Vintage Champagne, Alsace Riesling, Chablis Premier Cru, Condrieu, Mosel Spätlese or Penedès Chardonnay.

Mackerel

Hard or sharp white: Sauvignon Blanc from Bergerac or Touraine, Vinho Verde, White Rioja or Guinness.

Mullet, Red

A Chameleon, adaptable to good white or red (but avoid the liver).

Mussels

Muscadet Sur Lie, Chablis Premier Cru or Chardonnay.

Stuffed with garlic: See Escargots.

Perch, Sandre

Exquisite fish for finest wines: Bâtard-Montrachet Premiers Cru or noble Mossels. Top Swiss Fendant or Johannisberg.

Salmon (Fresh)

Fine white Burgundy: Puligny or Chassagne-Montrachet, Meursault, Corton-Charlemagne, Chablis Grand Cru; Condrieu, California, Idaho or New Zealand Chardonnay, Rheingau Kabinett/Spätlese, Australian Riesling or equivalent. Young Pinot Noir can be perfect too and Clarets are not bad.

Sardines (Fresh Grilled)

Very dry white: Vinho Verde, Soave or Muscadet.

Sashimi

If you are prepared to forego the wasabi, sparkling wines (including California's) will go, or Washington or Tasmanian Chardonnay, Chablis Grand Cru or Rheingau Riesling Halbtrocken. Otherwise, iced sake or beer.

Scallops

An inherently slightly sweet dish, best with medium dry whites.

In cream sauce: German Spätlese, a Montrachet or top Australian Chardonnay.

Grilled or fried: Hermitage Blanc, Gewürztraminer, GrünerVeltliner, Entre Deux Mers, Australian Riesling or Champagne.

Shad

White Graves, or Meursault or Hunter Sémillon.

Shellfish

Dry white with plain-bodied shellfish, richer wines with richer sauces.

Shrimp (Potted)

Fino Sherry, Chablis, Gavi or Long Island Chardonnay.

Skate with Black Butter

White with some pungency (*e.g.*, Menetou–Salon) or a clean straightforward one such as Muscadet or Arneis.

Snapper

Sauvignon Blanc from a New World Wine country.

Sole, Plaice, etc. (Plain, Grilled or Fried)

An ideal accompaniment for fine wines: white burgundy or its equivalent.

With sauce: Depending on the ingredients: sharp dry wine for tomato sauce, fairly rich for sole Véro-nique etc.

Sushi

Hot Wasabi is usually hidden in every piece. German QbA Trocken wines or simple Chablis are good enough or of course, sake or beer.

Swordfish

Dry white of whatever country you are in.

Trout

Delicate white wine (*e.g.*, Mosel—especially from Saar) or Alsace Pinot Blanc.

Smoked: A full-flavoured white: Gewürztraminer, Alsace Pinot Gris, Rhine Spätlese or Australian Hunter white.

Tuna (Grilled)

White red or rosé of fairly fruity character; a top St Véranor, White Hermitage or Côte du Rhône would be fine.

Turbot

Your best rich dry white: Meursault or Chassagne-Montrachet or its California, Australian or New Zealander equivalent. Condrieu, mature Rheingau Mosel or Nahe Spätlese or Auslese (not Trocken).

Whitebait

Crisp dry white: Muscadet, Sauvignon or Vordicchio.

26.4 MEAT, POULTRY AND MORE

Barbecues

Red with a slight rasp, therefore, young: Shiraz, Chianti, Navarra, Zinfandel or Turkish Buzbag. Bandol for a real treat.

Beef (Boiled)

Red Bordeaux (Bourg or Fronsac), Roussillon or Australian Shiraz. Gevrey-Chambertin, Côte Rôtie or top-notch beer. Roastan ideal partner for red wine of any kind.

Beef Stew

Sturdy red: Pomerol or St-Emilion, Hermitage, Cornas, Barbera, Shiraz, Napa Cabernet or Torres Gran Coronas.

Beef Stroganoff

Dramatic red: Barolo, Valpolicella Amarone, Cahors, Hermitage or late-harvest Zinfandel or even Moldovan Negru de Purkar.

Cabbage (Stuffed)

Hungarian Cabernet Franc/Kadarka or Bulgarian Cabernet.

Cajun Food

Fleurie or Brouilly. With gumbo: Amontillado or Mexican beer.

Cassoulet

Red from South West France (Madiran and Corbiéres), Barbera, Zinfandel or Australian Great Western Shiraz.

Chicken/Turkey/Guinea Fowl Roast

Virtually any wine, including very best bottles of dry/medium white and finest old reds (especially burgundy). The meat of fowl can be adapted with sauces to match almost any fine wine (*e.g.*, Coq au Vin red Burgundy). Avoid sauces that include tomato, if you want to taste any good bottles.

Chicken Casserole

Lirac, St-Joseph, Bordeaux or Chilean Pinot Noir.

Kiev: Alsace Riesling, Collio or Bergerac Rouge.

Chilli Con Carne

Young red: Gattinara, Beaujolais, Navarra or Zinfandel.

Chinese Food (Canton or Peking Style)

Dry to medium dry white Sauvignon Blanc or (better) Riesling can be good throughout a Chinese banquet (*e.g.*, Gewürztraminer). Dry sparkling (especially Cava) is good for cutting the oil. Eschew sweet/sour dishes, but try an 89/90 St-Emilion or St-Estéphe cru bourgeois, or Châteauneuf-du-Pape with duck. I often serve both white and red wines concurrently through Chinese meals.

Szechuan style: Muscadet, Alsace Pinot Blanc or chilled beer.

Choucroute Garnie

Alsace, Pinot Blanc, Pinot Gris or Riesling or beer.

Cold Meats

Generally taste better with full-flavored white wine than red. Mosel Spätlese or Hochheimer are ideal, and so is Beaujolais.

Confit d'Oie

Young tannic red Bordeaux Cru Bourgeois, helps in reducing the richness. Alsace Tokay Pinot Gris or Gewurztraminer marches it.

Coq au Vin

Red Burgundy: In an ideal world, one bottle of Chambertin in the dish, two on the table.

Corned Beef Hash

Zinfandel, Rioja Crianza or Côte du Rhône red

Curry

Medium (sweet white, very cold): Orvieto abboccato, California Chenin Blanc, Slovenian Traminer, Indian sparkling or emphasize the heat with a tannic Barolo or Barbaresco or deep flavoured reds, such as St-Emilion, Cornas, Shiraz-Cabernet or Valpolicella Amarone.

Duck or Goose

Rather rich white: Pfalz Spätlese or Alsace reserve exceptionelle; or mature gamey red: Morey St-Denis or Côte Rôtie, or Bordeaux or Burgundy. With oranges or peaches, the Sauternes propose drinking Sauternes, others Monbazillac or Auslese.

Peking: *See* Chinese food.

Wild duck (Big-scale red): Hermitage, Châteauneuf-du-Pape, Bandol, California or South. African Cabernet, Australian Shiraz–Grange, if you can find it.

With olives: Top-notch Chianti or Tuscan VdT.

Frankfurters

German, New York Riesling, Beaujolais or Budweiser.

Game Birds and Young Birds (Plain Roasted)

The best red wine you can afford.

Older birds in casseroles: Red (Gevrey-Chambertin, Pommard, Santé nay or Grand Cru St-Emilion, Napa Valley Cabernet Sauvignon).

Well-hung game: Vega Sicilia, great red Rhône or Château Musar.

Cold game: Mature vintage Champagne.

Game Pie

Hot red: Oregon Pinot Noir.
Cold: Equivalent white or Champagne.

Goulash

Flavoursome young red: Zinfandel, Bulgarian Cabernet, Hungarian Kadarka or young Australian Shiraz.

Grouse

See Game birds, but push the boat right out.

Haggis

Fruity red (*e.g.*, young claret), New Word Cabernet or malt whisky.

Ham

Softer red Burgundies: Volnay, Beaune; Chinon or Bourgueli; slightly sweet German white (Rhine Spätlese); Czech Müller-Thurgau; lightish Cabernet (*e.g.*, Chilean) or California Pinot Noir.

Hamburger

Young red: Beaujolais or Bulgarian Cabernet, Chianti, Zinfandel, Kadarka from Hungary or Coke or Pepsi.

Hare

Jugged hare call for flavourful red: Not too old Burgundy (try Vosne–Romanée) or Bordeaux, Rhône (*e.g.*, Gigondas), Bandol or a fine Rioja reserve. Australia's Grange would be an experience.

Heart-Stuffed

Full-bodied tannic red: Shiraz-Cabernet, Dao or Cornas.

Kebabs

Vigorous red: Greek Nemea or Naoussa, Turkish Buzbag, Chilean Cabernet, Zinfandel or Barossa Shiraz.

Kidneys

Red: St-Emilion or earthier versions: Nuits-St-Georges, Cornas, Barbaresco, Rioja, Spanish or Australian Cabernet or Portuguese Bairrada.

Lamb (Cutlet or Chops)

As for roast lamb, but a little less grand.

Roast: One of the traditional and best partners for very good red Bordeaux, or its Cabernet Equivalents from the New World. In Spain, the partner of the finest old Rioja Reservas.

Liver

Young red: Beaujolais-Villages, St-Joseph, Médoc, Italian Merlot, Breganze Cabernet, Zinfandel or Portuguese Bairrada.

Meatballs

Tangy medium-bodied red: Mercurey, Crozes-Hermitage, Madiran, Rubesco, Dao, Zinfandel or Cabernet.

Meatballs

Tangy medium-bodied red: Mercury, Crozes-Hermitage, Madiran, Rubesco, Dao, Zinfandel or Cabernet.

Mixed Grill

A fairly light, easily swallowable red: Bordeaux from Bourgongne, Fronsac or Premiére Côtes; Côtes de Buzet; Coteaux du Languedoc; Chianti; Chilean Cabernet or a Cru Beaujolais such as Juliénas.

Moussaka

Red or Rosé: Naoussa from Greece, Chianti, Cirbiéres, Côtes de Provence, Ajaccio or Patrimonio, Chilean Pinot Noir.

Oxtail or Ossobucco

Rather rich red: St-Emilion, Pomerol, Pommard, Nuits-St-Georges, Barolo or Rioja Reserva, California or Coonawarra Cabernet or a dry Rheingau Riesling Spätlese.

Paella

Young Spanish red, dry white or Rosé: Penedés or Rioja.

Pigeons or Squab

Lively red Burgundy: Chambolle-Musigny; Chianti Classico or California Pinot. Silvaner, Spätlese from Franken.

Pork (Roasted)

A good rich neutral background to a fairly light red or rich white. It deserves treatment—Médoc is fine. Portugal's famous suckling pig is eaten with Bairrada Garrafeira, Chinese pork dishes are good with Beaujolais.

Quail

As for pigeon, but does not harm finer reds.

Rabbit

Lively medium-bodied, young Italian red or Chiroubles, Chinon, Saumur-Champigny or Rhône Rosé.

Risotto

Pinot Grigio from Friuli, Gavi, youngish Sémillon, Dolcetto or Barberad'Alba.
With mushrooms Cahors, Madiran or Barbera.
With fungi Porcini finest mature Barolo or Barbaresco.

Satay

Australia's McLaren Vale Shiraz or Alsace or New Zealand Gewürztraminer.

Sauerkraut

Lager or Stout (*see also* Choucroute Garnie).

Sausages

See also Frankfurters, Salami.

The British banger requires a two and a half year old NE Italian Merlot (or a red wine, anyway).

Shepherd's Pie

Rough and really red seems most appropriate, *e.g.*, Barbera, but beer or dry cider is the real McCoy.

Spare Ribs

Vacqueyras or St-Joseph or Australian Old Vine Grenache or Zinfandel.

Steak au Poivre

A fairly young Rhône red or Cabernet.

Tartare Vodka or light young red: Beaujolais, Bergerac or Valpolicella.
Korean Yuk Whe (the world's best steak tartare) Sake.
Filet or tournedos, Any red (but not old wines with Béarnaise sauce).
T-bone reds of similar bone structure: Barolo, Hermitage, Australian Cabernet or Shiraz.
Fiorentina (Bistecca) Chianti Classico Riserva or Brunello.

Steak and Kidney Pie or Pudding

Red Rioja reserve premature Bordeaux wines.

Stew and Casseroles

Burgundy such as Chambolle-Musigny or Bonnes-Mares if fairly simple; otherwise, lusty full-flavoured red: young Côtes du Rhône, Corbiéres, Barbera, Shiraz, Zinfandel, etc.

Sweet Breads

A grand dish, so grand wine: Rhine Riesling or Franken Silvaner Spätlese, Alsace Grand Cru Pinot Gris or Condrieu, depending on sauce.

Tandoori Chicken

Sauvignon Blanc or young red Bordeaux.

Thai Food

Ginger and lemon grass call for Gewürztraminer.

Coconut curries Hunter Valley Chard; Alsace Pinot Blanc for refreshment.

Tongue

Good for any red or white of abundant character, especially Italian.

Tripe

Red, *e.g.*, Corbiéres, Roussillon or rather sweet white (*e.g.*, German Spätlese). Better: Western Australian Semillon-Chardonnay.

Veal (Roasted)

A good neutral background dish for any fine old red which may have faded with age (*e.g.*, a Rioja reserve) or a German or Austrian Riesling.

Venison

Big-scale-red: Rhône, Bordeaux or California Cab of a mature vintage; or rather rich white (Pfalz Spatlese or Alsace Tokay Pinot Grigio).

Vitello Tonatto

Light red (Valpolicella, Beaujolais) served cool.

26.5 VEGETARIAN DISHES

Bean Salad

Red Rioja Reserva.

Bean Stew

Bairrada from Portugal and Toro from Spain.

Broccoli Mornay

Crisp aromatic white: Sancerre, Riesling Spätlese or Muscat.

Cabbage (Including Bubble and Squeak)

Beer, Stout or Beaujolais Nouveau.
Choucroute, see also Sauerkraut.
Alsace Pinot Gris or Sylvaner.

Couscous

Young red with a bite: Shiraz, Corbiéres, Minerva's, etc.

Fennel-Based Dishes

Sauvignon: Pouilly-Fumé or one from New Zealand; Beaujolais.

Marrow, Stuffed

Fruity dry white: South African Chenin or Australian Marsanne.

'Meaty' Aubergine, Lentil or Mushroom Bakes

Corbiéres, Zinfandel.

Mushrooms (in Most Contexts)

Fleshy red; *e.g.*, Pomerol, California Merlot, Rioja reserve or Vega Sicilia.

On toast your best claret.

Wild Mushrooms

Barolo or Chianti Rufina or top Claret: Pauillac or St-Estéphe.

Onion/Leek Tart

Fruity dry white: Alsace Pinot Grigio or Gewurztraminer. Jurançon, Australian Riesling or Beaujolais or Loire red.

Peppers or Aubergines (Stuffed)

Vigorous red wine: Italian Chianti or Dolcetto, California Zinfandel, Bandol or Vacqueyras.

Ratatouille

Vigorous young red: Chianti, Bulgarian Cabernet or Merlot, Young red Bordeaux or Gigondas or Coteaux du Languedoc.

Spanish/Pasta Bakes

Valpolicella (its bitterness helps); Greco di Molise or Sicilian/Sardinian white.

26.6 DESSERTS

Apple Pie or Strudel

Sweet German, Austrian or Hungarian white.

Apples

Vintage port.

Banoffee Pie

Very sweet fortified wine such as Australian liqueur muscat or the sweetest of sherries.

Bread and Butter Pudding

10-year-old Barsac from a good Château.

Cakes

Bual or Malmsey Madeira, Oloroso or cream Sherry.

Cheesecake

Sweet white: Vouvray or Anjou, refreshing, but nothing special.

Chocolate Cake, Mousse, and Soufflés

Bual Madeira, Auslese, California orange muscat, Baumé-de-Venise or a tot of good rum.

Christmas Pudding, and Mince Pies

Tawny port, cream Sherry or Asti.

Creams, Custards, and Fools

Sauternes, Loupiac, Ste-Croix-du-Mont or Monbazillac.

Créme Brulée

Sauternes or Rhine Beerenauslese, best Madeira or Tokay (with concealed fruit, a more modest sweet wine).

Crêpes Suzette

Sweet Champagne or Asti spumante.

Fruit, Fresh

Sweet Coteaux du Layon, light sweet or liqueur muscat. Stewed apricots, pears etc. Sweet muscatel: try serving Muscat de Beaumes-de-Venise, Moscato di Pantelleria or Spanish dessert Tarragona.

Fruit Flans

Sauternes, Monbazillac or sweet Vouvray or Anjou.

Fruit Salads, Orange Salad

A fine sweet Sherry or any muscat-based wine.

Ice Cream

Fortified wine (*e.g.*, Banyuls) or sparkling sweet Asti spumante.

Mille-Feuille

Delicate medium—dry sparkling white such as Moscato d'Asti or Demi-Sec Champagne.

Nuts

Oloroso Sherry, Bual Madeira, Vintage or Tawny Port or Vin Santo.

Oranges (Caramelized)

Experiment with old Sauternes or California Orange Muscat.

Pears in Red Wine

A pause before the port or other fortified reds: Rivesaltes or Banyuls.

Raspberries (No Cream, Little Sugar)

Excellent with fine reds that themselves taste of raspberries: Beaujolais or a fruity Californian Rose.

Rice Pudding

Liqueur Muscat, Moscatel de Valencia or Loupiac.

Sorbets, Ice Creams

Asti or (better) Moscato d'Asti Naturale. Amaretto liqueur with vanilla; rum with chocolate.

Strawberries, Wild (No Cream)

Serve with red Bordeaux poured over them.

Strawberries and Cream

Sauternes or similar sweet Bordeaux, or Vouvray Moelleux.

Summer Pudding

Fairly young Sauternes of a good vintage.

Sweet Soufflés

Sauternes or Vouvray Moelleux. Sweet Champagne.

Tiramisu

Vin Santo, young tawny port or Beaumes-de-Venise.

Trifle

Should be sufficiently vibrant with its internal Sherry.

Walnuts

Nature's match for finest port, Madeira or Oloroso Sherry.

Zabaglione

Light gold Marsala or Australian botrytized Semillon.

26.7 WINE AND CHEESE

The notion that wine and cheese were married in heaven is not born out of experience. Fine red wines are slaughtered by strong cheeses: only sharp or sweet white wines survive. Principles to remember, despite exceptions, are first: the harder the cheese, the more tannin the wine can have. And the creamier it is, the more acidity is needed in the wine. The main exception constitutes a third principle: wines and cheese of a region usually go together. Cheese is classified by its texture and the nature of its rind, so its appearance is a guide to the type of wine to match it. Individual cheese mentioned below are only examples taken from the hundreds sold in good cheese shops.

Fresh, No Rind—Cream Cheese, Crème Fraiche, Mozzarella, Mascarpone

(Not layered with blue.)

Light crisp white-Côtes de Duras, Bergerac or Vinho Verde; or pink–Anjou or Rhône; or very light, young, fresh red Bordeaux, Bardolino or Beaujolais.

Hard cheeses, waxed or oiled, often showing marks from cheesecloth – Gruyere family, Manchego and Manu other Spanish cheeses, Parmesan, Chantal, old Gouda, Cheddar and most 'traditional' English cheese.

Particularly hard to generalize here; Gouda, Gruyere, some Spanish and a few English cheeses complement fine claret or Cab and great Shiraz/Syrah wines, but strong cheese need less refined wines, preferably local. Sugary and granular Old Dutch red Mimolette is perhaps the best of all for finest mature Bordeaux.

Blue Cheeses

Roquefort is wonderful with Sauternes, but do not extend the idea to other blues. It is the sweetness of Sauternes, especially old, which complements the saltiness of the cheese. Stilton and port, preferably tawny, is classic. Intensely flavoured old Oloroso, dry Amontillado, Madeira, dry Marsala and other fortified wines go with most blues.

Natural rind (mostly goat's cheese) with bluish-grey mould the rind becomes wrinkled when mature, sometimes dusted with ash–St-Marcellin.

Sancerre, Valencay. Light fresh Sauvignon, Jurançon, Savoy and Soave. Italian Chardonnay.

Bloomy rind soft cheeses, pure white rind if pasteurized or dotted with red: Brie, Camembert, Chaource or Bougon (goat's milk 'Camembert').

Full dry white burgundy or Rhône if cheese is white, immature; powerful, fruity St-Emilion, eastern European Pinot or young Australian (or Rhône) Shiraz/Syrah, if mature.

Washed-rind soft cheese, with rather sticky orange-red rind—Langres, mature Epoisses, Maroilles, Carrè de I'Est or Milleens.

Local reds, especially for burgundy cheeses; vigorous Languedoc, Cahors, Côtes du Frontonnais, Corsican, southern Italian or Sicilian, Bairrada.

Semi-soft cheese, grey pink thick rind—Livarot, Pont I'Evèque, Reblochon, Tomme de Savoie or St-Nectaire.

Powerful white Bordeaux, Chardonnay, Alsace Pinot Gris, dry Riesling, southern Italian and Sicilian white, aged white Rioja, dry Oloroso Sherry. However, the strongest of these cheeses kill most wines.

26.8 FOOD AND FINE WINE

With very special bottles, the wine sometimes guides the choice of food rather than the usual way round. The following suggestions are largely based on the gastronomic conventions of the wine regions producing these treasures, plus diligent research. They should help bring out the best in your best wines.

Red Wines

Red Bordeaux and other Cabernet Sauvignon-based wines

They are very old, light and delicate. Leg or rack of young lamb, roast with a hint of herbs (but not garlic); Entrecôte; roast Partridge or Grouse, Sweetbreads; or Cheese soufflé after the meat has been served.

Fully mature great vintage (*e.g.*, Bordeaux 5961)

Shoulder or saddle of lamb (including kidneys) with rich sauce, *e.g.*, Béarnaise. Fillet of beef marchand de Vin (with wine and bone marrow). Avoid Beef Wellington: pastry dulls the palate.

Merlot-based Bordeaux (Pomerol, Saint-Emilion)

Beef as above (fillet is richest) or venison.

Côte d'Or Red Burgundy

Consider the weight and texture, which grow lighter/more velvety with age. Also consider the character of the wine: Nuits is earthy, Musigny flowery, great Romanées can be exotic, Pommard renowned for its four-square qualities. Roast chicken, or better, capon, is safe standard with red burgundy; guineafowl for slightly stronger wines, then partridge, grouse or woodcock for those progressively more rich and pungent. Hare and Venison (Chevreuil) are the text alternatives.

Great Old Reds

The classic Burgundian formula is cheese: Epoisses (unfermented). It is a terrible waste of fine old wines.

Vigorous Younger Burgundy

Duck or goose roasted to minimize fat.

Great Syrahs: Heritage, Côte Rôtie, Grange, or Vega Sicilia

Beef, Venison, well-hung game; bone marrow on toast; English cheese (especially best farm Cheddar).

Rioja Gran Reserva, Pesquera

Richly flavoured roasts: wild boar or mutton.

Barolo, Barbaresco

Cheese risotto with white truffles; pasta with game sauce, porcini mushrooms or Parmesan.

White Wines

Very good Chablis, white burgundy, other top quality Chardonnays

White fish simply grilled or meunèire with Doria garnish of sautéed cucumber. Dover sole, Turbot and Rex sole are best. (Sea bass is too delicate; salmon passes, but does little for fine wine.)

Supreme white Burgundy (Le Montrachet, Corton-Charlemagne) or equivalent grades

Roast veal, capon or sweetbreads; richly sauced with fish or scallops as above or lobster or wild salmon.

Condrieu, Château Grillet or Hermitage Blanc

Very light pasta scented with herbs and tiny peas or broad beans.

Grand Cru Alsace, Riesling

Truite au bleu, smoked salmon or choucroutegarni.
Pinot Gris: roasted or grilled veal.
Gewürztraminer: Cheese soufflé (Munster cheese).
Vendange Tardive: Foie gras or Tarte Tatin.

Sauternes

Simple crisp buttery biscuits (*e.g.*, Langue due Chat), white peaches, nectarines or strawberries (without cream). Tropical fruit are not included. Pan-fried Foie gras. You may make some experiments with cheese.

Supreme Vouvray Moelleux etc.

Buttery biscuits, apples or apple tart.

Beerenauslese/TBA

Biscuits, peaches or green gages.

Finest Old Amontillado/Oloroso

Pecans.

Great Vintage Port or Madeira

Walnuts or pecans.

Old Vintage Champagne (Not Blanc de Blancs)

As an aperitif or with cold partridge, grouse or woodcock.

26.9 FAQs

1. Make a three-course French menu with appropriate wine pairing.
2. Make a five-course sea food menu using fine wines.
3. Give five fish dishes with an appropriate wine pairing.
4. Walnuts and desserts are generally served with__________. Give five desserts with their descriptions and appropriately pair them with wine.
5. Make a seven-course menu with description and pair with appropriate beverages, giving two options for the guest.

26.10 KEY TERMS

- Full Bodied
- Medium Bodied
- Pate

EQUIPMENT FOR SERVICE OF BEVERAGES

27

CHAPTER OUTLINE

As we have read in the earlier chapters, in this book, beverages are as old as the human civilization. The cavemen might have used their hands and probably making the first 'cup' used for drinking. However, as humans created a civilized society for better living, various tools and implements were used to make vessels. Those vessels were used for consuming food and beverages.

History points to many civilizations. One of those is the Indus valley civilization which existed in ancient India during the Bronze Age (3300–1300 BC). The vessels, which the residents of this civilization had used for their food and beverage needs, have been preserved in museums around the world.

27.1 HISTORY

The various types of glasses used in making modern-day glassware was first used in Mesopotamia in 3500 BC. Archaeological evidence points to Syria and ancient Egypt as well. Due to the Egyptians' greatest skill of preservation, many vessels are preserved till today. However, these glasses were not very transparent unlike modern-day glassware, but were a great improvement from the earlier containers and vessels.

As time progressed, the Venetians and Bohemians perfected the art of glass blowing. This led to mass production of wine bottles and goblets. The Venetians and Bohemian glassmakers had a unique secret skill to make coloured glass. This was used not only in the famed cathedrals but also in wine glasses.

More often the wine was not clear and hence a coloured glass helped mask the dull wine. Today's wines are brilliantly clear when bottled due to the advancements in science and technology, and hence the clearer the glassware the better the visual appeal.

27.2 STANDARD MEASUREMENTS FOR SERVING ALCOHOL

First let us understand the 'standard' measurements for serving the various alcoholic beverages from Table 27.1.

Once we are aware of the types of liqueurs and their standard serving, it will be easier to identify the glassware and associate it with its 'soul', which is the beverage.

Table 27.1 Standard Measurements for Serving Various Alcoholic Beverages

Alcoholic Beverages	Standard Serving Per Order
Spirits—Whisky, Gin, Rum, Vodka and Tequila (preferably large)	Single shot/Regular (30 ml) Double shot/Large (–60 ml)
Liqueurs	45 ml
Fortified wines	90 ml
Wines*	120 ml
Beer	330 or 500 ml

*Wines are served from the bottle, but the standard 'pour' per glass is 120 ml.

27.3 TYPES OF GLASSWARE

Each type of glass has its own unique shape and size, which is attributed to the spirit or beverage that is served in it (Table 27.2). For example, liqueur glasses are smaller than old-fashioned glasses, despite both being served in almost the same quantity. This is because liqueur glasses are used for serving liqueurs that are straight/neat, whereas old-fashioned glasses are used to serve whisky either straight, on the rocks or with soda or water.

About Libbey Inc.

Libbey is the leading producer of glass tableware products in the Western Hemisphere in addition to supplying key markets throughout the world. Libbey has the largest manufacturing, distribution and service network among the North American glass tableware manufacturers. They design and market an extensive line of high-quality glass tableware, ceramic dinnerware, metal flatware, hollowware and serveware, and plastic items to a broad group of customers in the foodservice, retail and business-to-business markets. They own and operate two glass tableware manufacturing plants in the United States as well as glass tableware manufacturing plants in the Netherlands, Portugal, China and Mexico. In addition, Libbey Inc. also import products from overseas countries in order to complement their line of manufactured items. The combination of manufacturing and procurement allows them to compete in the global tableware market by offering an extensive product line at competitive prices. In 2011, Libbey Inc's net sales totalled $817.1 million.

Based in Toledo, Ohio, since 1888, the company operates glass tableware manufacturing plants in the United States in Louisiana and Ohio, as well as in Mexico, China, Portugal and the Netherlands. Its Crisa subsidiary, which is located at Monterrey in Mexico, is the leading producer of glass tableware in Mexico. Its Royal Leerdam subsidiary, located in Leerdam, Netherlands, is among the world leaders in producing and selling glass stemware to retail, foodservice and industrial clients. Its Crisal subsidiary, located in Portugal, provides an expanded presence in Europe. Its 'Libbey China' subsidiary is located at Langfang in China. Its 'Syracuse China' subsidiary designs and distributes an extensive line of high-quality ceramic dinnerware, principally for foodservice establishments in the United States. Libbey Inc.'s 'World Tableware', subsidiary imports and sells a full-line of metal flatware and hollowware and an assortment of ceramic dinnerware and other tabletop items principally for foodservice establishments in the United States.

Table 27.2 Types of Glassware

Glassware	Volume	Usage	Image
Shot Glass	60 ml (2 Ounces)	Spirits	
Old Fashioned	240–360 ml (8–12 Ounces)	Whisky	
Highball Glass	240–300 ml (8–10 Ounces)	Spirits with chasers	
Tom Collins	330–360 ml (11–12 Ounces)	Tall drinks and cocktails	

Glassware	Volume	Usage	Image
Fancy Old-fashioned Glass	240–360 ml (8–12 Ounces)	Whisky	
Cocktail or Martini Glass	120 ml (4 Ounces)	Cocktails and martini	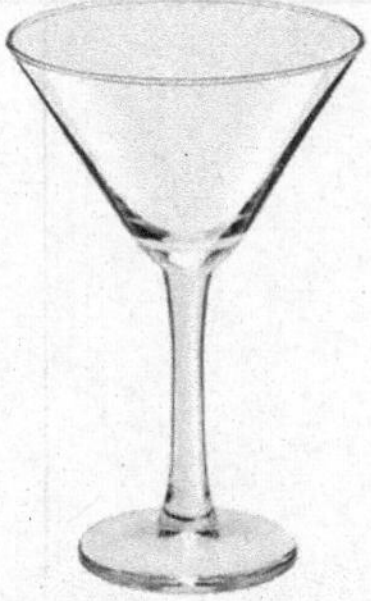
Sherry Copita	120 ml (4 Ounces)	Sherry	
Brandy Snifter	180–360 ml (6–12 ounces)	Brandy	

(*Continued*)

Table 27.2 Types of Glassware (Contd.)

Glassware	Volume	Usage	Image
Cognac Riddle	180–360 ml (6–12 ounces)	Cognac or brandy	
Beer Mug	330–360 ml (11–12 ounces)	Beer	
Beer Pilsner	330–360 ml (11–12 ounces)	Beer	
Beer Goblet	330–360 ml (11–12 ounces)	Beer	

Glassware	Volume	Usage	Image
White Wine Glass	330–360 ml (10–12 ounces)	White wine	
Red Wine Glass	240 ml (8 ounces)	Red wine	
'O' Glass (A new version of red wine glass without a stem, essentially used for serving the finest cognac or brandies.)	180–240 ml (6–8 ounces)	Wine/cognac and brandies	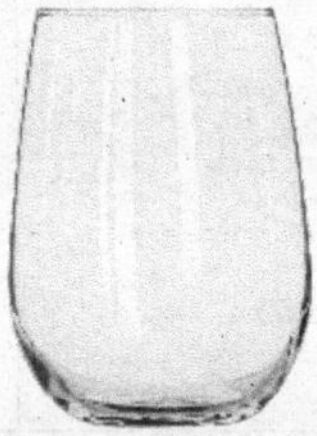
Water Goblet	120–180 ml (4–6 ounces)	Water	

(Continued)

Table 27.2 Types of Glassware (Contd.)

Glassware	Volume	Usage	Image
Bamboo Glass	480 ml (16 ounces)	Cocktails and tall drinks	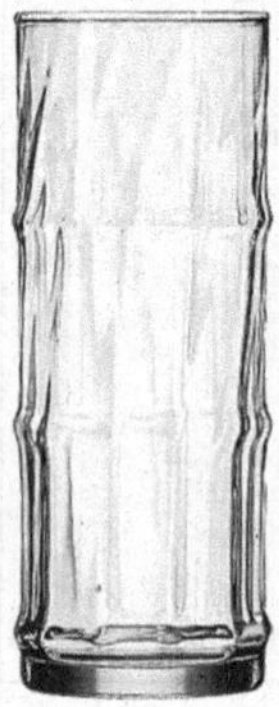
Paris Goblet	120 ml (6 ounces)	Eggnogs and cocktails	
Margarita Glass	150–180 ml (5–6 ounces)	Margarita cocktail	
Champagne Flute	120 ml (6 ounces)	Champagne	

Glassware	Volume	Usage	Image
Champagne Tulip	270 ml (9 ounces)	Champagne	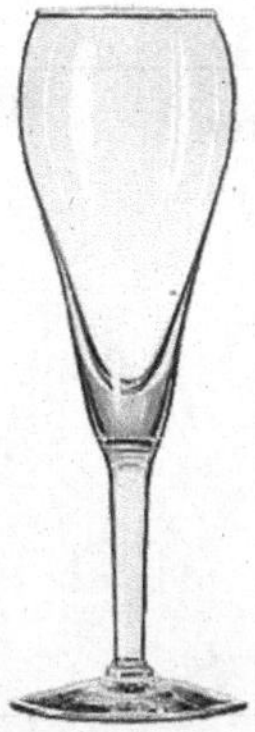
Champagne Saucer	180–240 ml (6–8 ounces)	Champagne or sparkling wine	
Liqueur Glasses	90–120 ml (3–4 ounces)	Liqueurs and aperitifs	
Water Jug	750 ml to 1 litre (25–30 ounces)	Serving water	

(*Continued*)

Table 27.2 Types of Glassware (Contd.)

Glassware	Volume	Usage	Image
Wine Decanter	1 Bottle of wine	Serving wine	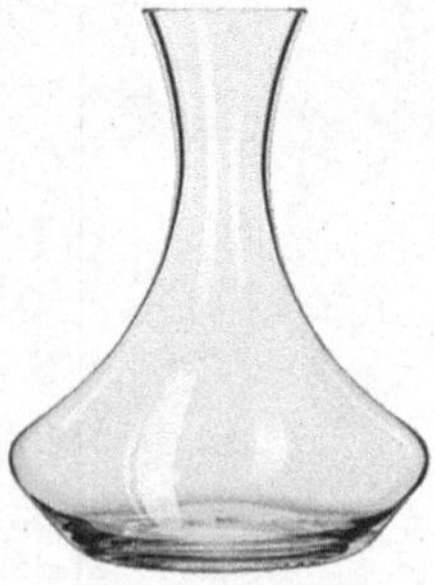
Soda/Water Decanter (Carafe)	300–330 ml (10–11 Ounces)		

Image Courtery: Libbey International Ltd.

27.4 OTHER BAR EQUIPMENT

Table 27.3 illustrates the other bar equipment. All this equipment is of utmost importance for the service of beverages in a restaurant or any food and beverage establishment.

Table 27.3 Other Bar Equipment

Equipment Name	Image
Wine Opener (waiters friend)	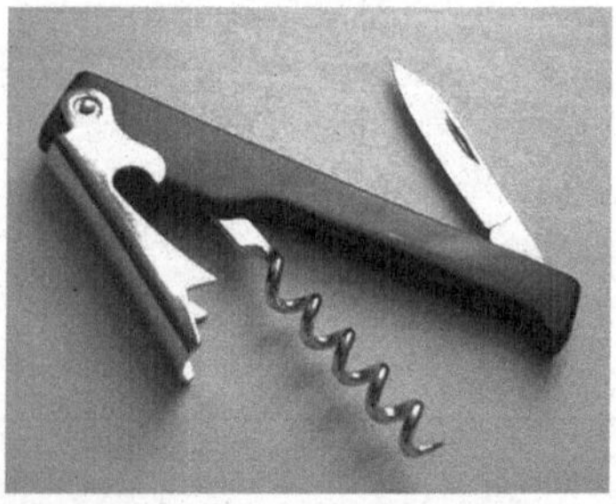

Equipment Name	Image
Wine Bucket	
Wine Opener (wing style)	
Wine Opener (automatic)	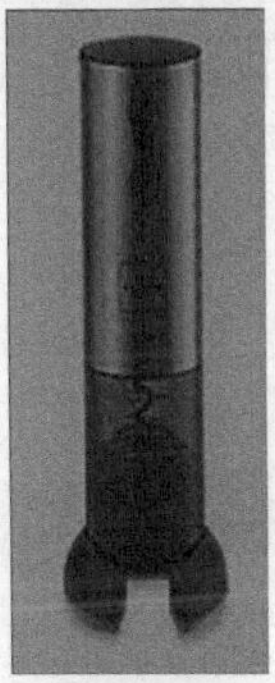
Wine Basket	

(Continued)

Table 27.3 Other Bar Equipment (Contd.)

Equipment Name	**Image**
Bar Spoon	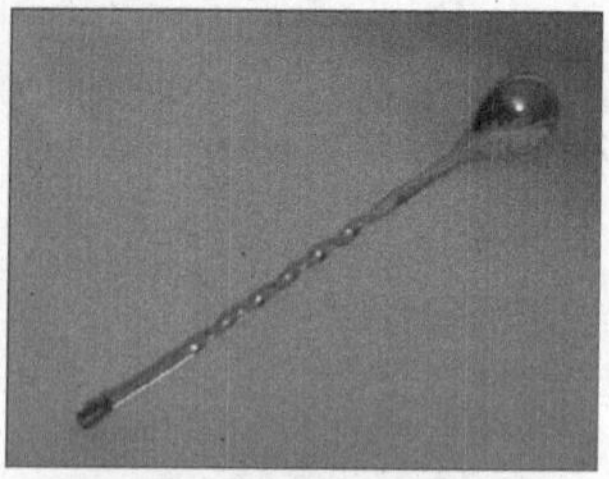
Cocktail Shaker	
Cocktail Strainer (Hawthorn strainer)	
Peg Measure	

Other Equipment Used for Serving Beverages

The other equipment used for serving beverages are depicted in Table 27.4.

Table 27.4 Other Equipment Used for Serving Beverages

Equipment Name	Image
Demi Tasse Cup and Saucer with Coffee Spoon	
Tea Cup and Saucer (Tasse)	
Strainer with Drip Bowl	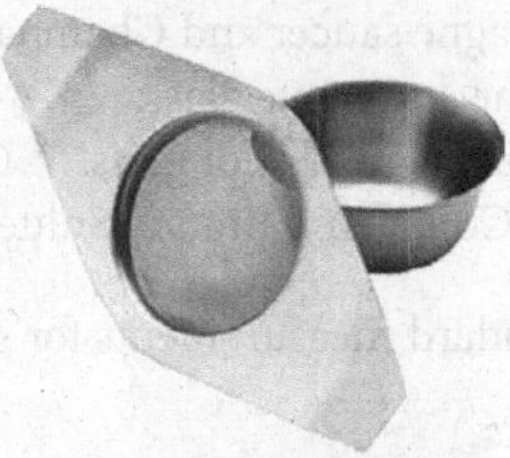
Creamer with Sugar Basin (with the Sugar Tong)	
Tea Pot	
Salver	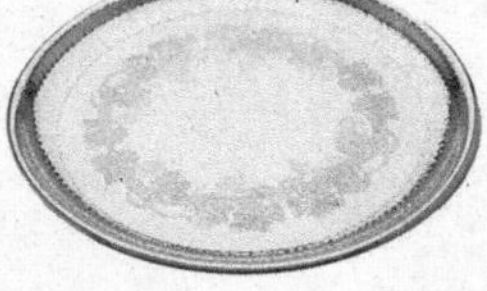

27.5 FAQs

1. Name and explain the usage of 10 bar equipments.
2. Why is a champagne flute preferred over a champagne saucer in restaurant service?
3. Give the capacity of the following glassware:
    i. 'O' Glass.
    ii. Champagne Tulip.
    iii. Old-fashioned glass.
    iv. Highball Glass.
    v. Brandy Snifter.
4. Draw a diagram of the following glassware:
    i. Pilsner.
    ii. Sherry copita.
    iii. Beer Goblet.
    iv. Red wine glass.
    v. White wine glass.
5. Differentiate between the following:
    i. Paris Goblet and Margarita glass.
    ii. Highball and Tom Collins.
    iii. Champagne saucer and Champagne Tulip.
    iv. Red wine and white glass.
    v. Liqueur glass and shot glass.
    vi. Sherry Copita and Brandy Snifter.
6. Give the standard measurements for serving the following alcohols:
    i. Liqueurs.
    ii. Beers.
    iii. Fortified wines.
    iv. Wines.
    v. Spirits.

27.6 KEY TERMS

- ML
- Demitasse
- Tasse

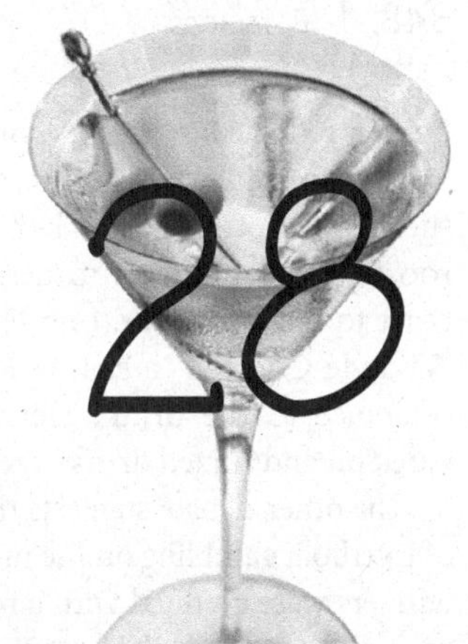

COCKTAILS

CHAPTER OUTLINE

LET'S DEFINE

'A cocktail is a concoction made with a combination of all or a choice of either of the following ingredients, namely, spirits, sugar, water, wines and other non-alcoholic beverages.'

A cocktail is a kind of drink which is a brilliant example of human's continuous desire to experiment and showcase their creativity using an array of ingredients, which include alcoholic and non-alcoholic beverages along with other flavouring agents. Cocktails can be made with one or more liquors; for example, gin, rum, vodka, whisky and tequila are referred to as *base spirits*.

In this chapter, we will discuss the history of this colourful and brilliant invention, along with the types of cocktails and the most famous classical cocktails of the world.

28.1 HISTORY

There are many stories claiming the invention of the 'cocktail'. A famous and widely accepted story is associated with Ms Betsy Flanagan's. She was a young tavern owner from New York, and it was her concoctions that were labelled as the first cocktails. The French and the American soldiers would gather at her bar to have her famous concoctions. One day, they were surprised when she teased them by decorating the liquor bottles at her bar with coloured hen and rooster feathers, given to her by her neighbour. In a toast to her brilliance, one French soldier exclaimed 'Vivre le Cocktail' meaning *long live the cocktail*—in reference to the drink. Hence, till today, the word stuck on and mixed drinks are called 'cocktails'.

The other debate suggests that during the wild days of riverboat gambling on the mighty Mississippi, the big winners were credited with a red cock's feather in their caps and were asked to mix up a concoction behind the bar. Their creation would be enjoyed in a cockerel-shaped glass with a spoon resembling its tail. Hence, giving the mixed concoction its name, 'the cocktail'.

The third story is that of French Creole Antoine Peychaud who used an eggcup (called *coquetier* in French) to measure out his spirits for his medicines. It is believed that the word cocktail was derived from the French word *Coquetel*, the name given to a certain mix of wines.

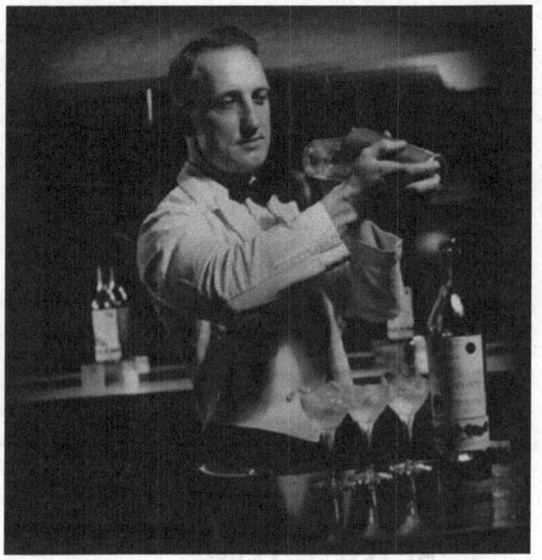

Bacardi cocktail competition. (Courtesy: *Bacardi International Limited.*)

28.2 BASIC COMPOSITION OF A COCKTAIL

There is a basic composition of a cocktail which is as follows:

1. **Base:** This refers to the liquor that is used to make this alcoholic beverage. It can be made using any spirit, beer or wine.
2. **Ingredients:** There are an array of ingredients which can be used and are broadly classified into four heads, which are as follows:
   - (i) **Fruit juices:** They can be fresh or canned.
   - (ii) **Syrups and colouring agents and smoothening agents:** These include alcoholic and non-alcoholic flavouring syrups, milk products, eggs etc., which may add flavour and smoothen the beverage.
   - (iii) **Aromatic agents:** These are some aromatic liqueurs, aperitifs or digestifs, which blend and add bouquet to the cocktail.
   - (iv) **Aerated beverages:** All types of aerated beverages are used.
3. **Garnish:** Each cocktail is exclusively served with its own garnish, mostly defined by its inventor. They add to the decorative value and at times give the cocktail its identity. For example, the classical martini has received its iconic status due to the olives at the end of a pick which are placed in the glass. Most classical cocktails have their own defined garnishes which we shall discuss later in this chapter.

   However, there is nothing worse than a cocktail without a garnish. It is like a new car without paint. Some famous garnishes and ingredients used to decorate cocktails are as follows:

   - **Citrus Twists:** To make a citrus twist, cut a thin slice of the fruit crosswise and simply twist to serve on the side of a glass or in it.

- **Citrus Peel Spirals:** To make a spiral of citrus peel, use a vegetable peeler to cut away the skin, working in a circular motion. Take care not to cut into the bitter pith.
- **Citrus Peel Knots:** Use strips of peel and carefully tie each strip into a knot. Drop into the drink for a nice garnish.
- **Cocktail Sticks:** These extremely useful wooden cocktail sticks are needed for spearing through pieces of fruit and cherries. These are not re-usable. However, plastic cocktail sticks are re-usable, provided they are washed and boiled.
- **Frosting/Rimming:** Margaritas and other mixed drinks often call for the rim of the glass to be coated with salt, sugar or some other ingredient. This is known as frosting or rimming. The easiest way to do this is to rub the rim of the glass with a slice of citrus fruit and then dip the very edge of the rim into a small bowl filled with sugar or salt.
- **Maraschino Cherries:** You should always have a plentiful supply of red maraschino cherries to decorate your cocktails with. These are the most widely used of decorations, as well as being available in multiple colours and flavours.
- **Olives or Onions:** Martinis are often garnished with olives or cocktail onions. Simply skewer one or two with a toothpick and drop into the drink.
- **Straws:** Straws are essential and go well with many cocktails. These, of course, should never be re-used.

Before we move on to the good part (recipes), we need to address the issue of bar safety and hygiene.

4. **Glassware:** The glassware used is defined very precisely as the quantity of a cocktail is directly proportional to the alcoholic strength of the cocktail. For example, the overall quantity of the *Martini* cocktail, which contains only alcoholic beverages, will be smaller and hence served in a cocktail glass.
   However, a rum-based *Planter's Punch* has more juice in its composition; hence, it is served in a larger highball. Listed above are the basic components of a cocktail.

28.3 METHODS OF MAKING COCKTAILS

Cocktails are unique creations. Some of them have become iconic names, even bigger than their creators. Before creating a cocktail, most people learn the techniques to create cocktails. The techniques popularly used are discussed in the following sections.

Shaking

Shaking is the method by which you use a cocktail shaker to mix ingredients together and chill them simultaneously. The objective of shaking is to almost freeze the drink while breaking down and combining the ingredients. Normally, this is done with ice cubes added to the shaker about three-fourth of the way to the top. Then, pour in the ingredients and hold the shaker in both hands with one hand on the top and the other hand supporting the base. Give the shaker a short, sharp and snappy shake. Do not rock your cocktail to sleep. When water has begun to condense on the surface of the shaker, the cocktail is chilled and ready to be strained.

Straining

Most cocktail shakers are sold with a build-in strainer or hawthorn strainer. When a drink calls for straining, ensure that you have used ice cubes, as crushed ice tends to clog the strainer of a standard shaker. If a drink is required shaken with crushed ice (*i.e.*, Shirley Temple), it is to be served unstrained.

Stirring

You can stir cocktails effectively with a metal or glass rod in a mixing glass. If you use ice, use them to prevent dilution and strain the contents into a glass when the surface of the mixing glass begins to collect condensation.

Muddling

To extract the most flavour from certain fresh ingredients such as fruit or mint garnishes, you should crush the ingredient with the muddler on the back end of your bar spoon or with a pestle.

Blending

An electric blender is often needed for recipes containing fruit or other ingredients that do not break down by shaking. Blending is a great way to combine these ingredients with others creating a smooth, ready-to-serve mixture. Some recipes call for ice to be placed in the blender in which case you would use a suitable amount of crushed ice to produce a smooth and pleasant tasting drink.

Building

When building a cocktail, the ingredients are poured into the glass in which the cocktail will be served. Usually, the ingredients are floated on top of each other, but occasionally, a swizzle stick is put in the glass, allowing the ingredients to be mixed.

Floating

This is a method of making a type of cocktail usually using an ice cream. The ice cream is gently added to the top of the beverage making it float.

Layering

To layer or float an ingredient such as cream liquor on top of another, use the rounded back part of a spoon and rest it against the inside of a glass. Slowly pour the liquor down the spoon and into the glass. The ingredient should run down the inside of the glass and remains separated from the ingredient below it.

Top-up

A cocktail made using a base liquor to which a *chaser* is added.

Flaming

Flaming is the method by which a cocktail or liquor is set alight (on fire), normally to enhance the flavour of a drink. It should only be attempted with caution, and for the above reason only, not to simply look fashionable.

A 'chaser' is the term generally used to describe the juice of the aerated beverage served along with a spirit. For example, a gin is served along with tonic water, which is its chaser. This should not be confused with a cocktail.

A 'shooter' is a mixed drink which comprises of a flavoured spirit. For example, Kahlua liqueur mixed with vodka and served in a shot glass with an approximate volume of 60 ml is called a shooter.

Some liquor will ignite quite easily if their proof is high. Heating a small amount of the liquor in a spoon will cause the alcohol to collect at the top, which can then be easily lit. You can then pour this over the prepared ingredients.

Do not add alcohol to ignited drinks and do not leave them unattended. Light them where they pose no danger to anybody else and ensure that no objects can possibly come into contact with any flames from the drink. Always extinguish a flaming drink before consuming it.

28.4 TYPES OF COCKTAILS

Box: Pour the drink into and out of a shaker, usually only once. This gives the drink a quick mixing without shaking.
Call Drink: Out of a liquor and a mixer, the liquor is a name brand (*i.e.*, Tanqueray and Tonic, Bacardi, Coke etc.).
Chaser: A chaser is a mixer that is consumed immediately after a straight shot of liquor to create a different taste.
Cobblers: Wine- and spirit-based cobblers are served with straws and decorated with fruit; for example, Gin Cobbler.
Cocktail: This can be any of various alcoholic beverages consisting usually of brandy, whiskey, vodka or gin combined with fruit juices or other liquors and often served chilled.
Collins: A drink similar to a sour, which is served in a tall glass with soda water or seltzer water.
Cooler: A drink consisting to ginger ale, soda water and a fresh spiral or twist of citrus fruit rind and served in a collins or highball glass.
Crusta: A sour-type drink served in a glass that is completely lined with an orange or a lemon peel cut in a continuous strip.
Cup: A punch-type drink that is made up in quantities of cups or glasses in preference to a punch bowl.
Daisy: An oversize drink of the sour type, normally made with rum or gin. It is served over crushed ice with a straw and sweetened with a fruit syrup.
Lace: Normally applies to the last ingredient in a recipe meaning to pour on top of the drink.
Eggnog: A traditional holiday drink containing a combination of eggs beaten with cream or milk, sugar and a liquor such as rum, brandy or bourbon.
Fix: A sour-type drink similar to the daisy made with crushed ice in a large goblet.
Fizz: An effervescent beverage—one which is carbonated and emits small bubbles.
Flip: A chilled and creamy drink made of eggs, sugar and a wine or spirit. Brandy and Sherry flips are two of the better known kinds of flips.
Frappe: This is a partially frozen often fruity drink. It is usually a mixture of ingredients served over a mound of crushed ice.
Grog: A rum-based beverage with water, fruit juice and sugar commonly served in a large mug.
Highball: Any spirit served with ice and soda in a medium to tall glass (a highball glass).
Julep: A drink made of bourbon, mint, sugar and crushed ice.
Lowball: A short drink made of spirits served with ice, water or soda in a small glass.
Mist: A liquor served over a glass filled with crushed ice—often as is the case with an after-dinner drink.

Mulls: A sweetened and spiced heated liquor, wine or beer served as a hot punch.
Neat: The consumption of a spirit as a straight and unaccompanied shot.
Nip: A quarter of a bottle.
Nightcap: Wine or liquor often consumed right before bedtime.
On the Rocks: A drink served over ice.
Pick-me-up: A drink designed to relieve the effects of overindulgence in alcohol.
Punch: A party-size beverage consisting of fruit, fruit juices, flavourings, sweeteners, soft drinks, and a wine or liquor base.
Rickey: A drink made of a liquor, usually gin, a half lime and soda water. It is sometimes sweetened and often served with ice.
Shooter: A straight shot of liquor taken neat.
Sling: A drink made with either brandy, whiskey or gin along with lemon juice, sugar and soda water. It is served both hot and cold.
Smashes: Smaller version of julep; for example, Brandy Smash.
Sour: A short drink consisting a liquor, lemon or lime juice and sugar.
Swizzles: They take the name from the stick used to stir the drink; sizzling creates a frost on the outside of the glass.
Toddy: A sweetened drink of liquor and hot water, often with spices.
Tot: A small amount of liquor.
Virgin: A non-alcoholic drink.
Well Drink: A liquor and a mixer of which neither are defined brands (*i.e.*, gin and tonic or rum and coke).

28.5 CLASSICAL COCKTAILS

Table 28.1 Recipes of Classical Cocktails

Sl. No.	Name	Base	Glass	Garnish	Ingredients	Method
1.	Godfather	Scotch whisky	Old-fashioned	None	(1) Scotch whisky (45 ml) (2) Amaretto (15 ml)	(1) Put ice in the old-fashioned glass. (2) Build with Scotch and Amaretto. (3) Serve.
2.	Rusty Nail	Scotch whisky	Old-fashioned	Lemon twist	(1) Scotch (Pouring Brand) (45 ml) (2) Drambuie (15 ml)	(1) Over ice, pour the Scotch and Drambuie. (2) Garnish and serve.

Sl. No.	Name	Base	Glass	Garnish	Ingredients	Method
				Rusty Nail cocktail. (Courtesy: *Drambuie International, UK*)		
3.	Rob Roy	Scotch whisky	Cocktail	Cocktail Cherry (maraschino only)	(1) Scotch whisky (pouring brand) (45 ml) (2) Angostura–Dash (3) Red Vermouth (15 ml)	(1) In a mixing glass, put ice. (2) Put a dash of Angostura, add whisky and Vermouth. (3) Stir, strain and pour. (4) Garnish with cocktail cherry and serve.
4.	Whisky Sour	Rye whisky	AP Wine	Slice of orange and cherry (maraschino only)	(1) Canadian/ American whisky (60 ml) (2) Lemon juice (45 ml) (3) Sugar syrup (30 ml) (4) Angostura–Dash (5) Egg white–half no.	(1) Fill shaker with ice. (2) Add egg white, lemon juice, sugar syrup, Angostura Bitters and the whiskey. (3) Shake, strain and pour. (4) Garnish and serve.
5.	Manhattan (served on the rocks)	Rye whiskey	Old-fashioned	Cocktail cherry (Maraschino only)	(1) Canadian whiskey (45 ml) (2) Red Vermouth (15 ml) (3) Angostura–dash	(1) Fill old-fashioned glass with ice. (2) Put a dash of Angostura Bitters. (3) Add whiskey and Vermouth. (4) Stir. (5) Garnish with a cocktail cherry and serve.

(*Continued*)

Table 28.1 Recipes of Classical Cocktails (*Contd.*)

Sl. No.	Name	Base	Glass	Garnish	Ingredients	Method
6.	Manhattan (served straight up)	Rye whiskey	Cocktail	Cocktail cherry (maraschino only)	(1) Canadian whiskey (45 ml) (2) Red Vermouth (15 ml) (3) Angostura–Dash	(1) In a mixing glass, put ice. (2) Put a dash of Angostura, add whiskey and Vermouth. (3) Stir; strain and pour. (4) Garnish with cocktail cherry and serve
7.	Old Fashioned	Bourbon whiskey	Old-fashioned	Cherry (maraschino only) and orange slice	(1) Cube Sugar (1 no.) (2) Angostura–Dash (3) Bourbon whiskey (60 ml) (4) Soda	(1) Put the sugar cube in the old-fashioned glass. (2) Add Angostura Bitters and Bourbon. (3) Muddle. (4) Fill with ice. (5) Top up with Soda. (6) Garnish and serve.
8.	Mint Julep	Bourbon whiskey	Highball glass	Spring of mint, two straws	(1) Bourbon whiskey (60 ml) (2) Castor sugar (1 tsp) (3) Mint leaf (6 nos.) (4) Soda (90 ml) (5) Crushed ice	(1) The mint is first muddled with Castor sugar. (2) The whiskey is added and then crushed ice is added and topped up with soda.
9.	Negroni	Gin	Old-fashioned	Lemon peel	(1) 30 ml gin (2) 30 ml sweet vermouth (3) 30 ml Campari (4) Ice	(1) The ingredients are first stirred and then strained.
10.	Dry Martini (served straight up)	Gin	Martini/Cocktail	Three-pitted olive on a cocktail sword.	(1) Dry Gin (60 ml) (2) Dry Vermouth (2 drops)	(1) In a mixing glass, add ice and ingredients. (2) Stir. (3) Strain into the martini/cocktail glass. (4) Garnish and serve.

Sl. No.	Name	Base	Glass	Garnish	Ingredients	Method
 Martini cocktail. (Courtesy: *Bacardi International Limited.*)						
11.	Pink Gin	Gin	Paris Goblet or Red Wine	None	(1) Gin (60 ml) (2) Angostura – dash (3) Water (30 ml) (check for guest preference on the quantity)	(1) Put a dash of Angostura Bitters, swirl the glass and lose excess. (2) Pour the gin. (3) Add water as per guests preference. (4) Serve.
 *Pink gin cocktail.* (Courtesy: *Angostura Bitters*)						

(*Continued*)

Table 28.1 Recipes of Classical Cocktails (*Contd.*)

Sl. No.	Name	Base	Glass	Garnish	Ingredients	Method
12.	Pink Lady	Gin	Cocktail	Cherry (Maraschino only)	(1) Gin (60 ml) (2) Grenadine (15 ml) (3) Egg white (half no.)	(1) In a shaker with ice, add egg white, gin and grenadine. (2) Shake. (3) Pour the drink into the cocktail glass. (4) Garnish and serve.
13.	Blue Lady	Gin	Cocktail	Lemon twist	(1) Gin (60 ml) (2) Blue Curacao (30 ml) (3) Egg white (half no.) (4) Lemon juice (15 ml)	(1) In a shaker with ice, add lemon juice, egg white, gin and Blue Curacao. (2) Shake. (3) Pour and garnish; serve.
14.	Gin Rickey	Gin	Old-fashioned	Lemon rind	(1) 60 ml gin (2) 15 ml lime juice (3) Soda	(1) Stirred and top with soda.
15.	White Lady	Gin	Cocktail	Lemon twist	(1) Gin–45 ml (2) Egg white–half no. (3) Cointreau (15 ml) (4) Lemon juice (15 ml)	(1) In a shaker, add ice, lemon juice, gin, Cointreau and egg white. (2) Shake. (3) Pour and garnish; serve.
16.	Singapore Sling	Gin	Highball	Cherry and orange slice	(1) Gin–45 ml (2) Cherry brandy (15 ml) (3) Lemon juice (15 ml) (4) Soda (30 ml)	(1) Shake gin, lemon juice and cherry brandy. (2) Pour over ice and top with soda. (3) Garnish and serve.

Sl. No.	Name	Base	Glass	Garnish	Ingredients	Method
17.	Tom Collins	Gin	Collins	Maraschino cherry and orange slice	(1) Gin–30 ml (2) Lemon juice (30 ml) (3) Sugar syrup (15 ml) (4) Angostura Orange Bitters (optional) (–5 ml) (5) Club soda–top up (6) Maraschino cherry and orange slice for garnish	(1) Pour the gin, lemon juice, sugar syrup and Angostura Orange Bitters in a collins glass with ice cubes. (2) Stir the glass. (3) Top up with club soda. (4) Garnish with the cherry and orange slice.
			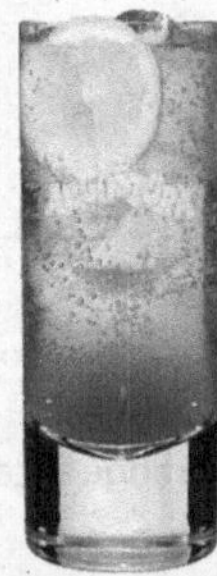 *Tom Collins cocktail.* (Courtesy: *Angostura Bitters*)			
18.	Gimlet	Gin	Cocktail	Lemon slice	(1) 45 ml gin (2) 15 ml lime juice (3) Ice	(1) All the ingredients need to be shaken and then stirred.
19.	Gin Cobbler	Gin	Red wine glass	Fruit, sprig of mint	(1) 30 ml gin (spirit) (2) 4 dash curacao (3) 1 tsp sugar (4) Ice	(1) All the ingredients need to be stirred.
20.	Martini (on the rocks)	Gin	Old-fashioned	Pitted olive on cocktail sword	(1) Dry Gin (60 ml) (2) Dry Vermouth (2 drops)	(1) Fill up the glass with ice. (2) For dry martini, just release the top and add two drops vermouth. (3) Add gin. (4) Garnish and serve.

(Continued)

Table 28.1 Recipes of Classical Cocktails (*Contd.*)

Sl. No.	Name	Base	Glass	Garnish	Ingredients	Method
21.	Screwdriver	Vodka	Highball	Orange slice	(1) Vodka (60 ml) (2) Orange juice (90 ml)	(1) Add ice into the highball glass. (2) Build with vodka and orange juice. (3) Garnish and serve.
22.	Black Russian	Vodka	Old-fashioned	None	(1) Vodka (45 ml) (2) Kahlua (15 ml)	(1) Add ice into the old-fashioned glass. (2) Build with vodka and Kahlua. (3) Serve.
23.	Harvey Wallbanger	Vodka	Highball	Cherry (Maraschino only) and orange slice	(1) Vodka (45 ml) (2) Orange juice (90 ml) (3) Galliano (15 ml	(1) Pour vodka over ice. (2) Add orange juice almost to the top. (3) Float Galliano over it. (4) Garnish and serve.
24.	Salty Dog	Vodka	Highball	Grapefruit slice	(1) Vodka (60 ml) (2) Grapefruit juice (90 ml)	(1) Rim the glass with salt. (2) Over ice, pour vodka and grapefruit juice. (3) Garnish and serve.
25.	Cosmo-politan	Vodka	Cocktail	Twist of orange peel rubbed on the rim	(1) Vodka (45 ml) (2) Cointreau (15 ml) (3) Cranberry juice (15 ml)	(1) In a shaker with ice, add ingredients. (2) Shake, strain and pour. (3) Garnish and serve.
26.	Moscow Mule	Vodka	Highball	Lemon slice	(1) 45 ml vodka (2) 15 ml lime juice (3) Ginger beer to top (4) Ice	(1) This is a topped up cocktail.

Sl. No.	Name	Base	Glass	Garnish	Ingredients	Method
27.	White Russian	Vodka	Old-fashioned	None	(1) Vodka (45 ml) (2) Kahlua (15 ml) (3) Double Cream (to float)	(1) Over the ice, build vodka and Kahlua. (2) Top with double cream. (3) Do not forget the swizzle stick. (4) Serve.
28.	Caipiroshka	Vodka	Old-fashioned	None	(1) 60 ml vodka (2) 20 gm brown sugar (3) ¼ lime cut into four	(1) First the lime segments and the sugar is muddled together. (2) Next the Vodka is poured on top. Crushed ice is used as an option.
 *Caipiroshka cocktail.* (Courtesy: *Bacardi International Limited*)						
29.	Vodka Daisy	Vodka	Beer Goblet	Spring of mint, fruit and straw	(1) Vodka (30 ml) (2) 1 tsp grenadine (3) 15 ml lemon juice (4) Soda (5) Ice	(1) All the ingredients are built up based on their densities.
30.	Bloody Mary	Vodka	Roly Poly	Celery Stick and lemon wedge	(1) Vodka (60 ml) (2) Tomato juice (120 ml) (3) Tabasco–one dash (4) Worcestershire sauce–2 dashes (5) Salt (6) Pepper (7) Lemon juice (15 ml)	(1) Salt rim the glass. (2) Add ice, salt, pepper, Tabasco, Worcester and lemon juice (or premix). (3) Stir. (4) Add tomato juice and pour vodka on top. (5) Garnish and serve.

(Continued)

Table 28.1 Recipes of Classical Cocktails (*Contd.*)

Sl. No.	Name	Base	Glass	Garnish	Ingredients	Method
31.	Sidecar	Brandy	Cocktail	Lemon twist	(1) Brandy (45 ml) (2) Cointreau (15 ml) (3) Lemon juice (15 ml)	(1) In a cocktail shaker, add ice. (2) Add the ingredients. (3) Shake. (4) Strain into the cocktail glass. (5) Garnish and serve.
32.	Eggnog	Brandy	Paris Goblet	Grated nutmeg	(1) 60 ml brandy (2) 1 Egg (3) 2 tbsp. sugar (4) 75 ml milk	(1) All the ingredients need to be shaken and then the milk is stirred.
33.	Stinger	Brandy	Cocktail	None	(1) Brandy (45 ml) (2) Crème de Menthe (white) (15 ml)	(1) In a cocktail shaker, add ice. (2) Add the ingredients. (3) Shake and strain. (4) Serve.
34.	Between the Sheets	Cognac	Cocktail	Lemon twist	(1) Brandy (30 ml) (2) Cointreau (15 ml) (3) White rum (15 ml) (4) Lemon juice (10 ml)	(1) In a cocktail shaker, add ice. (2) Add ingredients. (3) Shake and strain. (4) Garnish with a lemon twist. (5) Serve.
35.	Frozen Daiquiri	White Rum	Cocktail	Appropriate fruit	(1) White rum (60 ml) (2) Lemon juice (10 ml) (3) Sugar syrup (used if the flavouring used is tart) (4) Crushed ice	(1) In a blender, add crushed ice, lime juice, sugar syrup and rum. (2) Blend. (3) Garnish and serve. *Note:* Preferably fresh fruit or any fruit crush can be used to make various fruit daiquiris.

Sl. No.	Name	Base	Glass	Garnish	Ingredients	Method
36.	Cuba Libre	White Rum	Collins	None (since lemon wedge is squeezed and dropped into the glass)	(1) White rum (60 ml) (2) Cola–to top up (3) Lemon wedge	(1) Fill the glass with ice cubes. (2) Add the white rum. (3) Top up with cola. (4) Slightly squeeze the lemon wedge and drop inside. (5) Serve.
 *Cuba Libre.* (Courtesy: *Bacardi International Limited*)						
37.	Planters Punch	Dark Rum	Zombie/Any other tall	Orange slice and cherry (maraschino only)	(1) Dark rum (60 ml) (2) Pineapple and orange juices – equal quantities (3) Grenadine (15 ml)	(1) Pour the juices. (2) Add grenadine and float rum on top. (3) Serve.
38.	Daiquiri	White Rum	Cocktail	None	(1) White rum (60 ml) (2) Lemon juice (10 ml) (3) Sugar syrup	(1) Fill the shaker with ice. (2) Add lemon juice, sugar syrup and rum. Shake. (3) Strain into glass. (4) Serve.

(*Continued*)

Table 28.1 Recipes of Classical Cocktails (*Contd.*)

Sl. No.	Name	Base	Glass	Garnish	Ingredients	Method
 *Daiquiri cocktail.* (Courtesy: *Bacardi International Limited*)						
39.	Pina Colada	White Rum	Collins/ Cocktail	Pineapple slice and cherry (maraschino only)	(1) White rum (60 ml) (2) Caribbean coconut cream (60 ml) (3) Pineapple juice (80 ml)	(1) In a blender, add crushed ice. (2) Add the ingredients. Blend. (3) Pour into the glass. (4) Serve.
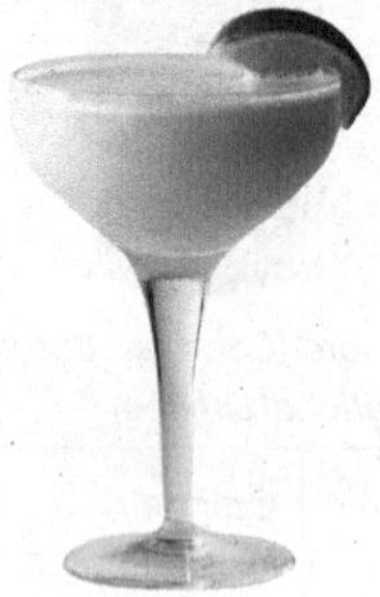 *A creole colada cocktail made with the same recipe as the pina colada with the addition of angostura bitters.* (Courtesy: *Angostura Bitters*)						
40.	Mojito	White Rum	Highball	Mint leaf	(1) White rum (60 ml) (2) Lemon juice (15 ml) (3) Mint leaves (5 nos.) (4) Castor sugar (5 g) (5) Soda–to top	(1) In a highball glass, put caster sugar, mint and little water (to moisten). (2) Muddle. Add crushed ice. (3) Pour the rum, lemon juice and top with soda. (4) Garnish and serve.

Sl. No.	Name	Base	Glass	Garnish	Ingredients	Method
Mojito cocktail. (Courtesy: *Angostura Bitters*)						
41.	Zombie	White Rum and Dark Rum	Zombie	Orange slice	(1) White rum (45 ml) (2) Dark rum (45 ml) (3) Caribbean coconut cream (60 ml) (4) Angostura (4 dash) (5) Apricot brandy (15 ml) (6) Pineapple juice–add till just below the rim	(1) Add the ingredients in a shaker. (2) Shake. (3) Pour into glass over crushed ice. (4) Float dark rum on top; place swizzle stick and straw in the glass. (5) Garnish and serve.
42.	Maitai	White Rum and Dark Rum	Old-fashioned glass	Maraschino cherry	(1) Light rum (30 ml) (2) Dark rum (30 ml) (3) Lime juice (15 ml) (4) Angostura Orange Bitters or orange-flavoured liqueur (10 ml) (5) Orgeat–Almond syrup (pronounced *'Or-zat'*) (5 ml) (6) Maraschino cherry for garnish	(1) Pour all the ingredients into the cocktail shaker without the dark rum. (2) Shake well. (3) Strain into an old-fashioned glass half filled with ice. (4) Top-up with the dark rum. (5) Garnish with the cherry.

(*Continued*)

Table 28.1 Recipes of Classical Cocktails (*Contd.*)

Sl. No.	Name	Base	Glass	Garnish	Ingredients	Method
Maitai cocktail. (Courtesy: *Angostura Bitters*)						
43.	Margarita	Tequila	Cocktail	None	(1) Tequila (45 ml) (2) Cointreau (15 ml) (3) Lime juice–dash	(1) Frost the rim of the glass with salt. (2) In a cocktail shaker, add ice. (3) Add ingredients. Shake and strain into the glass. (4) Serve.
 *Margarita cocktail.* (Courtesy: *Libbey's Glassware*)						

Sl. No.	Name	Base	Glass	Garnish	Ingredients	Method
44.	Frozen Margarita	Tequila	Cocktail	Lemon Twist	(1) Tequila (45 ml) (2) Cointreau (15 ml) (3) Crushed Ice (4) Flavouring (5) Lime juice (15 ml) (6) Sugar Syrup–if too tart	(1) Half salt rim the glass. (2) In a blender, add crushed ice. (3) Add ingredients. Add sugar syrup if too tart. (4) Blend and pour into glass. (5) Garnish and serve.
45.	Tequila Sunrise	Tequila	Collins	Slice of orange and cherry (maraschino only)	(1) Tequila (60 ml) (2) Grenadine (15 ml) (3) Orange juice	(1) Add ice into the Collins glass. (2) Pour orange juice with tequila over it. (3) Stir. Add grenadine. (4) Garnish and serve.
46.	Kir	White Wine	White wine	None	(1) Crème de Cassis (5 ml) (2) Dry White Wine–to top up	(1) Pour the Crème de Cassis into the wine glass. (2) Add the white wine. (3) Serve.
47.	Wine cooler	Red or White Wine	Highball	None	(1) 30 ml Red or White Wine (2) 4 dash grenadine ice and soda	(1) This is a built-up and top-up cocktail, first the grenadine is added to the glass. (2) Red wine is poured on top. (3) Ice and soda is used to top up.
48.	Sangria	Red Wine	Red Wine glass	None	(1) 60 ml Red Wine (2) Sliced apple, orange and lemon (3) 90 ml soda (4) Ice	(1) Soak wine and fruit together. (2) Add soda and ice before serving.

(Continued)

Table 28.1 Recipes of Classical Cocktails (*Contd.*)

Sl. No.	Name	Base	Glass	Garnish	Ingredients	Method
			Grande sangria, a version made with Angostura orange bitters. (Courtesy: *Angostura Bitters*)			
49.	Kir Royale	Champagne/ Sparkling Wine	Champagne flute	None	(1) Crème de Cassis (5 ml) (2) Champagne/sparkling wine–to top up	(1) Pour the Crème de Cassis into the Champagne flute. (2) Top with champagne/ sparkling wine. (3) Serve.
50.	Bucks Fizz	Champagne/ Sparkling Wine	Champagne flute	None	(1) Champagne/sparkling wine–to top up (2) Orange juice (120 ml)	(1) Pour the orange juice into the champagne flute. (2) Top with champagne/sparkling wine. (3) Serve.
51.	Mimosa	Champagne or Sparkling Wine	Champagne flute	None	(1) Champagne/sparkling wine–pour till just below the rim of the glass (2) Orange juice (120 ml) (3) Cointreau (15 ml)	(1) Pour the orange juice into the champagne flute. (2) Add the champagne/ sparkling wine. (3) Float Cointreau on top. (4) Serve.

Sl. No.	Name	Base	Glass	Garnish	Ingredients	Method
52.	Ducks Fizz	Champagne or Sparkling Wine	Champagne flute	None	(1) Champagne or sparkling wine (2) Grapefruit juice (1:1)	(1) Pour the grapefruit juice into the Champagne flute. (2) Top with Champagne/sparkling wine. (3) Serve.
53.	Bellini	Champagne/ Sparkling Wine	Champagne flute	None	(1) Peach juice (2) Peach schnapps–dash (3) Champagne or sparkling wine–to top up	(1) Add peach nectar, peach schnapps. (2) Top up with Champagne or sparkling wine. (3) Serve.
54.	Black Velvet	Champagne/ Sparkling Wine	Beer Goblet	None	(1) Champagne/sparkling wine–half (2) Guinness–half	(1) Pour Guinness into the beer goblet. (2) Add Champagne. (3) Serve.
55.	Champagne Cocktail	Champagne/ Sparkling Wine	Champagne flute	Orange slice and cherry (maraschino only)	(1) Sugar Cube (1 no.) (2) Angostura–dash (3) Brandy (30 ml) (4) Champagne/sparkling wine–to top up	(1) Build the ingredients in the order stated. (2) Garnish and serve.
56.	B-52	Liqueurs	Shot	None	(1) Kahlua (20 ml) (2) Bailey's Irish Cream (20 ml) (3) Cointreau (20 ml)	(1) Build the pousse café (in the order of ingredients) over the back of a spoon. (2) Serve.
57.	Long Island Iced Tea	White Spirits	Collins	Lemon slice	(1) Gin (15 ml) (2) White rum (15 ml) (3) Vodka (15 ml) (4) Tequila (15 ml) (5) Triple Sec/Cointreau (15 ml) (6) Lemon juice (30 ml) (7) Cola	(1) Fill the glass with ice. (2) Add lemon juice. (3) Add all the stated spirits. (4) Top up with cola. (5) Place the straw and swizzle stick in the glass. (6) Garnish and serve.

(Continued)

Table 28.1 Recipes of Classical Cocktails (*Contd.*)

Sl. No.	Name	Base	Glass	Garnish	Ingredients	Method
58.	Rusty Mule	Drambuie Liqueur	Collins	Wedge of lime	(1) Drambuie (30 ml) (2) Ginger beer (90–120 ml)	(1) Squeeze in the juice of 2 fresh lime wedges. (2) Pour the Drambuie and the ginger beer into the glass. (3) Serve with ice in an ice long glass.
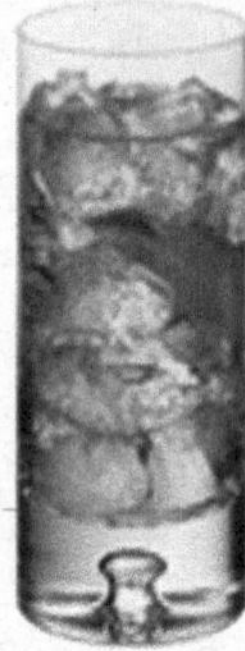 *Rusty Mule cocktail.* (Courtesy: *Drambuie, UK*)						
59.	Rusty Royale	Drambuie Liqueur	Champagne Flute	Black Berry and a twist of orange	(1) Drambuie (10 ml) (2) Champagne (120 ml)	(1) Pour the Champagne into a chilled flute containing Drambuie and stir. (2) Gently place the fruit on the rim of the glass to garnish.
 *Rusty Royale.* (Courtesy: *Drambuie, UK.*)						

Sl. No.	Name	Base	Glass	Garnish	Ingredients	Method
60.	Rusty Margarita	Drambuie Liqueur and Tequila	Cocktail	Orange peel	(1) Reposado tequila (35 ml) (2) Drambuie (20 ml) (3) Freshly squeezed lime juice (20 ml)	(1) Shake all the ingredients well and strain them into a chilled salt and pepper rimmed coupette. (2) Garnish with a lime wheel and a twist of orange.

Rusty Margarita cocktail (a version made using Drambuie liqueur). (Courtesy: *Drambuie, UK*)

Although many other cocktails are available in the market today, the list of cocktails shown here, are the classics, which will be a part of every beverage list in the world.

LET'S SUMMARIZE IN POINTS

- A cocktail is a concoction made with a combination of all or a choice of either of the following ingredients, namely, spirits, sugar, water, wines and other non-alcoholic beverages.
- A basic cocktail comprises of the following: base, ingredients, garnish and glassware.
- Built up, stirred, shaken, muddled, float and top-up are the basic methods of making cocktails.
- There are various types of cocktails are available in the market; for example, cobblers, collins, flips, eggnogs and many more.
- There are evergreen classical cocktails whose recipes are mentioned above. It is recommended to practise before preaching.

28.6 FAQs

Short-Answer Type Questions

1. Define cocktail.
2. Differentiate between a shooter and a chaser.
3. What are the methods of making cocktails?
4. What are the types of cocktails? Name five types of cocktails.
5. Name five classical cocktails.

Long-Answer Type Questions

1. Name five cocktails each with recipe and description.
   i. Rum based.
   ii. Gin based.
   iii. Whisky based.
   iv. Vodka based.
   v. Brandy based.
   vi. Wine based.

28.7 KEY TERMS

- Bar Spoon
- Base
- Blending
- Dash
- Float Stirring
- Hawthorn Strainer
- Long Drink
- Muddler
- Segments
- Shaker
- Shaking
- Twist
- Wheel

Service of Beverages in F&B Outlets

CHAPTER OUTLINE

According to the standards of food and beverage service, there are some particular ways for serving beverages in F&B establishments; hence in this book, we will discuss some general procedures of serving common alcoholic and non-alcoholic beverages.

29.1 SERVICE OF TEA

For serving a cup of tea, certain accompaniments are needed to make sure it is perfect. Moreover, some procedures are to be followed while serving tea.

The items, which have to be presented in a tray for a tea service, are:

1. Tea pot, containing infused tea.
2. Hot water pot, containing hot water in order to dilute tea.
3. Creamer, containing skimmed milk (for tea service, only skimmed milk is used at room temperature).

4. Sugar basin, containing sugar and sugar-free sachets.
5. Tea strainer set, which includes the strainer and drip bowl, to ensure clean and clear tea liquor in the cup.
6. Tea cup and saucer with a tea spoon.
7. Some cookies and pastries.
8. A quarter plate containing lemon (only for green tea and lemon tea), along with a fork to squeeze the lemon wedge.
9. Honey served along with chamomile tea and green tea.
10. Other teas such as Pu-erh, oolong and most herbal teas are served by themselves without any additives such as milk or cream.

Procedure for serving a cup of tea:

- Place tea cup and saucer in front of the guest from the right hand side of the guest and make sure that the handle of the cup is at a 4 O'clock position.
- Pour the tea in the tea cup and use a strainer, so that tea leaves do not gather in the cup (in case of black tea; it is not used in the case of green tea, chamomile tea and herbal tea). To avoid having the tea spill from the top of the pot, always place one hand on the lid, so that it does not slip. Pour slowly to avoid over-pouring.
- If the guest requires the tea liquor to be diluted, please adjust the brew with hot water.
- You may ask the guest if he or she wants some sugar/ sugar-free in his or her tea.
- In case of green tea and chamomile tea, honey is recommended instead of sugar.
- The lemon wedges along with the fork is placed on the upper right hand corner of the cover.
- Place the accompaniments such as cookies or pastries in the centre of the table.
- The temperature of tea at the time of serving should be approximately 95°C.

Lemon juice in a creamer
Monkey bowl with honey
Sugar bowl
Tea pot with green tea
Tea cup and saucer with a tea spoon

Service of green tea.

29.2 SERVICE OF COFFEE

There are several ways to serve coffee. Just like any business, serving coffee comes with a set of unspoken and expected rules to be followed. As mentioned above, there are several ways to serve coffee: black, with milk, with cream, with or without sugar etc. We can also add chocolate or cinnamon. It is always served warm; however, iced coffee beverages have recently begun to make their mark. The taste for coffee is not instant, but has to be acquired because it is strong and bitter.

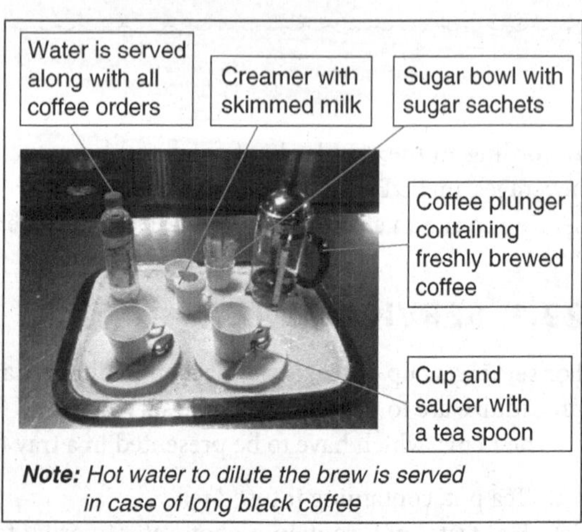

Service set up for freshly brewed coffee.

The items that are usually in a coffee service tray are as follows:

1. Coffee pot or French Press, containing brewed coffee with a temperature of 86 °C.
2. Cappuccino cup and saucer with a tea spoon on the right side of the saucer.
3. A pot of hot water to dilute the brew.
4. Creamer, containing either cream or hot/cold milk.
5. Sugar bowl, containing an assortment of white sugar, brown (Demerara sugar—recommended with coffee) and sugar-free sachets.
6. In case of readymade coffees, such as Cappuccinos, this procedure is not required as it is pre-poured into the cup. *Espressos are always served in a demitasse cup.*

Note: All coffees are accompanied with a glass of water to refresh the palate and enjoy the aromas.

Procedure for serving a cup of coffee either black, *café au lait* or *Vienna coffee* is:

- Serve the coffee on a serving tray with cappuccino cups and a teaspoon that you will have placed on the saucer.
- When serving coffee, leave the water glasses on the table, but remove the wine glasses. Coffee is served on the right hand side of the guest. The teaspoon is placed in the right side of the cup.
- Sugar, presented in a sugar bowl, is served with sugar tongs for sugar cubes. Provide an assortment of white and brown (Demerara) sugar.
- Skimmed milk is served in case of *café au lait*, cream is served in the case of Vienna coffee and hot water is served along with a long black. (A long black can be served with an espresso base along with a freshly brewed coffee base).
- Then only thing you have to notice, when you are serving coffee, is to pour the coffee to the cup and leave some room in order to add milk, cream and water.
- Voila, a freshly brewed cup of coffee is ready to be savoured.

29.3 SERVICE OF HOT CHOCOLATE

The terms hot cocoa and hot chocolate are often used interchangeably; however, technically they are as different as milk chocolate and bittersweet chocolate. Hot cocoa is made from cocoa powder, which is chocolate pressed, free of all its richness, namely the fat of cocoa butter. Whereas, hot chocolate is made from chocolate bars melted into cream. It is a rich decadent drink. The original hot chocolate recipe was a mixture of ground cocoa beans, water, wine and chilli peppers. It did not take long time for Spaniards to begin heating the mixture and sweetening it with sugar. After being introduced in England, milk was added to the then after-dinner treat, and now the hot chocolate is a mixture of cocoa powder, melted chocolate or chocolate sauce, milk and cream.

A cup of hot chocolate.

Service: To serve a cup of hot chocolate, you will need a cup and saucer (hot chocolate usually is served in mugs) and a tea spoon on the saucer and offer ground almonds or hazelnuts and whipped cream. It is pre-made in the kitchen and then poured into cups or mugs to savour. Hot chocolate is best enjoyed at a temperature ranging from 85–92°C.

29.4 SERVICE OF FRESHLIME SODA (SWEET, SALTED OR BOTH)

In A Historical Dictionary of Indian Food (Oxford University Press, 1998), author K.T. Acharya says that *fresh lime soda* was 'the supreme quencher of colonial thirst' in India. In hot weather, the body can lose a lot of salt through perspiration; therefore, a salty-sweet drink can be preferred (plus, the salt brings out the full flavour of lime). Salt and sugar always complement each other; it's just a matter of finding the right balance. To make a glass of fresh lime soda, fill a glass with ice cubes, then add simple syrup and lime juice. Add soda water. For serving a glass of fresh lime, you need the following accompaniments in your tray:

A glass of fresh lime soda with a slice of lime for garnish.

1. A glass of sweet, salted or sweet and salted lime soda.
2. A decanter of soda for adjusting the consistency of the drink.
3. A shot glass containing swizzle sticks, along with a straw holder with straws.
4. Sugar syrup and salt to make the guest able to adjust the sweetness or saltiness of the drink.
5. For garnishing, you can put a slice of lime on the rim of the glass.

29.5 SERVICE OF ICED TEA

Iced tea (sometimes known as *ice tea*) is a form of cold tea, usually served in a glass with ice. It may or may not be sweetened. It can be mixed with flavoured syrup, with common flavours including lemon, peach, raspberry, lime, passion fruit and cherry. While most iced teas get their flavour from tea leaves *(Camellia sinensis)*, other herb-infused beverages are also sometimes served cold and referred to as iced tea. To serve a glass of iced tea you need:

1. A glass filled with ice cubes, till the top of the Tom Collins glass.
2. Freshly brewed tea, preferably a black Assam tea or Darjeeling tea.
3. The hot tea is poured on the ice in the glass.
4. Ice tea is always served with lemon juice and sugar syrup for the guest to add as per his or her taste.
5. Iced tea is traditionally served with lemon slice; used as a garnish, which is often placed on the rim of the glass.

29.6 SERVICE OF BEER

Beer is a popular beverage item served in restaurants and it is essential to keep a few points in mind for the service of beer, which are mentioned below.

Temperature

Most people prefer drinking beer, which is chilled to about 2–5°C. This is the temperature that shows beer at its delicious best: cool enough to be refreshing, but not so cold that the nuances of flavour are suppressed. Its temperature is best obtained by storing it on the bottom shelf of the refrigerator, away

Presenting a bottle of beer and serving it in an appropriate glass with a cocktail napkin and a coaster.

from the freezer section or coldest compartment. Once removed from the refrigerator, beer should be served before it warms up.

For a large party, warm beer may be chilled in any large container—there are many attractive, jumbo, lightweight plastic containers that can be bought for a party and reused for storage, laundry or trash. The containers need to be filled with ice, let the ice melt and add cold water. Keep the beer bottles in this cold water. You can check the water temperature with a thermometer and add more ice if it's warming up.

Opening the Bottle

Open your bottles with care; be sure not to shake or agitate them. Use bottle openers that are in good condition. Faulty openers can cause chipping or cracking of bottles. Ensure to open the top of the can/bottle beer before approaching the guest, and you have one glass prepared for each beer ordered.

Choosing the Right Glass

Beer is more enjoyable when served in a clear glass vessel. The tall tapering pilsner and the graceful stemmed goblet are especially popular glasses for entertaining—they enable an elegant presentation of a relatively inexpensive beverage. Any trace of grease, soap or lint from a towel will cut down on beer enjoyment. If washed properly, there will be no bubbles clinging to the side of the glass. The foam will adhere to the inside of the glass in a ring design.

Pouring the Brew

There is an art to pour beer. Some people like a high foamy collar; some prefer a short one. You can obtain a fine creamy head by letting the beer splash into the glass. A good way to achieve the kind of foam you desire is to tilt the glass and begin pouring the beer down the side, then straighten the glass and pour into the centre.

- First proceed to the table to serve beer.
- Ask the guest politely, '*would you like me to pour your beer for you sir/madam.*' If they say no, place the beer can/bottle on the right hand side of the glass at 3 O'clock position. If the guest says yes, then proceed with the following steps.
- When filling the glass with beer, pour it at a slow steady pace and endeavour to pour the beer to flow down on the opposite side wall of the glass. Watch the glass filling with beer. If the beer starts appearing to have too large amount of head, stop for a few seconds, until the head subsides, then proceed with your right hand and begin to pour beer very slowly (ensure that the can/bottle does not touch the rim of the glass).
- Place the glass down on the right hand side of the guest.
- Stop pouring beer when the glass is already full. There should only be approximately 2–3 cm volume of head in the glass (though some guests may prefer a larger head).
- If there is some remaining beer in can/bottle place it on the right hand side of the guest at 3 O'clock position.
- Remove empty can/bottle with your right hand from the guest's right hand side and place it on your tray and return it to the bar or back of the house.
- When the beer glass has only 1/3 of beer remaining, politely ask the guest if he/she would care for another beer.

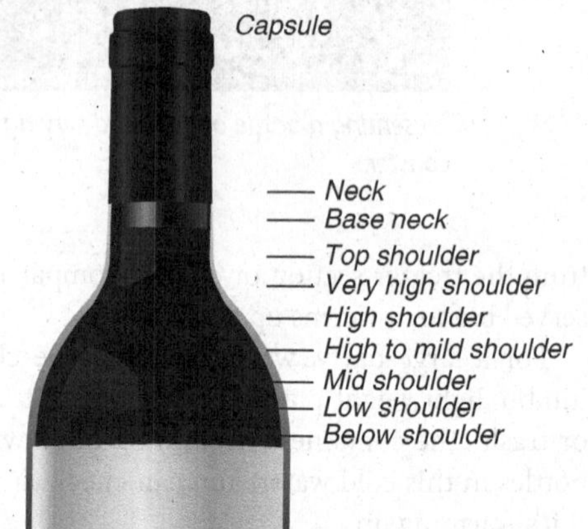

29.7 SERVICE OF WINE

Learning how to present and serve *wine* in a fine dining restaurant gives waiters and waitresses an important edge in earning bigger tips. Customers who enjoy wine will most likely appreciate a wine service performed with ease and grace, and will thank the server with a bigger tip. A server who takes their job seriously is always preferred. They always have a wine opener in the pocket, and a waiter's cloth made of fresh linen handy.

Table 29.1 Serving Temperatures for Different Types of Wine

Wine Type	°F	°C
Sparkling Wine	42–50	6–10
Rosé Wine	48–54	9–12
White Wine	48–58	9–14
Sherry (Light)	48–58	9–14
Sherry (Dark)	57–68	13–20
Fortified Wine	57–68	13–20
Red Wine	57–68	13–20

Wine Serving Order

1. **Serve young wines before old:** older wines are more robust than young wines.
2. **Serve white wines before red:** whites are usually more delicate.
3. **Serve light-bodied wines before full-bodied wines:** light-bodied wines are more subtle.
4. **Serve dry wines before sweet:** a dry wine following a sweet one will taste sour by comparison.

How to Present Wine

1. Put a collar for the bottle with the serviette.
2. Present the bottle from the right hand side of the host showing the label towards him or her.
3. Hold the bottle, so that the taster can easily read the label. Wait for him or her to approve the bottle.
4. Present the bottle of wine to the person who ordered it. Oftentimes, a woman dining out with a man will order the bottle of wine. It is insulting to her when the server assumes that the man will taste. However, sometimes it is unclear, for example, when a group of people at the table negotiate which wine they would like to share. In this case, it is fine to ask who would like to taste the wine when you return with the bottle.
5. Place a wine glass in front of each person who will be drinking the wine.

How to Open a Bottle of Wine at the Table

Once the bottle has been approved, the waiter will remove the cork with a corkscrew. The waiter is usually standing to the right of the wine host. Once the cork is removed, it will be placed next to the wine host for inspection.

Parts of a wine bottle.

1. Hold the bottle in one hand. Never put the bottle on the table or between your legs.
2. Hold a wine key in the other hand. Use the wine key's knife to remove foil or paper that is over the top of bottle. This must be done quickly and smoothly. Place the foil or paper in your pocket; it can be disposed of later. Wipe the mouth of the bottle with clean linen.
3. Insert the wine key's spiral at least 3/4 of the way into cork, and then anchor its arm on the lip of the bottle. Pull the cork out as smoothly and soundlessly as possible.
4. Sometimes you will find a cork you are unable to budge with an ordinary corkscrew. Therefore, what to do is, use the 'thief'. You put the longer side of the thief down one side of the cork, the shorter side down the other side, and wiggle it down. Then you twist it and pull it out in one motion. What it also may be useful for is when you have old bottles of wine with very fragile corks.

How to Pour Wine at the Table

When pouring wine, pour it gently and pour less than half a glass, so that you have got room to swirl it around if you want. What you do not want to do is pour it like mad and pour it more than half full, because then it goes all over the place and you make an awful mess on the carpet.

1. After removing the cork, untwist it from the spiral and place it to the right of the person tasting. Slip the wine key back into your pocket. Make certain that the wet end of the cork is facing the taster.
2. Give the person a moment to feel the cork if they so choose. This is to ascertain that the cork is wet. A dry cork could mean spoiled wine.
3. Some people choose to smell the cork. There is no reason to do this, but a good waiter will simply wait patiently. Also, some wines now have a 'cork' made out of rubber, or have switched to screw caps. In this case, the server should still simply place the 'cork' or cap to the right of the taster and continue the wine service.

4. Pour a small amount, about a half an inch up, into the taster's glass. Have the clean linen ready to wipe the lip of the bottle, so that no drops spill on the table. The taster will most likely swirl the wine, then drink it. Wait while he or she considers whether to accept the wine.
5. After the wine is accepted, pour the ladies' wine first, starting with the oldest lady and ending with the youngest. Then pour for the gentlemen at the table, starting with the oldest and ending with the youngest. Always pour the taster's wine last, regardless of gender and age.

How to Decant Wine

Some waitresses are lucky enough to work in restaurants that serve good wine and have decanters on hand. When this is not the case, it can be mentioned to the management as a possible improvement to the restaurant. Decanting a fine bottle of wine makes it easier to enjoy, and many diners will tip well for the service. A decanter is a glass bottle of sorts, usually very wide on the bottom. Many red wines become much tastier after they have been exposed to the air, or 'allowed to breathe.' The purpose of the decanter is to expose the wine to air more quickly; therefore, it opens up during dinner. 'Opens up' refers to the changes in the wine as it responds to air. Not all wines need to be decanted, but interesting, intricate and expensive reds should be.

1. Offer to decant the wine for the table.
2. At the table, hold the decanter at a 45° angle and pour the wine into the top.
3. Make sure the wine flows down the inside of the decanter.
4. Place the decanter on the table and remove the bottle.
5. Save the bottle in states in which customers can take an unfinished bottle home.

How to Deal with Bad Wine

Restaurant customers are not obligated to accept the wine. While infrequent, customers do reject bottles of wine. Sometimes there is something wrong with the wine, other times it is not to their taste. If the wine is rejected, be polite and ask if they would like to see the wine list again. The more the server knows about the wines in the restaurant, the better able he is to help the customer find something he will enjoy.

Tell management that the wine was rejected. Often, managers will send the bottle back for a credit to the restaurant's account with the wine merchant.

Customers who enjoy fine wine will appreciate any knowledge and understanding that a server displays.

Note: When it is time to pour the wine, proper etiquette is for the waiter to pour the wine for the ladies first, clockwise from the wine host, and the men in the same clockwise manner with the wine host last. An exception is that a guest of honour should be poured before other guests regardless of gender. In a banquet setting (eight or more guests at a table), the waiter may pour around the table clockwise from the wine host to all guests regardless of gender. If the number of guests is greater than five or six, the waiter may suggest to the host that another bottle is in order. Whatever the decision of the host, the waiter should ensure that all guests receive a nearly equal amount even if it means that guests receive less than a normal pour. Only a very poor waiter will run out of wine before making it around the table.

Serving Fortified and Aromatized Wines

These wines fall into the category of fortified wines meaning that brandy has been added to them after fermentation. Normally, they are strong and on the sweet side.

While they are not usually served with meals due to the strong flavours, they do make good additions to food in recipes and are often used in cooking. Fortified wines are normally served after dinner or at other times when relaxed conversation and a good wine can be enjoyed at a leisurely pace.

29.8 READING A WINE LABEL

Look for Five Elements

1. ***Grape Variety (or appellation):*** tells you the most about the body and complexity of the wine. For example, Cabernet Sauvignon and Nebbiolo are full-bodied, intense and tannic.
2. ***Region:*** hints the expected style, intensity and flavour. For example, Bordeaux wines are often more tannic and age better due to its cooler climate, rich soil and respect to appellation norms.
3. ***Producer/Vineyard:*** tells you most about the wine quality and expected consistency. For example, the names Chateau Laffite Rothschild, Chateau Latour, Margaux, and Haut-Brion—all classified Premier Crus (first growths) in 1855—indicate consistent quality.
4. ***Alcohol level:*** implies the body and sweetness of a bottle of wine. Above 14% wines are full-bodied and more tannic. Sweeter and lighter wines generally have alcoholic level below 11%. Sugar from grapes is transformed into alcohol during the fermentation process. Some Germany Riesling producers reduce fermentation time to attain sweeter wines.
5. ***Vintage or the year the wine is produced:*** reveals the best time to drink the wine. For example, a 1982 bottle of Chateau Lafite Rothschild Pauillac that ages well over 20–30 years is best drunk in the next couple of years.

Note: French and many European wines are described by appellation, rather than by grape variety. Appellation is the place of origin. In order to qualify for the appellation, the wine must be made from certain types of grapes. For example, Pauillac is predominantly composed of Cabernet Sauvignon and Merlot.

Recognize These Terms that Indicate a Good Wine Bottle

AOC/DOC: Appellation terminologies in multiple languages that indicate a higher or special quality wine are listed below:

1. **France:** Appellation d'Origine Contrôlée (AOC).
2. **Italy:** Denominazione di Origine Controllata e Garantita (DOCG) or Denominazione di Origine Controllata (DOC).
3. **Portugal:** Denominacao de'Origem Controlada (DOC) or Indicacao de Proveniencia Regulamentada (IPR).
4. **Spain:** Denominacion de Origen Calificada (DOC) or Denominacion de Origen (DO).

Grands Cru or Premier Cru: Commonly used in the French region to describe a vineyard of high quality. For example, in France, the top 1% of Burgundy wines would be labelled Grands Cru; and only 10% of Burgundy wines would fall into the Premier Cru category.

Gran Reserva: The wine is bottled for at least five years.

Mis en bouteille au chateau/domaine/a lapropriété/Gutsabfüllung (estate bottled): this means the wine is bottled in the estate. Traditionally, this label is affixed on wines that are estates' favourites.

Vieilles Vignes (old vines): the wine is made from grapes grown on old vines, usually over 40 years. Old vines have lower grape yield, but produces grapes with rich flavours.

Appellation French Wine Label

From the adjoining image, We get a clear understanding on the details of a French wine label. Each section of the label is generally followed by all manufacturers. Please note that the grower or producer who produced the wines may be identified by the terms Mis en bouteille au domaine, Mis au domaine or Mis en bouteille à la propriété.

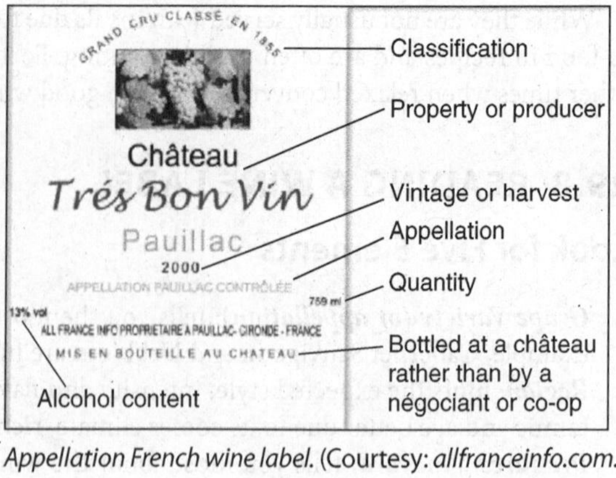

Appellation French wine label. (Courtesy: *allfranceinfo.com.*)

29.9 SERVICE OF WHISKY

Whisky is one of the alcoholic beverages found in most of the drinking parties. An alcoholic drink distilled out of fermented grain mash, whisky is manufactured in many countries, the most popular being the one produced in Scotland. The beverage produced there is termed as Scotch whisky. It is simply known as 'Scotch' as well, due to its origin. Equipment used (as shown in the image on next page) are:

1. Salver
2. Shot glass with a measure of whisky
3. Old-fashioned glass
4. Decanter for soda
5. Decanter for water
6. Ice bucket with ice cubes
7. Cocktail napkin and
8. Shot glass to keep swizzle sticks

Procedure to Serve Whisky

1. The best way to serve Scotch is 'on the rocks'. First, all the equipment mentioned above and glassware must be carried to the guest.
2. Next, the empty old-fashioned glass is placed in front of the guest.
3. The guest is asked for his or her preference with or without ice. If yes, then the ice cubes are put into the glass, 3–4 cubes on an average.
4. The whisky is always poured over the ice. Hence the name, 'on the rocks'.
5. Then as per guest's preference, water or soda is added if requested.
6. American whiskies especially bourbons, such as Jack Daniel's whisky, are served along with Coca-Cola.
7. Swizzle stick is placed in front of the guest along with the cocktail napkin.
8. In case you are serving water along with Scotch, make sure to use only spring water, because it is purer than other types of water and would have the least effect on the taste and aroma of the drink. Moreover, experts insist on the use of spring water, because the chlorinated taste and smell of tap water will distort the aroma and rich taste of Scotch.
9. For those who find Scotch to be too strong alone, you can serve cocktails. There are a large number of cocktails that are made with scotch, just check out online or in a recipe book.

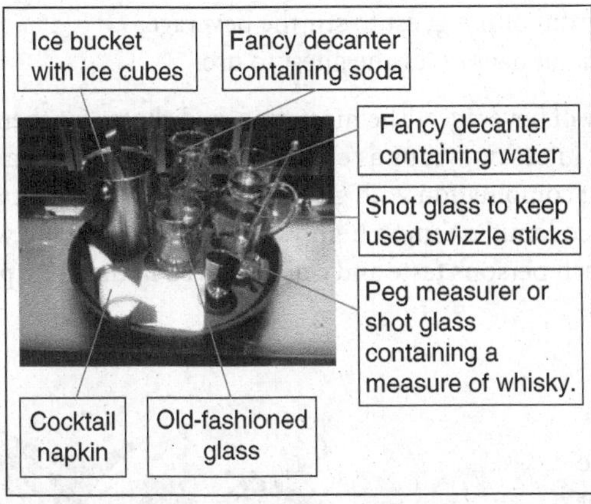

Service of whisky.

Image displaying a glass of whisky served on the rocks.

29.10 SERVICE OF GIN, RUM AND VODKA

Equipment used (as shown in the photo, below) are:

1. Salver
2. Tom Collins, Highball or Appropriate glassware
3. Ice bucket
4. Peg measure with a measure of rum, gin or vodka
5. A decanter containing Cola (for rum), tonic water (for gin) and Lemonade (for vodka)
6. Shot glass containing a swizzle stick, and
7. Cocktail Napkin

Procedure for Serving Rum, Gin or Vodka

1. First, the empty glass with the appropriate garnish is placed in front of the guest.
2. Next, the Ice cubes are added to the glass as per the guest's preference. Normally 3–4 cubes of ice are preferred.
3. The spirit is added on the ice from a shot glass or a peg measure.
4. Next the chasers follow, either Cola in case of rum, lemonade in case of vodka and tonic water in case of gin.

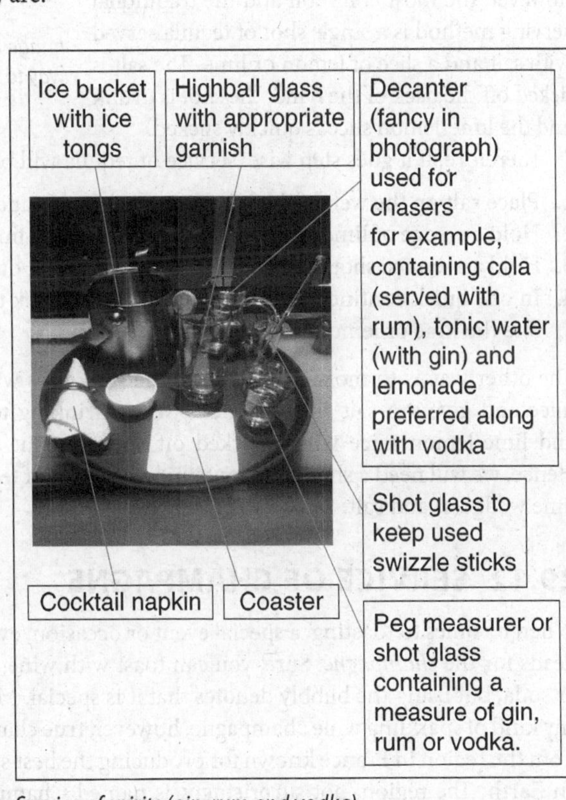

Service of spirits (gin, rum and vodka).

5. Swizzle sticks in a shot glass are placed in front of the guest to stir the beverage.
6. The drink is placed on a coaster with a cocktail napkin for the guest to use.

Gin, rum or vodka can be served with a variety of beverages. The most preferred chaser for them is mentioned in the procedure above. Many use fruit juices or syrups as chasers and are highly recommended. For example, Angostura bitters are an excellent combination with gin, whereas many prefer orange juice with a measure of vodka. Pineapple juice or coconut cream is highly appreciated by many with rum. Hence, chasers to these beverages vary from each person's taste and can be served in the same procedure as mentioned above.

29.11 SERVICE OF TEQUILA

Tequila is a distilled beverage made from the blue agave plant. When served neat (without any additional ingredients), tequila is most often served in a narrow shot glass called a caballito ('little horse' in Spanish), but can often be found in anything from a snifter to a tumbler.

Image displaying a service tray with shot glasses. A popular way to serve tequila.

There are various methods of serving tequila; however, the most common and the traditional serving method is a single shot of tequila served with salt and a slice of lemon or lime. The salt is licked off the back of the hand, the shot is drunk and the lime/lemon slice is quickly sucked.

Therefore, if it goes step wise, service of tequila will be:

1. Place salt on the web of the hand between thumb and forefinger.
2. Hold a wedge of lime or lemon with the same two fingers.
3. Hold a 1-ounce shot glass filled with tequila in the other hand.
4. In one quick continuous motion, lick the salt, drink the tequila, and bite the lime or lemon wedge.

The other way is to moisten the rim of the shot glass with lime/lemon juice and give it a salt rim; therefore, when drinking tequila, the salt and lime/lemon juice will be licked off and then the shot is drunk. Hence, we will need a shot glass containing one shot of tequila, a lemon/lime wedge(s) and salt.

29.12 SERVICE OF CHAMPAGNE

Champagne being poured gently into a champagne flute glass. The slow pouring ensures the effervescence remains in the beverage.

When it comes to toasting, a special event or occasion, everyone usually heads for the *champagne*. Sure, you can toast with wine, beer, cocktails or soda, but using the bubbly denotes that it is special. Most people call any kind of sparkling wine champagne; however, true champagne comes from the region in France known for producing the best sparkling wines on Earth. The region, not surprisingly, is named Champagne. The climate, soil and strict production regulations in Champagne ensure that the quality of sparkling wine there is unmatched. Because of the delicate nature of champagne and the occasions where it is typically served, it requires a little more than plastic cups or beer mugs to do it right. Champagne is a sparkling wine produced from grapes grown in the Champagne appellation of France following rules that demand secondary fermentation of the wine in the bottle to create carbonation.

Champagne Etiquette

The flute

Champagne is always served in tall, skinny and easily breakable flutes. If you do not have long-stemmed flutes, you can get away with a tulip-shaped wine glass. The reason champagne is served in a flute is because the design of the glass strengthens the aromas of the wine and aids the flow of bubbles, a key aspect of drinking sparkling wines. While the bubbly is served chilled, champagne flutes should always remain at room temperature.

The Chill

Serving champagne at the proper temperature is essential. Champagne should be served at a temperature between 4°–9°C. Non-vintage and sweeter champagnes can take the lower side of that scale; however, fine champagne should hover between 6–7°C. A wine refrigerator is the best way to get an exact temperature; however, a couple of hours in a regular refrigerator should get you close to where you need to be. You can also fill a wine bucket with half ice and half water for a 30-min rapid chill. Remember to always leave the bottle corked until it is time to serve. Never chill or ice the glass, as it would take away from the enjoyment of the wine.

The Battle of the Cork

When learning how to serve champagne, opening the bottle can be the trickiest part for a first-timer. The first thing you need to do is, remove the foil around the cork. There is about 80 Pounds per square inch of pressure behind the cork; therefore, carefully remove the foil covering. Do not remove the wire cage around the cork. Now, grasp the cork and wire cage securely with your left hand. Use your right hand to grasp the cork if you are left-handed. Uncork the champagne bottle slowly. Place a small dishtowel over the bottle before loosening the cork to prevent spills and to better grasp the cork. Hold the cork and slowly turn the champagne bottle to ease the cork out gradually. You will feel the pressure on the cork as it is released, but keep turning the bottle slowly, without letting the cork pop on its own. The cork should ease off quietly, so that you do not lose any of the champagne. Next ease the cork out, by securing the cork and turning the bottle (held at a 45° angle). Once the cork sighs open, you are ready to pour.

The Pour

After you have uncorked your champagne, which is best to do aimed away from people and glass, the next step, is the most fun–the pouring. You probably know that champagne is extremely bubbly, and the last thing you want to do is pour it, so that it flows over the glass and onto your guest. To prevent the champagne from foaming over, follow this simple technique. Start with just a little in the bottom and let the bubbles die down, then fill the glass about two-thirds full with a steady, even pour. Colder bottle temperatures also result in reduced loss of gas. Additionally, the industry is developing champagne glasses designed specifically to reduce the amount of gas lost. Moreover, consider the glasses you will be serving in. It is recommended that you use a champagne flute. However, if you do not have a champagne flute, use any narrow glass. A wide-mouthed glass would not preserve the bubbles for a long time.

29.13 SERVICE OF BRANDY

Traditional way of heating brandy. Now not commonly followed.

Brandy is served in brandy snifter. In general, a snifter holds approximately 8 fluid ounces. However, when serving brandy, no more than 3 ounces should ever be poured into the glass. In fact, if you were to lay a snifter on its side (with brandy in it), it should lay in such a way that the brandy would not fall out. Filling the glass with any more liquid would disrupt the oxidation and release of aromas.

Brandy may be served neat or on the rocks. It may be added to other beverages to make several popular cocktails; these include the Brandy Alexander, the Sidecar, the Brandy Daisy and the Brandy Old-fashioned.

In western countries, brandy is traditionally drunk neat at room temperature from a snifter or a tulip glass. In parts of Asia, it is usually drunk on the rocks. When drunk at room temperature, it is often slightly warmed by holding the glass cupped in the palm or by gently heating it. Sometimes when brandy is served, the snifter glass is heated beforehand by swirling hot water around in the glass. However, once the brandy is poured into the snifter, a napkin can then be placed over the narrow opening of the snifter to retain the heat. However, excessive heating of brandy may cause the alcohol vapour to become too strong, to the extent that its aroma may become overpowering. Brandy has a more pleasant aroma at a lower temperature, *e.g.*, 16°C (61°F). This would imply that brandy should be cooled, rather than heated, for maximum enjoyment.

29.14 SERVICE OF ABSINTHE

Absinthe historically described as a distilled, highly alcoholic (45–74% ABV) beverage. It is an anise-flavoured spirit derived from botanicals, including the flowers and leaves of *Artemisia absinthium* (also known as 'grand wormwood'), together with green anise, sweet fennel and other medicinal and culinary herbs. Absinthe traditionally has a natural green colour, but may also be colourless. It is commonly referred to in historical literature as '*la fée verte*' (the green fairy). Although it is sometimes mistakenly referred to as a liqueur, absinthe is not traditionally bottled with added sugar, and is, therefore, classified as a spirit. Absinthe is traditionally bottled at a high level of alcohol by volume, but is normally diluted with water prior to being consumed.

Traditional service equipment for serving Absinthe.

How to Serve Absinth

To serve absinth, you will need a tall glass, preferably wide open at the pouring end, a special slotted spoon (looks like a cake knife with holes in it), ice cold water and a lump of sugar. There are two popular methods for serving absinthe, the French way and the Czech way. Absinthe is usually quite bitter and strong; therefore, sugar is added to sweeten it and water to dilute it. Both methods require the use of an absinthe spoon. In a pinch, a large fork can work as well.

Service of Absinthe-Method One.

Method One: The Czech Absinthe Ritual (Flame Method)

1. Fill a glass with one shot of absinthe.
2. Dip a sugar cube in the absinthe quickly and pull it out. Light the sugar cube with a match over the drink. The sugar cube will burn and the caramelized sugar slowly drips into the drink.
3. When the sugar quits burning, drop the remainder in the absinthe.
4. The rest of the sugar is then stirred into the drink.

Pouring Absinthe over a spoon with a sugar cube placed above it.

Method Two: The French Absinthe Ritual (Louching)

1. Fill the glass with one shot of absinthe.
2. Put the spoon on top of the glass. Put the sugar cube on the spoon.
3. Pour 3–5 shots of cold water slowly over the sugar cube. The cold water will dissolve the sugar. When the sugar water hits the absinthe, it releases oils that turn the absinthe milky in appearance (the clear green liquid turns cloudy, as when water is added to Pastis). This is called the louche or louching.
4. The rest of the sugar is then stirred into the drink.

Variations on the French Absinthe Ritual

The Brouille Ritual

A brouilleur is a small glass lid, which is placed over the Absinthe glass. It is then filled with ice cubes and water is slowly poured into it. The water gets cooled and flows through a small hole in the bottom of the brouilleur into the Absinthe glass. Because of the extremely thin beam of water, the brouille method is the easiest way to achieve the best louche.

The Pipe Ritual

The pipe ritual has its roots in Bohemian culture. The glass pipe is filled with Absinthe and crushed ice, and the elixir is sucked up through the glass straw. It is comparable with an Absinthe shot; the effect is intensified as the Absinthe speeds into the mouth and creates a pleasant coolness and activation.

The Pipe used for the Pipe ritual.

DID YOU KNOW

Sales & Marketing companies, which deal in imported beverages (*i.e.*, wine, Spirits etc.), are setting up shops in India in a very big way. These companies will help in bringing the Indian consumers in direct contact with the best beverages across the globe.

One such company is Vinura Beverages Pvt Ltd. It is a VK Modi Group company, which has launched an array of high class international products – fine wines, sparkling wines and scotch whiskies and many more to come.

Vinura was setup in July 2012 with the intent to get the most brands of wines and spirits from around the world at affordable prices in the Indian market. What set them apart are the knowledge and understanding of consumers' taste palette and quick response to their evolving taste.

Its product portfolio comprises of Montiac French wines, Bernard Massard sparkling wines from Luxembourg and Highland Queen Range of blended and single malt whiskies. The entire range is available in several retail stores located at Gurgaon, Chandigarh and Punjab.

Vinura is virtually on a roll and will soon be adding the Just Wines range from France and the Italian Mango Sparkling Wine (Mamamango). Montiac is a fine range of varietal wines. Comprising wines from the Pays d'Oc, this range includes Chardonnay, Merlot, Sauvignon Blanc, Cinsault and Cabernet Sauvignon.

Vinura's Bernard Massard sparkling wine, produced in the banks of Luxembourg Moselle, is one of the most preferred varieties amongst the European wines. The Bernard Massard 'Brut', 'Demi-Sec', 'Ecusson' and 'Ecusson Rose' are produced from judiciously selected wines and according to the strictest rules of *Methode Traditionnelle*. This, along with competence of their creators, has guaranteed a consistent quality worthy of a great house.

Vinura is equally confident about the Highland Queen Scotch whisky range, which has been produced in Scotland for over 100 years. This range includes Highland Queen Blended Scotch 12 Year Old and 16 Year Old and single malt Majesty 12 Year Old, 16 Year Old and 40 Year Old.

The Indian markets looks forward to Vinura becoming a popular brand and help the Indian consumer to get an improved range of products from around the globe.

LET'S SUMMARIZE IN POINTS

- All beverages need to be served keeping various factors in mind, such as temperature, glassware, equipment and the consistency of the beverage.
- Tea, coffee and hot chocolate and hot cocoa are hot beverages, which need to be served in chinaware and not glassware.
- Cold beverages, which are served at room temperature or lower, need to be served in appropriate glassware.
- Popular beverages have to be served in a particular manner and procedure to achieve the desired results.
- Beverages need to be always served keeping the preference of their guests in mind and not be too rigid in following procedure over ruling guest's preference.

29.15 FAQs

Short-Answer Type Questions

1. Name the equipment required for serving tea.
2. Describe the following:
   i. Drip bowl and strainer.
   ii. Demitasse cup.
   iii. Tasse.
   iv. Demerara sugar.
   v. Diet sugar or sugar free.
   vi. Chamomile tea.
3. Give the difference between hot cocoa and hot chocolate.

Long-Answer Type Questions

1. Give the detailed procedure for serving coffee. Explain at least three types.
2. Give the procedure for serving oolong tea, Pu-erh tea.
3. Give the difference between service of black tea and green tea.
4. Give the detailed procedure along with the key factors influencing the service of beer.
5. Name the procedure for serving spirits.

29.16 KEY TERMS

- Sediments
- Wine Chiller

Tobacco

CHAPTER OUTLINE

The tobacco plant is harvested for its leaves and stems which is processed and rolled into cigars, shredded and used in cigarettes and smoking pipes. It is also processed into chewing tobacco or also sniffed, that is it is inhaled from the nose.

The tobacco industry is one of the most robust industries in the world, despite the various health regulations and increased taxation it continues to grow. This is due to the presence of the chemical nicotine which is very addictive.

30.1 HISTORY

In 1492, Christopher Columbus discovered the New World along with the discovery of Tobacco. The West Indian tribes gifted him a few leaves of Tobacco which he took to Europe where it grew in popularity. Tobacco cultivation existed in Brazil in 1548 and started in India in 1605.

In 1561, Jean Nicot is credited for defining tobacco and its chemical composition of Nicotine.

30.2 THE TOBACCO PLANT

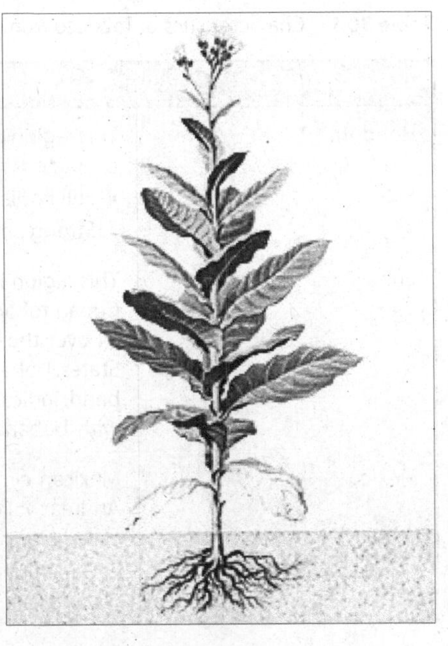
The tobacco plant.

The tobacco plant grows in two varieties, namely:

1. *Nicotiana tabacum* or cultivated tobacco and
2. *Nicotiana rustica* or wild tobacco.

N. rustica is commonly used in European countries for producing tobacco products, whereas *N. tabacum* is used all over the world for the commercial production of tobacco products.

Tobacco is grown in China, Java, India, Africa and Latin American countries. Though tobacco is grown and processed across the globe, the best quality tobacco is used in making cigars. The best tobacco is from Cuba, named after its capital, Havana. The finest Cuban tobacco comes from the Vuelta Abajo areas.

Tobacco cultivation requires the following appropriate conditions:

1. Tobacco cultivation requires good soil conditions and a warm climate.
2. It is grown in countries with tropical or semi-tropical climate such as Cuba, Indonesia, the Philippines, India and West Indies.
3. The area requires regular rain showers.
4. The local soil should be fertile and well drained.

30.3 TOBACCO FROM ACROSS THE WORLD

The characteristics of tobacco from places around the world are mentioned in Table 30.1.

Table 30.1 Characteristics of Tobacco from Across the World

Country	Characteristics
Dominican Republic	It is one of the major producers of top quality tobacco in the world. The principal growing area in the country is the Cibao River Valley region.
Connecticut Valley	It is famous for producing some of the world's finest wrapper tobacco leaves. The golden colour wrapper tobacco is famous all around the world and also praised by many famous cigar makers in the world.
Indonesia	It also has its own unique reputation for its wrapper tobacco leaves.
Brazil	Tobacco from Brazil has the following characteristics: • Dark • Rich • Smooth • Slight sweet flavour They will get a deep brown colour after their fermentation.

(*Continued*)

Table 30.1 Characteristics of Tobacco from Across the World (Contd.)

Country	Characteristics
Honduras	This region produces quality Cuban seed and Connecticut seed tobaccos. Its characteristics are: • Full bodied and • Strong and spicy flavour.
Cuba	This region is also very famous for its finest varieties of tobacco. Most of the Cuban tobaccos are used for making world-famous cigars and it is famous all over the world. The tobaccos of Cuba are even exported to the United States. Habana or Havana is a designation which, when inscribed on a cigar band, indicates that a cigar is Cuban. (*Note*: not all Cuban cigars are marked with 'Habana' or 'Havana'.)
Mexico	Mexican cigars are made from 100% of Mexican grown tobacco. The San Andreas valley of Mexico is world famous for producing a sun grown variety called *Mexican Sumatra*. Dark tobacco used for making the fillers and binders for the cigars are also grown here. This type of tobacco has a distinct peppery and light texture.

30.4 TYPES OF TOBACCO

1. **Flue-cured:** The tobacco is dried in closed barns into which heat is pumped from furnaces. The temperature is raised till leaves and stems are completely dry. It takes place for 1 week and the leaves turn lemon orange and slightly reddish in colour. The nicotine level is medium to high.
2. **Air-cured**: The leaves are hung on sticks in the barn allowing it to dry naturally in the air protected from wind and sun. The drying is carried out on the whole plant or as individual leaves. These barns are equipped with ventilators to control the temperature and humidity, as it takes 4–8 weeks where the leaves turn from green to yellow. Sugar is the by-product of this drying process.
   There are two categories in air curing, as:
   1. Light air-cured and
   2. Dark air-cured.

   For dark air-cured, the leaves are subjected to fermentation twice, whereas light air-cured has only one fermentation.
3. **Fire-cured**: Its natural drying is completed by a wood-fired fumigation in closed barns (oak is used by the traditionalists). The smoke imparts the smoky aroma and flavour. This process continues for 3–10 days. The colour is very dark and is full bodied.
4. **Sun-cured**: The leaves tied on strings are exposed to direct sunlight where they turn from dull yellow to rich red colour. Almost all of Oriental Tobaccos are cured by this method. Oriental tobaccos are grown in Greece, Turkey, Bulgaria and adjoining countries.

30.5 THE MANUFACTURING PROCESS

1. **Growing the tobacco:** Tobacco is initially grown in outdoor frames called seedbeds. In warm regions, the frames are covered with mulch or a cotton top sheet; in cooler regions, glass or plastic shields are installed to protect the plants. After 8–10 weeks, when the seedlings are almost 10 inches (25 cm) tall,

they are transplanted to the fields. Although transplanting machines are available, the vast majority of the world's tobacco plants are still planted manually. As the plants grow, the heads are broken off by hand so the leaves will grow fuller, a process called *topping*. The plants stay in the field 90–120 days before they are harvested.

2. **Harvesting the tobacco:** Tobacco plants are harvested by one of the two methods, *priming* or *stalk-cutting*. In the priming method, the leaves are gathered and brought to a curing barn as they ripen. In the stalk-cutting method, the entire plant is cut and the plants are allowed to wilt in the field before being taken to the curing barn.
3. **Curing the leaf:** Next, the leaves are carefully, gradually dried in a specially constructed barn by air-curing, flue-curing, sun-curing or fire-curing method. (The detailed description of different types of cured tobacco is given in the topic: Types of tobacco.)
4. **Moistening and stripping:** Cured tobacco leaves must be conditioned in moistening chambers so they do not break when they are handled. After moistening, the tobacco is stripped. During this process, the leaves are sprayed with additional moisture as a precaution against cracking or breaking.
5. **Sorting and auctioning:** After the leaves are moistened and stripped, they are sorted into grades based on size, colour, and quality, and tied in bundles for shipment. The farmers then bring the tobacco to warehouses, where it is placed in baskets, weighed, graded once again by a government inspector and, finally, auctioned to manufacturers of tobacco products.

30.6 CIGARETTES

Cigarette is a paper-wrapped roll of finely cut tobacco used for smoking. Cigarette tobacco is usually milder than cigar tobacco.

The Manufacturing Process

After the initial steps of processing tobacco are complete, the next few steps transform the tobacco into cigarettes.

1. **Conditioning, ageing and blending:** After they have purchased and transported the material to their factories, manufacturers treat and age the tobacco to enhance its flavour. First, the manufacturer re-dries the tobacco. This involves completely drying the leaves by air and then adding a uniform amount of moisture, they are then packed into barrels called hogsheads, the tobacco is then aged for one to three years, during which it develops its flavour and aroma. After it is aged, the tobacco leaves are again moistened and the stalks and other unwanted materials are removed. Leaves from different types of tobacco are mixed to create a particular flavour.
2. **Making the cigarettes:** After blending, the tobacco leaves are pressed and mechanically shredded. Fruit juices or menthol are added to give additional flavour. The final shredded tobacco is then dispersed over a continuous roll of cigarette paper. A machine rolls the shredded tobacco into the paper and cuts it to the desired length. A device then grabs each cigarette and fastens a filter on one end. Modern cigarette machines can produce 25–30 cigarettes a second.
3. **Packaging:** The final stage of cigarette manufacture is packaging. The completed cigarettes are packed 20 or 10 to a package. The hard or soft packs are mechanically sealed in cellophane and hand-placed in cartons.

Types of Cigarettes

- Hand-rolled cigarettes
- Straight cigarettes/unfiltered

- Regular-filtered cigarettes
- Light filtered cigarettes
- Ultra-light filtered cigarettes
- Regular filtered king size
- Light filtered king size
- Ultra-light filtered king size
- Regular slim—very long, skinny
- Light slim
- Ultra-light slim
- Menthols
- Slims–smaller diameter
- Wides–larger diameter

Colour Code

- **Red pack**–full flavour,
- **Gold/white pack**–lights,
- **Light blue/silver**–ultra lights,
- **Green pack**–menthols and
- **Very dark red**–unfiltered.

Brands

International brands

International brands of cigarettes are enumerated in Table 30.2.

Table 30.2 International Brands of Cigarettes

Country	Brand Names
UK	Rothmans, Marlboro, Dunhill, Benson & Hedges, Virginia Slims and 555
USA	Barclay, American Spirit, Basic, Cambridge, Camel, Chesterfield, Pall Mall, Kent, Kool, Virginia Slims, More, Newport (North Carolina), Parliament, Liggett Pyramid and Chesterfield
Peru	Manhattan
Nigeria	Aspen
Bangladesh	Gold Leaf
Paraguay	Hollywood and York
Germany	Cabinet

Indian brands

ITC Ltd. is a leading manufacturer of cigarettes in India. Some famous ITC brands along with others are mentioned in Table 30.3.

Table 30.3 Indian Brands of Cigarettes

Manufacturers	Brand Names
ITC Brands	Wills, Insignia, India Kings, Classic, Navy Cut, Gold Flake, Silk Cut and Scissors
Other Brands	Four Square, Panama, Capstan, Berkeley, Bristol and Flake

Service of Cigarettes in Hotels

Cigarettes should never be carried by hand to the customer but placed on a salver or quarterplates. The packet should be opened (pulling out few cigarettes partially). The waiter should stand by with a match to light the cigarette. It should be made sure that the ashtray is on the table. Ashtrays should never be allowed to collect too much of ash, it is the waiter's duty to exchange them frequently for fresh ones.

30.7 CIGARS

History of the Cigar

The history of the cigar goes back about two thousand years. Some scholars say the word cigar originated from *sikar*, the Mayan word for smoking. It is believed that the cigar has its origins within Central America, where smoking was practiced by the Mayans and later the Aztecs. They were known to have smoked tubes of loosely rolled tobacco leaves, similar to the present day cigars.

LET'S DEFINE

'A cigar is a rolled cylinder of tobacco that is wrapped in tobacco leaves or other substance that contains tobacco. Most cigars do not have filters at the end for the smoker to inhale the lit tobacco through, but a few companies do manufacture cigars with filters'.

After Columbus' discovery of the West Indies and other explorers visiting the American continent, numerous accounts were written of these New World people who smoked tobacco and also used it to chew and as a snuff for medicinal properties in their ceremonies.

Smoking came to Europe with the return of Columbus from the New World in 1492. He had been offered some dried leaves as a token of friendship and his men had witnessed how these leaves were used. Columbus himself was not particularly impressed by the custom, but soon Spanish and other European sailors fell for the habit, followed by the conquistadors and colonists. The introduction of tobacco seeds or plants is attributed to Ramon Pane, Columbus' priest on his second voyage. In due course the returning conquistadors introduced tobacco smoking to Spain and Portugal. The habit was considered a sign of wealth, and then it spread to France, through the French ambassador to Portugal, Jean Nicot in 1560 (from whom the herb was given its botanical name *Nicotiana tabacum*, the Latin name for tobacco).

Various people have been credited with being the first to smoke in England. We know tobacco was introduced into England at some time before 1565, when Hawkins returned from a voyage to America. Sir Walter Raleigh is believed to be chiefly responsible for making the smoking habit fashionable. Sailors were really the first to be seen smoking cigars around 1557.

By 1580s, smoking was coming into fashion among the upper classes, though for many years the habit was still frowned upon by their womenfolk to such an extent that the men had to take themselves off to the kitchen or the stables, or puff surreptitiously up the chimney, if they wished to smoke in their own homes.

Although the first tobacco plantations were set up in Virginia in 1612, and Maryland in 1631, tobacco was smoked only in pipes in the American colonies. The cigar itself is thought not to have arrived until after 1762, when Israel Putnam, an American general in the Revolutionary War, returned from Cuba, where he had been an officer in the British army. He came back to his home in Connecticut with a selection of Havana cigars, and large amounts of Cuban tobacco. Before long, cigar factories were set up in the Hartford area. Production of the leaves started in the 1820s, and Connecticut tobacco today provides among the best wrapper leaves to be found outside Cuba. By the early 19th century, not only were Cuban cigars being imported into the United States, but domestic production was also taking off.

By the mid-1800s, the cigar had become well accepted and in 1870, it was recorded that over half of the tobacco smoked in our towns was in the form of cigars.

During the depression in the early 1920s, the total consumption of tobacco fell and cigar manufacturers turned to 'promoting' their brands by including beautifully designed and coloured inserts in their packaging and boxes in order to attract cigar smokers, a tradition that continues to this day with some manufacturers.

Cuba led the way in the cigar industry. Early in the 16th century, Cuban peasants became tobacco growers. Later, the cigar became the country's national symbol and the Havana cigar became recognized as the world's finest.

The takeover by Fidel Castro and the subsequent US embargo were the start of events that began to challenge Havana's supremacy in the world of cigars. Many Cuban cigar-makers took their skills and seeds to the Caribbean, Dominican Republic, Honduras and Mexico and began producing high-quality premium and super-premium cigars for the American public. The Dominican Republic alone produces almost half of the handmade cigars sold in the United States.

Today, anyone can enjoy the taste of a premium cigar. Cigars handmade by experts from a choice blend of top-quality tobaccos and aged to perfection are referred to as premium cigars. Celebrities, industry leaders, politicians, sophisticated women and men are seen at dinners and at smoking clubs enjoying luxury cigars.

Parts of a Cigar

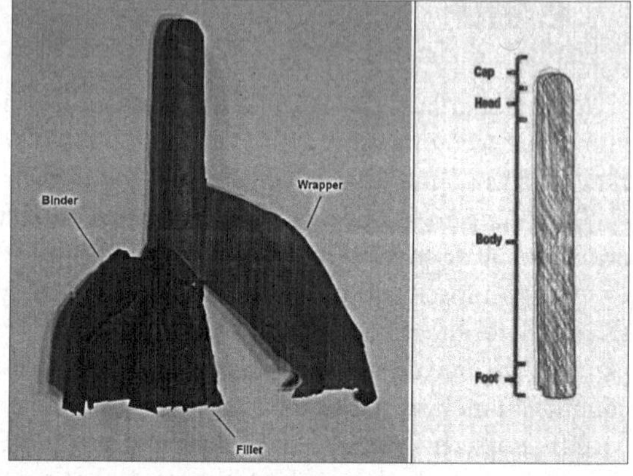

The various parts of a cigar.

Wrapper (capa): The outer wrapping of the cigar, made of the finest quality tobacco leaf. It gives the appearance to the cigar, together with a large proportion of the final aroma (Corojo plant). Leaves with elasticity are used to restrain the filler within the cigar. Good wrappers usually have no visible veins. Colours vary due to the maturing process.

Binder: It holds the filler together (Criollo plant) means the portion of leaf used to hold together the blend of filler leaves; with the wrapper and filler, it is one of the three main components in a cigar.

Filler: It is the inner core of the cigar (Criollo plant) means the individual tobacco used in the body of the cigar. A fine cigar usually contains from two to five different types of filler. Handmade cigars have long fillers, whereas machine made cigars usually contain smaller-cut leaf.

Common names to indicate various parts of cigars:

Head: The closed end of the cigar opposite from the end one lights.

Foot: The end of the cigar one lights. Most often it is pre-cut, except in the case of Torpedos and Perfectos. It is also called Tuck.

Barrel: The main body of the cigar.

Bunch: Up to four different types of filler tobacco blended to create the body of the cigar. The binder holds the bunch together.

Cap: A circular piece of wrapper leaf placed at the head of the cigar.

Classification of Cigars		
1. **Havana (a designation to indicate Cuban cigars)**		
(i) Bolivar	(ii) Larranga	(iii) Romeo
(iv) Romeo y Julieta	(v) Upman	(vi) Bock
(vii) La Corona (outstanding)	(viii) Havana	(ix) Henry
(x) Byrons	(xi) Canana	(xii) J.S. Murais
(xiii) Roman Allones	(xiv) Monte Cristo	(xv) Punch
2. **Jamaica**		
(i) Diplomat	(ii) Lainvicta	(iii) Flor De Nazenta
(iv) El Trovador	(v) Corona Deluxe	
3. **Manila**		
(i) Manila Gold	(ii) Manila Price	
4. **Holland**		
(i) Diplomat		
5. **American**		
(i) Robert Burns		
6. **Danish**		
(i) Ducados		
7. **Indian**		
(i) Bengal Tiger		
Some rare vintages are		
1. La Gloria Cubana	2. Avo	3. Macanudo

(According to country of origin)

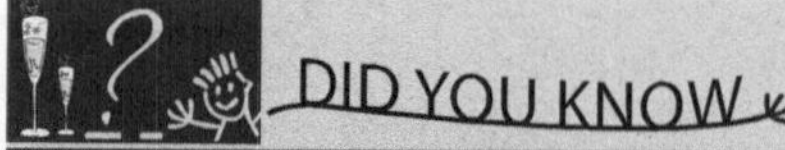

What is Ring Gauge?
Ring Gauge: The circumference of cigars. A measurement for the diameter of a cigar is based on 64ths of an inch. A 40-ring gauge cigar is 40/64ths of an inch thick.

Cigars are also classified by:

1. Shape and size,
2. Colour of the wrapper,
3. Country of origin and
4. Strength of the cigar.

Classification based on shape and size

The cigar is measured by length and ring gauge. The length is measured in inches. The ring gauge is measured in units of 1/64 of an inch. So the 64-ring cigar means 1 inch in diameter or a 52 ring means 52/64 = 0.8125 inch. Cigars have some basic shapes and some uncommon shapes also.

The ring gauge for cigars usually starts from 26–52. Common shapes of cigars with cigar shape charts are given in the photo (right).

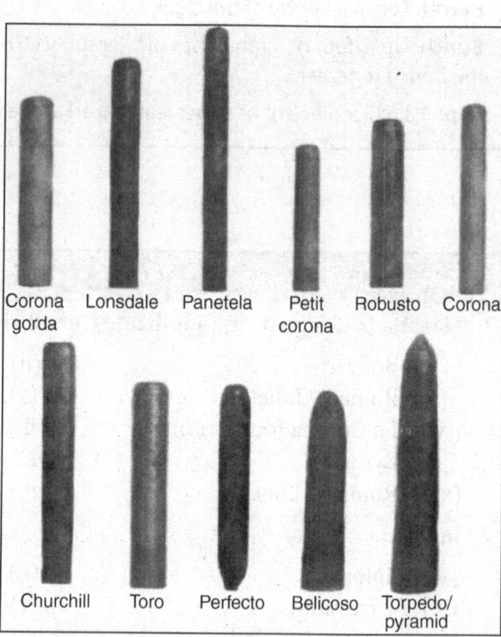

Cigar classification chart based on shape.

Various sizes of Cigars

Various sizes of cigars are listed in Table 30.4.

Classification Based on Wrapper

There are about a dozen shades, all variations of the basic colours from dull green to almost black wrappers. The wrapper leaf or the colour of the cigar accounts for less than 20% of cigars flavour. The wrapper does not indicate the kind of tobacco and the strength of cigars. There are six common colours of cigar wrappers as shown in Table 30.5. We should note that Double Claro is a type of Claro, and Colorado Claro is also a type of Colorado.

Table 30.4 Various Sizes of Cigars

Term	Length in Inches	Width in 64ths of an Inch
Rothschild	4 + 1/2	48
Robusto	4 + 7/8	50
Small Panatela	5	33
Petit Corona	5 + 1/8	42
Carlota	5 + 5/8	35
Corona	5 + 1/2	42
Corona Gorda	5 + 5/8	46
Panatela	6	38
Toro	6	50
Corona Grande	6 + 1/8	42
Lonsdale	6 + 1/2	42
Churchill	7	47–50
Double Corona	7 + 5/8	49
Presidente	8	50
Gran Corona	9 + 1/4	47

Table 30.5 Classification Based on Wrapper

Colour	Description
Double Claro	Very light, slightly greenish (also called candela, American market selection or jade); achieved by picking leaves before maturity and drying quickly; often grown in Connecticut.
Claro	Light tan or yellowish. Indicative of shade-grown tobacco.
Colorado	Reddish-brown (also called Rosado or 'Corojo').
Colorado Claro	Mid-brown; particularly associated with tobacco grown in the Dominican republic or in Cuba.
Colorado Maduro	Dark brown; particularly associated with Honduran or Cuba-grown tobacco.
Natural	Light brown to brown; generally sun-grown.
Maduro	Dark brown to very dark brown.
Oscuro	Also known as 'Double Maduro' black, often oily in appearance; mainly grown in Cuba, Nicaragua, Brazil, Mexico and Connecticut, USA.

Some manufacturers use alternative designations that are described in Table 30.6.

Table 30.6 Alternative Designations of Cigars

Designation	Acronym	Description
American Market Selection	AMS	Synonymous with double claro
English Market Selection	EMS	Can refer to any colour stronger than double claro but milder than Maduro
Spanish Market Selection	SMS	Either of the two darkest colours, Maduro and Oscuro

Classification as per Strength

Cigars can be classified as per the strength from mild to strong. Manufacturers import different types of tobaccos and blend them with their mature plants to create new taste and strengths some examples of cigars which are classified as per strength are as follows:

1. Mild cigars: Mostly Jamaican cigars are mild and to some extent Mexican also.
   (*e.g.* Fonseca, Dunhill Age.)
2. Mild to medium cigars:
   (*e.g.* Santa Rosa, Monte Cruz Natural Claro.)
3. Medium
   (*e.g.* Monte Cruz Don Diego.)
4. Medium to full:
   (*e.g.* Excalibur, Punch Deluxe.)
5. Full
   (*e.g.* Punch Henry Clay, La Gloria Cubana.)

30.8 HUMIDOR

A humidor is a room or a box, of varying sizes, designed to preserve or promote the proper storage and ageing of cigars by maintaining a relative humidity level of 70% and a temperature of approximately 65°–70°F.

In other words it is an enclosed device that keeps cigars in a tropical climate. A humidor can be a huge walk-in room, a box made of wood or Plexiglas, or something as simple as a sealed plastic bag—anything that maintains the relatively high level of airborne moisture, or humidity, cigars require to keep from drying out. Hygrometer—a device that indicates the humidity (percentage of moisture in the air), used to monitor humidor conditions.

A sketch of a cigar humidor.

Instruction for Storing Cigars in Humidors

1. Cigars should be stored at an optimum temperature of 16–18°C and relative humidity of 75–80%.
2. The humidor should be looked after carefully and the condition of the cigars within the humidor should be checked regularly.
3. The moisture source is the oasis located inside the cigar tray. When necessary this should be removed and dampened with distilled

water for about 10 seconds, then kept face upwards until the surface water is absorbed, wiped dry and replaced.

4. Do not use mineral water or tap water for wetting the moisture source for the cigars. The regularity with which you need to perform this task will vary with the weather, but the surest guide is the cigar itself. In general, this should be done every day.
5. It is essential that one member of staff is made responsible for the humidor. They must inspect it each day, not only to check condition but also to ensure that it is filled. Nothing destroys a sale faster than presenting the humidor with a flourish only to reveal a couple of lonely sticks of leaves.

30.9 CUTTING, LIGHTING AND SMOKING

1. The cigar should be cut half way through the cap using a cigar cutter or cigar scissors and should not be cut beneath the cap or the wrapper will start to unwind.
2. Do not pierce a hole in the cigar, it creates tar.
3. Cutting should take place at the table and executed with confidence.
4. A cigar should be lit with a butane gas lighter or with an ordinary long matchstick.
5. Cigars can also be lit with the thin cedar linings, which can be made from the cedar sheet available in the cigar box.
6. The cigar can be served to the guest; however, it is possible to present it ready lit to the guest without of course drawing on it yourself.
7. For lighting the cigar, hold the face of the cigar at 90° angle to the flames and rotate it. From time to time remove it from the flame and wave it in the air. Within a minute the cigar will be lit and ready to offer.
8. Do not offer to light the cigar unless asked. We do not inhale the smoke of cigars but taste it like a wine.
9. Do not pick up the extinguished cigar from the ashtray on the customers table unless asked.
10. Do not stub a cigar when finished smoking, let it die by itself in the ashtray.

Etiquettes of Cigar Smoking

1. Always let the customer decide what he wants to smoke and how he wants to smoke.
2. Never remove the band from the cigar since it is tightly secured and its removal might damage the wrapper.
3. In case the guest wishes to remove the band, suggest him to smoke 3/4th of the cigar for it to become soft for removal without damaging the wrapper.

30.10 SERVICE OF CIGARS

Cigars are served after a meal or during the sorbet course in the French classical menu.

1. **Offering the cigar:** Cigars are offered in humidors. The guest makes his/her selection by the colour, size and shape and judges the cigar before making the final decision.
2. **Cutting the cigar:** There are many types of cigar cutters that are used to cut off a portion of the cap. Regardless of which cutler is used, one should ensure that the

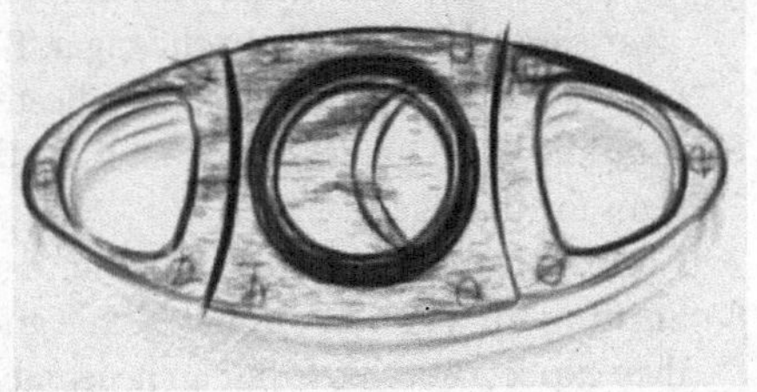

A sketch of a cigar cutter.

blades are sharp. If the blades are not sharp, the cigar could be crushed during the cutting time. Cutting is done in a quick way that requires experience. Care should be taken to avoid the cutting of the entire cap. If it happens so, the wrapper leaf unfoils during smoking. Some use a cigar punch or a drill, which is not a cutter but makes a hole at the head.

3. **Lighting the cigar:** The cigar can be lit using a cigar match or cigar lighter. The cigar match has a long stick as it takes time for a cigar to burn. Cigar gas lighters are those which have fuel without any odour and do not spoil the aroma of the cigar. For example, butane gas lighters. Before lighting a cigar, the foot of the cigar has to be warm using a lighter or match to ensure easy burning. The thicker the cigar, more time it takes to burn. When using match, allow the sulphur to burn-off before showing it to the cigar. A cigar is held at a 45° angle while showing it to the flame, simultaneously the cigar has to be rotated and puffed to make sure it burns evenly.
4. **Whether to remove the band or not?**
   It is the choice of the guest. Some guests prefer the band to be retained as it is a symbol of status. Removal of the band can damage the wrapper leaf because it is glued. If it has to be removed then that part of the cigar has to be heated a little so that the glue can loosen and it can be removed easily.

Accessories Required for Service of Cigars

1. Cigar cutter
2. Cigar match or cigar lighter
3. Cigar ashtray
4. Humidor box

30.11 JUDGING A CIGAR

1. **By the colour of ash:** Properly grown tobacco gives a whitish ash on the cigar, whereas low-quality tobacco gives a greyish ash on the cigar.
2. A whitish ash refers to a mild cigar. Grey connotes a strong cigar.
3. **Holding time of ash:** The ash of a premium handmade cigar holds on to the cigar for a long time before falling, whereas a cheaper cigar does not hold the ash and tends to fall frequently.
4. **Dryness:** The cigar should not be very dry. Rolling a cigar between both your palms near the ears is one method of judging the dryness. If there are crackling sounds, it means that the cigar is very dry.
5. **Bloom:** A fine whitish powder formed on the wrapper of the cigar caused by the oils in the cigar. Bloom can be brushed-off using a very soft brush. Bloom indicates that the cigar is alive.
6. **Mould:** Bluish green spots that stain the wrapper are not good signs for the cigar.
7. **Construction of cigars:** Inspect for any rack leaves and any loose caps.
8. **Sniffing for a good bouquet:** Some guests hold the cigar onto their nose and sniff it for the bouquet they expect. But this is not an acceptable practice. It is accepted to bring the humidor 3–4 inch away from the nose to get the entire bouquet of the cigar.

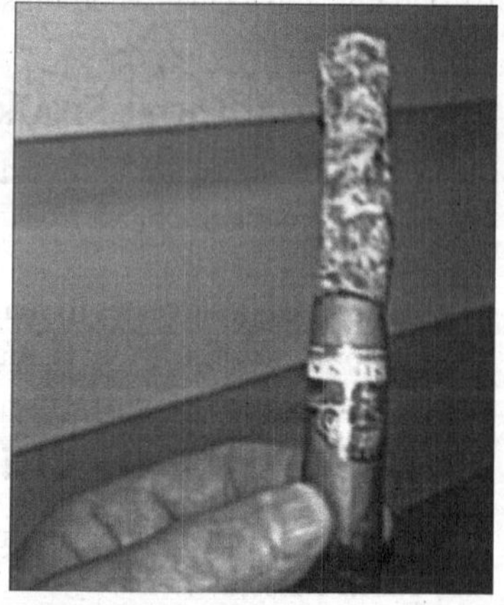

Holding of the ash.

30.12 INTERESTING FACTS ABOUT CIGARS

1. Arturo Fuente, a large cigar manufacturer based in the Dominican Republic, has also manufactured figurados in exotic shapes ranging from chili peppers to baseball bats and American footballs. They are highly collectible and extremely expensive, when publicly available.
2. In practice, the terms 'Torpedo' and 'Pyramid' are often used interchangeably, even among very knowledgeable cigar smokers.
3. Min Ron Nee, the Hong Kong-based cigar expert whose work *An Illustrated Encyclopedia of Post-Revolution Havana Cigars* is considered to be the definitive work on cigars and cigar terms, defines Torpedo as 'cigar slang'. Nee thinks the majority is right (because slang is defined by majority usage) and Torpedoes are Pyramids by another name.

LET'S SUMMARIZE IN POINTS

- In 1492, Christopher Columbus discovered the New World along with the discovery of tobacco.
- In 1561, Jean Nicot was credited for defining tobacco and its chemical composition of nicotine.
- The tobacco plant grows in two varieties, namely:
  - *Nicotiana tabacum* or cultivated tobacco and
  - *Nicotiana rustica* or wild tobacco.
- Cigarette is a paper-wrapped roll of finely cut tobacco used for smoking. Cigarette tobacco is usually milder than cigar tobacco.

30.13 FAQs

Short-Answer Type Questions

1. What is tobacco? Give the botanical name.
2. Name three brands of cigarettes from UK.
3. Describe the history of tobacco.
4. Give three parts of a cigar.
5. Name five factors while judging a cigar.

Long-Answer Type Questions

1. Give the manufacturing process for making a cigarette.
2. Give the manufacturing process of cigars.
3. How are cigars classified? Give at least three factors in detail.
4. Give the various sizes of cigars.
5. Give the various shapes of cigars.
6. Classify cigars on the basis of their country of origin.
7. Write a short note on storage of cigars.
8. What are the factors which help to judge the quality of a cigar?
9. Give the brands of cigars and cigarettes.
10. Explain cigar etiquette.

30.14 KEY TERMS

- Habana
- Bouquet
- Band
- Boite Nature Burros (*also* called bulks)
- Catador
- Draw
- Lance
- Piercer
- Bull's-Eye Piercer
- Oil
- Kent
- Mulch

Glossary

ABV	Alcohol by volume.
Acetobacter	It is an acetic acid bacterium which has the ability to convert ethanol to acetic acid in the presence of oxygen; thereby converting wine into vinegar.
Activated charcoal	Processed carbon, which is highly porous in nature; hence, having increased surface area available for adsorption. It is, therefore, used to remove unwanted odours, for example, in the production process of making vodka.
Adriatic Coast	A large inlet of the Mediterranean. The west coast runs through Italy, whereas, the east coast includes the shores of Slovenia, Croatia and Montenegro.
Aeration	The term refers to the soil aeration enabling increased exposure to nitrogen in the soil, making the roots of the vine grow faster.
Agraffes	The metallic strip used to secure the champagne cork, preventing it from releasing the bottle due to pressure.
Aguameil	The extracted juice of the *Agave plant, which is* used to make tequila.
Ale	A top-fermenting beer.
Amaretto	An almond-flavoured liqueur.
Amazon	The world's widest river, located in South America.
Amino acids	It is the name of the type of organic acids that make up the cell structure of proteins in living beings. They are as the building blocks of proteins.
Angel's share	During the maturation of spirits, a certain amount of them evaporates into the atmosphere, which is referred to as the Angel's share.
Antioxidants	These are substances that may protect cells from the damage caused by unstable molecules.
Aperitifs	Refers to a beverage normally served before a meal to stimulate the appetite.
Aquavit/Akuavit	It is a spirit produced in Scandinavian countries, predominantly flavoured with dill or caraway seeds.
Arabs	People native of the Arabian Peninsula or Saudi Arabia.
Aristotle	A Greek philosopher, thinker, educator and scientist and was one of the most influential thinkers in Western culture. He survived from 384–322 BC.
Aspergillus oryzae	A spore used for treating rice.
AVA	American Viticultural Area. It is an approved wine and grape-growing region in the United States of America.

Aztec Indians The famed Aztec tribes of South America who were the first to discover cocoa beans and referred to it as the drink of the gods, for its stimulating properties.

Band A paper ring around the head of most cigars. Cigar bands are often printed with the name of the brand, country of origin, and/or indication that the cigar is hand-rolled. They often have colourful graphics, which have made them a popular collector's item.

Bar Spoon The spoon used at the bar counter to stir cocktails and mocktails.

Base Refers to the base spirit used to make a cocktail.

Baume level A measuring system to check the level of sugar in a given liquid.

Beriech Refers to a district in Germany.

Bison grass It is also known as sweet grass, buffalo grass or holy grass (UK). It is an aromatic herb which grows in Eurasia and North America. It owes its sweet aromatic smell to the presence of coumarin.

Bodegas Bodega is a Spanish word, which refers to a wine cellar or a winery.

Boite Nature The cedar box in which many cigars are sold.

Bottling Refers to the process which involves putting the liquor in a bottle and sealing it.

Bouquet The smell or nose of a fine cigar. A badly stored cigar can lose its bouquet.

Bourbon Refers to an American whisky, which is made from corn and is barrel aged.

Bourbon whisky casks The casks or barrels used to age/mature Bourbon whisky.

Breathing of wine Refers to the wine being in contact with oxygen, and making it naturally develop and making it smoother to taste.

Brewing The process that is used in the making of beer.

Briskness Pleasing or tangy.

Brouillis/Bonne Chaffe Heart of the distillate.

Bull's-Eye Piercer A device used for opening the closed head of a cigar before smoking.

Burros (also called bulks) The piles or bulks, in which cigar tobacco is fermented.

Butts Refers to a wine barrel in the process of making sherry.

Caffeine It is a bitter stimulant found in tea, coffee, cocoa and various other seeds, leaves, parts and fruits. It is a chemical substance which temporarily wards off drowsiness and restores alertness.

Cardiovascular Refers to the blood vessels in human beings.

Caribbean Refers to crescent-shaped group of islands located off the coast of South America, also referred to as the West Indies.

Catador A professional cigar taster who determines a cigar's qualities of taste, texture and aroma.

Catechins A term used to refer to a group of flavonoids.

Cava Sparkling wines made in Spain using the Methode Champenoise.

Caviar It is a salted and non-fertilized sturgeon fish roe, which is processed and marketed as a luxury food.

Chaff The by-product of coffee making, which is obtained after the dry silver-coloured skin; it is removed after polishing the coffee bean.

Chalk Refers to the calcium carbonate in the soil.

Chaser The beverage accompanying a spirit, such as a juice, aerated soda or water

Chateau Refers to an estate.

Chicory It is often used as a substitute for coffee. The roots of this plant are baked and used to give coffee more body. Generally used in making south Indian filter coffee.

Claret British term used to describe wines from Bordeaux.

Clarification The method used to remove fine sediments in a wine, making it clear and appealing to the consumer.

Code of Hammurabi The earliest known writings on the production and distribution of beer.

Columbus Christopher Columbus was an explorer, a colonizer and a navigator who discovered the New World, referring to the western hemisphere.

Congeners These are also known as fusel oils. These are responsible for most of the aromas and flavours developed in an alcoholic beverage.

Connoisseurs Experts in the fields of food and beverage.

Continuous still Also known as a patent still or Coffey still.

Consejo Regulador Regulatory authority of Spain, governing the wine-making process and the quality of wine of a particular region.

Crema The essential oils of the coffee, which form a cream-ike layer on the surface of an espresso.

Crémant Refers to a sparkling wine not made in the Champagne region of France, but in any other region of France.

Crus A vineyard or growth of high quality

CTC Cut Tear Curl, refers to a method used in making tea.

Cuba Libre A famous rum-based cocktail.

Cubeb Peppers A pepper native to Java and Sumatra, hence, it is also known as Java peppers. It is very similar to the black pepper, but harvested with a tail.

Dash A small splash of a given ingredient, such as Angostura Bitters etc.

Decaffeination The process of removing caffeine from coffee beans.

Demineralize To remove all the minerals from water, usually done by the reverse osmosis (RO) method.

Demitasse It is a small cup used to serve espresso or Arabic coffee.

Digestif An alcoholic beverage served after a meal to aid in digestion.

Distillation A method of separating a substance, that is, in solution, from its solvent or of separating a liquid from a mixture of liquids having different boiling points. The liquid to be separated is evaporated (as by boiling), and its vapour is then collected after it condenses. The condensed vapour, which is the purified liquid, is called the distillate.

Draw The flow of smoke from a cigar.

Dry Refers to an alcoholic beverage with an overall higher percentage of alcohol in comparison to the amount of residual sugars in the beverage.

Dunder Dunder is a yeast-rich foam layer of one batch of rum, which is used as a starter culture for the next batch.

Eau de vie It is also spelled as eaux-de-vie. It is a colourless fruit brandy, which is produced by the means of fermentation and double distillation.

Edelfäule German word for noble rot.

Egrappage Egrappage refers to the steps where the grapes are passed through a mechanical device for de-stemming and crushing.

Elixir It is a clear and sweet, flavoured liquid used for medicinal purposes, intended to cure one's ills.

Enzymes These are biological molecules, which increase the rate of chemical reactions.

Epicatechin A strong antioxidant.

Eplusage Refers to the selective picking of grapes; practised for making the base wine for Champagne.

Esters Esters with low molecular weight are commonly used as fragrances and found in essential oils and pheromones.

Estufas These are hot houses used in a unique process of ageing Madeira wines.

Ethanol It is also called ethyl alcohol, grain alcohol or drinking alcohol. It is a potable, colourless and flammable liquid.

Evergreen drink Refers to whisky, which can be consumed in all seasons of the year.

Feints Also known as the tails of the distillate. *Please refer to tails.*

Fermentation The chemical reaction, which converts sugar to ethanol, carbon dioxide and heat energy due to the action of yeast.

Fining The process of adding a clarifying agent, which makes the finer sediments settle to the bottom of the liquid, thereby improving clarity and appeal.

Flavonoids Flavonoids are compounds found in fruits, vegetables, and certain beverages that have diverse beneficial biochemical and antioxidant effects. Their dietary intake is quite high compared to other dietary antioxidants such as vitamins C and E. The antioxidant activity of flavonoids depends on their molecular structure, and structural characteristics of certain flavonoids found in hops and beer confer surprisingly potent antioxidant activity exceeding that of red wine, tea, or soy.

Float Refers to a type of cocktail in which at least one ingredient has a lighter density; hence, floating on the surface of the liquid.

Flor It is a natural yeast film which develops on the surface of the wine.

Foreshots Also known as the heads of the distillate. *Please refer to heads.*

Frizzante Semi-sparkling wine made by the tank method from Italy.

Full bodied Having richness and intensity of flavour and aroma.

Gebeit Term used to describe a region in Germany.

Genievre French word for juniper.

Gold leaf A foil of pure gold used many times as a garnish.

Golden elixir Also known as an elixir of life, which is believed to possess properties that make a person immortal. This beverage is not a reality and is a belief and can be found in many mythical stories.

Gout de cuivre Coppery character of a wine.

Grappa An Italian brandy made from grape pomace.

Grinding Refers to the process in which the coffee beans are crushed into powder.

Grist Powdered barley, which is used to make a sugary liquid called wort.

Grosslage Term used to describe a sub-district in Germany.

Grover Vineyards One of the leading vineyards in India.

Gusano Refers to the worm found in certain tequila bottles.

Habana A designation which, when inscribed on a cigar band, indicates that a cigar is Cuban. (Note: Not all Cuban cigars are marked with 'Habana' or 'Havana.')

Hawthorn Strainer Also known as a cocktail strainer specially designed to strain cocktails.

Heads The non-potable part of the distillate usually collected in the beginning of the distillation process.

Hearts The potable part of the distillate collected by the still master after a close observation, preventing any heads or tails of the distillate from contaminating the liquid.

Heat Exchange The part of the still in which the vapours condense to a liquid distillate.

Heather honey Heather honey is made from nectar collected from the tiny purple bell-shaped flower of the common heather plant, so named because of its domination of many areas of heath and moorland, and also known as ling heather. Other heathers, such as the bell heather, flower earlier and are less common, which make them less viable for honey. The honey collected is used as a primary flavouring agent for Drambuie liqueur.

Hoccheimer/Hock German wine shipped to England in the 18th century.

Holland Another name used to refer to the country of the Netherlands.

Hops Hops are the female flower clusters (commonly called seed cones or strobiles), of a hop species, *Humuluslupulus*. They are used primarily as a flavouring and stabilizing agent in beer, to which they impart a bitter, tangy flavour, though hops are also used for various purposes in other beverages and herbal medicine.

Hymn of Ninkasi A prayer dedicated to the goddess of beer.

International Bitterness Units A measuring system used to calculate the bitterness levels of hops which influence the overall character of a beer.

Ice wine The frozen wine made in Canada similar to the German Iswein.

Infusion An infusion is the outcome of steeping plants that have desired chemical compounds or flavours in a solvent such as water, oil or alcohol.

Irish Whisky Whisky that is made in Ireland under the specific norms of the government of Scotland.

Ising Glass A clarifying agent used in the production process of wine or beer and other fermented beverages. It is obtained from the swim bladders of the sturgeon fish.

Jalisco State The state that is legally designated by Mexico to produce tequila.

Jamaican Rum Rum that is made in a specific Jamaican process, and is from Jamaica.

Juniper berries A juniper berry is the female seed cone produced by the various species of junipers. It is not a true berry but a cone with unusually fleshy and merged scales, which give it a berry-like appearance. The cones from a handful of species, especially *Juniperuscommunis*, are used as a spice, particularly in European cuisine, and also give gin its distinguishing flavour.

Kahlua A coffee-flavoured liqueur from Mexico.

Kent It is a brand of cigarettes, first to introduce smoke filters in 1952.

Kilning The process of baking or heating germinated barley or other grains.

Koji When steamed rice is treated with a special spore, *Aspergillusoryzae*, which converts the starch in the rice to sugar. This takes up to 30–35 hours to produce a culture called *Koji* that is rich in the enzyme.

Kojiki This is the oldest chronicle in Japan dating from the early 8th century (AD 711–712)

Koshiki Japanese rice-steaming tub.

Krausening A traditional method used by most German beer breweries to carbonate their beer using a secondary fermentation. This is done usually for lager styled beers.

La Champagne Refers to the famous sparkling wine from the Champagne region of France.

Lage Term in German referring to individual vineyards.

Lager The bottom-fermenting beer.

Lagres	Wooden pressing troughs used to produce Spanish wines
Lance	A cutter used to pierce a small hole in the closed end of a cigar. Also called a piercer.
Latte art	The art work now becoming a craze with almost all baristas (coffee masters) practising the art on the surface of a cappuccino or a café latte.
Lautering	The process of continuously passing the wort through the spent grain at the base of the tun
LBV	A type of port namely Late Bottled Vintage
LDL Cholesterol	Called 'bad cholesterol', very essential to have constant checks to ensure a healthy heart.
Le Champagne	Refers to the region of Champagne in France.
Lees	Refers to the deposits of dead or residual yeast and other particles that precipitate or are carried by the action of fining, to the bottom of the barrel after fermentation and ageing processes.
Licorice	It is the root of Glycyrrhiza from which a sweet flavour is extracted. It is not related to anise, star anise or fennel.
Long Drink	A type of cocktail that is made with a lot of ingredients, hence, having a larger volume.
Maceration	The process of the grape skins being left with the must to impart it colour and adds tannins.
Maduro	A Spanish term given to a dark brown, almost black, wrapper. The Maduro wrapper has the most taste and burns slower than any other wrapper.
Maguey	Generally refers to the blue *Agave* plant or the heart of the plant, which is used in making tequila.
Malolactic fermentation	This is a natural process that occurs during ageing of a wine. The malic acid present in the wine converts into a more palatable and smoother lactic acid. Therefore, a well-matured wine will be more palatable due to this process.
Malt wine	The first or second outcome of distillation, usually low in alcohol.
Maltings	The firms that malt the grain for whisky production firms of Scotland. These firms work only for local or small-scale units, as the larger organizations have their own malting units.
Marry/Marrying	To perfectly match or blend two different batches of the same type of alcohol, namely wine, whisky etc.
Mashing	The process of subjecting the grist to hot water making a mash that is then processed to form beer.
Meal	Refers to the American name used to describe grist-powdered barley.
Medieval Period	Sometimes referred to as the Middle Ages, encompassing the 5th to the 15th centuries and is marked by the collapse of the Western Roman Empire.

Medium Bodied	Term used to describe a wine with a less aromas and flavours.
Methode Champenoise	The traditional method used in making sparkling wine from the Champagne region of France. Other regions of the world have adopted this method but their end products cannot be called champagnes.
Mezcal plant	The blue *Agave* plant.
ML	Millilitre.
Molasses	The sweet and black coloured by-product of sugar manufacturing, which acts as the base(after dilution) for making rum.
Monasteries	The residence of monks.
Monk	A hermit who normally has dedicated his life to a spiritual pursuit.
Moonshine liquor/ Bathtub Liquor	The liquor made under the garb of night to prevent the authorities from taxing the locally produced gin, after the prohibition was imposed in Britain.
Moto	When *Koji* is added to a thin paste of rice and water, it slowly multiplies feeding on the sugar produced by the *Koji*, resulting a fully ripened *Moto*.
Muddler	Usually a wooden piece of equipment used to crush lemon or mint, thereby, releasing the flavours into the cocktail.
Mulch	A protective covering, usually of organic matter such as leaves, straw or peat, placed around plants to prevent the evaporation of moisture, the freezing of roots and the growth of weeds.
Must	The grape juice extracted after crushing is referred to as the must.
Mustimeter	The instrument used to check the sugar level or Baume levels in the must
Musto	The Spanish word to describe must.
New World	The countries which are relatively new to the wine world. They comprise of the countries such as Australia, New Zealand, USA, Chile, Argentina and South Africa. India and China are becoming a part of these countries.
Ninhonshu	Japanese name for sake–spirit of rice'.
Noble Rot	Refers to a vine disease. *Please refer to vine diseases in the Chapter 17.*
Normandy	A region in France famous for producing pears and perry.
Oak	The wood used for ageing most alcoholic beverages including wine and spirits.
Oil	The mark of a well-humidified cigar. Even well-aged cigars secrete oil at 70–72 % relative humidity, the level at which they should be stored.
Okolehao	Also known as Oke and made on the Islands of Hawaii. It is a fermented and distilled beverage made from the roots of the sacred *Ti plant.*
Old World	Refers to the European countries those have mastered the art of making wine for a number of centuries. France, Italy, Portugal, Spain and Germany would be included in this list.
Ordinario	Cloudy, milky first liquid that is the result of the first distillation process of a pot still.

Oxidation Combination of a substance with oxygen.

P.X. A short abbreviation for the Pedro Ximinez grapes used to make sherry.

Palatinate Refers to the Palatinate of the Rhine in Germany, a historic state of the holy Roman Empire.

Panniers Baskets for carrying grapes.

Parchment The outer fruit pulp and skin on the coffee bean when removed exposes the coffee bean.

Pasteurization It is the process of sterilization of a liquid to a specific temperature for a definite length of time and cooling it immediately. This process slows the spoilage due to microbial growth in the food.

Pate Paste made from poultry, meat, fish and vegetables often appearing on the appetizer menu.

Patent still Also known as the continuous still or Coffey still. *Please refer to Chapter 8 on distillation for working.*

Peat A type of vegetable charcoal used to kiln malted barley used to make Scotch or Irish whisky.

Peptides Short polymers of Amino acids. They are distinguished from proteins on the basis of size.

Percolation To filter through or trickle through, concerns the movement and filtering of fluids through porous materials. Used to describe the percolation method used in making percolated coffee.

PFA Act Prevention of Food Adulteration Act of India.

Phylloxera A vine disease. *Please refer to Chapter 17 on viticulture.*

Piercer A cutter used to pierce a small hole in the closed end of a cigar. Also called a lance.

Pimms A famous spirit made from a gin base.

Pinas The heart of the mezcal plant.

Pint A measure of serving beer. In India, it refers to a 330-ml serving.

Pisco A Peruvian brandy.

Plunger Another name for the French Press used to make freshly brewed coffee.

Plymouth gin Heavier, strongly flavoured gin as compared to the London dry gin.

Pommace/Pommage The pressed pulp of apples or pears.

Pompeii It is a partially buried Roman city located near modern Naples in the Italian region of Campania in the territory of the commune of Pompeii. This city was buried under 4–6 meters of volcanic ash in the eruption of Mout Vesuvius in AD 79.

Portus Cale The Port of Cale.

Pot still An onion shaped still made of copper. The first type of still used to distill spirits which is used to make flavourful whiskies and other spirits.

Poteen Term used to describe Illicit distilled Irish whisky.

Premiere Chauffe The French term used for the lower wines in the distillation process of Cognac

Proving The system which is used to evaluate the levels of alcohol in a given bottle.

Pulque The alcoholic beverage made by fermenting the sap of the mezcal plant. This is further distilled to make vino mezcal, the best into mezcals are classified as Tequilas.

Quinine Substance which is used to flavour tonic water, the traditional accompaniment of gin. Quinine has properties to fight malaria.

Quintas Place where vines are grown in Portugal.

Quiote The 20–30 feet long stem of the blue *Agave* plant, which grows as the plant matures. It is undesirable for the tequila producer as this consumes all the starch in the plant.

Rabelos Sailboats used to transport casks on the Duorao river to Oporto.

Racking The process of removing the clearer wine without mixing it with the sediments which have settled at the bottom of the barrel or Vat.

Raya Meaning Stroke, referring to the classification of wines to make sherry.

Redistilling A double distillation process, usually done to gin with the addition of flavouring agents. A practice with various liqueurs as well.

Reinheitgebod The first Purity law of 1516 adopted by William IV- the Duke of Bavaria.

Removing the Lees The process of removing the sediments which have settled to the base of the barrel or Vat. Also known as Racking.

Remuage This process is also called ridling. It is the process of removing the dead yeast cells and other sediments after the Champagne has undergone its secondary fermentation. *Please refer to Chapter 19 for the detailed working.*

Remuer Refers to a worker who works in the estate.

Riddling It is one step in the traditional method of making Champagne or sparkling wine that helps to consolidate sediments prior to removal.

Rum An alcoholic spirit made from a sugar cane base.

Rye Whisky A type of whisky produced with Rye, predominantly in Canada.

Saccharum officinarum Botanical name of the sugarcane plant.

Saccharometer A measuring device used to check the sugar level in the wort or molasses before fermentation.

Saccharomyces vodermani A string of yeast culture.

Sakuzi Ceramic bowls used to sip sake which hold an ounce of sake.

Scotch whisky	The whisky produced in Scotland as per the guidelines of the Scottish government.
Scurvy	A disease in which an individual has a deficiency of Vitamin C.
Sediments	The large particles of dead yeast cells, grape skin etc. which cloud a wine.
Segments	Refers to parts of a citrus fruit like oranges, lemon etc.
Sekt	A German Sparkling wine.
Semi-automatic espresso machine	A machine used to make espresso and cappuccino. It involves the maker to acquire a skill to make the coffee.
Shaker	Equipment used to shake a cocktail.
Shaking	Refers to the method in which the cocktail ingredients are shaken to create a homogenous mixture.
Sherry	A fortified wine from Spain
Skimmed Milk	Milk with a fat content lesser than 0.1%, used to accompany freshly brewed tea and coffee.
Slaves	Refers to people who were part of the slavery system which treated people as property to be bought and sold and were forced to work.
Smoky character	A characteristic to some Single malt whiskies carrying a smoky after taste.
Solera	A specialized system of blending sherry
Sparging	The process of spraying hot water over the spent grain extracting any residual sugars
Spumante	A sparkling wine from Spain
Stirring	A method using a bar spoon to stir the ingredients.
Stomping	The manual method of crushing grapes by foot.
Sucrose	A type of simple sugar
Sugarcane Plantation	A plantation area where Sugarcane crop is grown in abundance.
Sulphured Barriques	The barrels which have been treated with sulphur to prevent any natural yeasts from spoiling the contents of the barrel.
Sweet	Refers to a wine in which there are more residual sugars
Swirling the glass	The method of drinking wine, in which the wine is swirled (moved) in a glass thereby allowing the aromas of the wine to emerge.
Tails	The non-potable part of the distillate containing the burnt base wine.
Tasse	Refers to a cup used to serve tea of coffee.
Tennessee	A region in USA which is famous for making whisky.
Tequila city	The city of Tequila located in the Region of Jalisco
Terminal Bud	The top most bud of a plant. The terminal bud of the tea plant is used to make the beverage

Terroir	The term used to describe the collective conditions required to propagate the grape vine.
Ti plant	The plant grown on the Islands of Hawaii used to make Okolehao.
Tia Maria	A coffee liqueur
Tokkuri	Small ceramic bottles used to serve Sake.
Treading	*See Stomping*
Troken	Refers to a Dry German wine.
Tsar	It is a title used to designate certain European Slavic monarchs or Supreme rulers.
Tulloch Mhor	A region in Scotland
Twist	A twist of lemon is a common garnish used in many cocktails
Uisge Beatha/Uisge Baugh	The Scottish and Irish names of Whisky
UK Proof	A type of Proof which is 7/4 times the Alcohol by Volume system
Umechu	Japanese medicinal wine
Umeshu	Japanese plum wine
US Proof	Alcoholic proof defined as twice the value of ABV
Vielle Reserve	A type of classification for Cognac
Vineyard	A place where grapes are cultivated.
Vino Mezcal	Pulque after distillation is called vino mezcal
Virgin Islands	A group of Islands located
Vitis Vinifera	The genus of the grape vine used to produce grapes meant for making wine.
VQA	Vintners Quality Alliance
Wheel	A slice of lemon used to garnish glassware
Whirlpool separator	A step in the manufacture of beer which separates the hops from the wort before fermentation begins.
Wine Chiller	A refrigerator used to maintain the optimum temperature for storage of wine.
WOK	A steel vessel popularly used in Chinese cookery
Wormwood	The principle flavouring agent used to produce Vermouth which is an Aromatized wine.
Wort	The sugary sweet liquid made from powdered barley, when fermented produces beer.
Yeast	Yeasts are classified in the kingdom of fungi with 1500 species currently. Most are unicellular with a few exceptions.